LAW, CRIME AND LAW ENFORCEMENT

# A BOOK ABOUT LAWYERS

# LAW, CRIME AND LAW ENFORCEMENT

Additional books and e-books in this series can be found
on Nova's website under the Series tab.

LAW, CRIME AND LAW ENFORCEMENT

# A BOOK ABOUT LAWYERS

JOHN CORDY JEAFFRESON

snova
New York

**Library of Congress Cataloging-in-Publication Data**

ISBN: 978-1-53619-329-9

*Published by Nova Science Publishers, Inc. † New York*

# CONTENTS


| | | |
|---|---|---|
| **Preface** | | **ix** |
| **Part 1.** | **Houses and Householders** | **1** |
| **Chapter 1** | Ladies in Law Colleges | **3** |
| **Chapter 2** | The Last of the Ladies | **7** |
| **Chapter 3** | York House and Powis House | **13** |
| **Chapter 4** | Lincoln's Inn Fields | **17** |
| **Chapter 5** | The Old Law Quarter | **23** |
| **Part 2.** | **Loves of the Lawyers** | **31** |
| **Chapter 6** | A Lottery | **33** |
| **Chapter 7** | Good Queen Bess | **37** |
| **Chapter 8** | Rejected Addresses | **43** |
| **Chapter 9** | "Cicero" upon His Trial | **49** |
| **Chapter 10** | Brothers in Trouble | **53** |
| **Chapter 11** | Early Marriages | **61** |
| **Part 3.** | **Money** | **67** |
| **Chapter 12** | Fees to Counsel | **69** |
| **Chapter 13** | Retainers General and Special | **79** |
| **Chapter 14** | Judicial Corruption | **85** |
| **Chapter 15** | Gifts and Sales | **95** |

| | | |
|---|---|---|
| **Chapter 16** | A Rod Pickled by William Cole | **99** |
| **Chapter 17** | Chief Justice Popham | **103** |
| **Chapter 18** | Judicial Salaries | **107** |
| **Part 4.** | **Costume and Toilet** | **115** |
| **Chapter 19** | Bright and Sad | **117** |
| **Chapter 20** | Millinery | **121** |
| **Chapter 21** | Wigs | **123** |
| **Chapter 22** | Bands and Collars | **131** |
| **Chapter 23** | Bags and Gowns | **135** |
| **Chapter 24** | Hats | **141** |
| **Part 5.** | **Music** | **147** |
| **Chapter 25** | The Piano in Chambers | **149** |
| **Chapter 26** | The Battle of the Organs | **151** |
| **Chapter 27** | A Thickness in the Throat | **159** |
| **Part 6.** | **Amateur Theatricals** | **163** |
| **Chapter 28** | Actors at the Bar | **165** |
| **Chapter 29** | "The Play's the Thing" | **169** |
| **Chapter 30** | The River and the Strand by Torchlight | **175** |
| **Chapter 31** | Anti-Prynne | **179** |
| **Chapter 32** | An Empty Grate | **185** |
| **Part 7.** | **Legal Education** | **189** |
| **Chapter 33** | Inns of Court and Inns of Chancery | **191** |
| **Chapter 34** | Lawyers and Gentlemen | **197** |
| **Chapter 35** | Law-French and Law-Latin | **205** |
| **Chapter 36** | Student Life in Old Time | **211** |
| **Chapter 37** | Readers and Mootmen | **219** |
| **Chapter 38** | Pupils in Chambers | **225** |
| **Part 8.** | **Mirth** | **231** |
| **Chapter 39** | Wit of Lawyers | **233** |

**Chapter 40** Humorous Stories **245**

**Chapter 41** Wits in 'Silk' and Punsters in 'Ermine' **257**

**Chapter 42** Witnesses **267**

**Chapter 43** Circuiteers **275**

**Chapter 44** Lawyers and Saints **285**

**Part 9. At Home: In Court: And in Society 293**

**Chapter 45** Lawyers at Their Own Tables **295**

**Chapter 46** Wine **303**

**Chapter 47** Law and Literature **309**

**Index 315**

# PREFACE[*]

*A Book About Lawyers* provides a glimpse into the history of lawyers in London in the $19^{th}$ century.

[*] This is an edited, augmented, and reformatted version of "A Book About Lawyers," by John Cordy Jeaffreson, originally published by G.W. Carleton & Co., dated 1807.

# PART 1. HOUSES AND HOUSEHOLDERS

*Chapter 1*

# LADIES IN LAW COLLEGES

A law-student of the present day finds it difficult to realize the brightness and domestic decency which characterized the Inns of Court in the sixteenth, seventeenth, and eighteenth centuries. Under existing circumstances, women of character and social position avoid the gardens and terraces of Gray's Inn and the Temple.

Attended by men, or protected by circumstances that guard them from impertinence and scandal, gentlewomen can without discomfort pass and repass the walls of our legal colleges; but in most cases a lady enters them under conditions that announce even to casual passers the object of her visit. In her carriage, during the later hours of the day, a barrister's wife may drive down the Middle Temple Lane, or through the gate of Lincoln's Inn, and wait in King's Bench Walk or New Square, until her husband, putting aside clients and papers, joins her for the homeward drive. But even thus placed, sitting in her carriage and guarded by servants, she usually prefers to fence off inquisitive eyes by a bonnet-veil, or the blinds of her carriage-windows. On Sunday, the wives and daughters of gentle families brighten the dingy passages of the Temple, and the sombre courts of Lincoln's Inn: for the musical services of the grand church and little chapel, are amongst the religious entertainments of the town. To those choral celebrations ladies go, just as they are accustomed to enter any metropolitan church; and after service they can take a turn in the gardens of either Society, without drawing upon themselves unpleasant attention. So also, unattended by men, ladies are permitted to inspect the floral exhibitions with which Mr. Broome, the Temple gardener, annually entertains London sightseers.

But, save on these and a few similar occasions and conditions, gentlewomen avoid an Inn of Court as they would a barrack-yard, unless they have secured the special attendance of at least one member of the society. The escort of a barrister or student, alters the case. What barrister, young or old, cannot recall mirthful eyes that, with quick shyness, have turned away from his momentary notice, as in answer to the rustling of silk, or stirred by sympathetic consciousness of women's noiseless presence, he has raised his face from a volume of reports, and seen two or three timorous girls peering through the golden haze of a London morning, into the library of his Inn? What man, thus drawn away for thirty seconds from prosaic toil, has not in that half minute remembered the faces of happy rural homes,—has not recalled old days when his young pulses beat cordial welcome to similar intruders upon the stillness of the Bodleian, or the tranquil seclusion of Trinity library? What occupant of dreary chambers in the Temple, reading this page, cannot look back to a bright day, when young, beautiful, and pure as sanctity, Lilian, or Kate, or Olive, entered his room radiant with smiles, delicate in attire, and musical with gleesome gossip about country neighbors, and the life of a joyous home?

Seldom does a Templar of the present generation receive so fair and innocent a visitor. To him the presence of a gentlewoman in his court, is an occasion for ingenious conjecture; encountered on his staircase she is a cause of lively astonishment. His guests are men, more or less addicted to tobacco; his business callers are solicitors and their clerks; in his vestibule the masculine emissaries of tradesmen may sometimes be found—head-waiters from neighboring taverns, pot-boys from the 'Cock' and the 'Rainbow.' A printer's devil may from time to time knock at his door. But of women—such women as he would care to mention to his mother and sisters—he sees literally nothing in his dusty, ill-ordered, but not comfortless rooms. He has a laundress, one of a class on whom contemporary satire has been rather too severe.

Feminine life of another sort lurks in the hidden places of the law colleges, shunning the gaze of strangers by daylight; and even when it creeps about under cover of night, trembling with a sense of its own incurable shame. But of this sad life, the bare thought of which sends a shivering through the frame of every man whom God has blessed with a peaceful home and wholesome associations, nothing shall be said in this page.

In past time the life of law-colleges was very different in this respect. When they ceased to be ecclesiastics, and fixed themselves in the hospices which soon after the reception of the gowned tenants, were styled Inns of Courts; our lawyers took unto themselves wives, who were both fair and discreet. And having so made women flesh of their flesh and bone of their bone, they brought them to homes within the immediate vicinity of their collegiate walls, and sometimes within the walls themselves. Those who would appreciate the life of the Inns in past centuries, and indeed in times within the memory of living men, should bear this in mind. When he was not on circuit, many a counsellor learned in the law, found the pleasures not less than the business of his existence within the bounds of his 'honorable society.' In the fullest sense of the words, he took his ease in his Inn; besides being his workshop, where clients flocked to him for advice, it was his club, his place of pastime, and the shrine of his domestic affections. In this generation a successful Chancery barrister, or Equity draftsman, looks upon Lincoln's Inn merely as a place of business, where at a prodigious rent he holds a set of rooms in which he labors over cases, and satisfies the demands of clients and pupils. A century or two centuries since the case was often widely different. The rising barrister brought his bride in triumph to his 'chambers,' and in them she received the friends who hurried to congratulate her on her new honors. In those rooms she dispensed graceful hospitality, and watched her husband's toils. The elder of her children first saw the light in those narrow quarters; and frequently the lawyer, over his papers, was disturbed by the uproar of his heir in an adjoining room.

Young wives, the mistresses of roomy houses in the western quarters of town, shudder as they imagine the discomforts which these young wives of other days must have endured. "What! live in chambers?" they exclaim with astonishment and horror, recalling the smallness and cheerless aspect of their husbands' business chambers. But past usages must not be hastily condemned,—allowance must be made for the fact that our ancestors set no very high price on the luxuries of elbow-room and breathing-room. Families in opulent circumstances were wont to dwell happily, and receive whole regiments of jovial visitors in little houses nigh the Strand and Fleet Street, Ludgate Hill and Cheapside;—houses hidden in narrow passages and sombre courts—houses, compared with which the lowliest residences in a "genteel suburb" of our own time would appear capacious mansions. Moreover, it must be borne in mind that the married barrister, living a century since with his wife in chambers—either within or hard-by an Inn or Court—was, at a comparatively low rent, the occupant of far more ample quarters than those for which a working barrister now-a-days pays a preposterous sum. Such a man was tenant of a 'set of rooms' (several rooms, although called 'a chamber') which, under the present system, accommodates a small colony of industrious 'juniors' with one office and a clerk's room attached. Married ladies, who have lived in Paris or Vienna, in the 'old town' of Edinburgh, or Victoria Street, Westminster, need no assurance that life 'on a flat' is not an altogether deplorable state of existence. The young couple in chambers had six rooms at their disposal,—a chamber for business, a parlor, not unfrequently a drawing-room, and a trim, compact little kitchen. Sometimes they had two 'sets of rooms,' one above another; in which case the young wife could have her bridesmaids to stay with her, or could offer a bed to a friend from the country. Occasionally during the last fifty years of the last century, they were so fortunate as to get possession of a small detached house, originally built by a nervous bencher, who disliked the sound of footsteps on the stairs outside his door. Time was when the Inns comprised numerous detached houses, some of them snug dwellings, and others imposing mansions, wherein great dignitaries lived with proper ostentation. Most of them have bean pulled down, and their sites covered with collegiate 'buildings;' but a few of them still remain, the grand piles having long since been partitioned off into chambers, and the little houses striking the eye as quaint, misplaced, insignificant blocks of human habitation. Under the trees of Gray's Inn gardens may be seen two modest tenements, each of them comprising some six or eight rooms and a vestibule. At the present time they are occupied as offices by legal practitioners, and many a day has passed since womanly taste decorated their windows with flowers and muslin curtains; but a certain venerable gentleman, to whom the writer of this page is indebted for much information about the lawyers of the last century, can remember when each of those cottages was inhabited by a barrister, his young wife, and three or four lovely children. Into some such a house near Lincoln's Inn, a young lawyer who was destined to hold the seals for many years, and be also the father of a Lord Chancellor, married in the year of our Lord, 1718. His name was Philip Yorke: and though he was of humble birth, he had made such a figure in his profession that great men's doors, were open to him. He was asked to dinner by learned judges, and invited to balls by their ladies. In Chancery Lane, at the house of Sir Joseph Jekyll, Master of the Rolls, he met Mrs. Lygon, a beauteous and wealthy widow, whose father was a country squire, and whose mother was the sister of the great Lord Somers. In fact, she was a lady of such birth, position, and jointure, that the young lawyer—rising man though he was—seemed a poor match for her. The lady's family thought so; and if Sir Joseph Jekyll had not cordially supported the suitor with a letter of recommendation, her father would have rejected him as a man too humble in rank and fortune. Having won the lady and married her, Mr. Philip Yorke brought her home to a 'very small house' near Lincoln's Inn; and in that lowly dwelling, the ground-floor of which was the barrister's office, they spent the first years of their wedded life. What would be said of the rising barrister who, now-a-days, on his marriage with a rich squire's rich daughter and a peer's niece, should propose to set up his household gods in a tiny crip just outside Lincoln's Inn gate, and to use the parlor of the 'very small house' for professional purposes? Far from being guilty of unseemly parsimony in this arrangement, Philip Yorke paid proper consideration to his wife's social advantages, in taking her to a separate house. His contemporaries amongst the junior bar would have felt no astonishment if he had fitted up a set of chambers for his wealthy and well-descended bride. Not merely in his day, but for long years afterward, lawyers of gentle birth and comfortable means, who married women scarcely if at all inferior to Mrs. Yorke in social condition, lived upon the flats of Lincoln's Inn and the Temple.

*Chapter 2*

# THE LAST OF THE LADIES

Whatever its drawbacks, the system which encouraged the young barrister to marry on a modest income, and make his wife 'happy in chambers,' must have had special advantages. In their Inn the husband was near every source of diversion for which he greatly cared, and the wife was surrounded by the friends of either sex in whose society she took most pleasure—friends who, like herself, 'lived in the Inn,' or in one of the immediately adjacent streets. In 'hall' he dined and drank wine with his professional compeers and the wits of the bar: the 'library' supplied him not only with law books, but with poems and dramas, with merry trifles written for the stage, and satires fresh from the Row; 'the chapel'—or if he were a Templer, 'the church'—was his habitual place of worship, where there were sittings for his wife and children as well as for himself; on the walks and under the shady trees of 'the garden' he sauntered with his own, or, better still, a friend's wife, criticising the passers, describing the new comedy, or talking over the last ball given by a judge's lady. At times those gardens were pervaded by the calm of collegiate seclusion, but on 'open days' they were brisk with life. The women and children of the legal colony walked in them daily; the ladies attired in their newest fashions, and the children running with musical riot over lawns and paths. Nor were the grounds mere places of resort for lawyers and their families. Taking rank amongst the pleasant places of the metropolis, they attracted, on 'open days,' crowds from every quarter of the town—ladies and gallants from Soho Square and St. James's Street, from Whitehall and Westminster; sightseers from the country and gorgeous alderwomic dowagers from Cheapside. From the days of Elizabeth till the middle, indeed till the close, of the eighteenth century the ornamental grounds of the four great Inns were places of fashionable promenade, where the rank and talent and beauty of the town assembled for display and exercise, even as in our own time they assemble (less universally) in Hyde Park and Kensington Gardens.

When ladies and children had withdrawn, the quietude of the gardens lured from their chambers scholars and poets, who under murmuring branches pondered the results of past study, or planned new works. Ben Jonson was accustomed to saunter beneath the elms of Lincoln's Inn; and Steele—alike on 'open' and 'close' days—used to frequent the gardens of the same society. "I went," he writes in May, 1809, "into Lincoln's Inn Walks, and having taking a round or two, I sat down, according to the allowed familiarity of these places, on a bench." In the following November he alludes to the privilege that he enjoyed of walking there as "a favor that is indulged me by several of the benchers, who are very intimate friends, and grown in the neighborhood."

But though on certain days, and under fixed regulations, the outside public were admitted to the college gardens, the assemblages were always pervaded by the tone and humor of the law. The courtiers and grand ladies from 'the west' felt themselves the guests of the lawyers; and the humbler folk, who by special grant had acquired the privilege of entry, or whose decent attire and aspect satisfied the janitors of their respectability, moved about with watchfulness and gravity, surveying the counsellors and their ladies with admiring eyes, and extolling the benchers whose benevolence permitted simple tradespeople to take the air side by side with 'the quality.' In 1736, James Ralph, in his 'New Critical Review of the Publick Buildings,' wrote about the square and gardens of Lincoln's Inn in a manner which testifies to the respectful gratitude of the public for the liberality which permitted all outwardly decent persons to walk in the grounds. "I may safely add," he says, "that no area anywhere is kept in better order, either for cleanliness and beauty by day, or illumination by night; the fountain in the middle is a very pretty decoration, and if it was still kept playing, as it was some years ago, 'twould preserve its name with more propriety." In his remarks on the chapel the guide observes, "The raising this chapel on pillars affords a pleasing, melancholy walk underneath, and by night, particularly, when illuminated by the lamps, it has an effect that may be felt, but not described." Of the gardens Mr. Ralph could not speak in high praise, for they were ill-arranged and not so carefully kept as the square; but he observes, "they are convenient; and considering their situation cannot be esteemed to much. There is something hospitable in laying them open to public use; and while we share in their pleasures, we have no title to arraign their taste."

The chief attraction of Lincoln's Inn gardens, apart from its beautiful trees, was for many years the terrace overlooking 'the Fields,' which was made *temp.* Car. II. at the cost of nearly £1000. Dugdale, speaking of the recent improvements of the Inn, says, "And the last was the enlargement of their garden, beautifying with a large tarras walk on the west side thereof, and raising the wall higher towards Lincoln's Inne Fields, which was done in An. 1663 (15 Car. II.), the charge thereof amounting to a little less than a thousand pounds, by reason that the levelling of most part of the ground, and raising the tarras, required such great labor." A portion of this terrace, and some of the old trees, were destroyed to make room for the new dining-hall.

The old system supplied the barrister with other sources of recreation. Within a stone's throw of his residence was the hotel where his club had its weekly meeting. Either in hall, or with his family, or at a tavern near 'the courts,' it was his use, until a comparatively recent date, to dine in the middle of the day, and work again after the meal. Courts sat after dinner as well as before; and it was observable that counsellors spoke far better when they were full of wine and venison than when they stated the case in the earlier part of the day. But in the evening the system told especially in the barrister's favor. All his many friends lying within a small circle, he had an abundance of congenial society. Brother-circuiteers came to his wife's drawing-room for tea and chat, coffee and cards. There was a substantial supper at half-past eight or nine for such guests (supper cooked in my lady's little kitchen, or supplied by the 'Society's cook'); and the smoking dishes were accompanied by foaming tankards of ale or porter, and followed by superb and richly aromatic bowls of punch. On occasions when the learned man worked hard and shut out visitors by sporting his oak, he enjoyed privacy as unbroken and complete as that of any library in Kensington or Tyburnia. If friends stayed away, and he wished for diversion, he could run into the chambers of old college-chums, or with his wife's gracious permission could spend an hour at Chatelin's or Nando's, or any other coffeehouse in vogue with members of his profession. During festive seasons, when the judges' and leaders' ladies gave their grand balls, the young couple needed no carriage for visiting purposes. From Gray's Inn to the Temple they walked—if the weather was fine. When it rained they hailed a hackney-coach, or my lady was popped into a sedan and carried by running bearers to the frolic of the hour.

Of course the notes of the preceding paragraphs of this chapter are but suggestions as to the mode in which the artistic reader must call up the life of the old lawyers. Encouraging him to realize the manners and usages of several centuries, not of a single generation, they do not attempt to entertain the student with details. It is needless to say that the young couple did not use hackney-coaches in times prior to the introduction of those serviceable vehicles, and that until sedans were invented my lady never used them.

It is possible, indeed it is certain, that married ladies living in chambers occasionally had for neighbors on the same staircase women whom they regarded with abhorrence. Sometimes it happened that a dissolute barrister introduced to his rooms a woman more beautiful than virtuous, whom he had not married, though he called her his wife. People can no more choose their neighbors in a house broken up into sets of chambers, than they can choose them in the street. But the cases where ladies were daily liable to meet an offensive neighbor on their common staircase were comparatively rare; and when the annoyance actually occurred, the discipline of the Inn afforded a remedy.

Uncleanness too often lurked within the camp, but it veiled its face; and though in rare cases the error and sin of a powerful lawyer may have been notorious, the preccant man was careful to surround himself with such an appearance of respectability that society should easily feign ignorance of his offence. An Elizabethan distich—familiar to all barristers, but too rudely worded for insertion in this page—informs us that in the sixteenth century Gray's Inn had an unenviable notoriety amongst legal hospices for the shamelessness of its female inmates. But the pungent lines must be regarded as a satire aimed at certain exceptional members, rather than as a vivacious picture of the general tone of morals in the society. Anyhow the fact that Gray's Inn[1] was alone designated as a home for infamy—whilst the Inner Temple was pointed to as the hospice most popular with rich men, the Middle Temple as the society frequented by Templars of narrow means, and Lincoln's Inn as the abode of gentlemen—is, of itself, a proof that the pervading manners of the last three institutions were outwardly decorous. Under the least favorable circumstances, a barrister's wife living in chambers, within or near Lincoln's Inn, or the Temple, during Charles II.'s reign, fared as well in this respect as she would have done had Fortune made her a lady-in-waiting at Whitehall.

A good story is told of certain visits paid to William Murray's chambers at No. 5, King's Bench Walk Temple, in the year 1738. Born in 1705, Murray was still a young man when in 1738 he made his brilliant speech in behalf of Colonel Sloper, against whom Colley Cibber's rascally son had brought an action for *crim. con.* with his wife—the lovely actress who was the rival of Mrs. Clive. Amongst the many clients who were drawn to Murray by that speech, Sarah, Duchess of Marlborough, was neither the least powerful nor the least distinguished. Her grace began by sending the rising advocate a general retainer, with a fee of a thousand guineas; of which sum he accepted only the two-hundredth part, explaining to the astonished duchess that "the professional fee, with a general retainer, could neither be less nor more than five guineas." If Murray had accepted the whole sum he would not have been overpaid for his trouble; for her grace persecuted him with calls at most unseasonable hours. On one occasion, returning to his chambers after "drinking champagne with the wits," he found the duchess's carriage and attendants on King's Bench Walk. A numerous crowd of footmen and link-bearers surrounded the coach; and when the barrister entered his chambers he encountered the mistress of that army of lackeys. "Young man," exclaimed the grand lady, eying the future Lord Mansfield with a look of warm displeasure, "if you mean to rise in the world, you must not sup out." On a subsequent night Sarah of Marlborough called without appointment at the same chambers, and waited till past midnight in the hope that she would see the lawyer ere she went to bed. But Murray being at an unusually late supper-party, did not return till her grace had departed in an over-powering rage. "I could not make out, sir, who she was," said Murray's clerk, describing her grace's appearance and

[1] The scandalous state of Gray's Inn at this period is shown by the following passage in Dugdale's 'Origines:'—"In 23 Eliz. (30 Jan.) there was an order made that no laundress, nor women called victuallers, should thenceforth come into the gentlemen's chambers of this society, until they were full forty years of age, and not send their maid-servants, of what age soever, in the said gentlemen's chambers, upon penalty, for the first offence of him that should admit of any such, to be put out of Commons: and for the second, to be expelled the House." The stringency and severity of this order show a determination on the part of the authorities to cure the evil.

manner, "for she would not tell me her name; *but she swore so dreadfully that I am sure she must be a lady of quality*."

Perhaps the Inns of Court may still shelter a few married ladies, who either from love of old-world ways, or from stern necessity, consent to dwell in their husbands' chambers. If such ladies can at the present time be found, the writer of this page would look for them in Gray's Inn—that straggling caravansary for the reception of money-lenders, Bohemians, and eccentric gentlemen—rather than in the other three Inns of Court, which have undoubtedly quite lost their old population of lady-residents. But from those three hospices the last of the ladies must have retreated at a comparatively recent date. Fifteen years since, when the writer of this book was a beardless undergraduate, he had the honor of knowing some married ladies, of good family and unblemished repute, who lived with their husbands in the Middle Temple. One of those ladies—the daughter of a country magistrate, the sister of a distinguished classic scholar—was the wife of a common law barrister who now holds a judicial appointment in one of our colonies. The women of her old home circle occasionally called on this young wife: but as they could not reach her quarters in Sycamore Court without attracting much unpleasant observation, their visits were not frequent. Living in a barrack of unwed men, that charming girl was surrounded by honest fellows who would have resented as an insult to themselves an impertinence offered to her. Still her life was abnormal, unnatural, deleterious; it was felt by all who cared for her that she ought not to be where she was; and when an appointment with a good income in a healthy and thriving colony was offered to her husband, all who knew her, and many who had never spoken to her, rejoiced at the intelligence. At the present time, in the far distant country which looks up to her as a personage of importance, this lady—not less exemplary as wife and mother than brilliant as a woman of society—takes pleasure in recalling the days when she was a prisoner in the Temple.

One of the last cases of married life in the Temple, that came before the public notice, was that of a barrister and his wife who incurred obloquy and punishment for their brutal conduct to a poor servant girl. No one would thank the writer for re-publishing the details of that nauseous illustration of the degradation to which it is possible for a gentleman and scholar to sink. But, however revolting, the case is not without interest for the reader who is curious about the social life of the Temple.

The portion of the Temple in which the old-world family life of the Inns held out the longest, is a clump of commodious houses lying between the Middle Temple Garden and Essex Street, Strand. Having their entrance-doors in Essex Street, these houses are, in fact, as private as the residences of any London quarter. The noise of the Strand reaches them, but their occupants are as secure from the impertinent gaze or unwelcome familiarities of law-students and barristers' clerks, as they would be if they lived at St. John's Wood. In Essex Street, on the eastern side, the legal families maintained their ground almost till yesterday. Fifteen years since the writer of this page used to be invited to dinners and dances in that street—dinners and dances which were attended by prosperous gentlefolk from the West End of the town. At that time he often waltzed in a drawing-room, the windows of which looked upon the spray of the fountain—at which Ruth Pinch loved to gaze when its jet resembled a wagoner's whip. How all old and precious things pass away! The dear old 'wagoner's whip' has been replaced by a pert, perky squirt that will never stir the heart or brain of a future Ruth.

*Chapter 3*

# York House and Powis House

Whilst the great body of lawyers dwelt in or hard by the Inns, the dignitaries of the judicial bench, and the more eminent members of the bar, had suitable palaces or mansions at greater or less distances from the legal hostelries. The ecclesiastical Chancellors usually enjoyed episcopal or archiepiscopal rank, and lived in the London palaces attached to their sees or provinces. During his tenure of the seals, Morton, Bishop of Ely, years before he succeeded to the archbishopric of Canterbury, and received the honors of the Cardinalate, grew strawberries in his garden on Holborn Hill, and lived in the palace surrounded by that garden. As Archbishop of Canterbury, Chancellor Warham maintained at Lambeth Palace the imposing state commemorated by Erasmus.

When Wolsey made his first progress to the Court of Chancery in Westminster Hall, a progress already alluded to in these pages, he started from the archiepiscopal palace, York House or Place—an official residence sold by the cardinal to Henry VIII. some years later; and when the same superb ecclesiastic, towards the close of his career, went on the memorable embassy to France, he set out from his palace at Westminster, "passing through all London over London Bridge, having before him of gentlemen a great number, three in rank in black velvet livery coats, and the most of them with great chains of gold about their necks."

At later dates Gardyner, whilst he held the seals, kept his numerous household at Winchester House in Southwark; and Williams, the last clerical Lord Keeper, lived at the Deanery, Westminster.

The lay Chancellors also maintained costly and pompous establishments, apart from the Inns of Court. Sir Thomas More's house stood in the country, flanked by a garden and farm, in the cultivation of which ground the Chancellor found one of his chief sources of amusement. In Aldgate, Lord Chancellor Audley built his town mansion, on the site of the Priory of the Canons of the Holy Trinity of Christ Church. Wriothesley dwelt in Holborn at the height of his unsteady fortunes, and at the time of his death. The infamous but singularly lucky Rich lived in Great St. Bartholomew's, and from his mansion there wrote to the Duke of Northumberland, imploring that messengers might be sent to him to relieve him of the perilous trust of the Great Seal. Christopher Hatton wrested from the see of Ely the site of Holborn, whereon he built his magnificent palace. The reluctance with which the Bishop of Ely surrendered the ground, and the imperious letter by which Elizabeth compelled the prelate to comply with the wish of her favorite courtier, form one of the humorous episodes of that queen's reign. Hatton House rose over the soil which had yielded strawberries to Morton; and of that house—where the dancing Chancellor received Elizabeth as a visitor, and in which he died of "diabetes *and* grief of mind"—the memory is preserved by Hatton Garden, the name of the street where some of our wealthiest jewelers and gold assayers have places of business.

Public convenience had long suggested the expediency of establishing a permanent residence for the Chancellors of England, when either by successive expressions of the royal will, or by the individual choice of several successive holders of the *Clavis Regni*, a noble palace on the northern bank of the Thames came to be regarded as the proper domicile for the Great Seal. York House, memorable as the birthplace of Francis Bacon, and the scene of his brightest social splendor, demands a brief notice. Wolsey's 'York House' or Whitehall having passed from the province of York to the crown, Nicholas Heath, Archbishop of York, established himself in another York House on a site lying between the Strand and the river. In this palace (formerly leased to the see of Norwich as a bishop's Inn, and subsequently conferred on Charles Brandon by Henry VIII.) Heath resided during his Chancellorship; and when, in consequence of his refusal to take the oath of supremacy, Elizabeth deprived him of his archbishopric, York House passed into the hands of her new Lord Keeper, Sir Nicholas Bacon. On succeeding to the honors of the Marble Chair, Hatton did not move from Holborn to the Strand; but otherwise all the holders of the Great Seal, from Heath to Francis Bacon inclusive, seem to have occupied York House; Heath, of course, using it by right as Archbishop of York, and the others holding it under leases granted by successive archbishops of the northern province. So little is known of Bromley, apart from the course which he took towards Mary of Scotland, that the memory of old York House gains nothing of interest from him. Indeed it has been questioned whether he was one of its tenants. Puckering, Egerton, and Francis Bacon certainly inhabited it in succession. On Bacon's fall it was granted to Buckingham, whose desire to possess the picturesque palace was one of the motives which impelled him to blacken the great lawyer's reputation. Seized by the Long Parliament, it was granted to Lord Fairfax. In the following generation it passed into the hands of the second Duke of Buckingham, who sold house and precinct for building-ground. The bad memory of the man who thus for gold surrendered a spot of earth sacred to every scholarly Englishman is preserved in the names of *George* Street, *Duke* Street, *Villiers* Street, *Buckingham* Street.

The engravings commonly sold as pictures of the York House, in which Lord Bacon kept the seals, are likenesses of the building after it was pulled about, diminished, and modernized, and in no way whatever represent the architecture of the original edifice. Amongst the art-treasures of the University of Oxford, Mr. Hepworth Dixon fortunately found a rough sketch of the real house, from which sketch Mr. E.M. Ward drew the vignette that embellishes the title-page of 'The Story of Lord Bacon's Life.'

After the expulsion of the Great Seal from old York House, it wandered from house to house, manifesting, however, in its selections of London quarters, a preference for the grand line of thoroughfare between Charing Cross and the foot of Ludgate Hill. Escaping from the Westminster Deanery, where Williams kept it in a box, the *Clavis Regni* inhabited Durham House, Strand, whilst under Lord Keeper Coventry's care. Lord Keeper Littleton, until he made his famous ride from London to York, lived in Exeter House. Clarendon resided in Dorset House, Salisbury Court, Fleet Street, and subsequently in Worcester House, Strand, before he removed to the magnificent palace which aroused the indignation of the public in St. James's Street. The greater and happier part of his official life was passed in Worcester House. There he held councils in his bedroom when he was laid up with gout; there King Charles visited him familiarly, even condescending to be present to the bedside councils; and there he was established when the Great Fire of London caused him, in a panic, to send his most valuable furniture to his Villa at Twickenham. Thanet House, Aldersgate Street, is the residence with which Shaftesbury, the politician, is most generally associated; but whilst he was Lord Chancellor he occupied Exeter House, Strand, formerly the abode of Keeper Littleton. Lord Nottingham slept with the seals under his pillow in Great Queen Street, Lincoln's Inn Fields, the same street in which his successor, Lord Guildford, had the establishment so racily described by his brother, Roger North. And Lord Jeffreys moving westward, gave noisy dinners in Duke Street, Westminster, where he opened a court-house that was afterwards consecrated as a place of worship, and is still known as the Duke Street Chapel. Says Pennant, describing the Chancellor's residence, "It is easily known by a large flight of stone steps, which his royal master permitted to be made into the park adjacent for the accommodation of his lordship. These steps terminate above in a small court, on three sides of which stands the house." The steps still remain, but their history is unknown to many of the habitual frequenters of the chapel. After Jefferys' fall the spacious and imposing mansion, where the *bon-vivants* of the bar used to drink inordinately with the wits and buffoons of the London theatres, was occupied by Government; and there the Lords of the Admiralty had their offices until they moved to their quarters opposite Scotland Yard. Narcissus Luttrell's Diary contains the following entry:—"April 23, 1690. The late Lord Chancellor's house at Westminster is taken for the Lords of the Admiralty to keep the Admiralty Office at."

William III., wishing to fix the holders of the Great Seal in a permanent official home, selected Powis House (more generally known by the name of Newcastle House), in Lincoln's Inn Fields, as a residence for Somers and future Chancellors. The Treasury minute books preserve an entry of September 11, 1696, directing a Privy Seal to "discharge the process for the apprised value of the house, and to declare the king's pleasure that the Lord Keeper or Lord Chancellor for the time being should have and enjoy it for the accommodation of their offices." Soon after his appointment to the seals, Somers took possession of this mansion at the north-west corner of the Fields; and after him Lord Keeper Sir Nathan Wright, Lord Chancellor Cowper, and Lord Chancellor Harcourt used it as an official residence. But the arrangement was not acceptable to the legal dignitaries. They preferred to dwell in their private houses, from which they were not liable to be driven by a change of ministry or a grist of popular disfavor. In the year 1711 the mansion was therefore sold to John Holles, Duke of Newcastle, to whom it is indebted for the name which it still bears. This large, unsightly mansion is known to every one who lives in London, and has any knowledge of the political and social life of the earlier Georgian courtiers and statesmen.

*Chapter 4*

# LINCOLN'S INN FIELDS

The annals of the legal profession show that the neighborhood of Guildhall was a favorite place of residence with the ancient lawyers, who either held judicial offices within the circle of the Lord Mayor's jurisdiction, or whose practice lay chiefly in the civic courts. In the fifteenth and sixteenth centuries there was quite a colony of jurists hard by the temple of Gogmagog and Cosineus—or Gog and Magog, as the grotesque giants are designated by the unlearned, who know not the history of the two famous effigies, which originally figured in an Elizabethan pageant, stirring the wonder of the illiterate, and reminding scholars of two mythical heroes about whom the curious reader of this paragraph may learn further particulars by referring to Michael Drayton's 'Polyolbion.'

In Milk Street, Cheapside, lived Sir John More, judge in the Court of King's Bench; and in Milk street, A.D. 1480, was born Sir John's famous son Thomas, the Chancellor, who was at the same time learned and simple, witty and pious, notable for gentle meekness and firm resolve, abounding with tenderness and hot with courage. Richard Rich—who beyond Scroggs or Jeffreys deserves to be remembered as the arch-scoundrel of the legal profession—was one of Thomas More's playmates and boon companions for several years of their boyhood and youth. Richard's father was an opulent mercer, and one of Sir John's near neighbors; so the youngsters were intimate until Master Dick, exhibiting at an early age his vicious propensities, came to be "esteemed very light of his tongue, a great dicer and gamester, and not of any commendable fame."

On marrying his first wife Sir Thomas More settled in a house in Bucklersbury, the City being the proper quarter for his residence, as he was an under-sheriff of the city of London, in which character he both sat in the Court of the Lord Mayor and Sheriffs, and presided over a separate court on the Thursday of each week. Whilst living in Bucklersbury he had chambers in Lincoln's Inn. On leaving Bucklersbury he took a house in Crosby Place, from which he moved, in 1523, to Chelsea, in which parish he built the house that was eventually pulled down by Sir Hans Sloane in the year 1740.

A generation later, Sir Nicholas Bacon was living in Noble Street, Foster Lane, where he had built the mansion known as Bacon House, in which he resided till, as Lord Keeper, he took possession of York House. Chief Justice Bramston lived, at different parts of his career, in Whitechapel; in Philip Lane, Aldermanbury; and (after his removal from Bosworth Court) in Warwick Lane, Sir John Bramston (the autobiographer) married into a house in Charterhouse Yard, where his father, the Chief Justice, resided with him for a short time.

But from an early date, and especially during the seventeenth and eighteenth centuries, the more prosperous of the working lawyers either lived within the walls of the Inns, or in houses lying near the law colleges. Fleet Street, the Strand, Holborn, Chancery Lane, and the good streets leading into those thoroughfares, contained a numerous legal population in the times between Elizabeth's death and George III.'s first illness. Rich benchers and Judges wishing for more commodious quarters than they could obtain at any cost within college-walls, erected mansions in the immediate vicinity of their Inns; and their example was followed by less exalted and less opulent members of the bar and judicial bench. The great Lord Strafford first saw the light in Chancery Lane, in the house of his maternal grandfather, who was a bencher of Lincoln's Inn. Lincoln's Inn Fields was principally built for the accommodation of wealthy lawyers; and in Charles II.'s reign Queen Street, Lincoln's Inn Fields was in high repute with legal magnates. Sir Edward Coke lived alternately in chambers, and in Hatton House, Holborn, the palace that came to him by his second marriage. John Kelyng's house stood in Hatton Garden, and there he died in 1671. In his mansion in Lincoln's Inn Fields, Sir Harbottle Grimston, on June 25, 1660 (shortly before his appointment to the Mastership of the Rolls, for which place he is said to have given Clarendon £8000), entertained Charles II and a grand gathering of noble company. After his marriage Francis North took his high-born bride into chambers, which they inhabited for a short time until a house in Chancery Lane, near Serjeants' Inn, was ready for their use. On Nov. 15, 1666,—the year of the fire of London, in which year Hyde had his town house in the Strand—Glyn died in his house, in Portugal Row, Lincoln's Inn Fields. On June 15, 1691, Henry Pollexfen, Chief Justice of Common Pleas, expired in his mansion in Lincoln's Inn Fields. These addresses—taken from a list of legal addresses lying before the writer—indicate with sufficient clearness the quarter of the town in which Charles II.'s lawyers mostly resided.

Under Charles II the population of the Inns was such that barristers wishing to marry could not easily obtain commodious quarters within College-walls. Dugdale observes "that all but the benchers go two to a chamber: a bencher hath only the privilege of a chamber to himself." He adds—"if there be any one chamber consisting of two parts, and the one part exceeds the other in value, and he who hath the best part sells the same, yet the purchaser shall enter into the worst part; for it is a certain rule that the auntient in the chamber—*viz.*, he who was therein first admitted, without respect to their antiquity in the house, hath his choice of either part." This custom of sharing chambers gave rise to the word 'chumming,' an abbreviation of 'chambering.' Barristers in the present time often share a chamber—i.e., set of rooms. In the seventeenth century an utter-barrister found the half of a set of rooms inconveniently narrow quarters for himself and wife. By arranging privately with a non-resident brother of the long robe, he sometimes obtained an entire "chamber," and had the space allotted to a bencher. When he could not make such an arrangement, he usually moved to a house outside the gate, but in the immediate vicinity of his inn, as soon as his lady presented him with children, if not sooner.

Of course working, as well as idle, members of the profession were found in other quarters. Some still lived in the City; others preferred more fashionable districts. Roger North, brother of the Lord Keeper and son of a peer, lived in the Piazza of Covent Garden, in the house formerly occupied Lely the painter. To this house Sir Dudley North moved from his costly and dark mansion in the City, and in it he shortly afterwards died, under the hands of Dr. Radcliffe and the prosperous apothecary, Mr. St. Amand. "He had removed," writes Roger, "from his great house in the City, and came to that in the Piazza which Sir Peter Lely formerly used, and I had lived in alone for divers years. We were so much together, and my incumbrances so small, that so large a house might hold us both." Roger was a practicing barrister and Recorder of Bristol.

During his latter years Sir John Bramston (the autobiographer) kept house in Greek Street, Soho.

In the time of Charles II the wealthy lawyers often maintained suburban villas, where they enjoyed the air and pastimes of the country. When his wife's health failed, Francis North took a villa for her at Hammersmith, "for the advantage of better air, which he thought beneficial for her;" and whilst his household tarried there, he never slept at his chambers in town, "but always went home to his family, and was seldom an evening without company agreeable to him." In his latter years, Chief Justice Pemberton had a rural mansion in Highgate, where his death occurred on June 10, 1699, in the 74th year of his age. A pleasant chapter might be written on the suburban seats of our great lawyers from the Restoration down to the present time. Lord Mansfield's 'Kenwood' is dear to all who are curious in legal *ana*. Charles Yorke had a villa at Highgate, where he entertained his political and personal friends. Holland, the architect, built a villa at Dulwich for Lord Thurlow; and in consequence of a quarrel between the Chancellor and the builder, the former took such a dislike to the house, that after its completion he never slept a night in it, though he often passed his holidays in a small lodge standing in the grounds of the villa. "Lord Thurlow," asked a lady of him, as he was leaving the Queen's Drawing-room, "when are you going into your new house?" "Madam," answered the surly Chancellor, incensed by her curiosity, "the Queen has asked me that impudent question, and I would not answer her; I will not tell you." For years Loughborough and Erskine had houses in Hampstead. "In Lord Mansfield's time," Erskine once said to Lord Campbell, "although the King's Bench monopolized all the common-law business, the court often rose at one or two o'clock—the papers, special, crown, and peremptory, being cleared; and then I refreshed myself by a drive to my villa at Hampstead." It was on Hampstead Heath that Loughborough, meeting Erskine in the dusk, said, "Erskine, you must not take Paine's brief;" and received the prompt reply, "But I have been retained, and I will take it, by G-d!" Much of that which is most pleasant in Erskine's career occurred at his Hampstead villa. Of Lord Kenyon's weekly trips from his mansion in Lincoln's Inn Fields to his farm-house at Richmond notice has been taken in a previous chapter. The memory of Charles Abbott's Hendon villa is preserved in the name, style, and title of Lord Tenterden, of Hendon, in the county of Middlesex. Indeed, lawyers have for many generations manifested much fondness for fresh air; the impure atmosphere of their courts in past time apparently whetting their appetites for wholesome breezes.

Throughout the eighteenth century Lincoln's Inn Fields, an open though disorderly spot, was a great place for the residence of legal magnates. Somers, Nathan Wright, Cowper, Harcourt, successively inhabited Powis House. Chief Justice Parker (subsequently Lord Chancellor Macclesfield) lived there when he engaged Philip Yorke (then an attorney's articled clerk, but afterwards Lord Chancellor of England) to be his son's law tutor. On the south side of the square, Lord Chancellor Henley kept high state in the family mansion that descended to him on the death of his elder brother, and subsequently passed into the hands of the Surgeons, whose modest but convenient college stands upon its site. Wedderburn and Erskine had their mansions in Lincoln's Inn Fields, as well as their suburban villas. And between the lawyers of the Restoration and the judges of George III's reign, a large proportion of our most eminent jurists and advocates lived in that square and the adjoining streets; such as Queen Street on the west, Serle Street, Carey Street, Portugal Street, Chancery Lane, on the south and south-east. The reader, let it be observed, may not infer that this quarter was confined to legal residents. The lawyers were the most conspicuous and influential occupants; but they had for neighbors people of higher quality, who, attracted to the square by its openness, or the convenience of its site, or the proximity of the law colleges, made it their place of abode in London. Such names as those of the Earl of Lindsey and the Earl of Sandwich in the seventeenth, and of the Duke of Ancaster and the Duke of Newcastle in the eighteenth century, establish the patrician character of the quarter for many years. Moreover, from the books of popular antiquaries, a long list might be made of wits, men of science, and minor celebrities, who, though in no way personally connected with the law, lived during the same period under the shadow of Lincoln's Inn.

Whilst Lincoln's Inn Fields took rank amongst the most aristocratic quarters of the town, it was as disorderly a square as could be found in all London. Royal suggestions, the labors of a learned committee especially appointed by James I. to decide on a proper system of architecture, and Inigo Jones's magnificent but abortive scheme had but a poor result. In Queen Anne's reign, and for twenty years later, the open space of the fields was daily crowded with beggars, mountebanks, and noisy rabble; and it was the scene of constant uproar and frequent riots. As soon as a nobleman's coach drew up before one of the surrounding mansions, a mob of half-naked rascals swarmed about the equipage, asking for alms in alternate tones of entreaty and menace. Pugilistic encounters, and fights resembling the faction fights of an Irish row, were of daily occurrence there; and when the rabble decided on torturing a bull with dogs, the wretched beast was tied to a stake in the centre of the wide area, and there baited in the presence of a ferocious multitude, and to the diversion of fashionable ladies, who watched the scene from their drawing-room windows. The Sacheverell outrage was wildest in this chosen quarter of noblemen and blackguards; and in George II.'s reign, when Sir Joseph Jekyll, the Master of the Rolls, made himself odious to the lowest class by his Act for laying an excise upon gin, a mob assailed him in the middle of the fields, threw him to the ground, kicked him over and over, and savagely trampled upon him. It was a marvel that he escaped with his life; but with characteristic good humor, he soon made a joke of his ill-usage, saying that until the mob made him their football he had never been master of *all* the *rolls*. Soon after this outbreak of popular violence, the inhabitants enclosed the middle of the area with palisades, and turned the enclosure into an ornamental garden. Describing the Fields in 1736, the year in which the obnoxious Act concerning gin became law, James Ralph says, "Several of the original houses still remain, to be a reproach to the rest; and I wish the disadvantageous comparison had been a warning to others to have avoided a like mistake.... But this is not the only quarrel I have to Lincoln's Inn Fields. The area is capable of the highest improvement, might be made a credit to the whole city, and do honor to those who live round it; whereas at present no place can be more contemptible or forbidding; in short, it serves only as a nursery for beggars and thieves, and is a daily reflection on those who suffer it to be in its abandoned condition."

During the eighteenth century, a tendency to establish themselves in the western portion of the town was discernible amongst the great law lords. For instance, Lord Cowper, who during his tenure of the seals resided in Powis House, during his latter years occupied a mansion in Great George Street, Westminster—once a most fashionable locality, but now a street almost entirely given up to civil engineers, who have offices there, but usually live elsewhere. In like manner, Lord Harcourt, moving westwards from Lincoln's Inn Fields, established himself in Cavendish Square. Lord Henley, on retiring from the family mansion in Lincoln's Inn Fields, settled in Grosvenor Square. Lord Camden lived in Hill Street, Berkeley Square. On being entrusted with the sole custody of the seals, Lord Apsley (better known as Lord Chancellor Bathurst) made his first state-progress to Westminster Hall from his house in Dean Street, Soho; but afterwards moving farther west, he built Apsley House (familiar to every Englishman as the late Duke of Wellington's town mansion) upon the site of Squire Western's favorite inn—the 'Hercules' Pillars.'

*Chapter 5*

# THE OLD LAW QUARTER

Fifteen years since the writer of this page used to dine with a conveyancer—a lawyer of an old and almost obsolete school—who had a numerous household, and kept a hospitable table in Lincoln's Inn Fields; but the conveyancer was almost the last of his species. The householding legal *resident* of the Fields, like the domestic resident of the Temple, has become a feature of the past. Among the ordinary nocturnal population of the square called Lincoln's Inn Fields, may be found a few solicitors who sleep by night where they work by day, and a sprinkling of young barristers and law students who have residential chambers in grand houses that less than a century since were tenanted by members of a proud and splendid aristocracy; but the gentle families have by this time altogether disappeared from the mansions.

But long before this aristocratic secession, the lawyers took possession of a new quarter. The great charm of Lincoln's Inn Fields had been the freshness of the air which played over the open space. So also the recommendation of Great Queen Street had been the purity of its rural atmosphere. Built between 1630 and 1730, that thoroughfare—at present hemmed in by fetid courts and narrow passages—caught the keen breezes of Hampstead, and long maintained a character for salubrity as well as fashion. Of those fine squares and imposing streets which lie between High Holborn and Hampstead, not a stone had been laid when the ground covered by the present Freemason's Tavern was one of the most desirable sites of the metropolis. Indeed, the houses between Holborn and Great Queen Street were not erected till the mansions on the south side of the latter thoroughfare—built long before the northern side—had for years commanded an unbroken view of Holborn Fields. Notwithstanding many gloomy predictions of the evils that would necessarily follow from over-building, London steadily increased, and enterprising architects deprived Lincoln's Inn Fields and Great Queen Street of their rural qualities. Crossing Holborn, the lawyers settled on a virgin plain beyond the ugly houses which had sprung up on the north of Great Queen Street, and on the country side of

Holborn. Speedily a new quarter arose, extending from Gray's Inn on the east to Southampton Row on the West, and lying between Holborn and the line of Ormond Street, Red Lion Street, Bedford Row, Great Ormond Street, Little Ormond Street, Great James Street, and Little James Street were amongst its best thoroughfares; in its centre was Red Lion Square, and in its northwestern corner lay Queen's Square. Steadily enlarging its boundaries, it comprised at later dates Guildford Street, John's Street, Doughty Street, Mecklenburgh Square, Brunswick Square, Bloomsbury Square, Russell Square, Bedford Square—indeed, all the region lying between Gray's Inn Lane (on the east), Tottenham Court Road (on the west), Holborn (on the south), and a line running along the north of the Foundling Hospital and 'the squares.' Of course this large residential district was more than the lawyers required for themselves. It became and long remained a favorite quarter with merchants, physicians,[2] and surgeons; and until a recent date it comprised the mansions of many leading members of the aristocracy. But from its first commencement it was so intimately associated with the legal profession that it was often called the 'law quarter;' and the writer of this page has often heard elderly ladies and gentlemen speak of it as the 'old law quarter.'

Although lawyers were the earliest householders in this new quarter, its chief architect encountered at first strong opposition from a section of the legal profession. Anxious to preserve the rural character of their neighborhood, the gentlemen of Gray's Inn were greatly displeased with the proposal to lay out Holborn Fields in streets and squares. Under date June 10, 1684, Narcissus Luttrell wrote in his diary—"Dr. Barebone, the great builder, having some time since bought the Red Lyon Fields, near Graie's Inn walks, to build on, and having for that purpose employed severall workmen to goe on with the same, the gentlemen of Graie's Inn took notice of it, and, thinking it an injury to them, went with a considerable body of 100 persons; upon which the workmen assaulted the gentlemen, and flung bricks at them, and the gentlemen at them again. So a sharp engagement ensued, but the gentlemen routed them at last, and brought away one or two of the workmen to Graie's Inn; in this skirmish one or two of the gentlemen and servants of the house were hurt, and several of the workmen."

James Ralph's remarks on the principal localities of this district are interesting. "Bedford Row," he says, "is one of the most noble streets that London has to boast of, and yet there is not one house in it which deserves the least attention." He tells us that "Ormond Street is another place of pleasure, and that side of it next the Fields is, beyond

---

[2] Dr. Clench lived in Brownlow Street, Holborn; and until his death, in 1831, John Abernethy occupied in Bedford Row the house which is still inhabited by an eminent surgeon, who was Abernethy's favorite pupil. Of Dr. Clench's death in January, 1691-2, Narcissus Luttrell gives the following account: "The 5th, last night, Dr. Clench, the physician, was strangled in a coach; two persons came to his house in Brownlow Street, Holborn, in a coach, and pretended to carry him to a patient's in the City; they drove backward and forward, and after some time stopt by Leadenhall, and sent the coachman to buy a couple of fowls for supper, who went accordingly; and in the meantime they slipt away, and the coachman when he returned found Dr. Clench with a handkerchief tyed about his neck, with a hard sea-coal twisted in it, and clapt against his windpipe; he had spirits applied to him and other means, but too late, he having been dead some time." Dr. Clench's murderer, one Mr. Harrison, a man of gentle condition, was apprehended, tried, found guilty, and hung in chains.

question, one of the most charming situations about town." This 'place of pleasure' is now given up for the most part to hospitals and other charitable institutions, and to lodging-houses of an inferior sort. Passing on to Bloomsbury Square, and speaking of the Duke of Bedford's residence, which stood on the North side of the square, he says, "Then behind it has the advantage of most agreeable gardens, and a view of the country, which would make a retreat from the town almost unnecessary, besides the opportunity of exhibiting another prospect of the building, which would enrich the landscape and challenge new approbation." This was written in 1736. At that time the years of two generations were appointed to pass away ere the removal of Bedford House should make way for Lower Bedford Place, leading into Russell Square.

So late as the opening years of George III.'s reign, Queen's Square enjoyed an unbroken prospect in the direction of Highgate and Hampstead. 'The Foreigner's Guide: or a Necessary and Instructive Companion both to the Foreigner and Native, in their Tours through the Cities of London and Westminster' (1763), contains the following passage:—"Queen's Square, which is pleasantly situated at the extreme part of the town, has a fine open view of the country, and is handsomely built, as are likewise the neighboring streets—viz., Southampton Row, Ormond Street, &c. In this last is Powis House, so named from the Marquis of Powis, who built the present stately structure in the year 1713. It is now the town residence of the Earl of Hardwicke, late Lord Chancellor. The apartments are noble, and the whole edifice is commendable for its situation, and the fine prospect of the country. Not far from thence is Bloomsbury Square. This square is commendable for its situation and largeness. On the North side is the house of the Duke of Bedford. This building was erected from a design of Inigo Jones, and is very elegant and spacious." From the duke's house in Bloomsbury Square and his surrounding property, the political party, of which he was the Chief, obtained the nickname of the Bloomsbury Gang.

Chief Justice Holt died March 5, 1710, at his house[3] in Bedford Row. In Red Lion Square Chief Justice Raymond had the town mansion wherein he died on April 15, 1733; twelve years after Sir John Pratt, Lord Camden's father, died at his house in Ormond Street. On December 15, 1761, Chief Justice Willes died at his house in Bloomsbury Square. Chagrin at missing the seals through his own arrogance, when they had been actually offered to him, was supposed to be a principal cause of the Chief Justice's death. His friends represented that he died of a broken heart; to which assertion flippant enemies responded that no man ever had a heart after living seventy-four years. Murray for many years inhabited a handsome house in Lincoln's Inn Fields; but his name is more generally associated with Bloomsbury Square, where stood the house which was sacked and burnt by the Gordon rioters. In Bloomsbury Square our grandfathers used to lounge, watching

[3] Holt's country seat was Redgrave Hall, formerly the home of the Bacons. It was on his manor of Redgrave, that Sir Nicholas Bacon entertained Queen Elizabeth, when she remarked that her Lord Keeper's house was too small for him, and he answered—"Your Majesty has made me too great for my house."

the house of Edward Law, subsequently Lord Ellenborough, in the hope of seeing Mrs. Law, as she watered the flowers of her balcony. Mrs. Law's maiden name was Towry, and, as a beauty, she remained for years the rage of London. Even at this date there remain a few aged gentlemen whose eyes sparkle and whose checks flush when they recall the charms of the lovely creature who became the wife of ungainly Edward Law, after refusing him on three separate occasions.

On becoming Lord Ellenborough and Chief Justice, Edward Law moved to a great mansion in St. James's Square, the size of which he described to a friend by saying: "Sir, if you let off a piece of ordnance in the hall, the report is not heard in the bedrooms." In this house the Chief Justice expired, on December 13, 1818. Speaking of Lord Ellenborough's residence in St. James's Square, Lord Campbell says: "This was the first instance of a common law judge moving to the 'West End.' Hitherto all the common law judges had lived within a radius of half a mile from Lincoln's Inn; but they are now spread over the Regent's Park, Hyde Park Gardens, and Kensington Gore."

Lord Harwicke and Lord Thurlow have been more than once mentioned as inhabitants of Ormond Street.

Eldon's residences may be noticed with advantage in this place. On leaving Oxford and settling in London, he took a small house for himself and Mrs. Scott in Cursitor Street, Chancery Lane. About this dwelling he wrote to his brother Henry:—"I have got a house barely sufficient to hold my small family, which (so great is the demand for them here) will, in rent and taxes, cost me annually six pounds." To this house he used to point in the days of his prosperity, and, in allusion to the poverty which he never experienced, he would add, "There was my first perch. Many a time have I run down from Cursitor Street to Fleet Market and bought sixpenn'orth of sprats for our supper." After leaving Cursitor Street, he lived in Carey Street, Lincoln's Inn Fields, where also, in his later years, he believed himself to have endured such want of money that he and his wife were glad to fill themselves with sprats. When he fixed this anecdote upon Carey Street, the old Chancellor used to represent himself as buying the sprats in Clare Market instead of Fleet Market. After some successful years he moved his household from the vicinity of Lincoln's Inn, and took a house in the law quarter, selecting one of the roomy houses (No. 42) of Gower Street, where he lived when as Attorney General he conducted the futile prosecutions of Hardy, Horne Tooke, and Thelwall, in 1794.

On quitting Gower Street, Eldon took the house in Bedford Square, which witnessed so many strange scenes during his tenure of the seals, and also during his brief exclusion from office. In Bedford Square he played the part of chivalric protector to the Princess of Wales, and chuckled over the proof-sheets of that mysterious 'book' by the publication of which the injured wife and the lawyer hoped to take vengeance on their common enemy. There the Chancellor, feeling it well to protract his flirtation with the Princess of Wales, entertained her in the June of 1808, with a grand banquet, from which Lady Eldon was compelled by indisposition to be absent. And there, four years later, when he was satisfied that her Royal Highness's good opinion could be of no service to him, the crafty, self-seeking minister gave a still more splendid dinner to the husband whose vices he had professed to abhor, whose meanness of spirit he had declared the object of his contempt. "However," writes Lord Campbell, with much satiric humor, describing this alliance between the selfish voluptuary and the equally selfish lawyer, "he was much comforted by having the honor, at the prorogation, of entertaining at dinner his Royal Highness the Regent, with whom he was now a special favorite, and who, enjoying the splendid hospitality of Bedford Square, forgot that the Princess of Wales had sat in the same room; at the same table; on the same chair; had drunk of the same wine; out of the same cup; while the conversation had turned on her barbarous usage, and the best means of publishing to the world *her* wrongs and *his* misconduct."

Another of the Prince Regent's visits to Bedford Square is surrounded with comic circumstances and associations. In the April of 1815, a mastership of chancery became vacant by the death of Mr. Morris; and forthwith the Chancellor was assailed with entreaties from every direction for the vacant post. For two months Eldon, pursuing that policy of which he was a consummate master, delayed to appoint; but on June 23, he disgusted the bar and shocked the more intelligent section of London society, by conferring the post on Jekyll, the courtly *bon vivant* and witty descendant of Sir Joseph Jekyll, Master of the Rolls. Amiable, popular, and brilliant, Jekyll received the congratulations of his numerous personal friends; but beyond the circle of his private acquaintance the appointment created lively dissatisfaction—dissatisfaction which was heightened rather than diminished by the knowledge that the placeman's good fortune was entirely due to the personal importunity of the Prince Regent, who called at the Chancellor's house, and having forced his way into the bedroom, to which Eldon was confined by an attack of gout, refused to take his departure without a promise that his friend should have the vacant place. How this royal influence was applied to the Chancellor, is told in the 'Anecdote Book.'

Fortunately Jekyll was less incompetent for the post than his enemies had declared, and his friends admitted. He proved a respectable master, and held his post until age and sickness compelled him to resign it; and then, sustained in spirits by the usual retiring pension, he sauntered on right mirthfully into the valley of the shadow of death. On the day after his retirement, the jocose veteran, meeting Eldon in the street, observed:—"Yesterday, Lord Chancellor, I was your master; to-day I am my own."

From Bedford Square, Lord Eldon, for once following the fashion, moved to Hamilton Place, Piccadilly. With the purpose of annoying him the 'Queen's friends,' during the height of the 'Queen Caroline agitation,' proposed to buy the house adjoining the Chancellor's residence in Hamilton Place, and to fit it up for the habitation of that not altogether meritorious lady. Such an arrangement would have been an humiliating as well as exasperating insult to a lawyer who, as long as the excitement about the poor woman lasted, would have been liable to affront whenever he left his house or looked through the windows facing Hamilton Place. The same mob that delighted in hallooing round whatever house the Queen honored with her presence, would have varied their 'hurrahs' for the lady with groans for the lawyer who, after making her wrongs the stalking-horse of his ambition, had become one of her chief oppressors. Eldon determined to leave Hamilton Place on the day which should see the Queen enter it; and hearing that the Lords of the Treasury were about to assist her with money for the purchase of the house, he wrote to Lord Liverpool, protesting against an arrangement which would subject him to annoyance at home and to ridicule out of doors. "I should," he wrote, "be very unwilling to state anything offensively, but I cannot but express my confidence that Government will not aid a project which must remove the Chancellor from his house the next hour that it takes effect, and from his office at the same time." This decided attitude caused the Government to withdraw their countenance from the project; whereupon a public subscription was opened for its accomplishment. Sufficient funds were immediately proffered; and the owner of the mansion had verbally made terms with the patriots, when the Chancellor, outbidding them, bought the house himself. "I had no other means," he wrote to his daughter, "of preventing the destruction of my present house as a place in which I could live, or which anybody else would take. The purchase-money is large, but I have already had such offers, that I shall not, I think, lose by it."

Russell Square—where Lord Loughborough (who knows aught of the Earl of Rosslyn?) had his town house, after leaving Lincoln's Inn Fields, and where Charles Abbott (Lord Tenterden) established himself on leaving the house in Queen Square, into which he married during the summer of 1795—maintained a quasi-fashionable repute much later than the older and therefore more interesting parts of the 'old law quarter.' Theodore Hook's disdain for Bloomsbury is not rightly appreciated by those who fail to bear in mind that the Russell Square of Hook's time was tenanted by people who—though they were unknown to 'fashion,' in the sense given to the word by men of Brummel's habit and tone—had undeniable status amongst the aristocracy and gentry of England. With some justice the witty writer has been charged with snobbish vulgarity because he ridiculed humble Bloomsbury for being humble. His best defence is found in the fact that his extravagant scorn was not directed at helpless and altogether obscure persons so much as at an educated and well-born class who laughed at his caricatures, and gave dinners at which he was proud to be present. Though it fails to clear the novelist of the special charge, this apology has a certain amount of truth; and in so far as it palliates some of his offences against good taste and gentle feeling, by all means let him have the full benefit of it. Criticism can afford to be charitable to the clever, worthless man, now that no one admires or tries to respect him. Again, it may be advanced, in Hook's behalf, that political animosity—a less despicable, though not less hurtful passion than love of gentility—contributed to Hook's dislike of the quarter on the north side of Holborn. As a humorist he ridiculed, as a panderer to fashionable prejudices he sneered at, Bloomsbury; but as a tory he cherished a genuine antagonism to the district of town that was associated in the public mind with the wealth and ascendency of the house of Bedford. Anyhow, the Russell Square neighborhood—although it was no longer fashionable, as Belgravia and Mayfair are fashionable at the present day—remained the locality of many important families, at the time when Mr. Theodore Hook was pleased to assume that no one above the condition of a rich tradesman or second-rate attorney lived in it. Of the lawyers whose names are mournfully associated with the square itself are Sir Samuel Romilly and Sir Thomas Noon Talfourd. In 1818, the year of his destruction by his own hand, Sir Samuel Romilly lived there; and Talfourd had a house on the east side of the square up to the time of his lamented death in 1854.

That Theodore Hook's ridicule of Bloomsbury greatly lessened for a time the value of its houses there is abundant evidence. When he deluged the district with scornful satire, his voice was a social power, to which a considerable number of honest people paid servile respect. His clever words were repeated; and Bloomsbury having become a popular by-word for contempt, aristocratic families ceased to live, and were reluctant to invest money, in its well-built mansions. But Hook only accelerated a movement which had for years been steadily though silently making progress. Erskine knew Red Lion Square when every house was occupied by a lawyer of wealth and eminence, if not of titular rank; but before he quitted the stage, barristers had relinquished the ground in favor of opulent shopkeepers. When an ironmonger became the occupant of a house in Red Lion Square on the removal of a distinguished counsel, Erskine wrote the epigram—

> "This house, where once a lawyer dwelt,
> Is now a smith's,—alas!
> How rapidly the iron age
> Succeeds the age of brass."

These lines point to a minor change in the social arrangements of London, which began with the century, and was still in progress when Erskine had for years been mouldering in his grave. In 1823, the year of Erskine's death, Chief Baron Richards expired in his town house, in Great Ormond Street. In the July of the following year Baron Wood—i.e., George Wood, the famous special pleader—died at his house in Bedford Square, about seventeen months after his resignation of his seat in the Court of Exchequer to John Hullock.

At the present time the legal fraternity has deserted Bloomsbury. The last of the Judges to depart was Chief Baron Pollock, who sold his great house in Queen Square at a quite recent date. With the disappearance of this venerable and universally respected judge, the legal history of the neighborhood may be said to have closed. Some wealthy solicitors still live in Russell Square and the adjoining streets; a few old-fashioned barristers still linger in Upper Bedford Place and Lower Bedford Place. Guilford Street and Doughty Street, and the adjacent thoroughfares of the same class, still number a sprinkling of rising juniors, literary barristers, and fairly prosperous attorneys. Perhaps the ancient aroma of the 'old law quarter'—Mesopotamia, us it is now disrespectfully termed—is still strong and pleasant enough to attract a few lawyers who cherish a sentimental fondness for the past. A survey of the Post Office Directory creates an impression that, compared with other neighborhoods, the district north and northeast of Bloomsbury Square still possesses more than an average number of legal residents; but it no longer remains the quarter of the lawyers.

There still resides in Mecklenburgh Square a learned Queen's Counsel, for whose preservation the prayers of the neighborhood constantly ascend. To his more scholarly and polite neighbors this gentleman is an object of intellectual interest and anxious affection. As the last of an extinct species, as a still animate Dodo, as a lordly Mohican who has outlived his tribe, this isolated counselor of her Gracious Majesty is watched by heedful eyes whenever he crosses his threshold. In the morning, as he paces from his dwelling to chambers, his way down Doughty Street and John Street, and through Gray's Inn Gardens, is guarded by men anxious for his safety. Shreds of orange-peel are whisked from the pavement on which he is about to tread; and when he crosses Holborn he walks between those who would imperil their lives to rescue him from danger. The gatekeeper in Doughty Street daily makes him low obeisance, knowing the historic value and interest of his courtly presence. Occasionally the inhabitants of Mecklenburgh Square whisper a fear that some sad morning their Q.C. may flit away without giving them a warning. Long may it be before the residents of the 'Old Law Quarter' shall wail over the fulfillment of this dismal anticipation!

# PART 2. LOVES OF THE LAWYERS

*Chapter 6*

# A LOTTERY

"I would compare the multitude of women which are to be chosen for wives unto a bag full of snakes, having among them a single eel; now if a man should put his hand into this bag, he may chance to light on the eel; but it is an hundred to one he shall be stung by a snake."

These words were often heard from the lips of that honest judge, Sir John More, whose son Thomas stirred from brain to foot by the bright eyes, and snowy neck, and flowing locks of *cara Elizabetha* (the *cara Elizabetha* of a more recent Tom More was 'Bessie, my darling')—penned those warm and sweetly-flowing verses which delight scholars of the present generation, and of which the following lines are neither the least musical nor the least characteristic:—

> "Jam subit illa dies quæ ludentem obtulit olim
> Inter virgineos te mibi prima choros.
> Lactea cum flavi decuerunt colla capilli,
> Cum gena par nivibus visa, labella rosis:
> Cum tua perstringunt oculos duo sydera nostros
> Perque oculos intrant in mea corda meos."

The goddess of love played the poet more than one droll trick. Having approached her with musical flattery, he fled from her with fear and abhorrence. For a time the highest and holiest of human affections was to his darkened mind no more than a carnal appetite; and he strove to conquer the emotions which he feared would rouse within him a riot of impious passions. With fasting and cruel discipline he would fain have killed the devil that agitated him, whenever he passed a pretty girl in the street. As a lay Carthusian he wore a hair-shirt next his skin, disciplined his bare back with scourges, slept on the cold ground or a hard bench, and by a score other strong measures sought to preserve his spiritual by ruining his bodily health. But nature was too powerful for unwholesome doctrine and usage, and before he rashly took a celibatic vow, he knelt to fair Jane Colt—and rising, kissed her on the lips.

When spiritual counsel had removed his conscientious objections to matrimony, he could not condescend to marry for love, but must, forsooth, choose his wife in obedience to considerations of compassion and mercy. Loving her younger sister, he paid his addresses to Jane, because he shrunk from the injustice of putting the junior above the older of the two girls. "Sir Thomas having determined, by the advice and direction of his ghostly father, to be a married man, there was at that time a pleasant conceited gentleman of an ancient family in Essex, one Mr. John Colt, of New Hall, that invited him into his house, being much delighted in his company, proffering unto him the choice of any of his daughters, who were young gentlewomen of very good carriage, good complexions, and very religiously inclined; whose honest and sweet conversation and virtuous education enticed Sir Thomas not a little; and although his affection most served him to the second, for that he thought her the fairest and best favored, yet when he thought within himself that it would be a grief and some blemish to the eldest to have the younger sister preferred before her, he, out of a kind of compassion, settled his fancy upon the eldest, and soon after married her with all his friends' good liking."

The marriage was a fair happy union, but its duration was short. After giving birth to four children Jane died, leaving the young husband, who had instructed her sedulously, to mourn her sincerely. That his sorrow was poignant may be easily believed; for her death deprived him of a docile pupil, as well as a dutiful wife.

"Virginem duxit admodum puellam," Erasmus says of his friend, "claro genere natam, rudem adhuc utpote ruri inter parentes ac sorores semper habitam, quo magis illi liceret illam ad suos mores fingere. Hanc et literis instruendam curavit, et omni musices genere doctam reddidit." Here is another insight into the considerations which brought about the marriage. When he set out in search of a wife, he wished to capture a simple, unsophisticated, untaught country girl, whose ignorance of the world should incline her to rely on his superior knowledge, and the deficiencies of whose intellectual training should leave him an ample field for educational experiments. Seeking this he naturally turned his steps toward the eastern countries; and in Essex he found the young lady, who to the last earnt with intelligence and zeal the lessons which he set her.

More's second choice of a wife was less fortunate than his first. Wanting a woman to ke care of his children and preside over his rather numerous establishment, he made an er to a widow, named Alice Middleton. Plain and homely in appearance and taste, tress Alice would have been invaluable to Sir Thomas as a superior domestic servant, his good judgment and taste deserted him when he decided to make her a closer anion. Bustling, keen, loquacious, tart, the good dame scolded servants and petty men with admirable effect; but even at this distance of time the sensitive ear is by her sharp, garrulous tongue, when its acerbity and virulence are turned against ific and scholarly husband. A smile follows the recollection that he endeavored to soften her manners and elevate her nature by a system of culture similar to that by which Jane Colt, 'admodum puella,' had been formed and raised into a polished gentlewoman. Past forty years of age, Mistress Alice was required to educate herself anew. Erasmus assures his readers that "though verging on old age, and not of a yielding temper," she was prevailed upon "to take lessons on the lute, the cithara, the viol, the monochord, and the flute, which she daily practised to him."

It has been the fashion with biographers to speak bitterly of this poor woman, and to pity More for his cruel fate in being united to a termagant. No one has any compassion for her. Sir Thomas is the victim; Mistress Alice the shrill virago. In those days, when every historic reprobate finds an apologist, is there no one to say a word in behalf of the Widow Middleton, whose lot in life and death seems to this writer very pitiable? She was quick in temper, slow in brain, domineering, awkward. To rouse sympathy for such a woman is no easy task; but if wretchedness is a title to compassion, Mistress Alice has a right to charity and gentle usage. It *was not* her fault that she could not sympathize with her grand husband, in his studies and tastes, his lofty life and voluntary death; it *was* her misfortune that his steps traversed plains high above her own moral and intellectual level. By social theory they were intimate companions; in reality, no man and woman in all England were wider apart. From his elevation he looked down on her with commiseration that was heightened by curiosity and amazement; and she daily writhed under his gracious condescension and passionless urbanity; under her own consciousness of inferiority and consequent self-scorn. He could no more sympathize with her petty aims, than she with the high views and ambitions; and conjugal sympathy was far more necessary to her than to him. His studious friends and clever children afforded him an abundance of human fellowship; his public cares and intellectual pursuits gave him constant diversion. He stood in such small need of her, that if some benevolent fairy had suddenly endowed her with grace, wisdom, and understanding, the sum of his satisfaction would not have been perceptibly altered. But apart from him she had no sufficient enjoyments. His genuine companionship was requisite for her happiness; but for this society nature had endowed her with no fitness. In the case of an unhappy marriage, where the unhappiness is not caused by actual misconduct, but is solely due to incongruity of tastes and capacities, it is cruel to assume that the superior person of the ill-assorted couple has the stronger claim to sympathy.

Finding his wife less tractable than he wished, More withheld his confidence from her, taking the most important steps of his life, without either asking for her advice, or even announcing the course which he was about to take. His resignation of the seals was announced to her on the day *after* his retirement from office, and in a manner which, notwithstanding its drollery, would greatly pain any woman of ordinary sensibility. The day following the date of his resignation was a holiday; and in accordance with his usage the ex-Chancellor, together with his household, attended service in Chelsea Church. On her way to church, Lady More returned the greetings of her friends with a stateliness not unseemly at that ceremonious time in one who was the lady of the Lord High Chancellor. At the conclusion of service, ere she left her pew, the intelligence was broken to her in a jest that she had lost her cherished dignity. "And whereas upon the holidays during his High Chancellorship one of his gentlemen, when the service of the church was done, ordinarily used to come to my lady his wife's pew-door, and say unto her '*Madam, my lord is gone*,' he came into my lady his wife's pew himself, and making a low courtesy, said unto her, 'Madam, my lord is gone,' which she, imagining to be but one of his jests, as he used many unto her, he sadly affirmed unto her that it was true. This was the way he thought fittest to break the matter unto his wife, who was full of sorrow to hear it."

Equally humorous and pathetic was that memorable interview between More and his wife in the Tower, when she, regarding his position by the lights with which nature had endowed her, counseled him to yield even at that late moment to the king. "What the goodyear, Mr. More!" she cried, bustling up to the tranquil and courageous man. "I marvel that you, who have been hitherto always taken for a wise man, will now so play the fool as to lie here in this close, filthy prison, and be content to be shut up thus with mice and rats, when you might be abroad at your liberty, with the favor and good-will both of the king and his council, if you would but do as the bishops and best learned of his realm have done; and, seeing you have at Chelsea a right fair house, your library, your books, your gallery, and all other necessaries so handsome about you, where you might, in company with me, your wife, your children, and household, be merry, I muse what, in God's name, you mean, here thus fondly to tarry." Having heard her out—preserving his good-humor, he said to her, with a cheerful countenance, "I pray thee, good Mrs. Alice, tell me one thing!" "What is it?" saith she, "Is not this house as near heaven as my own?"

Sir Thomas More was looking towards heaven.

Mistress Alice had her eye upon the 'right fair house' at Chelsea.

*Chapter 7*

# GOOD QUEEN BESS

Amongst the eminent men who are frequently mentioned as notorious suitors for the personal affection of Queen Elizabeth, a conspicuous place is awarded to Hatton, by the scandalous memoirs of his time and the romantic traditions of later ages. Historians of the present generation have accepted without suspicion the story that Hatton was Elizabeth's amorous courtier, that the fanciful letters of 'Lydds' were fervent solicitations for response to his passion; that he won her favor and his successive promotions by timely exhibition of personal grace and steady perseverance in flattery. Campbell speaks of the queen and her chancellor as 'lovers;' and the view of the historian has been upheld by novelists and dramatic writers.

The writer of this page ventures to reject a story which is not consistent with truth, and casts a dark suspicion on her who was not more powerful as a queen than virtuous as a woman.

For illustrations of lovers' pranks amongst the Elizabethan lawyers, the reader must pass to two great judges, the inferior of whom was a far greater man than Christopher Hatton. Rivals in law and politics, Bacon and Coke were also rivals in love. Having wooed the same proud, lovely, capricious, violent woman, the one was blessed with failure, and the other was cursed with success.

Until a revolution in the popular estimate of Bacon was effected by Mr. Hepworth Dixon's vindication of that great man, it was generally believed that love was no appreciable element in his nature. Delight in vain display occupied in his affections the place which should have been held by devotion to womanly beauty and goodness; he had sneered at love in an essay, and his cold heart never rebelled against the doctrine of his clever brain; he wooed his notorious cousin for the sake of power, and then married Alice

Barnham for money. Such was the theory, the most solid foundation of which was a humorous treatise,[4] misread and misapplied.

The lady's wealth, rank, and personal attractions were in truth the only facts countenancing the suggestion that Francis Bacon proffered suit to his fair cousin from interested motives. Notwithstanding her defects of temper, no one denies that she was a woman qualified by nature to rouse the passion of man. A wit and beauty, she was mistress of the arts which heighten the powers of feminine tact and loveliness. The daughter of Sir Thomas Cecil, the grandchild of Lord Burleigh, she was Francis Bacon's near relation; and though the Cecils were not inclined to help him to fortune, he was nevertheless one of their connection, and consequently often found himself in familiar conversation with the bright and fascinating woman. Doubtless she played with him, persuading herself that she merely treated him with cousinly cordiality, when she was designedly making him her lover. The marvel was that she did not give him her hand; that he sought it is no occasion for surprise—or for insinuations that he coveted her wealth. Biography is by turns mischievously communicative and vexatiously silent. That Bacon loved Sir William Hatton's widow, and induced Essex to support his suit, and that rejecting him she gave herself to his enemy, we know; but history tells us nothing of the secret struggle which preceded the lady's resolution to become the wife of an unalluring, ungracious, peevish, middle-aged widower. She must have felt some tenderness for her cousin, whose comeliness spoke to every eye, whose wit was extolled by every lip. Perhaps she, like many others, had misread the essay 'Of Love,' and felt herself bound in honor to bring the philosopher to his knees at her feet. It is credible that from the outset of their sentimental intercourse, she intended to win and then to flout him. But coquetry cannot conquer the first laws of human feeling. To be a good flirt, a woman must have nerve and a sympathetic nature; and doubtless the flirt in this instance paid for her triumph with the smart of a lasting wound. Is it fanciful to argue that her subsequent violence and misconduct, her impatience of control and scandalous disrespect for her aged husband, may have been in some part due to the sacrifice of personal inclination which she made in accepting Coke at the entreaty of prudent and selfish relations—and to the contrast, perpetually haunting her, between what she was as Sir Edward's termagant partner, and what she might have been as Francis Bacon's wife?

She consented to a marriage with Edward Coke, but was so ashamed of her choice, that she insisted on a private celebration of their union, although Archbishop Whitgift had

---

[4] To readers who have no sense of humor and irony, the essay 'Of Love' unquestionably gives countenance to the theory that Francis Bacon was cold and passionless in all that concerned woman. Of the many strange constructions put upon this essay, not the least amusing and perverse is that which would make it a piece of adroit flattery to Elizabeth, who never permitted love "to check with business," though she is represented to have used it as a diversion in idle moments. If Sir Thomas More's 'Utopia' had been published a quarter of a century after 1518 (the date of its appearance), a similar construction would have been put on the passage, which urges that lovers should not be bound by an indissoluble tie of wedlock, until mutual inspection has satisfied each of the contracting parties that the other does not labor under any grave personal defect. If it were possible to regard the passage containing this proposal as an interpolation in the original romance, it might then be regarded as an attempt to palliate Henry VIII.'s conduct to Anne of Cleves.

recently raised his voice against the scandal of clandestine weddings, and had actually forbidden them. In the face of the primate's edict the ill-assorted couple were united in wedlock, without license or publication of banns, by a country parson, who braved the displeasure of Whitgift, in order that he might secure the favor of a secular patron. The wedding-day was November 24, 1598, the bridegroom's first wife having been buried on the 24th of the previous July.[5] On learning the violation of his orders, the archbishop was so incensed that he resolved to excommunicate the offenders, and actually instituted for that purpose legal proceedings, which were not dropped until bride and bridegroom humbly sued for pardon, pleading ignorance of law in excuse of their misbehavior.

The scandalous consequences of that marriage are known to every reader who has laughed over the more pungent and comic scenes of English history. Whilst Lady Hatton gave masques and balls in the superb palace which came into her possession through marriage with Sir Christopher Hatton's nephew, Coke lived in his chambers, working at cases and writing the books which are still carefully studied by every young man who wishes to make himself a master of our law. In private they had perpetual squabbles, and they quarrelled with equal virulence and indecency before the world. The matrimonial settlement of their only and ill-starred daughter was the occasion of an outbreak on the part of husband and wife, that not only furnished diversion for courtiers but agitated the council table. Of all the comic scenes connected with that unseemly *fracas*, not the least laughable and characteristic was the grand festival of reconciliation at Hatton House, when Lady Hatton received the king and queen in Holborn, and expressly forbade her husband to presume to show himself among her guests. "The expectancy of Sir Edward's rising," says a writer of the period,[6] "is much abated by reason of his lady's liberty,[7] who

---

[5] When due allowance has been made for the difference between the usages of the sixteenth century and the present time, decency was signally violated by this marriage, which followed so soon upon Mrs. Coke's death, and still sooner upon the death of Lady Hatton's famous grandfather, at whose funeral the lawyer made the first overtures for her hand. Mrs. Coke died June 27, 1598, and was buried at Huntingfield, co. Suffolk, July 24, 1598. Lord Burleigh expired on August 4, of the same year. Coke's first marriage was not unhappy; and on the death of his wife by that union, he wrote in his note-book:—"Most beloved and most excellent wife, she well and happily lived, and, as a true handmaid of the Lord, fell asleep in the Lord, and now lives and reigns in heaven." In after years he often wished most cordially that he could say *as much* for his second wife.

[6] Strafford's Letters and Despatches, I. 5.

[7] Lady Hatton never used her second husband's name either before or after his knighthood. A good case, touching the customary right of a married lady to bear the name, and take her title from the rank of a former husband, is that of Sir Dudley North, Charles II.'s notorious sheriff of London. The son of an English peer, he married Lady Gunning, the widow of a wealthy civic knight, and daughter of Sir Robert Cann, "a morose old merchant of Bristol"—the same magistrate whom Judge Jeffreys, in terms not less just than emphatic, upbraided for his connection with, or to speak moderately, his connivance at, the Bristol kidnappers. It might be thought that the merchant's daughter, on her marriage with a peer's son, would be well content to relinquish the title of Lady Gunning; but Roger North tells us that his brother Dudley accepted knighthood, in order that he might avoid giving offence to the city, and also, in order that his wife might be called Lady North, and not Lady Gunning.—*Vide Life of the Hon. Sir Dudley North.* After Sir Thomas Wilde (subsequently Lord Truro), married Augusta Emma d'Este, the daughter of the duke of Sussex and Lady Augusta Murray, that lady, of whose legitimacy Sir Thomas had vainly endeavored to convince the House of Lords, retained her maiden surname. In society she was generally known as the Princess d'Este, and the bilious satirists of the Inns of Court used to speak of Sir Thomas as 'the Prince.' It was said that one of Wilde's familiar associates, soon after the lawyer's marriage, called at his house and asked if the Princess d'Este was at home. "No, sir," replied the servant, "the Princess d'Este is not at home, but the Prince is!" That this malicious story obtained a wide

was brought in great honor to Exeter House by my Lord of Buckingham from Sir William Craven's, whither she had been remanded, presented by his lordship to the king, received gracious usage, reconciled to her daughter by his Majesty, and her house in Holborn enlightened by his presence at a dinner, where there was a royal feast; and to make it more absolutely her own, express commandment given by her ladyship, that neither Sir Edward Coke nor any of his servants should be admitted."

If tradition may be credited, the law is greatly indebted to the class of women whom it was our forefathers' barbarous wont to punish with the ducking-stool. Had Coke been happy in his second marriage, it is assumed that he would have spent more time in pleasure and fewer hours at his desk, that the suitors in his court would have had less careful decisions, and that posterity would have been favored with fewer reports. If the inference is just, society may point to the commentary on Littleton, and be thankful for the lady's unhappy temper and sharp tongue. In like manner the wits of the following century maintained that Holt's steady application to business was a consequence of domestic misery. The lady who ruled his house in Bedford Row, is said to have been such a virago, that the Chief Justice frequently retired to his chambers, in order that he might place himself beyond reach of her voice. Amongst the good stories told of Radcliffe, the Tory physician, is the tradition of his boast, that he kept Lady Holt alive out of pure political animosity to the Whig Chief Justice. Another eminent lawyer, over whose troubles people have made merry in the same fashion, was Jeffrey Gilbert, Baron of the Exchequer. At his death, October 14, 1726, this learned judge left behind him that mass of reports, histories, and treatises by which he is known as one of the most luminous, as well as voluminous of legal writers. None of his works passed through the press during his life, and when their number and value were discovered after his departure to another world, it was whispered that they had been composed in hours of banishment from a hearth where a *scolding wife* made misery for all who came within the range of her querulous notes.

Disappointed in his suit to his beautiful and domineering cousin, Bacon let some five or six years pass before he allowed his thoughts again to turn to love, and then he wooed and waited for nearly three years more, ere, on a bright May day, he met Alice Barnham in Marylebone Chapel, and made her his wife in the presence of a courtly company. In

---

currency is not wonderful; that it is a truthful anecdote the writer of this book would not like to pledge his credit. The case of Sir John Campbell and Lady Strathedon, was a notable instance of a lawyer and his wife bearing different names. Raised to the peerage, with the title of Baroness Stratheden, the first Lord Abinger's eldest daughter was indebted to her husband for an honor that made him her social inferior. Many readers will remember a droll story of a misapprehension caused by her ladyship's title. During an official journey, Sir John Campbell and Baroness Stratheden slept at lodgings which he had frequently occupied as a circuiteer. On the morning after his arrival, the landlady obtained a special interview with Campbell, and in the baroness's absence thus addressed him, with mingled indignation and respectfulness:—"Sir John Campbell, I am a lone widow, and live by my good name. It is not in my humble place to be too curious about the ladies brought to my lodgings by counsellors and judges. It is not in me to make remarks if a counsellor's lady changes the color of her eyes, and her complexion every assizes. But, Sir John, a gentleman ought not to bring a lady to a lone widow's lodgings, unless so long as he 'okkipies' the apartments he makes all honorable professions that the lady is his wife, and as such gives her the use of his name."

the July of 1603, he wrote to Cecil:—"For this divulged and almost prostituted title of knighthood, I could, without charge by your honor's mean, be content to have it, both because of this late disgrace, and because I have three new knights in my mess in Gray's Inn Commons, and because I have found out an alderman's daughter, a handsome maiden, to my liking. So as if your honor will find the time, I will come to the court from Gorhambury upon any warning." This expression, 'an alderman's daughter,' contributed greatly, if it did not give rise to, the misapprehension that Bacon's marriage was a mercenary arrangement. In these later times the social status of an alderman is so much beneath the rank of a distinguished member of the bar, that a successful queen's counsel, who should make an offer to the daughter of a City magistrate, would be regarded as bent upon a decidedly unambitious match; and if in a significant tone he spoke of the lady as 'an alderman's daughter' his words might be reasonably construed as a hint that her fortune atoned for her want of rank. But it never occurred to Bacon's contemporaries to put such a construction on the announcement. Far from using the words in an apologetic manner, the lover meant them to express concisely that Alice Barnham was a lady of suitable condition to bear a title as well as to become his bride. Cecil regarded them merely as an assurance that his relative meditated a suitable and even advantageous alliance, just as any statesman of the present day would read an announcement that a kinsman, making his way in the law-courts, intended to marry 'an admiral's daughter' or a 'bishop's daughter.' That it was the reverse of a mercenary marriage, Mr. Hepworth Dixon has indisputably proved in his eighth chapter of 'The Story of Lord Bacon's Life,' where he contrasts Lady Bacon's modest fortune with her husband's personal acquisitions and prospects.

*Chapter 8*

# REJECTED ADDRESSES

No lawyer of the Second Charles's time surpassed Francis North in love of money, or was more firmly resolved not to marry, without due and substantial consideration.

His first proposal was for the daughter of a Gray's Inn money-lender. Usury was not a less contemptible vocation in the seventeenth century than it is at the present time; and most young barristers of gentle descent and fair prospects would have preferred any lot to the degradation of marriage with the child of the most fortunate usurer in Charles II.'s London. But the Hon. Francis North was placed comfortably *beneath* the prejudices of his order and time of life. He was of noble birth, but quite ready to marry into a plebeian family; he was young, but loved money more than aught else. So his hearing was quickened and his blood beat merrily when, one fine morning, "there came to him a recommendation of a lady, who was an only daughter of an old usurer in Gray's Inn, supposed to be a good fortune in present, for her father was rich; but, after his death, to become worth, nobody could tell what." One would like to know how that 'recommendation of a lady' reached the lawyer's chambers; above all, who sent it?

"His lordship," continues Roger North, "got a sight of the lady, and did not dislike her; thereupon he made the old man a visit, and a proposal of himself to marry his daughter." By all means let this ingenuous, high-spirited Templar have a fair judgment. He would not have sold himself to just any woman. He required a *maximum* of wealth with a *minimum* of personal repulsiveness. He therefore 'took a sight of the lady' (it does not appear that he talked with her) before he committed himself irrevocably by a proposal. The *sight* having been taken, as he did not dislike her (mind, he did not positively like her) he made the old man a visit. Loving money, and believing in it, this 'old man' wished to secure as much of it as possible for his only child; and therefore looking keenly at the youthful admirer of a usurer's heiress, "asked him what estate his father intended to settle upon him for present maintenance, jointure, and provision for children." Mildly and not unjustly Roger calls this "an inauspicious question." It was so inauspicious that Mr. Francis North abruptly terminated the discussion by wishing the usurer good-morning. So ended Love Affair No. 1.

Having lost his dear companion, Mr. Edward Palmer, son of the powerful Sir Geoffry Palmer, Mr. Francis North soon regarded his friend's wife with tender longing. It was only natural that he should desire to mitigate his sorrow for the dead by possession of the woman who was "left a flourishing widow, and very rich." But the lady knew her worth, as well she might, for "never was lady more closely besieged with wooers: she had no less than five younger sons sat down before her at one time, and she kept them well in hand, as they say, giving no definite answers to any of one of them." Small respect did Mistress Edward Palmer show her late husband's most intimate friend. For weeks she tortured the wretched, knavish fellow with coquettish tricks, and having rendered him miserable in many ways, made him ludicrous by jilting him. "He was held at the long saw above a month, doing his duty as well as he might, and that was but clumsily; for he neither dressed nor danced, when his rivals were adroit at both, and the lady used to shuffle her favors amongst them affectedly, and on purpose to mortify his lordship, and at the same time be as civil to him, with like purpose to mortify them." Poor Mr. Francis! Well may his brother write indignantly, "It was very grievous to him—that had his thoughts upon his clients' concerns, which came in thick upon him—to be held in a course of bo-peep play with a crafty widow." At length, "after a clancular proceeding," this crafty widow, by marrying "a jolly knight of a good estate," set her victims free; and Mr. Francis was at liberty to look elsewhere for a lapful of money.

Roger North tells the story of the third affair so concisely and pithily that his exact words must be put before the reader:—"Another proposition came to his lordship," writes the fraternal biographer, giving Francis North credit for the title he subsequently won, although at the time under consideration he was plain *Mister* North, on the keen look-out for the place of Solicitor General, "by a city broker, from Sir John Lawrence, who had many daughters, and those reputed beauties; and the fortune was to be £6000. His lordship went and dined with the alderman, and liked the lady, who (as the way is) was dressed out for a muster. And coming to treat, the portion shrank to £5000, and upon that his lordship parted, and was not gone far before Mr. Broker (following) came to him, and said Sir John would give £500 more at the birth of the first child; but that would not do, for his lordship hated such screwing. Not long after this dispute, his lordship was made the King's Solicitor General, and then the broker came again, with news that Sir John would give £10,000. 'No,' his lordship said, 'after such usage he would not proceed if he might have £20,000.'" The intervention of the broker in this negotiation is delightfully suggestive. More should have been said about him—his name, address, and terms for doing business. Was he paid for his services on all that he could save from a certain sum beyond which his employer would not advance a single gold-piece for the disposal of his child? Were there, in olden time, men who avowed themselves 'Heart and Jointure Brokers, Agents for Lovers of both Sexes, Contractors of Mutual Attachments,

Wholesale and Retail Dealers in Reciprocal Affection, and General Referees, Respondents, and Insurers in all Sentimental Affairs, Clandestine or otherwise?'

After these mischances Francis North made an eligible match under somewhat singular circumstances. As co-heiresses of Thomas, Earl of Down, three sisters, the Ladies Pope, claimed under certain settlements large estates of inheritance, to which Lady Elizabeth Lee set up a counter claim. North, acting as Lady Elizabeth Lee's counsel, effected a compromise which secured half the property in dispute to his client, and diminished by one-half the fortunes to which each of the three suitors on the other side had maintained their right. Having thus reduced the estate of Lady Frances Pope to a fortune estimated at about £14,000, the lawyer proposed for her hand, and was accepted. After his marriage, alluding to his exertions in behalf of Lady Elizabeth Lee's very disputable claim, he used to say that "he had been counsel against himself;" but Roger North frankly admits that "if this question had not come to such a composition, which diminished the ladies' fortunes, his brother had never compassed his match."

It was not without reluctance that the Countess of Downs consented to the union of her daughter with the lawyer who had half ruined her, and who (though he was Solicitor General and in fine practice) could settle only £5000 upon the lady. "I well remember," observes Roger, "the good countess had some qualms, and complained that she knew not how she could justify what she had done (meaning the marrying her daughters with no better settlement)." To these qualms Francis North, with lawyer-like coolness, answered—"Madam, if you meet with any question about that, *say* that your daughter has £1000 per annum jointure."

The marriage was celebrated in Wroxton Church; and after bountiful rejoicings with certain loyalist families of Oxfordshire, the happy couple went up to London and lived in chambers until they moved into a house in Chancery Lane.

It may surprise some readers of this book to learn that George Jeffreys, the odious judge of the Bloody Circuit, was a successful gallant. Tall, well-shaped, and endowed by nature with a pleasant countenance and agreeable features, Jeffreys was one of the most fascinating men of his time. A wit and a *bon-vivant*, he could hit the humor of the roystering cavaliers who surrounded the 'merry monarch;' a man of gallantry and polite accomplishments, he was acceptable to women of society. The same tongue that bullied from the bench, when witnesses were perverse or counsel unruly, could flatter with such melodious affectation of sincerity, that he was known as a most delightful companion. As a musical connoisseur he spoke with authority; as a teller of good stories he had no equal in town. Even those who detested him did not venture to deny that in the discharge of his judicial offices he could at his pleasure assume a dignity and urbane composure that well became the seat of justice. In short, his talents and graces were so various and effective, that he would have risen to the bench, even if he had labored under the disadvantages of pure morality and amiable temper.

Women declared him irresistible. At court he had the ear of Nell Gwyn and the Duchess of Portsmouth—the Protestant favorite and the Catholic mistress; and before he attained the privilege of entering Whitehall—at a time when his creditors were urgent, and his best clients were the inferior attorneys of the city courts—he was loved by virtuous girls. He was still poor, unknown, and struggling with difficulties, when he induced an heiress to accept his suit,—the daughter of a rural squire whose wine the barrister had drunk upon circuit. This young lady was wooed under circumstances of peculiar difficulty; and she promised to elope with him if her father refused to receive him as a son-in-law. Ill-luck befell the scheme; and whilst young Jeffreys was waiting in the Temple for the letter which should decide his movements, an intimation reached him that elopement was impossible and union forbidden. The bearer of this bad news was a young lady—the child of a poor clergyman—who had been the confidential friend and paid companion of the squire's daughter.

The case was hard for Jeffreys, cruel for the fair messenger. He had lost an advantageous match, she had lost her daily bread. Furious with her for having acted as the *confidante* of the clandestine lovers, the squire had turned this poor girl out of his house; and she had come to London to seek for employment as well as to report the disaster.

Jeffreys saw her overpowered with trouble and shame—penniless in the great city, and disgraced by expulsion from her patron's roof. Seeing that her abject plight was the consequence of amiable readiness to serve him, Jeffreys pitied and consoled her. Most young men would have soothed their consciences and dried the running tears with a gift of money or a letter recommending the outcast to a new employer. As she was pretty, a libertine would have tried to seduce her. In Jeffreys, compassion roused a still finer sentiment: he loved the poor girl and married her. On May 23, 1667, Sarah Neesham was married to George Jeffreys of the Inner Temple; and her father, in proof of his complete forgiveness of her *escapade*, gave her a fortune of £300—a sum which the poor clergyman could not well afford to bestow on the newly married couple.

Having outlived Sarah Neesham, Jeffreys married again—taking for his second wife a widow whose father was Sir Thomas Bludworth, ex-Lord Mayor of London. Whether rumor treated her unjustly it is impossible to say at this distance of time; but if reliance may be put on many broad stories current about the lady, her conduct was by no means free from fault. She was reputed to entertain many lovers. Jeffreys would have created less scandal if, instead of taking her to his home, he had imitated the pious Sir Matthew Hale, who married his maid-servant, and on being twitted by the world with the lowliness of his choice, silenced his censors with a jest.

Amongst the love affairs of seventeenth-century lawyers place must be made for mention of the second wife whom Chief Justice Bramston brought home from Ireland, where she had outlived two husbands (the Bishop of Clogher and Sir John Brereton), before she gave her hand to the judge who had loved her in his boyhood. "When I see her," says the Chief Justice's son, who describes the expedition to Dublin, and the return to London, "I confess I wondered at my father's love. She was low, fatt, red-faced; her dress, too, was a hat and ruff, which tho' she never changed to death. But my father, I believe, seeing me change countenance, told me it was not beautie, but virtue, he courted. I believe she had been handsome in her youth; she had a delicate, fine hand, white and plump, and indeed proved a good wife and mother-in-law, too." On her journey to Charles I.'s London, this elderly bride, in her antiquated attire, rode from Holyhead to Beaumaris on a pillion behind her step-son. "As she rode over the sandes," records her step-son, "behind mee, and pulling off her gloves, her wedding ringe fell off, and sunk instantly. She caused her man to alight; she sate still behind me, and kept her eye on the place, and directed her man, but he not guessing well, she leaped off, saying she would not stir without her ringe, it being the most unfortunate thinge that could befall any one to lose the wedding-ringe—made the man thrust his hand into the sands (the nature of which is not to bear any weight but passing), he pulled up sand, but not the ringe. She made him strip his arme and put it deeper into the sand, and pulled up the ringe; and this done, he and shee, and all that stood still, were sunk almost to the knees, but we were all pleased that the ringe was found."

In the legal circle of Charles the Second's London, Lady King was notable as a virago whose shrill tongue disturbed her husband's peace of mind by day, and broke his rest at night. Earning a larger income than any other barrister of his time, he had little leisure for domestic society; but the few hours which he could have spent with his wife and children, he usually preferred to spend in a tavern, beyond the reach of his lady's sharp querulousness. "All his misfortune," says Roger North, "lay at home, in perverse consort, who always, after his day-labor done, entertained him with all the chagrin and peevishness imaginable; so that he went home as to his prison, or worse; and when the time came, rather than go home, he chose commonly to get a friend to go and sit in a free chat at the tavern, over a single bottle, till twelve or one at night, and then to work again at five in the morning. His fatigue in business, which, as I said, was more than ordinary to him, and his no comfort, or rather, discomfort at home, and taking his refreshment by excising his sleep, soon pulled him down; so that, after a short illness, he died." On his death-bed, however, he forgave the weeping woman, who, more through physical irritability than wicked design, had caused him so much undeserved discomfort; and by his last will and testament he made liberal provision for her wants. Having made his will, "he said, I am glad it is done," runs the memoir of Sir John King, written by his father, "and after took leave of his wife, who was full of tears; seeing it is the will of God, let us part quietly in friendship, with submissiveness to his will, as we came together in friendship by His will."

*Chapter 9*

# "CICERO" UPON HIS TRIAL

A complete history of the loves of lawyers would notice many scandalous intrigues and disreputable alliances, and would comprise a good deal of literature for which the student would vainly look in the works of our best authors. From the days of Wolsey, whose amours were notorious, and whose illegitimate son became Dean of Wells, down to the present time of brighter though not unimpeachable morality, the domestic lives of our eminent judges and advocates have too frequently invited satire and justified regret. In the eighteenth century judges, without any loss of *caste* or popular regard, openly maintained establishments that in these more decorous and actually better days would cover their keepers with obloquy. Attention could be directed to more than one legal family in which the descent must be traced through a succession of illegitimate births. Not only did eminent lawyers live openly with women who were not their wives, and with children whom the law declined to recognize as their offspring; but these women and children moved in good society, apparently indifferent to shame that brought upon them but few inconveniences. In Great Ormond Street, where a mistress and several illegitimate children formed his family circle, Lord Thurlow was visited by bishops and deans; and it is said that in 1806, when Sir James Mansfield, Chief Justice of the Common Pleas, was invited to the woolsack and the peerage, he was induced to decline the offer more by consideration for his illegitimate children than by fears for the stability of the new administration.

Speaking of Lord Thurlow's undisguised intercourse with Mrs. Hervey, Lord Campbell says, "When I first knew the profession, it would not have been endured that any one in a judicial situation should have had such a domestic establishment as Thurlow's; but a majority of judges had married their mistresses. The understanding then was that a man elevated to the bench, if he had a mistress, must either marry her or put her away. For many years there has been no necessity for such an alternative." Either Lord Campbell had not the keen appetite for professional gossip, with which he is ordinarily credited, or his conscience must have pricked him when he wrote, "For many years there has been no necessity for such an alternative." To show how far his lordship erred through want of information or defect of candor is not the duty of this page; but without making any statement that can wound private feeling, the present writer may observe that 'the understanding,' to which Lord Campbell draws attention, has affected the fortune of ladies within the present generation.

That the bright and high-minded Somers was the debauchee that Mrs. Manley and Mr. Cooksey would have us believe him is incredible. It is doubtful if Mackey in his 'Sketch of Leading Characters at the English Court' had sufficient reasons for clouding his sunny picture of the statesman with the assertion that he was "something of a libertine." But there are occasions when prudence counsels us to pay attention to slander.

Having raised himself to the office of Solicitor General, Somers, like Francis Bacon, found an alderman's daughter to his liking; and having formed a sincere attachment for her, he made his wishes known to her father. Miss Anne Bawdon's father was a wealthy merchant, styled Sir John Bawdon—a man proud of his civic station and riches, and thinking lightly of lawyers and law. When Somers stated his property and projects, the rental of his small landed estate and the buoyancy of his professional income, the opulent knight by no means approved the prospect offered to his child. The lawyer might die in the course of twelve months; in which case the Worcestershire estate would be still a small estate, and the professional income would cease. In twelve mouths Mr. Solicitor might be proved a scoundrel, for at heart all lawyers were arrant rogues; in which case matters would be still worse. Having regarded the question from these two points of view, Sir John Bawdon gave Somers his dismissal and married Miss Anne to a rich Turkey merchant. Three years later, when Somers had risen to the woolsack, and it was clear that the rich Turkey merchant would never be anything grander than a rich Turkey merchant, Sir John saw that he had made a serious blunder, for which his child certainly could not thank him. A goodly list might be made of cases where papas have erred and repented in Sir John Bawdon's fashion. Sir John Lawrence would have made his daughter a Lord Keeper's lady and a peeress, if he and his broker had dealt more liberally with Francis North. Had it not been for Sir Joseph Jekyll's counsel, Mr. Cocks, the Worcestershire squire, would have rejected Philip Yorke as an ineligible suitor, in which case *plain* Mrs. Lygon would never have been Lady Hardwicke, and worked her husband's twenty purses of state upon curtains and hangings of crimson velvet. And, if he were so inclined, this writer could point to a learned judge, who in his days of 'stuff' and 'guinea fees' was deemed an ineligible match for a country apothecary's pretty daughter. The country doctor being able to give his daughter £20,000, turned away disdainfully from the unknown 'junior,' who five years later was leading his circuit, and quickly rose to the high office which he still fills to the satisfaction of his country.

Disappointed in his pursuit of Anne Bawdon, Somers never again made any woman an offer of marriage; but scandalous gossip accused him of immoral intercourse with his housekeeper. This woman's name was Blount; and while she resided with the Chancellor, fame whispered that her husband was still living. Not only was Somers charged with open adultery, but it was averred that for the sake of peace he had imprisoned in a madhouse his mistress's lawful husband, who was originally a Worcester tradesman. The chief authority for this startling imputation is Mrs. Manley, who was encouraged, if not actually paid, by Swift to lampoon his political adversaries. In her 'New Atalantis'—the 'Cicero' of which scandalous work was understood by its readers to signify 'Lord Somers,'—this shameless woman entertained quid-nuncs and women of fashion by putting this abominable story in written words, the coarseness of which accorded with the repulsiveness of the accusation.

At a time when honest writers on current politics were punished with fine and imprisonment, the pillory and the whip, statesmen and ecclesiastics were not ashamed to keep such libellers as Mrs. Manley in their pay. That the reader may fully appreciate the change which time has wrought in the tone of political literature, let him contrast the virulence and malignity of this unpleasant passage from the New Atalantis, with the tone which recently characterized the public discussion of the case which is generally known by the name of 'The Edmunds Scandal.'

Notwithstanding her notorious disregard of truth, it is scarcely credible that Mrs. Manley's scurrilous charge was in no way countenanced by facts. At the close of the seventeenth century to keep a mistress was scarcely regarded as an offence against good morals; and living in accordance with the fashion of the time, it is probable that Somers did that which Lord Thurlow, after an interval of a century, was able to do without rousing public disapproval. Had his private life been spotless, he would doubtless have taken legal steps to silence his traducer; and unsustained by a knowledge that he dared not court inquiry into his domestic arrangements, Mrs. Manley would have used her pen with greater caution. But all persons competent to form an opinion on the case have agreed that the more revolting charges of the indictment were the baseless fictions of a malicious and unclean mind.

*Chapter 10*

# BROTHERS IN TROUBLE

In the 'Philosophical Dictionary,' Voltaire, laboring under misapprehension or carried away by perverse humor, made the following strange announcement:—"Il est public en Angleterre, et on voudroit le nier en vain, que le Chancelier Cowper épousa deux femmes, qui vécurent ensemble dans sa maison avec une concorde singulière qui fit honneur à tous trois. Plusieurs curieux ont encore le petit livre que ce Chancelier composa en faveur de la Polygamie." Tickled by the extravagant credulity or grotesque malice of this declaration, an English wit, improving upon the published words, represented the Frenchman as maintaining that the custodian of the Great Seal of England was called the *Lord Keeper*, because, by English law, he was permitted to keep as many wives as he pleased.

The reader's amusement will not be diminished by a brief statement of the facts to which we are indebted for Voltaire's assertions.

William Cowper, the first earl of his line, began life with a reputation for dissipated tastes and habits, and by unpleasant experience he learned how difficult it is to get rid of a bad name. The son of a Hertfordshire baronet, he was still a law student when he formed a reprehensible connection with an unmarried lady of that county—Miss (or, as she was called by the fashion of the day Mistress) Elizabeth Culling, of Hertingfordbury Park. But little is known of this woman. Her age is an affair of uncertainty, and all the minor circumstances of her intrigue with young William Cowper are open to doubt and conjecture; but the few known facts justify the inference that she neither merited nor found much pity in her disgrace, and that William erred through boyish indiscretion rather than from vicious propensity. She bore him two children, and he neither married her nor was required by public opinion to marry her. The respectability of their connections gave the affair a peculiar interest, and afforded countenance to many groundless reports. By her friends it was intimated that the boy had not triumphed over the lady's virtue until he had made her a promise of marriage; and some persons even went so far as to assert that they were privately married. It is not unlikely that at one time the boy intended to make her his wife as soon as he should be independent of his father, and free to please himself. Beyond question, however, is it that they were never united in wedlock, and that Will Cowper joined the Home Circuit with the tenacious fame of a scapegrace and *roué*.

That he was for any long period a man of dissolute morals is improbable; for he was only twenty-four years of age when he was called to the bar, and before his call he had married (after a year's wooing) a virtuous and exemplary young lady, with whom he lived happily for more than twenty years. A merchant's child, whose face was her fortune—Judith, the daughter of Sir Robert Booth, is extolled by biographers for reclaiming her young husband from a life of levity and culpable pleasure. That he loved her sincerely from the date of their imprudent marriage till the date of her death, which occurred just about six months before his elevation to the woolsack, there is abundant evidence.

Judith died April 2, 1705, and in the September of the following year the Lord Keeper married Mary Clavering, the beautiful and virtuous lady of the bedchamber to Caroline Wilhelmina Dorothea, Princess of Wales. This lady was the Countess Cowper whose diary was published by Mr. Murray in the spring of 1864; and in every relation of life she was as good and noble a creature as her predecessor in William Cowper's affection. Of the loving terms on which she lived with her lord, conclusive testimony is found in their published letters and her diary. Frequently separated by his professional avocations and her duties of attendance upon the Princess of Wales, they maintained, during the periods of personal severance, a close and tender intercourse by written words; and at all other times, in sickness not less than in health, they were a fondly united couple. One pathetic entry in the countess's diary speaks eloquently of their nuptial tenderness and devotion:—"April 7th, 1716. After dinner we went to Sir Godfrey Kneller's to see a picture of my lord, which he is drawing, and is the best that was ever done for him; it is for my drawing-room, and in the same posture that he watched me so many weeks in my great illness."

Lord Cowper's second marriage was solemnized with a secrecy for which his biographers are unable to account. The event took place September, 1706, about two months before his father's death, but it was not announced till the end of February, 1707, at which time Luttrell entered in his diary, "The Lord Keeper, who not long since was privately married to Mrs. Clavering of the bishoprick of Durham, brought her home this day." Mr. Foss, in his 'Judges of England,' suggests that the concealment of the union "may not improbably be explained by the Lord Keeper's desire not to disturb the last days of his father, who might perhaps have been disappointed that the selection had not fallen on some other lady to whom he had wished his son to be united." But this conjecture, notwithstanding its probability, is only a conjecture. Unless they had grave reasons for their conduct, the Lord Keeper and his lady had better have joined hands in the presence of the world, for the mystery of their private wedding nettled public curiosity, and gave new life to an old slander.

Cowper's boyish *escapade* was not forgotten by the malicious. No sooner had he become conspicuous in his profession and in politics, than the story of his intercourse with Miss Culling was told in coffee-rooms with all the exaggerations that prurient fancy could devise or enmity dictate. The old tale of a secret marriage—or, still worse, of a mock marriage—was caught from the lips of some Hertford scandal-monger, and conveyed to the taverns and drawing-rooms of London. In taking Sir Robert Booth's daughter to Church, he was said to have committed bigamy. Even while he was in the House of Commons he was known by the name of 'Will Bigamy;' and that *sobriquet* clung to him ever afterwards. Twenty years of wholesome domestic intercourse with his first wife did not free him from the abominable imputation, and his marriage with Miss Clavering revived the calumny in a new form. Fools were found to believe that he had married her during Judith Booth's life and that their union had been concealed for several years instead of a few months. The affair with Miss Culling was for a time forgotten, and the charge preferred against the keeper of the queen's conscience was bigamy of a much more recent date.

In various forms this ridiculous accusation enlivens the squibs of the pamphleteers of Queen Anne's reign. In the 'New Atalantis' Mrs. Manley certified that the fair victim was first persuaded by his lordship's sophistries to regard polygamy as accordant with moral law. Having thus poisoned her understanding, he gratified her with a form of marriage, in which his brother Spencer, in clerical disguise, acted the part of a priest. It was even suggested that the bride in this mock marriage was the lawyer's ward. Never squeamish about the truth, when he could gain a point by falsehood, Swift endorsed the spiteful fabrication, and in the *Examiner*, pointing at Lord Cowper, wrote—"This gentleman, knowing that marriage fees were a considerable perquisite to the clergy, found out a way of improving them cent. per cent for the benefit of the Church. His invention was to marry a second wife while the first was alive; convincing her of the lawfulness by such arguments as he did not doubt would make others follow the same example. *These he had drawn up in writing with intention to publish for the general good, and it is hoped he may now have leisure to finish them.*" It is possible that the words in italics were the cause of Voltaire's astounding statement: "Plusieurs curieux ont encore le petit livre que ce Chancelier composa en faveur de la Polygamie." On this point Lord Campbell, confidently advancing an opinion which can scarcely command unanimous assent, says, "The fable of the '*Treatise*' is evidently taken from the panegyric on 'a plurality of wives,' which Mrs. Manley puts into the mouth of Lord Cowper, in a speech supposed to be addressed by Hernando to Lousia." But whether Voltaire accepted the 'New Atalantis,' or the *Examiner*, as an authority for the statements of his very laughable passage, it is scarcely credible that he believed himself to be penning the truth. The most reasonable explanation of the matter appears to be, that tickled by Swift's venomous lines, the sarcastic Frenchman in malice and gaiety adopted them, and added to their piquancy by the assurance that the Chancellor's book was not only published, but was preserved by connoisseurs as a literary curiosity.

Like his elder brother, the Chancellor, Spencer Cowper married at an early age, lived to wed a second wife, and was accused of immorality that was foreign to his nature. The offence with which the younger Cowper was charged, created so wide and profound a sensation, and gave rise to such a memorable trial, that the reader will like to glance at the facts of the case.

Born in 1669, Spencer Cowper was scarcely of age when he was called to the bar, and made Comptroller of the Bridge House Estate. The office, which was in the gift of the corporation of London, provided him with a good income, together with a residence in the Bridge House, St. Olave's, Southwark, and brought him in contact with men who were able to bring him briefs or recommend him to attorneys. For several years the boy-barrister was thought a singularly lucky fellow. His hospitable house was brightened by a young and lovely wife (Pennington, the daughter of John Goodeve), and he was so much respected in his locality that he was made a justice of the peace. In his profession he was equally fortunate: his voice was often heard at Westminster and on the Home Circuit, the same circuit where his brother William practised and his family interest lay. He found many clients.

Envy is the shadow of success; and the Cowpers were watched by men who longed to ruin them. From the day when they armed and rode forth to welcome the Prince of Orange, the lads had been notably fortunate. Notwithstanding his reputation for immorality William Cowper had sprung into lucrative practice, and in 1695 was returned to Parliament as representative for Hartford, the other seat for the borough being filled by his father, Sir William Cowper.

In spite of their comeliness and complaisant manners, the lightness of their wit and the *prestige* of their success, Hertford heard murmurs that the young Cowpers were *too* lucky by half, and that the Cowper interest was dangerously powerful in the borough. It was averred that the Cowpers were making unfair capital out of liberal professions: and when the Hertford Whigs sent the father and son to the House of Commons, the vanquished party cursed in a breath the Dutch usurper and his obsequious followers.

It was resolved to damage the Cowpers:—by fair means or foul, to render them odious in their native town.

Ere long the malcontents found a good cry.

Scarcely less odious to the Hertford Tories than the Cowpers themselves was an influential Quaker of the town, named Stout, who actively supported the Cowper interest. A man of wealth and good repute, this follower of George Fox exerted himself enthusiastically in the election contest of 1695: and in acknowledgment of his services the Cowpers honored him with their personal friendship. Sir William Cowper asked him to dine at Hertford Castle—the baronet's country residence; Sir William's sons made calls on his wife and daughter. Of course these attentions from Cowpers to 'the Shaker' were offensive to the Tory magnates of the place: and they vented their indignation in whispers, that the young men never entered Stout's house without kissing his pretty daughter.

While these rumors were still young, Mr. Stout died leaving considerable property to his widow, and to his only child—the beauteous Sarah; and after his death the intercourse between the two families became yet more close and cordial. The lawyers advised the two ladies about the management of their property: and the baronet gave them invitations to his London House in Hatton Garden, as well as to Hertford Castle. The friendship had disastrous consequences. Both the brothers were very fascinating men—men, moreover, who not only excelled in the art of pleasing, but who also habitually exercised it. From custom, inclination, policy, they were very kind to the mother and daughter; probably paying the latter many compliments which they would never have uttered had they been single men. Coming from an unmarried man the speech is often significant of love, which on the lips of a husband is but the language of courtesy. But, unfortunately, Miss ('Mistress' is her style in the report of a famous trial) Sarah Stout fell madly in love with Spencer Cowper notwithstanding the impossibility of marriage.

Not only did she conceive a dangerous fondness for him, but she openly expressed it—by speech and letters. She visited him in the Temple, and persecuted him with her embarrassing devotion whenever he came to Hertford. It was a trying position for a young man not thirty years of age, with a wife to whom he was devotedly attached, and a family whose political influence in his native town might be hurt by publication of the girl's folly. Taking his elder brother into his confidence, he asked what course he ought to pursue. To withdraw totally and abruptly from the two ladies, would be cruel to the daughter, insulting to the mother; moreover, it would give rise to unpleasant suspicions and prejudicial gossip in the borough. It was decided that Spencer must repress the girl's advances—must see her loss frequently—and, by a reserved and frigid manner, must compel her to assume an appearance of womanly discretion. But the plan failed.

At the opening of the year 1699 she invited him to take up his quarters in her mother's house, when he came to Hertford at the next Spring Assizes. This invitation he declined, saying that he had arranged to take his brother's customary lodgings in the house of Mr. Barefoot, in the Market Place, but with manly consideration he promised to call upon her. "I am glad," Sarah wrote to him on March 5, 1699, "you have not quite forgot there is such a person as I in being: but I am willing to shut my eyes and not see anything that looks like unkindness in you, and rather content myself with what excuses you are pleased to make, than be inquisitive into what I must not know: I am sure the winter has been too unpleasant for me to desire the continuance of it: and I wish you were to endure the sharpness of it but for one short hour, as I have done for many long nights and days, and then I believe it would move that rocky heart of yours that can be so thoughtless of me as you are."

On Monday, March 13, following the date of the words just quoted, Spencer Cowper rode into Hertford, alighted at Mrs. Stout's house, and dined with the ladies. Having left the house after dinner, in order that he might attend to some business, he returned in the evening and supped with the two women. Supper over, Mrs. Stout retired for the night, leaving her daughter and the young barrister together. No sooner had the mother left the room, than a distressing scene ensued.

Unable to control or soothe her, Spencer gently divided the clasp of her hands, and having freed himself from her embrace, hastened from the room and abruptly left the house. He slept at his lodgings; and the next morning he was horror-struck on hearing that Sarah Stout's body had been found drowned in the mill-stream behind her old home. That catastrophe had actually occurred. Scarcely had the young barrister reached the Market Place, when the miserable girl threw herself into the stream from which her lifeless body was picked on the following morning. At the coroner's inquest which ensued, Spencer Cowper gave his evidence with extreme caution, withholding every fact that could be injurious to Sarah's reputation; and the jury returned a verdict that the deceased gentlewoman had killed herself whilst in a state of insanity.

In deep dejection Spencer Cowper continued the journey of the circuit.

But the excitement of the public was not allayed by the inquest and subsequent funeral. It was rumored that it was no case of self-murder, but a case of murder by the barrister, who had strangled his dishonored victim, and had then thrown her into the river. Anxious to save their sect from the stigma of suicide the Quakers concurred with the Tories in charging the young man with a hideous complication of crimes. The case against Spencer was laid before Chief Justice Holt, who at first dismissed the accusation as absurd, but was afterwards induced to commit the suspected man for trial; and in the July of 1699 the charge actually came before a jury at the Hertford Assizes. Four prisoners—Spencer Cowper, two attorneys, and a law-writer—were placed in the dock on the charge of murdering Sarah Stout.

On the present occasion there is no need to recapitulate the ridiculous evidence and absurd misconduct of the prosecution in this trial; though criminal lawyers who wish to know what unfairness and irregularities were permitted in such inquiries in the seventeenth century cannot do better than to peruse the full report of the proceedings, which may be found in every comprehensive legal library. In this place it is enough to say that though the accusation was not sustained by a shadow of legal testimony, the prejudice against the prisoners, both on the part of a certain section of the Hertford residents and the presiding judge, Mr. Baron Hatsel, was such that the verdict for acquittal was a disappointment to many who heard it proclaimed by the foreman of the jury. Narcissus Luttrell, indeed, says that the verdict was "to the satisfaction of the auditors;" but in this statement the diarist was unquestionably wrong, so far as the promoters of the prosecution were concerned. Instead of accepting the decision without demur, they attempted to put the prisoners again on their trial by the obsolete process of "appeal of murder;" but this endeavor proving abortive, the case was disposed of, and the prisoners' minds set at rest.

The barrister who was thus tried on a capital charge, and narrowly escaped a sentence that would have consigned him to an ignominious death, resumed his practice in the law courts, sat in the House of Commons and rose to be a judge in the Court of Common Pleas. It is said that he "presided on many trials for murder; ever cautious and mercifully inclined—remembering the great peril which he himself had undergone."

The same writer who aspersed Somers with her unchaste thoughts, and reiterated the charge of bigamy against Lord Chancellor Cowper, did not omit to give a false and malicious version to the incidents which had acutely wounded the fine sensibilities of the younger Cowper. But enough notice has been taken of the 'New Atalantis' in this chapter. To that repulsive book we refer those readers who may wish to peruse Mrs. Manley's account of Sarah Stout's death.

A distorted tradition of Sarah Stout's tragic end, and of Lord Cowper's imputed bigamy, was contributed to an early number of the 'European' by a clerical authority—the Rev. J. Hinton, Rector of Alderton, in Northamptonshire. "Mrs. Sarah Stout," says the writer, "whose death was charged upon Spencer Cowper, was strangled accidentally by drawing the steenkirk too tight upon her neck, as she, with four or five young persons, were at a game of romp upon the staircase; but it was not done by Mr. Cowper, though one of the company. Mrs. Clavering, Lord Chancellor Cowper's second wife, whom he married during the life of his first, was there too; they were so confounded with the accident, that they foolishly resolved to throw her into the water, thinking it would pass that she had drowned herself." This charming paragraph illustrates the vitality of scandal, and at the same time shows how ludicrously rumor and tradition mistell stories in the face of evidence.

Spencer Cowper's second son, the Rev. John Cowper, D.D., was the father of William Cowper, the poet.

*Chapter 11*

# EARLY MARRIAGES

Notwithstanding his illustrious descent, Simon Harcourt raised himself to the woolsack by his own exertions, and was in no degree indebted to powerful relatives for his elevation. The son of a knight, whose loyalty to the House of Stuart had impoverished his estate, he spent his student-days at Pembroke, Oxford, and the Inner Temple, in resolute labor, and with few indulgences. His father could make him but a slender allowance; and when he assumed the gown of a barrister, the future Chancellor, like Erskine in after years, was spurred to industry by the voices of his wife and children. Whilst he was still an undergraduate of the university, he fell in love with Rebecca Clark, daughter of a pious man, of whose vocation the modern peerages are ashamed. Sir Philip Harcourt (the Chancellor's father) in spite of his loyalty quarrelled with the Established Church, and joined the Presbyterians: and Thomas Clark was his Presbyterian chaplain, secretary, and confidential servant. Great was Sir Philip's wrath on learning that his boy had not only fallen in love with Rebecca Clark, but had married her privately. It is probable that the event lowered the worthy knight's esteem for the Presbyterian system; but as anger could not cut the nuptial bond, the father relented—gave the young people all the assistance he could, and hoped that they would live long without repenting their folly. The match turned out far better than the old knight feared. Taking his humble bride to modest chambers, young Harcourt applied sedulously to the study of the law; and his industry was rewarded by success, and by the gratitude of a dutiful wife. In unbroken happiness they lived together for a succession of years, and their union was fruitful of children.

Harcourt fared better with his love-match than Sergeant Hill with his heiress, Miss Medlycott of Cottingham, Northamptonshire. On the morning of his wedding the eccentric sergeant, having altogether forgotten his most important engagement for the day, received his clients in chambers after his usual practice, and remained busy with professional cares until a band of devoted friends forcibly carried him to the church, where his bride had been waiting for him more than an hour. The ceremony having been duly performed, he hastened back to his chambers, to be present at a consultation. Notwithstanding her sincere affection for him, the lady proved but an indifferent wife to the black-letter lawyer. Empowered by Act of Parliament to retain her maiden-name after marriage, she showed her disesteem for her husband's patronymic by her mode of exercising the privilege secured to her by special law; and many a time the sergeant indignantly insisted that she should use his name in her signatures. "My name is Hill, madam; my father's name was Hill, madam; all the Hills have been named Hill, madam; Hill is a good name—and by ——, madam, you *shall* use it." On other matters he was more compliant—humoring her old-maidish fancies in a most docile and conciliating manner. Curiously neat and orderly, Mrs. Medlycott took great pride in the faultlessness of her domestic arrangements, so far as cleanliness and precise order were concerned. To maintain the whiteness of the pipe-clayed steps before the front door of her Bedford Square mansion was a chief object of her existence; and to gratify her in this particular, Sergeant Hill use daily to leave his premises by the kitchen steps. Having outlived the lady, Hill observed to a friend who was condoling with him on his recent bereavement, "Ay, my poor wife is gone! She was a good sort of woman—in *her* way a *very* good sort of woman. I do honestly declare my belief that in *her* way she had no equal. But—but—I'll tell you something in confidence. If ever I marry again, *I won't marry merely for money*." The learned sergeant died in his ninety-third year without having made a second marriage.

Like Harcourt, John Scott married under circumstances that called forth many warm expressions of censure; and like Harcourt, he, in after life, reflected on his imprudent marriage as one of the most fortunate steps of his earlier career. The romance of the law contains few more pleasant episodes than the story of handsome Jack Scott's elopement with Bessie Surtees. There is no need to tell in detail how the comely Oxford scholar danced with the banker's daughter at the Newcastle assemblies; how his suit was at first recognised by the girl's parents, although the Scotts were but rich 'fitters,' whereas Aubone Surtees, Esquire, was a banker and gentleman of honorable descent; how, on the appearance of an aged and patrician suitor for Bessie's hand, papa and mamma told Jack Scott not to presume on their condescension, and counseled Bessie to throw her lover over and become the lady of Sir William Blackett; how Bessie was faithful, and Jack was urgent; how they had secret interviews on Tyne-side and in London, meeting clandestinely on horseback and on foot, corresponding privately by letters and confidential messengers; how, eventually, the lovers, to the consternation of 'good society' in Newcastle, were made husband and wife at Blackshiels, North Britain. Who is ignorant of the story? Does not every visitor to Newcastle pause before an old house in Sandhill, and look up at the blue pane which marks the window from which Bessie descended into her lover's arms?

Jack and Bessie were not punished with even that brief period of suffering and uncertainty which conscientious novelists are accustomed, for the sake of social morals, to assign to run-away lovers before the merciful guardian or tender parent promises forgiveness and a liberal allowance, paid in quarterly installments. In his old age Eldon used to maintain that their plight was very pitiable on the third morning after their rash union. "Our funds were exhausted: we had not a home to go to, and we knew not whether our friends would ever speak to us again." In this strain ran the veteran's story, which, like all other anecdotes from the same source, must be received with caution. But even the old peer, ever ready to exaggerate his early difficulties, had not enough effrontery to represent that their dejection lasted more than three days. The fathers of the bride and bridegroom soon met and came to terms, and with the beginning of the new year Bessie Scott was living in New Inn Hall, Oxford, whilst her husband read Vinerian Lectures, and presided over that scholastic house. The position of Scott at this time was very singular. He was acting as substitute for Sir Robert Chambers, the principal of New Inn Hall and Vinerian Professor of Law, who contrived to hold his university preferments, whilst he discharged the duties of a judge in India. To give an honest color to this indefensible arrangement, it was provided that the lectures read from the Vinerian Chair should actually be written by the Professor, although they were delivered by deputy. Scott, therefore, as the Professor's mouth-piece, on a salary of £60 a year, with free quarters in the Principal's house, was merely required to read a series of treatises sent to him by the absent teacher. "The law-professor," the ex-Chancellor used to relate with true Eldonian humor and *fancy*—"sent me the first lecture, which I had to read immediately to the students, and which I began without knowing a single word that was in it. It was upon the statute (4 and 5 P. and M. c. 8), 'of young men running away with maidens.' Fancy me reading, with about 140 boys and young men all giggling at the Professor! Such a tittering audience no one ever had." If this incident really occurred on the occasion of his 'first reading,' the laughter must have been inextinguishable; for, of course, Jack Scott's run-away marriage had made much gossip in Oxford Common Rooms, and the singular loveliness of his girlish wife (described by an eye-witness as being "so very young as to give the impression of childhood,") stirred the heart of every undergraduate who met her in High Street.

There is no harm done by laughter at the old Chancellor's romantic fictions about the poverty which he and his Bessie encountered, hand in hand, at the outset of life; for the laughter blinds no one to the genuine affection and wholesome honesty of the young husband and wife. One has reason to wish that marriages such as theirs were more frequent amongst lawyers in these ostentatious days. At present the young barrister, who marries before he has a clear fifteen hundred a year, is charged with reckless imprudence; and unless his wife is a woman of fortune, or he is able to settle a heavy sum of money upon her, his anxious friends terrify him with pictures of want and sorrow stored up for him in the future. Society will not let him live after the fashion of 'juniors' eighty or a hundred years since. He must maintain two establishments—his chambers for business, his house in the west-end of town for his wife. Moreover, the lady must have a brougham and liberal pin money, or four or five domestic servants and a drawing-room well furnished with works of art and costly decorations. They must give state dinners and three or four routs every season; and in all other matters their mode of life must be, or seem to be, that of the upper ten thousand. Either they must live in this style, or be pushed aside and forgotten. The choice for them lies between very expensive society or none at all—that is to say, none at all amongst the rising members of the legal profession, and the sort of people with whom young barristers, from prudential motives, wish to form acquaintance. Doubtless many a fair reader of this page is already smiling at the writer's simplicity, and is saying to herself, "Here is one of the advocates of marriage on three hundred a year."

But this writer is not going to advocate marriage on that or any other particular sum. From personal experience he knows what comfort a married man may have for an outlay of three or four hundred per annum; and from personal observation he knows what privations and ignominious poverty are endured by unmarried men who spend twice the larger of those sums on chamber-and-club life. He knows that there are men who shiver at the bare thought of losing caste by marriage with a portionless girl, whilst they are complacently leading the life which, in nine cases out of ten, terminates in the worst form of social degradation—matrimony where the husband blushes for his wife's early history, and dares not tell his own children the date of his marriage certificate. If it were his pleasure he could speak sad truths about the bachelor of modest income, who is rich enough to keep his name on the books of two fashionable clubs, to live in a good quarter of London, and to visit annually continental capitals, but far too poor to think of incurring the responsibilities of marriage. It could be demonstrated that in a great majority of instances this wary, prudent, selfish gentleman, instead of being the social success which many simple people believe him, is a signal and most miserable failure; that instead of pursuing a career of various enjoyments and keen excitements, he is a martyr to *ennui*, bored by the monotony of an objectless existence, utterly weary of the splendid clubs, in which he is presumed by unsophisticated admirers to find an ample compensation for want of household comfort and domestic affection: that as soon as he has numbered forty years, he finds the roll of his friends and cordial acquaintances diminish, and is compelled to retire before younger men, who snatch from his grasp the prizes of social rivalry; and that, as each succeeding lustre passes, he finds the chain of his secret disappointments and embarrassments more galling and heavy.

It is not a question of marriage on three hundred a year without prospects, but a marriage on five or six hundred a year with good expectations. In the Inns of Court there are, at the present time, scores of clever, industrious fine-hearted gentlemen who have sure incomes of three or four hundred pounds per annum. In Tyburnia and Kensington there is an equal number of young gentlewomen with incomes varying between £150 and

£300 a year. These men and women see each other at balls and dinners, in the parks and at theatres; the ladies would not dislike to be wives, the men are longing to be husbands. But that hideous tyrant, social opinion, bids them avoid marriage.

In Lord Eldon's time the case was otherwise. Society saw nothing singular or reprehensible in his conduct when he brought Bessie to live in the little house in Cursitor Street. No one sneered at the young law-student, whose home was a little den in a dingy thoroughfare. At a later date, the rising junior, whose wife lived over his business chambers in Carey Street, was the object of no unkind criticism because his domestic arrangements were inexpensive, and almost frugal. Had his success been tardy instead of quick and decisive, and had circumstances compelled him to live under the shadow of Lincoln's Inn wall for thirty years on a narrow income, he would not on that account have suffered from a single disparaging criticism. Amongst his neighbors in adjacent streets, and within the boundaries of his Inn, he would have found society for himself and wife, and playmates for his children. Good fortune coming in full strong flood, he was not compelled to greatly change his plan of existence. Even in those days, when costly ostentation characterized aristocratic society—he was permitted to live modestly—and lay the foundation of that great property which he transmitted to his ennobled descendants.

When satire has done its worst with the miserly propensities of the great lawyer and his wife, their long familiar intercourse exhibits a wealth of fine human affection and genuine poetry which sarcasm cannot touch. Often as he had occasion to regret Lady Eldon's peculiarities—the stinginess which made her grudge the money paid for a fish or a basket of fruit; the nervous repugnance to society, which greatly diminished his popularity; and the taste for solitude and silence which marked her painfully towards the close of her life—the Chancellor never even hinted to her his dissatisfaction. When their eldest daughter, following her mother's example, married without the permission of her parents, it was suggested to Lord Eldon that her ladyship ought to take better care of her younger daughter, Lady Frances, and entering society should play the part of a vigilant *chaperon*. The counsel was judicious; but the Chancellor declined to act upon it, saying,—"When she was young and beautiful, she gave up everything for me. What she is, I have made her; and I cannot now bring myself to compel her inclinations. Our marriage prevented her mixing in society when it afforded her pleasure; it appears to give pain now, and why should I interpose?" In his old age, when she was dead, he visited his estate in Durham, but could not find heart to cross the Tyne bridge and look at the old house from which he took her in the bloom and tenderness of her girlhood. An urgent invitation to visit Newcastle drew from him the reply—"I know my fellow-townsmen complain of my not coming to see them; but *how can I pass that bridge?*" After a pause, he added, "Poor Bessie! if ever there was an angel on earth she was one. The only reparation which one man can make to another for running away with his daughter, is to be exemplary in his conduct towards her."

In pecuniary affairs not less prudent than his brother, Lord Stowell in matters of sentiment was capable of indiscretion. In the long list of legal loves there are not many episodes more truly ridiculous than the story of the older Scott's second marriage. On April 10, 1813, the decorous Sir William Scott, and Louisa Catharine, widow of John, Marquis of Sligo, and daughter of Admiral Lord Howe, were united in the bonds of holy wedlock, to the infinite amusement of the world of fashion, and to the speedy humiliation of the bridegroom. So incensed was Lord Eldon at his brother's folly, that he refused to appear at the wedding; and certainly the Chancellor's displeasure was not without reason, for the notorious absurdity of the affair brought ridicule on the whole of the Scott family connexion. The happy couple met for the first time in the Old Bailey, when Sir William Scott and Lord Ellenborough presided at the trial of the marchioness's son, the young Marquis of Sligo, who had incurred the anger of the law by luring into his yacht, in Mediterranean waters, two of the king's seamen. Throughout the hearing of that *cause célèbre*, the marchioness sat in the fetid court of the Old Bailey, in the hope that her presence might rouse amongst the jury or in the bench feelings favorable to her son. This hope was disappointed. The verdict having been given against the young peer, he was ordered to pay a fine of £5000, and undergo four months' incarceration in Newgate, and—worse than fine and imprisonment—was compelled to listen to a parental address from Sir William Scott on the duties and responsibilities of men of high station. Either under the influence of sincere admiration for the judge, or impelled by desire for vengeance on the man who had presumed to lecture her son in a court of justice, the marchioness wrote a few hasty words of thanks to Sir William Scott for his salutary exhortation to her boy. She even went so far as to say that she wished the erring marquis could always have so wise a counsellor at his side. This communication was made upon a slip of paper, which the writer sent to the judge by an usher of the court. Sir William read the note as he sat on the bench, and having looked towards the fair scribe, he received from her a glance and smile that were fruitful of much misery to him. Within four months the courteous Sir William Scott was tied fast to a beautiful, shrill, voluble termagant, who exercised marvellous ingenuity in rendering him wretched and contemptible. Reared in a stately school of old-world politeness, the unhappy man was a model of decorum and urbanity. He took reasonable pride in the perfection of his tone and manner; and the marchioness—whose malice did not lack cleverness—was never more happy than when she was gravely expostulating with him, in the presence of numerous auditors, on his lamentable want of style, tact, and gentlemanlike bearing. It is said that, like Coke and Holt under similar circumstances, Sir William preferred the quietude of his chambers to the society of an unruly wife, and that in the cellar of his Inn he sought compensation for the indignities and sufferings which he endured at home. Fifty years since the crusted port of the Middle Temple could soothe the heart at night, without paining the head in the morning.

# PART 3. MONEY

*Chapter 12*

# FEES TO COUNSEL

From time immemorial popular satire has been equally ready to fix the shame of avarice upon Divinity Physic, and Law; and it cannot be denied that in this matter the sarcasms of the multitude are often sustained by the indisputable evidence of history. The greed of the clergy for tithes and dues is not more widely proverbial than the doctor's thirst for fees, or the advocate's readiness to support injustice for the sake of gain. Of Guyllyam of Horseley, physician to Charles VI of France, Froissart says, "All his dayes he was one of the greatest nygardes that ever was;" and the chronicler adds, "With this rodde lightly all physicians are beaten." In his address to the sergeants who were called soon after his elevation to the Marble Chair, the Lord Keeper Puckering, directing attention to the grasping habits which too frequently disgraced the leaders of the bar, observed: "I am to exhort you also not to embrace multitude of causes, or to undertake more places of hearing causes than you are well able to consider of or perform, lest thereby you either disappoint your clients when their causes be heard, or come unprovided, or depart when their causes be in hearing. For it is all one not to come, as either to come unprovided, or depart before it be ended." Notwithstanding Lingard's able defence of the Cardinal, scholars are still generally of opinion that Beaufort—the Chancellor who lent money on the king's crown, the bishop who sold the Pope's soldiers for a thousand marks—is a notable instance of the union of legal covetousness and ecclesiastical greed.

The many causes which affect the value of money in different ages create infinite perplexity for the antiquarian who wishes to estimate the prosperity of the bar in past times; but the few disjointed data, that can be gathered from old records, create an impression that in the fourteenth, fifteenth and sixteenth centuries the ordinary fees of eminent counsel were by no means exorbitant, although fortunate practitioners could make large incomes.

Dugdale's 'Baronage' describes with delightful quaintness William de Beauchamp's interview with his lawyers when that noble (on the death of John Hastings, Earl of Pembroke, *temp.* Richard II., without issue), claimed the earl's estates under an entail, in opposition to Edward Hastings, the earl's heir-male of the half-blood. "Beauchamp," says Dugdale, "invited his learned counsel to his house in Paternoster Row, in the City of London; amongst whom were Robert Charlton (then a judge), William Pinchbek, William Branchesley, and John Catesby (all learned lawyers); and after dinner, coming out of his chapel, in an angry mood, threw to each of them a piece of gold, and said, 'Sirs, I desire you forthwith to tell me whether I have any right or title to Hastings' lordship and lands.' Whereupon Pinchbek stood up (the rest being silent, fearing that he suspected them), and said, 'No man here nor in England dare say that you have any right in them, except Hastings do quit his claim therein; and should he do it, being now under age, it would be of no validitie.'" Had Charlton, the Chief Justice of the Common Pleas, taken gold for his opinion on a case put before him in his judicial character, he would have violated his judicial oath. But in the earl's house in Paternoster Row he was merely a counsellor learned in the law, not a judge. Manifest perils attend a system which permits a judge in his private character to give legal opinions concerning causes on which he may be required to give judgment from the bench; but notwithstanding those perils, there is no reason for thinking that Charlton on this occasion either broke law or etiquette. The fair inference from the matter is, that in the closing years of the fourteenth century judges were permitted to give opinions for money to their private clients, although they were forbidden to take gold or silver from any person having "plea or process hanging before them."

In the year of our Lord 1500 the corporation of Canterbury paid for advice regarding their civic interests 3*s.* 4*d.* to each of three sergeants, and gave the Recorder of London 6*s.* 8*d.* as a retaining-fee. Five years later, Mr. Serjeant Wood received a fee of 10*s.* from the Goldsmiths' Company; and it maybe fairly assumed, that so important and wealthy a body paid the sergeant on a liberal scale. In the sixteenth century it was, and for several generations had been, customary for clients to provide food and drink for their counsel. Mr. Foss gives his readers the following list of items, taken from a bill of costs, made in the reign of Edward IV:—

| | *s.* | *d.* |
|---|---|---|
| For a breakfast at Westminster spent on our counsel | 1 | 6 |
| To another time for boat-hire in and out, and a breakfast for two days | 1 | 6 |

In like manner the accountant of St. Margaret's, Westminster, entered in the parish books, "Also, paid to Roger Fylpott, learned in the law, for his counsel given, 3*s.* 8*d.*, with 4*d.* for his dinner."

A yet more remarkable custom was that which enabled clients to hire counsel to plead for them at certain places, for a given time, in whatever causes their eloquence might be required. There still exists the record of an agreement by which, in the reign of Henry VII, Sergeant Yaxley bound himself to attend the assizes at York, Nottingham and Derby, and speak in court at each of those places, whenever his client, Sir Robert Plumpton—"that perpetual and always unfortunate litigant," as he is called by Sergeant Manning—required him to do so. This interesting document runs thus—"This bill, indented at London the 18th day of July, the 16th yeare of the reigne of King Henry the 7th, witnesseth that John Yaxley, Sergeant-at-Law, shall be at the next assizes to be holden at York, Nottin., and Derb., if they be holden and kept, and there to be of council with Sir Robert Plumpton, knight, such assizes and actions as the said Sir Robert shall require the said John Yaxley, for the which premises, as well as for his costs and his labours, John Pulan, gentleman, bindeth him by thease presents to content and pay to the said John Yaxley 40 marks sterling at the feast of the Nativetie of our Lady next coming, or within eight days next following, with 5 li paid aforehand, parcell of paiment of the said 40 marks. Provided alway that if the said John Yaxley have knowledg and warning only to cum to Nottin and Derby, then the said John Yaxley is agread by these presents to take only xv li besides the 5 li aforesaid. Provided alwaies that if the said John Yaxley have knowledg and warning to take no labour in this matter, then he to reteine and hold the said 5 li resaived for his good will and labour. In witness hereof, the said John Yaxley, serjeant, to the part of this indenture remaining with the said John Pulan have put his seale the day and yeare above-written. Provided also that the said Robert Plumpton shall beare the charges of the said John Yaxley, as well at York as at Nottingham and Derby, and also to content and pay the said money to the said John Yaxley comed to the said assizes att Nott., Derb., and York. John Yaxley."

This remarkable agreement—made after Richard III had vainly endeavored to compose by arbitration the differences between Sir Robert and Sir Robert's heir-general—certifies that Sir Robert Plumpton engaged to provide the sergeant with suitable entertainment at the assize towns, and also throws light upon the origin of retaining-fees. It appears from the agreement that in olden time a retaining fee was merely part (surrendered in advance) of a certain sum stipulated to be paid for certain services. In principle it was identical with the payment of the shilling, still given in rural districts, to domestic servants on an agreement for service, and with the transfer of the queen's shilling given to every soldier on enlistment. There is no need to mention the classic origin of this ancient mode of giving force to a contract.

From the 'Household and Privy Purse Expenses of the Le Stranges of Hunstanton,' published in the Archæologia, may be gleamed some interesting particulars relating to the payment of counsel in the reign of Henry VIII. In 1520, Mr. Cristofer Jenney received from the Le Stranges a half-yearly fee of ten shillings; and this general retainer was continued on the same terms till 1527, when the fee was raised from £1 per annum to a yearly payment of £2 13*s.* 4*d.* To Mr. Knightley was paid the sum of 8*s.* 11*d.* "for his fee, and that money yt he layde oute for suying of Simon Holden;" and the same lawyer also received at another time 14*s.* 3*d.* "for his fee and cost of sute for iii termes." A fee of 6*s.* 8*d.* was paid to "Mr. Spelman, s'jeant, for his counsell in makyng my answer in ye Duchy Cham.;" and the same serjeant received a fee of 3*s.* 4*d.* "for his counsell in putting in of the answer." Fees of 3*s.* 4*d.* were in like manner given "for counsell" to Mr. Knightley and Mr. Whyte; and in 1534, Mr. Yelverton was remunerated "for his counsell" with the unusually liberal honorarium of twenty shillings. From the household book of the Earl of Northumberland, it appears that order was made, in this same reign, for "every oone of my lordes counsaill to have c's. fees, if he have it in household and not by patent." After the earl's establishment was reduced to forty-two persons, it still retained "one of my lordes counsaill for annswering and riddying of causes, whenne sutors cometh to my lord." At a time when every lord was required to administer justice to his tenants and the inferior people of his territory, a counsellor learned in the law, was an important and most necessary officer in a grand seigneur's retinue.

Whilst Sir Thomas More lived in Bucklersbury, he "gained, without grief, not so little as £400 by the year." This income doubtless accrued from the emoluments of his judicial appointment in the City, as well as from his practice at Westminster and elsewhere. In Henry VIII.'s time it was a very considerable income, such as was equalled by few leaders of the bar not holding high office under the Crown.

In Elizabeth's reign, and during the time of her successor, barristers' fees show a tendency toward increase; and the lawyers who were employed as advocates for the Crown, or held judicial appointments, acquired princely incomes, and in some cases amassed large fortunes. Fees of 20*s.* were more generally paid to counsel under the virgin queen, than in the days of her father; but still half that fee was not thought too small a sum for an opinion given by Her Majesty's Solicitor General. Indeed, the ten-shilling fee was a very usual fee in Elizabeth's reign; and it long continued an ordinary payment for one opinion on a case, or for one speech in a cause of no great importance and of few difficulties. 'A barrister is like Balaam's ass, only speaking when he sees the angel,' was a familiar saying in the seventeenth century. In Chancery, however, by an ordinance of the Lords Commissioners passed in 1654, to regulate the conduct of suits and the payments to masters, counsel, and solicitors, it was arranged that on the hearing of a cause, utter-barristers should receive £1 fees, whilst the Lord Protector's counsel and sergeants-at-law should receive £2 fees, i.e., 'double fees.'

The archives of Lyme Regis show that under Elizabeth the usage was maintained of supplying counsel with delicacies of the table, and also of providing them with means of locomotion. Here are some items in an old record of disbursements made by the corporation of Lyme Regis:—"A.D. Paid for Wine carried with us to Mr. Poulett—£0 3*s.* 6*d.*; Wine and sugar given to Mr. Poulett, £0 3*s.* 4*d.*; Horse-hire, and for the Sergeant to ride to Mr. Walrond, of Bovey, and for a loaf of sugar, and for conserves given there to

Mr. Poppel, £1 1*s.* 0*d.*; Wine and sugar given to Judge Anderson, £0 3*s.* 4*d.* A bottle and sugar given to Mr. Gibbs (a lawyer)."

Under Elizabeth, the allowance made to Queen's Sergeants was £26 6*s.* 8*d.* for fee, reward, and robes; and £20. for his services whenever a Queen's Sergeant travelled circuit as Justice of Assize. The fee for her Solicitor General was £50. When Francis Bacon was created King's Counsel to James I., an annual salary of forty pounds was assigned to him from the royal purse; and down to William IV.'s time, King's Counsel received a stipend of £40 a year, and an allowance for stationery. Under the last mentioned monarch, however, the stipend and allowance were both withdrawn; and at present the status of a Q.C. is purely an affair of professional precedence, to which no fixed emolument is attached.

But a list of the fees, paid from the royal purse to each judge or crown lawyer under James I., would afford no indication as to the incomes enjoyed by the leading members of the bench and bar at that period. The salaries paid to those officers were merely retaining fees, and their chief remuneration consisted of a large number of smaller fees. Like the judges of prior reigns, King James's judges were forbidden to accept *presents* from actual suitors; but no suitor could obtain a hearing from any one of them, until he had paid into court certain fees, of which the fattest was a sum of money for the judge's personal use. At one time many persons labored under an erroneous impression, that as judges were forbidden to accept presents from actual suitors, the honest judge of past times had no revenue besides his specified salary and allowance. Like the king's judges, the king's counsellors frequently made great incomes by fees, though their nominal salaries were invariably insignificant. At a time when Francis Bacon was James's Attorney General, and received no more than £81 6*s.* 8*d.* for his yearly salary, he made £6000 per annum in his profession; and of that income—a royal income in those days—the greater portion consisted of fees paid to him for attending to the king's business. "I shall now," Bacon wrote to the king, "again make oblation to your Majesty,—first of my heart, then of my service; thirdly, of my place of Attorney, which I think is honestly worth £6000 per annum; and fourthly, of my place in the Star Chamber, which is worth £1600 per annum, and with the favor and countenance of a Chancellor, much more." Coke had made a still larger income during his tenure of the Attorney's place, the fees from his private official practice amounting to no loss a sum than seven thousand pounds in a single year.

At later periods of the seventeenth century barristers made large incomes, but the fees seem to have been by no means exorbitant. Junior barristers received very modest payments, and it would appear that juniors received fees from eminent counsel for opinions and other professional services. Whilst he acted as treasurer of the Middle Temple, at an early period of his career, Whitelock received a fee from Attorney General Noy. "Upon my carrying the bill," writes Whitelock, "to Mr. Attorney General Noy for his signature, with that of the other benchers, he was pleased to advise with me about a patent the king had commanded him to draw, upon which he gave me a fee for it out of his little purse, saying, 'Here, take those single pence,' which amounted to eleven groats, 'and I give you more than an attorney's fee, because you will be a better man than the Attorney General. This you will find to be true.' After much other drollery, wherein he delighted and excelled, we parted, abundance of company attending to speak to him all this time." Of course the payment itself was no part of the drollery to which Whitelock alludes, for as a gentleman he could not have taken money proffered to him in jest, unless etiquette encouraged him to look for it, and allowed him to accept it. The incident justifies the inference that the services of junior counsel to senior barristers—services at the present time termed 'devilling'—were formerly remunerated with cash payments.

Toward the close of Charles I.'s reign—at a time when political distractions were injuriously affecting the legal profession, especially the staunch royalists of the long robe—Maynard, the Parliamentary lawyer, received on one round of the Western Circuit, £700, "which," observes Whitelock, to whom Maynard communicated the fact, "I believe was more than any one of our profession got before."

Concerning the incomes made by eminent counsel in Charles II.'s time, many *data* are preserved in diaries and memoirs. That a thousand a year was looked upon as a good income for a flourishing practitioner of the 'merry monarch's' Chancery bar, may be gathered from a passage in 'Pepys's Diary,' where the writer records the compliments paid to him regarding his courageous and eloquent defence of the Admiralty, before the House of Commons, in March, 1668. Under the influence of half-a-pint of mulled sack and a dram of brandy, the Admiralty clerk made such a spirited and successful speech in behalf of his department, that he was thought to have effectually silenced all grumblers against the management of his Majesty's navy. Compliments flowed in upon the orator from all directions. Sir William Coventry pledged his judgment that the fame of the oration would last forever in the Commons; silver-tongued Sir Heneage Finch, in the blandest tones, averred that no other living man could have made so excellent a speech; the placemen of the Admiralty vied with each other in expressions of delight and admiration; and one flatterer, whose name is not recorded, caused Mr. Pepys infinite pleasure by saying that the speaker who had routed the accusers of a government office, might easily earn a thousand a year at the Chancery bar.

That sum, however, is insignificant when it is compared with the incomes made by the most fortunate advocates of that period. Eminent speakers of the Common Law Bar made between £2000 and £3500 per annum on circuit and at Westminster, without the aid of king's business; and still larger receipts were recorded in the fee-books of his Majesty's attorneys and solicitors. At the Chancery bar of the second Charles, there was at least one lawyer, who in one year made considerably more than four times the income that was suggested to Pepys's vanity and self-complacence. At Stanford Court, Worcestershire, is preserved a fee-book kept by Sir Francis Winnington, Solicitor-General to the 'merry monarch,' from December 1674 to January 13, 1679, from the entries of which record the reader may form a tolerably correct estimate of the professional revenues of successful lawyers at that time. In Easter Term, 1671, Sir Francis pocketed £459; in Trinity Term £449 10s.; in Michaelmas Term £521; and in Hilary Term 1672, £361 10s.; the income for the year being £1791, without his earnings on the Oxford Circuit and during vacation. In 1673, Sir Francis received £3371; in 1674, he earned £3560;[8] and in 1675—i.e., the first year of his tenure of the Solicitor's office—his professional income wars £4066, of which sum £429 were office fees. Concerning the Attorney-General's receipts about this time, we have sufficient information from Roger North, who records that his brother, whilst Attorney General, made nearly seven thousand pounds in one year, from private and official business. It is noteworthy that North, as Attorney General, made the same income which Coke realized in the same office at the commencement of the century. But under the Stuarts this large income of £7000—in those days a princely revenue—was earned by work so perilous and fruitful of obloquy, that even Sir Francis, who loved money and cared little for public esteem, was glad to resign the post of Attorney and retire to the Pleas with £4000 a year. That the fees of the Chancery lawyers under Charles II were regulated upon a liberal scale we know from Roger North, and the record of Sir John King's success. Speaking of his brother Francis, the biographer says: "After he, as king's counsel, came within the bar, he began to have calls into the Court of Chancery; which he liked very well, because the quantity of the business, *as well as the fees*, was greater; but his home was the King's Bench, where he sat and reported like as other practitioners." And in Sir John King's memoirs it is recorded that in 1676 he made £4700, and that he received from £40 to £50 a day during the last four days of his appearance in court. Dying in 1677,[9] whilst his supremacy in his own court was at its height, Sir John King was long spoken of as a singularly successful Chancery barrister.

Of Francis North's mode of taking and storing his fees, the 'Life of Lord Keeper Guildford' gives the following picture: "His business increased, even while he was Solicitor, to be so much as to have overwhelmed one less dexterous; but when he was made Attorney General, though his gains by his office were great, they were much greater by his practice; for that flowed in upon him like an orage, enough to overset one that had not an extraordinary readiness in business. His skull-caps, which he wore when he had leisure to observe his constitution, as I touched before, were now destined to lie in a drawer to receive the money that came in by fees. One had the gold, another the crowns

---

[8] In his 'Survey of the State of England in 1685,' Macauley—giving one of those misleading references with which his history abounds—says: "A thousand a year was thought a large income for a barrister. Two thousand a year was hardly to be made in the Court of King's Bench, except by crown lawyers." Whilst making the first statement, he doubtless remembered the passage in 'Pepys's Diary.' For the second statement, he refers to 'Layton's Conversation with Chief Justice Hale.' It is fair to assume that Lord Macauley had never seen Sir Francis Winnington's fee-book.

[9] In the fourth day of his fever, he being att the Chancery Bar, he fell so ill of the fever, that he was forced to leave the Court and come to his chambers in the Temple, with one of his clerks, which constantly wayted on him and carried his bags of writings for his pleadings, and there told him that he should return to every clyent his breviat and his fee, for he could serve them no longer, for he had done with this world, and thence came home to his house in Salisbury Court, and took his bed.... And there he sequestered himself to meditation between God and his own soul, without the least regret, and quietly and patiently contented himself with the will of God.—*Vide Memoir of Sir John King, Knt., written by his Father.*

and half-crowns, and another the smaller money. When these vessels were full, they were committed to his friend (the Hon. Roger North), who was constantly near him, to tell out the cash, and put it into the bags according to the contents; and so they went to his treasurers, Blanchard and Child, goldsmiths, Temple Bar."[10] In the days of wigs, skull-caps like those which Francis North used as receptacles for money, were very generally worn by men of all classes and employments. On returning to the privacy of his home, a careful citizen usually laid aside his costly wig, and replaced it with a cheap and durable skull-cap, before he sat down in his parlor. So also, men careful of their health often wore skull-caps *under* their wigs, on occasions when they were required to endure a raw atmosphere without the protection of their beavers. In days when the law-courts were held in the open hall of Westminster, and lawyers practising therein, were compelled to sit or speak for hours together, exposed to sharp currents of cold air, it was customary for wearers of the long robe to place between their wigs and natural hair closely-fitting caps, made of stout silk or soft leather. But more interesting than the money-caps, are the fees which they contained. The ringing of the gold pieces, the clink of the crowns with the half-crowns, and the rattle of the smaller money, led back the barrister to those happier and remote times, when the 'inferior order' of the profession paid the superior order with 'money down;' when, the advocate never opened his mouth till his fingers had closed upon the gold of his trustful client; when 'credit' was unknown in transactions between counsel and attorney;—that truly *golden* age of the bar, when the barrister was less suspicious of the attorney, and the attorney held less power over the barrister.

Having profited by the liberal payments of Chancery whilst he was an advocate, Lord Keeper Guildford destroyed one source of profit to counsel from which Francis North, the barrister, had drawn many a capful of money. Saith Roger, "He began to rescind all motions for speeding and delaying the hearing of causes besides the ordinary rule of court; and this lopped off a limb of the motion practice. I have heard Sir John Churchill, a

---

[10] The lawyers of the seventeenth century were accustomed to make a show of their fees to the clients who called upon them. Hudibras's lawyer (Hud., Part iii. cant. 3) is described as sitting in state with his books and money before him:

"To this brave man the knight repairs
For counsel in his law affairs,
And found him mounted in his pew,
With books and money placed for shew,
Like nest-eggs, to make clients lay,
And for his false, opinion pay:
To whom the knight, with comely grace,
Put off his hat to put his case,
Which he as proudly entertain'd
As the other courteously strain'd;
And to assure him 'twas not that
He looked for, bid him put on's hat."

Under Victoria, the needy junior is compelled, for the sake of appearances, to furnish his shelves with law books, and cover his table with counterfeit briefs. Under the Stuarts, he placed a bowl of spurious money amongst the sham papers that lay upon his table.

famous Chancery practitioner, say, that in his walk from Lincoln's Inn down to the Temple Hall, where, in the Lord Keeper Bridgman's time, causes and motions out of term were heard, he had taken £28. with breviates only for motions and defences for hastening and retarding hearings. His lordship said, that the rule of the court allowed time enough for anyone to proceed or defend; and if, for special reasons, he should give way to orders for timing matters, it would let in a deluge of vexatious pretenses, which, true or false, being asserted by the counsel with equal assurance, distracted the court and confounded the suitors."

Let due honor be rendered to one Caroline, lawyer, who was remarkable for his liberality to clients, and carelessness of his own pecuniary interests. From his various biographers, many pleasant stories may be gleaned concerning Hale's freedom from base love of money. In his days, and long afterward, professional etiquette permitted clients and counsel to hold intercourse without the intervention of an attorney. Suitors, therefore, frequently addressed him personally and paid for his advice with their own hands, just as patients are still accustomed to fee their doctors. To these personal applicants, and also to clients who approached him by their agents, he was very liberal. "When those who came to ask his counsel gave him a piece, he used to give back the half, and to make ten shillings his fee in ordinary matters that did not require much time or study." From this it may be inferred that whilst Hale was an eminent member of the bar, twenty shillings was the usual fee to a leading counsel, and an angel the customary honorarium to an ordinary practitioner. As readers have already been told, the angel[11] was a common fee in the seventeenth century; but the story of Hale's generous usage implies that his more distinguished contemporaries were wont to look for and accept a double fee. Moreover, the anecdote would not be told in Hale's honor, if etiquette had fixed the double fee as the minimum of remuneration for a superior barrister's opinion. He was frequently employed in arbitration cases, and as an arbitrator he steadily refused payment for his services to legal disputants, saying, in explanation of his moderation, "In these cases I am made a judge, and a judge ought to take no money." The misapprehension as to the nature of an arbitrator's functions, displayed in these words, gives an instructive insight into the mental constitution of the judge who wrote on natural science, and at the same time exerted himself to secure the conviction of witches. A more pleasant and commendable illustration of his conscientiousness in pecuniary matters, is found in the steadiness with which he refused to throw upon society the spurious coin which he had taken from his

[11] In the 'Serviens ad Legem,' Mr. Sergeant Manning raises question concerning the antiquity of *guineas* and half-guineas, with the following remarks:—"Should any cavil be raised against this jocular allusion, on the ground that guineas and half-guineas were unknown to sergeants who flourished in the sixteenth century, the objector might be reminded, that in antique records, instances occur in which the 'guianois d'or,' issued from the ducal mint at Bordeaux, by the authority of the Plantagenet sovereigns of Guienne, were by the same authority, made current among their English subjects; and it might be suggested that those who have gone to the coast of Africa for the origin of the modern guinea, need not have carried their researches beyond the Bay of Biscay. *Quære*, whether the Guinea Coast itself may not owe its name to the 'guianois d'or' for which it furnished the raw material."

clients. In a tone of surprise that raises a smile at the average morality of our forefathers, Bishop Burnet tells of Hale: "Another remarkable instance of his justice and goodness was, that when he found ill money had been put into his hands, he would never suffer it to be vented again; for he thought it was no excuse for him to put false money in other people's hands, because some had put it into his. A great heap of this he had gathered together, for many had so abused his goodness as to mix base money among the fees that were given him." In this particular case, the judge's virtue was its own reward. His house being entered by burglars, this accumulation of bad money attracted the notice of the robbers, who selected it from a variety of goods and chattels, and carried it off under the impression that it was the lawyer's hoarded treasure. Besides large sums expended on unusual acts of charity, this good man habitually distributed amongst the poor a tithe of his professional earnings.

In the seventeenth century, General Retainers were very common, and the counsel learned in the law, were ready to accept them from persons of low extraction and questionable repute. Indeed, no upstart deemed himself properly equipped for a campaign at court, until he had recorded a fictitious pedigree at the Herald's College, taken a barrister as well as a doctor into regular employment, and hired a curate to say grace daily at his table. In the summer of his vile triumph, Titus Oates was attended, on public occasions, by a robed counsel and a physician.

*Chapter 13*

# Retainers General and Special

Pemberton's fees for his services in behalf of the Seven Bishops show that the most eminent counsel of his time were content with very modest remuneration for advice and eloquence. From the bill of an attorney employed in that famous trial, it appears that the ex-Chief Justice was paid a retaining-fee of five guineas, and received twenty guineas with his brief. He also pocketed three guineas for a consultation. At the present date, thirty times the sum of these paltry payments would be thought an inadequate compensation for such zeal, judgment, and ability as Francis Pemberton displayed in the defence of his reverend clients.

But, though lawyers were paid thus moderately in the seventeenth century, the complaints concerning their avarice and extortions were loud and universal. This public discontent was due to the inordinate exactions of judges and place-holders rather than to the conduct of barristers and attorneys; but popular displeasure seldom cares to discriminate between the blameless and the culpable members of an obnoxious system, or to distinguish between the errors of ancient custom and the qualities of those persons who are required to carry out old rules. Hence the really honest and useful practitioners of the law endured a full share of the obloquy caused by the misconduct of venal justices and corrupt officials. Counsel, attorneys, and even scriveners came in for abuse. It was averred that they conspired to pick the public pocket; that eminent conveyancers not less than copying clerks, swelled their emoluments by knavish tricks. They would talk for the mere purpose of protracting litigation, injure their clients by vexations and bootless delays, and do their work so that they might be fed for doing it again. Draughtsmen find their clerks wrote loosely and wordily, because they were paid by the folio. "A term," writes the quaint author of 'Saint Hillaries Teares,' in 1642, "so like a vacation; the prime court, the Chancery (wherein the clerks had wont to dash their clients out of countenance with long dashes); the examiners to take the depositions in hyperboles, and roundabout *Robinhood* circumstances with *saids* and *aforesaids*, to enlarge the number of sheets."

'Hudibras' contains, amongst other pungent satires against the usages of lawyers, an allusion to this characteristic custom of legal draughtsmen, who being paid by the sheet, were wont

> "To make 'twixt words and lines large gaps,
> Wide as meridians in maps;
> To squander paper and spare ink,
> Or cheat men of their words some think."

In the following century the abuses consequent on the objectionable system of folio-payment were noticed in a parliamentary report (bearing date November 8, 1740), which was the most important result of an ineffectual attempt to reform the superior courts of law and to lessen the expenses of litigation.

More is known about the professional receipts of lawyers since the Revolution of 1688 than can be discovered concerning the incomes of their precursors in Westminster Hall. For six years, commencing with Michaelmas Term, 1719, Sir John Cheshire, King's Sergeant, made an average annual income of 3241*l.* Being then sixty-three years of age, he limited his practice to the Common Pleas, and during the next six years made in that one court 1320*l.* per annum. Mr. Foss, to whom the present writer is indebted for these particulars with regard to Sir John Cheshire's receipts, adds: "The fees of counsel's clerks form a great contrast with those that are now demanded, being only threepence on a fee of half-a-guinea, sixpence for a guinea, and one shilling for two guineas." Of course the increase of clerk's fees tells more in favor of the master than the servant. At the present time the clerk of a barrister in fairly lucrative practice costs his master nothing. Bountifully paid by his employer's clients, he receives no salary from the counsellor whom he serves; whereas, in old times, when his fees were fixed at the low rate just mentioned, the clerk could not live and maintain a family upon them, unless his master belonged to the most successful grade of his order.

Horace Walpole tells his readers that Charles Yorke "was reported to have received 100,000 guineas in fees;" but his fee-book shows that his professional rise was by no means so rapid as those who knew him in his sunniest days generally supposed. The story of his growing fortunes is indicated in the following statement of successive incomes:—1st year of practice at the bar, 121*l.* 2nd, 201*l.*; 3rd and 4th, between 300*l.* and 400*l.* per annum; 5th, 700*l.*; 6th, 800*l.*; 7th, 1000*l.*; 9th, 1600*l.*; 10th, 2500*l.* Whilst Solicitor General he made 3400*l.* in 1757; and in the following year he earned 5000*l.* His receipts during the last year of his tenure of the Attorney Generalship amounted to 7322*l.* The reader should observe that as Attorney General he made but little more than Coke had realized in the same office,—a fact serving to show how much better paid were Crown lawyers in times when they held office like judges during the Sovereign's pleasure, than in these latter days when they retire from place together with their political parties.

The difference between the incomes of Scotch advocates and English barristers was far greater in the eighteenth century than at the present time, although in our own day the receipts of several second-rate lawyers of the Temple and Lincoln's Inn far surpass the revenues of the most successful advocates of the Edinburgh faculty. A hundred and thirty years since a Scotch barrister who earned 500*l.* per annum by his profession was esteemed notably successful.

Just as Charles Yorke's fee-book shows us the pecuniary position of an eminent English barrister in the middle of the last century, John Scott's list of receipts displays the prosperity of a very fortunate Crown lawyer in the next generation. Without imputing motives the present writer, may venture to say that Lord Eldon's assertions with regard to his earnings at the bar, and his judicial incomes, were not in strict accordance with the evidence of his private accounts. He used to say that his first year's earnings in his profession amounted to half-a-guinea, but there is conclusive proof that he had a considerable quantity of lucrative business in the same year. "When I was called to the bar," it was his humor to say, "Bessie and I thought all our troubles were over, business was to pour in, and we were to be rich almost immediately. So I made a bargain with her that during the following year all the money I should receive in the first eleven months should be mine, and whatever I should get in the twelfth month should be hers. That was our agreement, and how do you think it turned out? In the twelfth month I received half-a-guinea—eighteenpence went for charity, and Bessy got nine shillings. In the other eleven months I got one shilling." John Scott, be it remembered, was called to the bar on February 9, 1776, and on October 2, of the same year, William Scott wrote to his brother Henry—"My brother Jack seems highly pleased with his circuit business. I hope it is only the beginning of future triumphs. All appearances speak strongly in his favor." There is no need to call evidence to show that Eldon's success was more than respectable from the outset of his career, and that he had not been called many years before he was in the foremost rank of his profession. His fee-book gives the following account of his receipts in thirteen successive years:—1786, 6833*l.* 7*s.*; 1787, 7600*l.* 7*s.*; 1788, 8419*l.* 14*s.*; 1789, 9559*l.* 10*s.*; 1790, 9684*l.* 15*s.*; 1791, 10,213*l.* 13*s.* 6*d.*; 1792, 9080*l.* 9*s.*; 1793, 10,330*l.* 1*s.* 4*d.*; 1794, 11,592*l.*; 1795, 11,149*l.* 15*s.* 4*d.*; 1796, 12,140*l.* 15*s.* 8*d.*; 1797, 10,861*l.* 5*s.* 8*d*; 1798, 10,557*l.* 17*s.* During the last six of the above-mentioned years he was Attorney General, and during the preceding four years Solicitor General.

Although General Retainers are much less general than formerly, they are by no means obsolete. Noblemen could be mentioned who at the present time engage counsel with periodical payments, special fees of course being also paid for each professional service. But the custom is dying out, and it is probable that after the lapse of another hundred years it will not survive save amongst the usages of ancient corporations. Notice has already been taken of Murray's conduct when he returned nine hundred and ninety-five out of a thousand guineas to the Duchess of Marlborough, informing her that the professional fee with the general retainer was neither more nor less than five guineas. The annual salary of a Queen's Counsel in past times was in fact a fee with a general retainer; but this periodic payment is no longer made to wearers of silk.

In his learned work on 'The Judges of England,' Mr. Foss observes: "The custom of retaining counsel in fee lingered in form, at least in one ducal establishment. By a formal deed-poll between the proud Duke of Somerset and Sir Thomas Parker, dated July 19, 1707, the duke retains him as his 'standing counsell in ffee,' and gives and allows him 'the yearly ffee of four markes, to be paid by my solicitor' at Michaelmas, 'to continue during my will and pleasure.'" Doubtless Mr. Foss is aware that this custom still 'lingers in form;' but the tone of his words justifies the opinion that he underrates the frequency with which general retainers are still given. The 'standing counsel' of civic and commercial companies are counsel with general retainers, and usually their general retainers have fees attached to them.

The payments of English barristers have varied much more than the remunerations of English physicians. Whereas medical practitioners in every age have received a certain definite sum for each consultation, and have been forbidden by etiquette to charge more or less than the fixed rate, lawyers have been allowed much freedom in estimating the worth of their labor. This difference between the usages of the two professions is mainly due to the fact, that the amount of time and mental effort demanded by patients at each visit or consultation is very nearly the same in all cases, whereas the requirements of clients are much more various. To get up the facts of a law-case may be the work of minutes, or hours, or days, or even weeks; to observe the symptoms of a patient, and to write a prescription, can be always accomplished within the limits of a short morning call. In all times, however, the legal profession has adopted certain scales of payment—that fixed the *minimum* of remuneration, but left the advocate free to get more, as circumstances might encourage him to raise his demands. Of the many good stories told of artifices by which barristers have delicately intimated their desire for higher payment, none is better than an anecdote recorded of Sergeant Hill. A troublesome case being laid before this most erudite of George III.'s sergeants, he returned it with a brief note, that he "saw more difficulty in the case than, *under all the circumstances*, he could well solve." As the fee marked upon the case was only a guinea, the attorney readily inferred that its smallness was one of the circumstances which occasioned the counsel's difficulty. The case, therefore, was returned, with a fee of two guineas. Still dissatisfied, Sergeant Hill wrote that "he saw no reason to change his opinion."

By the etiquette of the bar no barrister is permitted to take a brief on any circuit, save that on which he habitually practises, unless he has received a special retainer; and no wearer of silk can be specially retained with a less fee than three hundred guineas. Erskine's first special retainer was in the Dean of St. Asaph's case, his first speech in which memorable cause was delivered when he had been called to the bar but little more than five years. From that time till his elevation to the bench he received on an average twelve special retainers a year, by which at the minimum of payment he made £3600 per annum. Besides being lucrative and honorable, this special employment greatly augmented his practice in Westminster Hall, as it brought him in personal contact with attorneys in every part of the country, and heightened his popularity amongst all classes of his fellow-countrymen. In 1786 he entirely withdrew from ordinary circuit practice, and confined his exertions in provincial courts to the causes for which he was specially retained. No advocate since his time has received an equal number of special retainers; and if he did not originate the custom of special retainers,[12] he was the first English barrister who ventured to reject all other briefs.

There is no need to recapitulate all the circumstances of Erskine's rapid rise in his profession—a rise due to his effective brilliance and fervor in political trial: but this chapter on lawyers' fees would be culpably incomplete, if it failed to notice some of its pecuniary consequences. In the eighth month after his call to the bar he thanked Admiral Keppel for a splendid fee of one thousand pounds. A few years later a legal gossip wrote: "Everybody says that Erskine will be Solicitor General, and if he is, and indeed whether he is or not, he will have had the most rapid rise that has been known at the bar. It is four years and a half since he was called, and in that time he has cleared £8000 or £9000, besides paying his debts—got a silk gown, and business of at least £3000 a year—a seat in Parliament—and, over and above, has made his brother Lord Advocate."

Merely to mention large fees without specifying the work by which they were earned would mislead the reader. During the railway mania of 1845, the few leaders of the parliamentary bar received prodigious fees; and in some cases the sums were paid for very little exertion. Frequently it happened that a lawyer took heavy fees in causes, at no stage of which he either made a speech or read a paper in the service of his too liberal employers. During that period of mad speculation the committee-rooms of the two Houses were an El Dorado to certain favored lawyers, who were alternately paid for speech and *silence* with reckless profusion. But the time was so exceptional, that the fees received and the fortunes made in it by a score of lucky advocates and solicitors cannot be fairly cited as facts illustrating the social condition of legal practitioners. As a general rule, it may be stated that large fortunes are not made at the bar by large fees. Our richest lawyers have made the bulk of their wealth by accumulating sufficient but not exorbitant payments. In most cases the large fee has not been a very liberal remuneration for the work done. Edward Law's retainer for the defence of Warren Hastings brought with it £500—a sum which caused our grandfathers to raise their hands in astonishment at the nabob's munificence; but the sum was in reality the reverse of liberal. In all, Warren Hastings paid his leading advocate considerably less than four thousand pounds; and if Law had not contrived to win the respect of solicitors by his management of the defence, the case could not be said to have paid him for his trouble. So also the eminent advocate,

[12] Lord Campbell observes: "Some say that special retainers began with Erskine; but I doubt the fact." It is strange that there should be uncertainty as to the time when special retainers—unquestionably a comparatively recent innovation in legal practice—came into vogue.

who in the great case of Small *v.* Attwood received a fee of £6000, was actually underpaid. When he made up the account of the special outlay necessitated by that cause, and the value of business which the burdensome case compelled him to decline, he had small reason to congratulate himself on his remuneration.

A statement of the incomes made by chamber-barristers, and of the sums realized by counsel in departments of the profession that do not invite the attention of the general public, would astonish those uninformed persons who estimate the success of a barrister by the frequency with which his name appears in the newspaper reports of trials and suits. The talkers of the bar enjoy more *éclat* than the barristers who confine themselves to chamber practice, and their labors lead to the honors of the bench; but a young lawyer, bent only on the acquisition of wealth, is more likely to achieve his ambition by conveyancing or arbitration-business than by court-work. Kenyon was never a popular or successful advocate, but he made £3000 a year by answering cases. Charles Abbott at no time of his life could speak better than a vestryman of average ability; but by drawing informations and indictments, by writing opinions on cases, he made the greater part of the eight thousand pounds which he returned as the amount of his professional receipts in 1807. In our own time, when that popular common law advocate, Mr. Edwin James, was omnipotent with juries, his income never equalled the incomes of certain chamber-practitioners whose names are utterly unknown to the general body of English society.

*Chapter 14*

# JUDICIAL CORRUPTION

To a young student making his first researches beneath the surface of English history, few facts are more painful and perplexing than the judicial corruption which prevailed in every period of our country's growth until quiet recent times—darkening the brightest pages of our annals, and disfiguring some of the greatest chieftains of our race.

Where he narrates the fall and punishment of De Weyland towards the close of the thirteenth century, Speed observes: "While the Jews by their cruel usuries had in one way eaten up the people, the justiciars, like another kind of Jews, had ruined them with delay in their suits, and enriched themselves with wicked convictions." Of judicial corruption in the reigns of Edward I and Edward II a vivid picture is given in a political ballad, composed in the time of one or the other of those monarchs. Of this poem Mr. Wright, in his 'Political Songs,' gives a free version, a part of which runs thus:—

> "Judges there are whom gifts and favorites control,
> Content to serve the devil alone and take from him a toll;
> If nature's law forbids the judge from selling his decree,
> How dread to those who finger bribes the punishment shall be.
>
> "Such judges have accomplices whom frequently they send
> To get at those who claim some land, and whisper as a friend,
> "Tis I can help you with the judge, if you would wish to plead,
> Give me but half, I'll undertake before him you'll succeed.'
>
> "The clerks who sit beneath the judge are open-mouthed as he,
> As if they were half-famished and gaping for a fee;
> Of those who give no money they soon pronounce the state,
> However early they attend, they shall have long to wait.

"If comes some noble lady, in beauty and in pride,
With golden horns upon her head, her suit he'll soon decide;
But she who has no charms, nor friends, and is for gifts too poor,
Her business all neglected, she's weeping shown the door.

"But worse than all, within the court we some relators meet,
Who take from either side at once, and both their clients cheat;
The ushers, too, to poor men say, 'You labor here in vain,
Unless you tip us all around, you may go back again.'

"The sheriff's hard upon the poor who cannot pay for rest,
Drags them about to every town, on all assizes press'd
Compell'd to take the oath prescrib'd without objection made,
For if they murmur and can't pay, upon their backs they're laid.

"They enter any private house, or abbey that they choose,
Where meat and drink and all things else are given as their dues;
And after dinner jewels too, or this were all in vain,
Bedels and garçons must receive, and all that form the train.

"And next must gallant robes be sent as presents to their wives,
Or from the manor of the host someone his cattle drives;
While he, poor man, is sent to gaol upon some false pretence,
And pays at last at double cost, ere he gets free from thence.

"I can't but laugh to see their clerks, whom once I knew in need,
When to obtain a bailiwick they may at last succeed;
With pride in gait and countenance and with their necks erect
They lands and houses quickly buy and pleasant rents collect.

"Grown rich they soon the poor despise, and new-made laws display,
Oppress their neighbors and become the wise men of their day;
Unsparing of the least offence, when they can have their will,
The hapless country all around with discontent they fill."

In the fourteenth century judicial corruption was so general and flagrant, that cries came from every quarter for the punishment of offenders. The Knights Hospitallers' Survey, made in the year 1338, gives us revelations that confound the indiscreet admirers of feudal manners. From that source of information it appears that regular stipends were paid to persons "tam in curia domini regis quam justiciariis, clericis, officiariis et aliis ministris, in diversis curiis suis, ac etiam aliis familaribus magnatum tam pro terris tenementis redditbus et libertatibus Hospitalis, quam Templariorum, et maxime pro terris Templariorum manutenendis."

Of pensions to the amount of £440 mentioned in the account, £60 were paid to judges, clerks, and minor officers of courts. Robert de Sadington, the Chief Baron, received 40 marks annually; twice a year the Knights Hospitallers presented caps to one hundred and forty officers of the Exchequer; and they expended 200 marks *per annum* on gifts that were distributed in law courts, "*pro favore habendo*, et pro placitis habendis, et expensis parliamentorum." In that age, and for centuries later, it was customary for wealthy men and great corporations to make valuable presents to the judges and chief servants the king's courts; but it was always presumed that the offerings were simple expressions of respect—not tribute rendered, "pro favore habendo."

Bent on purifying the moral atmosphere of his courts, Edward III raised the salaries of his judges, and imposed upon them such oaths that none of their order could pervert justice, or even encourage venal practices, without breaking his solemn vow[13] to the king's majesty.

From the amounts of the *royal* fees or stipends paid to Edward III.'s judges, it may be vaguely estimated how far they were dependent on gifts and *court* fees for the means of living with appropriate state. John Knyvet, Chief Justice of the King's Bench, has £40 and 100 marks per annum. The annual fee of Thomas de Ingleby, the solitary puisne judge of the King's Bench at that time, was at first 40 marks; but he obtained an additional £40 when the 'fees' were raised, and he received moreover £20 a year as a judge of assize. The Chief of the Common Pleas, Robert de Thrope, received £40 per annum, payable during his tenure of office, and another annual sum of £40 payable during his life. John de Mowbray, William de Wychingham, and William de Fyncheden, the other judges of the Common Pleas, received 40 marks each as official salary, and £20 per annum for their services at assizes. Mowbray's stipend was subsequently increased by 40 marks, whilst Wychingham and Fyncheden received an additional £40 par annum.

---

[13] A portion of the oath prescribed for judges in the 'Ordinances for Justices,' 20 Edward III., will show the reader the evils which called for correction and the care taken to effect their cure. "Ye shall swear," ran the injunction to which each judge was required to vow obedience, "that well and lawfully ye shall serve our lord the king and his people in the office of justice; ... and that ye take not by yourself or by other, privily or apertly, gift or reward of gold or silver, nor any other thing which may turn to your profit, unless it be meat nor drink, and that of small value, *of any man that shall have plea or process before you, as long as the same process shall be so hanging, nor after for the same cause: and that ye shall take no fee as long as ye shall be justice, nor robes of any man, great or small*, but of the king himself: and that ye give none advice or counsel to no man, great or small, in any case where the king is party; &c. &c. &c." The clause forbidding the judge to receive gifts of actual suitors was a positive recognition of his right to customary gifts rendered by persons who had no process hanging before him. It should, moreover, be observed that in the passage, "ye shall take no fee as long as ye shall be justice, nor robes of any man," the word "fee" signifies "salary," and not a single payment or gratuity. The Judge was forbidden to receive from any man a fixed stipend (by the acceptance of which he would become the donor's servant), or robes (the assumption of which would be open declaration of service); but he was at liberty to accept the offerings which the public were wont to make to men of his condition, as well as the sums (or 'fees,' as they would be termed at the present day) due on different processes of his court. That the word 'fee' is thus used in the ordinance may be seen from the words "for this cause we have increased the fees (les feez) of the same our justices, in such manner as it ought reasonably to suffice them," by which language attention is drawn to the increase of judicial salaries.

To the Chief Baron and the other two Barons of the Exchequer annual fees of 40 marks each were paid, the Chief Baron receiving £20 per annum as Justice of Assize, and one of the puisne Barons, Almaric de Shirland, getting an additional 40 marks for certain special services. The 'Issue Roll of 44 Edward III, 1370,' also shows that certain sergeants-at-law acted as Justices of Assize, receiving for their service £20 per annum.

Throughout his reign Edward III. strenuously exerted himself to purge his law courts of abuses, and to secure his subjects from evils wrought by judicial dishonesty; and though there is reason to think that he prosecuted his reforms, and punished offending judges with more impulsiveness than consistency—with petulance rather than firmness[14]—his action must have produced many beneficial results. But it does not seem to have occurred to him that the system adopted by his predecessors, and encouraged by the usages of his own time, was the real source of the mischief, and that so long as judges received the greater part of their remuneration from suitors, fees and the donations of the public, enactments and proclamations would be comparatively powerless to preserve the streams of justice from pollution. The fee-system poisoned the morality of the law-courts. From the highest judge to the lowest usher, every person connected with a court of justice was educated to receive small sums of money for trifling services, to be always looking out for paltry dues or gratuities, to multiply occasions for demanding, and reasons for pocketing petty coins, to invent devices for legitimate peculation. In time the system produced such complications of custom, right, privilege, claim, that no one could say definitely how much a suitor was actually bound to pay at each stage of a suit. The fees had an equally bad influence on the public. Trained to approach the king's judges with costly presents, to receive them on their visits with lavish hospitality, to send them offerings at the opening of each year, the rich and the poor learnt to look on judicial decisions as things that were bought and sold. In many cases this impression was not erroneous. Judges were forbidden to accept gifts from actual suitors, or to take payments *for* judgments after their delivery; but on the judgment-seat they were often influenced by recollections of the conduct of suitors who *had been* munificent before the commencement of proceedings, and most probably would be equally munificent six months after delivery of a judgment favorable to their claims. Humorous anecdotes heightened the significance of patent facts. Throughout a shire it would be told how this suitor won a judgment by a sumptuous feast; how that suitor bought the justice's favor with a flask of rare wine, a horse of excellent breed, a hound of superior sagacity.

In the fifteenth century the judge whose probity did not succumb to an excellent dinner was deemed a miracle of virtue. "A lady," writes Fuller of Chief Justice Markham, who was dismissed from his place in 1470, "would traverse a suit of law against the will of her husband, who was contented to buy his quiet by giving her her will therein, though

[14] Mr. Foss observes: "In 1350, William de Thrope, Chief Justice of the King's Bench, was convicted on his own confession of receiving bribes to stay justice; but though his property was forfeited to the Crown on his condemnation, the king appears to have relented, and to have made him second Baron of the Exchequer in May, 1352, unless I am mistaken in supposing the latter to have been the same person."

otherwise persuaded in his judgment the cause would go against her. This lady, dwelling in the shire town, invited the judge to dinner, and (though thrifty enough herself) treated him with sumptuous entertainment. Dinner being done, and the cause being called, the judge gave it against her. And when, in passion, she vowed never to invite the judge again, 'Nay, wife,' said he, 'vow never to invite a *just judge* anymore.'" It may be safely affirmed that no English lady of our time ever tried to bribe Sir Alexander Cockburn or Sir Frederick Pollock with a dinner *à la Russe*.

By his eulogy of Chief Justice Dyer, who died March 24, 1582, Whetstone gives proof that in Elizabethan England purity was the exception rather than the rule with judges:—

> "And when he spake he was in speeche reposde;
> His eyes did search the simple suitor's harte;
> To put by bribes his hands were ever closde,
> His processe juste, he tooke the poore man's parte.
> He ruld by lawe and listened not to arte,
> Those foes to truthe—loove, hate, and private gain,
> Which most corrupt, his conscience could not staine."

There is no reason to suppose that the custom of giving and receiving presents was more general or extravagant in the time of Elizabeth than in previous ages; but the fuller records of her splendid reign give greater prominence to the usage than it obtained in the chronicles of any earlier period of English history. On each New Year's day her courtiers gave her costly presents—jewels, ornaments of gold or silver workmanship, hundreds of ounces of silver-gilt plate, tapestry, laces, satin dresses, embroidered petticoats. Not only did she accept such costly presents from men of rank and wealth, but she graciously received the donations of tradesmen and menials. Francis Bacon made her majesty "a poor oblation of a garment;" Charles Smith, the dustman, threw upon the pile of treasure "two bottes of cambric." The fashion thus countenanced by the queen was followed in all ranks of society; all men, from high to low, receiving presents, as expressions of affection when they came from their equals, as declarations of respect when they came from their social inferiors. Each of her great officers of state drew a handsome revenue from such yearly offerings. But though the burdens and abuses of this system were excessive under Elizabeth, they increased in enormity and number during the reigns of the Stuarts.

That the salaries of the Elizabethan judges were small in comparison with the sums which they received in presents and fees may be seen from the following Table of stipends and allowances annually paid, towards the close of the sixteenth century:—

| | £ | *s.* | *d.* |
|---|---|---|---|
| The Lord Cheefe Justice of England:— | | | |
| Fee, Reward and Robes | 208 | 6 | 8 |
| Wyne, 2 tunnes at £5 the tunne | 10 | 0 | 0 |
| Allowance for being Justice of Assize | 20 | 0 | 0 |
| The Lord Cheefe Justice of the Common Pleas:— | | | |
| Fee, Reward, and Robes | 141 | 13 | 4 |
| Wyne, two tunnes | 8 | 0 | 0 |
| Allowance as Justice of Assize | 20 | 0 | 0 |
| Fee for keeping the Assize in the Augmentation Court | 12 | 10 | 8 |
| Each of the three Justices in these two Courts:— | | | |
| Fee, Reward and Robes | 123 | 6 | 8 |
| Allowance as Justice of Assize | 20 | 0 | 0 |
| The Lord Cheefe Baron of the Exchequer:— | | | |
| Fee | 100 | 0 | 0 |
| Lyvery | 12 | 17 | 8 |
| Allowance as Justice of the Assize | 20 | 0 | 0 |
| Each of the three Barons:— | | | |
| Fee | 46 | 12 | 4 |
| Lyvery a peece | 12 | 17 | 4 |
| Allowance as Justice of Assize | 20 | 0 | 0 |

Prior to and in the earlier part of Elizabeth's reign, the sheriffs had been required to provide diet and lodging for judges travelling on circuit, each sheriff being responsible for the proper entertainment of judges within the limits of his jurisdiction. This arrangement was very burdensome upon the class from which the sheriffs were elected, as the official host had not only to furnish suitable lodging and cheer for the justices themselves, but also to supply the wants of their attendants and servants. The ostentatious and costly hospitality which law and public opinion thus compelled or encouraged them to exercise towards circuiteers of all ranks had seriously embarrassed a great number of country gentlemen; and the queen was assailed with entreaties for a reform that should free a sheriff of small estate from the necessity of either ruining himself, or incurring a reputation for stinginess. In consequence of these urgent representations, an order of council, bearing date February 21, 1574, decided "the justices shall have of her majesty several sums of money out of her coffers for their daily diet." Hence rose the usage of 'circuit allowances.' The sheriffs, however, were still bound to attend upon the judges, and make suitable provision for the safe conduct of the legal functionaries from assize town to assize town;—the sheriff of each county being required to furnish a body-guard for the protection of the sovereign's representatives. This responsibility lasted till the other day, when an innovation (of which Mr. Arcedeckne, of Glevering Hall, Suffolk, was the most notorious, though not the first champion), substituted guards of policemen, paid by county-rates, for bands of javelin-men equipped and rewarded by the sheriffs. In some counties the javelin-men—remote descendants of the mail-clad knights and stalwart men-at-arms who formerly mustered at the summons of sheriffs—still do duty with long wands and fresh rosettes; but they are fast giving way to the wielders of short staves.

Amongst the bad consequences of the system of gratuities was the color which it gave to idle rumors and malicious slander against the purity of upright judges.

When Sir Thomas More fell, charges of bribery were preferred against him before the Privy Council. A disappointed suitor, named Parnell, declared that the Chancellor had been bribed with a gift-cup to decide in favor of his (Parnell's) adversary. Mistress Vaughan, the successful suitor's wife, had given Sir Thomas the cup with her own hands. The fallen Chancellor admitting that "he had received the cup as a New Year's Gift," Lord Wiltshire cried, with unseemly exultation, "Lo! did I not tell you, my lords, that you would find this matter true?" It seemed that More had pleaded guilty, for his oath did not permit him to receive a New Year's Gift from an actual suitor. "But, my lords," continued the accused man, with one of his characteristic smiles, "hear the other part of my tale. After having drunk to her of wine, with which my butler had filled the cup, and when she had pledged me, I restored it to her, and would listen to no refusal." It is possible that Mistress Vaughan did not act with corrupt intention, but merely in ignorance of the rule which forbade the Chancellor to accept her present. As much cannot be said in behalf of Mrs. Croker, who, being opposed in a suit to Lord Arundel, sought to win Sir Thomas More's favor by presenting him with a pair of gloves containing forty angels. With a courteous smile he accepted the gloves, but constrained her to take back the gold. The gentleness of this rebuff is charming; but the story does not tell more in favor of Sir Thomas than to the disgrace of the lady and the moral tone of the society in which she lived.

Readers should bear in mind the part which New Year's Gifts and other customary gratuities played in the trumpery charges against Lord Bacon. Adopting an old method of calumny, the conspirators against his fair fame represented that the gifts made to him, in accordance with ancient usage, were bribes. For instance Reynel's ring, presented on New Year's day, was so construed by the accusers; and in his comment upon the charge, Bacon, who had inadvertently accepted the gift during the progress of a suit, observes, "This ring was received certainly *pendente lite*, and though it were at New Year's tide, yet it was too great a value for a New Year's Gift, though, as I take it, nothing near the value mentioned in the articles." So also Trevor's gift was a New Year's present, of which Bacon says, "I confess and declare that I received at New Year's tide an hundred pounds from Sir John Trevor, and because it came as a New Year's Gift, I neglected to inquire whether the cause was ended or depending; but since I find that though the cause was then dismissed to a trial at law, yet the equity is reserved, so as it was in that kind *pendente lite*." Bacon knew that this explanation would be read by men familiar with the history of New Year's Gifts, and all the circumstances of the ancient usage; and it is needless to say that no man of honor thought the less highly of Bacon at that time, because his pure and guiltless acceptance of customary presents was by ingenious and unscrupulous adversaries made to assume an appearance of corrupt compliance.

How far the Chancellors of the sixteenth and seventeenth centuries depended upon customary gratuities for their revenues may be seen from the facts which show the degree of state which they were required to maintain, and the inadequacy of the ancient fees for the maintenance of that pomp. When Elizabeth pressed Hatton for payment of the sums which he owed her, the Chancellor lamented his inability to liquidate her just claims, and urged in excuse that the *ancient fees* were very inadequate to the expenses of the Chancellor's office. But though Elizabethan Chancellors could not live upon their ancient fees, they kept up palaces in town and country, fed regiments of lackeys, and surpassed the ancient nobility in the grandeur of their equipages. Egerton—the needy and illegitimate son of a rural knight, a lawyer who fought up from the ranks—not only sustained the costly dignities of office, but left to his descendants a landed estate worth £8000 per annum. Bacon's successor in the 'marble chair,' Lord Keeper Williams, assured Buckingham that in Egerton's time the Chancellor's lawful income was less than three thousand per annum. "The lawful revenue of the office stands thus," wrote Williams, speaking from his intimate knowledge of Ellesmere's affairs, "or not much above it at anytime:—in fines certain, £1300 per annum, or thereabouts; in fines casual, £1250 or thereabouts; in greater writs, £140; for impost of wine, £100—in all, £2790; and these are all the true means of that great office." It is probable that Williams under-stated the revenue, but it is certain that the income, apart from gratuities, was insufficient.

The Chancellor was not more dependent on customary gratuities than the chief of the three Common Law courts. At Westminster and on circuit, whenever he was required to discharge his official functions, the English judge extended his hand for the contributions of the well-disposed. No one thought of blaming judges for their readiness to take customary benevolences. To take gifts was a usage of the profession, and had its parallel in the customs of every calling and rank of life. The clergy took dues in like manner: from the earliest days of feudal life the territorial lords had supplied their wants in the same way; amongst merchants and yeomen, petty traders and servants, the system existed in full force. These presents were made without any secrecy. The aldermen of borough towns openly voted presents to the judges; and the judges received their offerings—not as benefactions, but as legitimate perquisites. In 1620—just a year before Lord Bacon's fall—the municipal council of Lyme Regis left it to the "mayor's discretion" to decide "what gratuity he will give to the Lord Chief Baron and his men" at the next assizes. The system, it is needless to say, had disastrous results. Empowering the chief judge of every court to receive presents not only from the public, but from subordinate judges, inferior officers, and the bar; and moreover empowering each place-holder to take gratuities from persons officially or by profession concerned in the business of the courts, it produced a complicated machinery for extortion. By presents the chief justices bought their places from the crown or a royal favorite; by presents the puisne justices, registrars, counsel bought place or favor from the chief; by presents the attorneys, sub-registrars, and outside public sought to gain their ends with the humbler place-holders. The meanest ushers of Westminster Hall took coins from ragged scriveners. Hence every place was actually bought and sold, the sum being in most cases very high. Sir James Ley offered the Duke of Buckingham £10,000 for the Attorney's place. At the same period the Solicitor General's office was sold for £4000. Under Charles I. matters grew still worse than they had been under his father. When Sir Charles Cæsar consulted Laud about the worth of the vacant Mastership of the Rolls, the archbishop frankly said, "that as things then stood, the place was not likely to go without more money than he thought any wise man would give for it." Disregarding this intimation, Sir Charles paid the king £15,000 for the place, and added a loan of £2000. Sir Thomas Richardson, at the opening of the reign, gave £17,000 for the Chiefship of the Common Pleas. If judges needed gifts before the days when vacant seats were put up to auction, of course they stood all the more in need of them when they bought their promotions with such large sums. It is not wonderful that the wearers of ermine repaid themselves by venal practices. The sale of judicial offices was naturally followed by the sale of judicial decisions. The judges having submitted to the extortions of the king, the public had to endure the extortions of the judges. Corruption on the bench produced corruption at the bar. Counsel bought the attention and compliance of 'the court,' and in some cases sold their influence with shameless rascality. They would take fees to speak from one side in a cause and fees to be silent from the other side—selling their own clients as coolly as judges sold the suitors of their courts. Sympathizing with the public, and stung by personal experience of legal dishonesty, the clergy sometimes denounced from the pulpit the extortions of corrupt judges and unprincipled barristers. The assize sermons of Charles I.'s reign were frequently seasoned with such animadversions. At Thetford Assizes, March, 1630, the Rev. Mr. Ramsay, in the assize-sermon, spoke indignantly of judges who "favored causes," and of "counsellors who took fees to be silent." In the summer of 1631, at the Bury Assizes, "one Mr. Scott made a sore sermon in discovery of corruption in judges and others." At Norwich, the same authority, viz., 'Sir John Rous's Diary,' informs us—"Mr. Greene was more plaine, insomuch that Judge Harvey, in his charge, broke out thus: 'It seems by the sermon that we are corrupt, but we know that we can use conscience in our places as well as the best clergieman of all.'"

In his 'Life and Death of Sir Matthew Hale,' Bishop Burnet tells a good story of the Chief's conduct with regard to a customary gift. "It is also a custom," says the biographer, "for the Marshall of the King's Bench to present the judges of that court with a piece of plate for a New Year's Gift, that for the Chief Justice being larger than the rest. This he intended to have refused, but the other judges told him it belonged to his office, and the refusing it would be a prejudice to his successors; so he was persuaded to take it, but he sent word to the marshall, that instead of plate he should bring him the value of it in money, and when he received it, he immediately sent it to the prisons for the relief and discharge of the poor there."

*Chapter 15*

# GIFTS AND SALES

By degrees the public ceased to make presents to the principal judges of the kingdom; but long after the Chancellor and the three Chiefs had taken the last offerings of general society, they continued to receive yearly presents from the subordinate judges, placemen, and barristers of their respective courts. Lord Cowper deserves honor for being the holder of the seals who, by refusing to pocket these customary donations, put an end to a very objectionable system, so far as the Court of Chancery was concerned.

On being made Lord Keeper, he resolved to depart from the custom of his predecessors for many generations, who on the first day of each new year had invariably entertained at breakfast the persons from whom tribute was looked for. Very droll were these receptions in the old time. The repast at an end, the guests forthwith disburdened themselves of their gold—the payers approaching the holder of the seals in order of rank, and laying on his table purses of money, which the noble payee accepted with his own hands. Sometimes his lordship was embarrassed by a ceremony that required him to pick gold from the fingers of men, several of whom he knew to be in indigent circumstances. In Charles II.'s time it was observed that the silver-tongued Lord Nottingham on such occasions always endeavored to hide his confusion under a succession of nervous smiles and exclamations—"Oh, Tyrant Cuthtom!—Oh, Tyrant Cuthtom!"

It is noteworthy that in relinquishing the benefit of these exactions, the Lord Keeper feared unfriendly criticism much more than he anticipated public commendation. In his diary, under date December 30, Cowper wrote:—"I acquainted my Lord Treasurer with my design to refuse New Year's Gifts, if he had no objection against it, as spoiling, in some measure, a place of which he had the conferring. He answered it was not expected of me, but that I might do as my predecessors had done; but if I refused, he thought nobody could blame me for it." Anxious about the consequences of his innovation, the new Lord Keeper gave notice that on January 1, 1705-6, he would receive no gifts; but notwithstanding this proclamation, several officers of Chancery and counsellors came to his house with tribute, and were refused admittance. "New Year's Gifts turned back," he wrote in his diary at the close of the eventful day, "and pray God it doth me more credit and good than hurt, by making secret enemies *in fæce Romuli*." His fears were in a slight degree fulfilled. The Chiefs of the three Common Law Courts were greatly displeased with an innovation which they had no wish to adopt; and their warm expressions of dissatisfaction induced the Lord Keeper to cover his disinterestedness with a harmless fiction. To pacify the indignant Chiefs and the many persons who sympathized with them, he pretended that though he had declined intentionally the gifts of the Chancery barristers, he had not designed to exercise the same self-denial with regard to the gifts of Chancery officers.[15]

The common law chiefs were slow to follow in the Lord Keeper's steps, and many years passed before the reform, effected in Chancery by accident or design, or by a lucky combination of both, was adopted in the other great courts. In his memoir of Lord Cowper, Campbell observes: "His example with respect to New Year's Gifts was not speedily followed; and it is said that till very recently the Chief Justice of the Common Pleas invited the officers of his court to a dinner at the beginning of the year, when each of them deposited under his plate a present in the shape of a Bank of England note, instead of a gift of oxen roaring at his levee, as in ruder times." There is no need to remind the reader in this place of the many veracious and the many apocryphal stories concerning the basket justices of Fielding's time—stories showing that in law courts of the lowest sort applicants for justice were accustomed to fee the judges with victuals and drink until a comparatively recent date.

Lucky would it have been for the first Earl of Macclesfield if the custom of selling places in Chancery had been put an end to forever by the Lord Keeper who abolished the custom of New Year's Gifts; but the judge who at the sacrifice of one-fourth of his official income swept away the pernicious usage which had from time immemorial marked the opening of each year, saw no reason why he should purge Chancery of another scarcely less objectionable practice. Following the steps of their predecessors, the Chancellors Cowper, Harcourt, and Macclesfield sold subordinate offices in their court; and whereas all previous Chancellors had been held blameless for so doing, Lord Macclesfield was punished with official degradation, fine, imprisonment, and obloquy.

By birth as humble[16] as any layman who before or since his time has held the seals, Thomas Parker raised himself to the woolsack by great talents and honorable industry. As

---

[15] It should be observed that many persons are of opinion that the Lord Keeper's assertion on this point was not an artifice, but a simple statement of fact. To those who take this view, his lordship's position seems alike ridiculous and respectable—respectable because he actually intended to forbear from taking the barrister's money; ridiculous because, through clumsy and inadequate arrangements, he missed the other and not less precious gifts which he did not mean to decline. Anyhow, the critics admit that credit is due to him for persisting in a change—wrought in the first instance partly by honorable design and partly by accident.

[16] The cases of John Scott, Philip Yorke, and Edward Sugden are before the mind of the present writer, when he pens the sentence to which this note refers. The social extraction of the English bar will be considered in a later chapter of this work.

an advocate he won the respect of society and his profession; as a judge he ranks with the first expositors of English law. Although for imputed corruption he was hurled with ignominy from his high place, no one has ventured to charge him with venality on the bench. That he was a spotless character, or that his career was marked by grandeur of purpose, it would be difficult to establish; but few Englishmen could at the present time be found to deny that he was in the main an upright peer, who was not wittingly neglectful of his duty to the country which had loaded him with wealth and honors.

Amongst the many persons ruined by the bursting of the South Sea Bubble were certain Masters of Chancery, who had thrown away on that wild speculation large sums of which they were the official guardians. Lord Macclesfield was one of the victims on whom the nation wreaked its wrath at a crisis when universal folly had produced universal disaster. To punish the masters for their delinquencies was not enough; greater sacrifices than a few comparatively obscure placemen were demanded by the suitors and wards whose money had been squandered by the fraudulent trustees. The Lord Chancellor should be made responsible for the Chancery defalcations. That was the will of the country. No one pretended that Lord Macclesfield had originated the practice which permitted Masters in Chancery to speculate with funds placed under their care; attorneys and merchants were well aware that in the days of Harcourt, Cowper, Wright, and Somers, it had been usual for masters to pocket interest accruing from suitors' money; notorious also was it that, though the Chancellor was theoretically the trustee of the money confided to his court, the masters were its actual custodians. Had the Chancellor known that the masters were trafficking in dangerous investments to the probable loss of the public, duty would have required him to examine their accounts and place all trust-moneys beyond their reach; but until the crash came, Lord Macclesfield knew neither the actual worthlessness of the South Sea Stock, nor the embarrassed circumstances of the defaulting masters, nor the peril of the persons committed to his care. The system which permitted the masters to speculate with money not their own was execrable, but the Lord Chancellor was not the parent of that system.

Infuriated by the national calamity, in which they were themselves great sufferers, the Commons impeached the Chancellor, charging him with high crimes and misdemeanors, of which the peers unanimously declared him guilty. In this famous trial the great fact established against his lordship was that he had sold masterships to the defaulters. It appeared that he had not only sold the places, but had stood out for very high prices; the inference being, that in consideration of these large sums he had left the purchasers without the supervision usually exercised by Chancellors over such officers, and had connived at the practices which had been followed by ruinous results. To this it was replied, that if the Chancellor had sold the places at higher prices than his predecessors, he had done so because the places had become much more valuable; that at the worst he had but sold them to the highest bidder, after the example of his precursors; that the inference was not supported by any direct testimony.

Very humorous was some of the evidence by which the sale of the masterships was proved. Master Elde deposed that he bought his office for 5000 guineas, the bargain being finally settled and fulfilled after a personal interview with the accused lord. Master Thurston, another purchaser at the high rate of 5000 guineas, paid his money to Lady Macclesfield. It must be owned that these sums were very large, but their magnitude does not fix fraudulent purpose upon the Chancellor. That he believed himself fairly entitled to a moderate present on appointing to a mastership is certain; that he regarded £2000 as the gratuity which he might accept, without blushing at its publication, may be inferred from the restitution of £3250 which he made to one of the purchasers for £5250 at a time when he anticipated an inquiry into his conduct; that he felt himself acting indiscreetly if not wrongfully in pressing for such large sums is testified by the caution with which he conferred with the purchasers and the secrecy with which he accepted their money.

His defence before the peers admitted the sales of the places, but maintained that the transactions were legitimate.

The defence was of no avail. When the question of guilty or not guilty was put to the peers, each of the noble lords present answered, "Guilty, upon my honor." Sentenced to pay a fine of £30,000, and undergo imprisonment until the mulct was paid, the unfortunate statesman bitterly repented the imprudence which had exposed him to the vengeance of political adversaries and to the enmity of the vulgar. Whilst the passions roused by the prosecution were at their height, the fallen Chancellor was treated with much harshness by Parliament, and with actual brutality by the mob. Ever ready to vilify lawyers, the rabble seized on so favorable an occasion for giving expression to one of their strongest prejudices. Amongst the crowds who followed the Earl to the Tower with curses, voices were heard to exclaim that "Staffordshire had produced the three greatest scoundrels of England—Jack Sheppard, Jonathan Wilde, and Tom Parker." Jonathan Wilde was executed in 1725—the year of Lord Macclesfield's impeachment; and Jack Sheppard died on the gallows at Tyburn, November 16, 1724.

Throughout the inquiry, and after the adverse verdict, George I. persisted in showing favor to the disgraced Chancellor; and when the violent emotions of the crisis had passed away it was generally admitted by enlightened critics of public events that Lord Macclesfield had been unfairly treated. The scape-goat of popular wrath, he suffered less for his own faults, than for the evil results of a bad system; and at the present time—when the silence of more than a hundred and thirty years rests upon his tomb—Englishmen, with one voice, acknowledge the valuable qualities that raised him to eminence, and regret the proceedings which consigned him in his old age to humiliation and gloom.

*Chapter 16*

# A Rod Pickled by William Cole

"A proneness to take bribes may be generated from the habit of taking fees," said Lord Keeper Williams in his Inaugural Address, making an ungenerous allusion to Francis Bacon, whilst he uttered a statement which was no calumny upon King James's Bench and Bar, though it is signally inapplicable to lawyers of the present day.

Of Williams, tradition preserves a story that illustrates the prevalence of judicial corruption in the seventeenth century, and the jealousy with which that Right Reverend Lord Keeper watched for attempts to tamper with his honesty. Whilst he was taking exercise in the Great Park of Nonsuch House, his attention was caught by a church recently erected at the cost of a rich Chancery suitor. Having expressed satisfaction with the church, Williams inquired of George Minors, "Has he not a suit depending in Chancery?" and on receiving an answer in the affirmative, observed, "he shall not fare the worse for building of churches." These words being reported to the pious suitor, he not illogically argued that the Keeper was a judge likely to be influenced in making his decisions by matters distinct from the legal merits of the case put before him. Acting on this impression, the good man forthwith sent messengers to Nonsuch House, bearing gifts of fruits and poultry to the holder of the seals. "Nay, carry them back," cried the judge, looking with a grim smile from the presents to George Minors; "nay, carry them back, George, and tell your friend that he shall not fare the better for sending of presents."

Rich in satire directed against law and its professors, the literature of the Commonwealth affords conclusive testimony of the low esteem in which lawyers were held in the seventeenth century by the populace, and shows how universal was the belief that wearers of ermine and gentlemen of the long robe would practice any sort of fraud or extortion for the sake of personal advantage. In the pamphlets and broadsides, in the squibs and ballads of the period, may be found a wealth of quaint narrative and broad invective, setting forth the rascality of judges and attorneys, barristers and scriveners. Any literary effort to throw contempt upon the law was sure of success. The light jesters, who made merry with the phraseology and costumes of Westminster Hall, were only a few degrees less welcome than the stronger and more indignant scribes who cried aloud against the sins and sinners of the courts. When simple folk had expended their rage in denunciations of venal eloquence and unjust judgments, they amused themselves with laughing at the antiquated verbiage of the rascals who sought to conceal their bad morality under worse Latin. 'A New Modell, or the Conversion of the Infidell Terms of the Law: For the Better promoting of misunderstanding according to Common Sense,' is a publication consisting of a cover or fly-leaf and two leaves, that appeared about a year before the Restoration. The wit is not brilliant; its humor is not free from uncleanness; but its comic renderings[17] of a hundred law terms illustrate the humor of the times.

More serious in aim, but not less comical in result, is William Cole's 'A Rod for the Lawyers. London, Printed in the year 1659.' The preface of this mad treatise ends thus—"I do not altogether despair but that before I dye I may see the Inns of Courts, or dens of Thieves, converted into Hospitals, which were a rare piece of justice; that as they formerly have immured those that robbed the poor of houses, so they may at last preserve the poor themselves."

Another book touching on the same subject and belonging to the same period, is, 'Sagrir, or Doomsday drawing nigh; With Thunder and Lightning to Lawyers, (1653) by John Rogers.'

Violent, even for a man holding Fifth-Monarchy views, John Rogers prefers a lengthy indictment against lawyers, for whose delinquencies and heinous offence he admits neither apology nor palliation. In his opinion all judges deserve the death of Arnold and Hall, whose last moments were provided for by the hangman. The wearers of the long robe are perjurers, thieves, enemies of mankind; their institutions are hateful, and their usages abominable. In olden time they were less powerful and rapacious. But prosperity soon exaggerated all their evil qualities. Sketching the rise of the profession, the author observes—"These men would get sometimes Parents, Friends, Brothers, Neighbors, sometimes *others* to be (in their absence) Agents, Factors, or Solicitors for them at Westminster, and as yet they had no stately houses or mansions to live in, as they have now (called Inns of Court), but they lodged like countrymen or strangers in ordinary Inns. But afterwards, when the interests of lawyers began to look big (as in Edward III.'s days), they got mansions or colleges, which they called Inns, and by the king's favor had an addition of honor, whence they were called Inns of Court."[18]

---

[17] Of these renderings the subjoined may be taken as favorable specimens:—"Breve originale, original sinne; capias, a catch to a sad tune; alias capias, another to the same (sad tune); habeas corpus, a trooper; capias ad satisfaciend., a hangman: latitat, bo-peep; nisi prius, first come first served; demurrer, hum and haw; scandal. magnat., down with the Lords."

[18] Even vacations stink in the nostrils of Mr. Rogers; for he maintains that they are not so much periods when lawyers cease from their odious practices, as times of repose and recreation wherein they gain fresh vigor and daring for the commission of further outrages, and allow their unhappy victims to acquire just enough wealth to render them worth the trouble of despoiling.

The familiar anecdotes which are told as illustrations of Chief Justice Hale's integrity are very ridiculous, but they serve to show that the judges of his time were believed to be very accessible to corrupt influences. During his tenure of the Chiefship of the Exchequer, Hale rode the Western Circuit, and met with the loyal reception usually accorded to judges on circuit in his day. Amongst other attentions offered to the judges on this occasion was a present of venison from a wealthy gentleman who was concerned in a cause that was in due course called for hearing. No sooner was the call made than Chief Baron Hale resolved to place his reputation for judicial honesty above suspicion, and the following scene occurred:—

> "*Lord Chief Baron.*—'Is this plaintiff the gentleman of the same name who hath sent me the venison?' *Judge's servant.*—'Yes, please you, my lord.' *Lord Chief Baron.*—'Stop a bit, then. Do not yet swear the jury. I cannot allow the trial to go on till I have paid him for his buck!' *Plaintiff.*—'I would have your lordship to know that neither myself nor my forefathers have ever sold venison, and I have done nothing to your lordship which we have not done to every judge that has come this circuit for centuries bygone.' *Magistrate of the County.*—'My lord, I can confirm what the gentleman says for truth, for twenty years back.' *Other Magistrates.*—'And we, my lord, know the same.' *Lord Chief Baron.*—'That is nothing to me. The Holy Scripture says, 'A gift perverteth the ways of judgment.' I will not suffer the trial to go on till the venison is paid for. Let my butler count down the full value thereof.' *Plaintiff.*—'I will not disgrace myself and my ancestors by becoming a venison butcher. From the needless dread of *selling* justice, your lordship *delays* it. I withdraw my record.'"

As far as good taste and dignity were concerned, the gentleman of the West Country was the victor in this absurd contest: on the other hand, Hale had the venison for nothing, and was relieved of the trouble of hearing the cause.

In the same manner Hale insisted on paying for six loaves of sugar which the Dean and Chapter of Salisbury sent to his lodgings, in accordance with ancient usage. Similar cases of the judge's readiness to construe courtesies as bribes may be found in notices of trials and books of *ana*.

*A propos* of these stories of Hale's squeamishness, Lord Campbell tells the following good anecdote of Baron Graham: "The late Baron Graham related to me the following anecdote to show that he had more firmness than Judge Hale:—'There was a baronet of ancient family with whom the judges going the Western Circuit had always been accustomed to dine. When I went that circuit I heard that a cause, in which he was plaintiff, was coming on for trial: but the usual invitation was received, and lest the people might suppose that judges could be influenced by a dinner; I accepted it. The defendant, a neighboring squire, being dreadfully alarmed by this intelligence, said to himself, 'Well, if Sir John entertains the judge hospitably, I do not see why I should not do the same by the jury.' So he invited to dinner the whole of the special jury summoned to try the cause. Thereupon the baronet's courage failed him, and he withdrew the record, so that the cause was not tried; and although I had my dinner, I escaped all suspicion of partiality."

This story puts the present writer in mind of another story which he has heard told in various ways, the wit of it being attributed by different narrators to two judges who have left the bench for another world, and a Master of Chancery who is still alive. On the present occasion the Master of Chancery shall figure as the humorist of the anecdote.

Less than twenty years since, in one of England's southern counties, two neighboring landed proprietors differed concerning their respective rights over some unenclosed land, and also about certain rights of fishing in an adjacent stream. The one proprietor was the richest baronet, the other the poorest squire of the county; and they agreed to settle their dispute by arbitration. Our Master in Chancery, slightly known to both gentlemen, was invited to act as arbitrator after inspecting the localities in dispute. The invitation was accepted and the master visited the scene of disagreement, on the understanding that he should give up two days to the matter. It was arranged that on the first day he should walk over the squire's estate, and hear the squire's uncontradicted version of the case, dining at the close of the day with both contendents at the squire's table; and that on the second day, having walked over the baronet's estate, and heard without interruption the other side of the story, he should give his award, sitting over wine after dinner at the rich man's table. At the close of the first day the squire entertained his wealthy neighbor and the arbitrator at dinner. In accordance with the host's means, the dinner was modest but sufficient. It consisted of three fried soles, a roast leg of mutton, and vegetables; three pancakes, three pieces of cheese, three small loaves of bread, ale, and a bottle of sherry. On the removal of the viands, three magnificent apples, together with a magnum of port, were placed on the table by way of dessert. At the close of the second day the trio dined at the baronet's table, when it appeared that, struck by the simplicity of the previous day's dinner, and rightly attributing the absence of luxuries to the narrowness of the host's purse, the wealthy disputant had resolved not to attempt to influence the umpire by giving him a superior repast. Sitting at another table the trio dined on exactly the same fare,—three fried soles, a roast leg of mutton, and vegetables; three pancakes, three pieces of cheese, three small loaves of bread, ale, and a bottle of sherry; and for dessert three magnificent apples, together with a magnum of port. The dinner being over, the apples devoured, and the last glass of port drunk, the arbitrator (his eyes twinkling brightly as he spoke) introduced his award with the following exordium:—"Gentlemen, I have with all proper attention considered your *sole* reasons: I have taken due notice of your *joint* reasons, and I have come to the conclusion that your *des(s)erts* are about equal."

*Chapter 17*

# CHIEF JUSTICE POPHAM

One of the strangest cases of corruption amongst English Judges still remains to be told on the slender authority which is the sole foundation of the weighty accusation. In comparatively recent times there have not been many eminent Englishmen to whom 'tradition's simple tongue' has been more hostile than Queen Elizabeth's Lord Chief Justice, Popham. The younger son of a gentle family, John Popham passed from Oxford to the Middle Temple, raised himself to the honors of the ermine, secured the admiration of illustrious contemporaries, in his latter years gained abundant praise for wholesome severity towards footpads, and at his death left behind him a name—which, tradition informs us, belonged to a man who in his reckless youth, and even after his call to the bar, was a cut-purse and highwayman. In mitigation of his conduct it is urged by those who credit the charge, that young gentlemen of his date were so much addicted to the lawless excitement of the road, that when he was still a beardless stripling, an act (1 Ed. VI. c. 12, s. 14) was passed, whereby any peer of the realm or lord of parliament, on a first conviction for robbery, was entitled to benefit of clergy, though he could not read. But bearing in mind the liberties which rumor is wont to take with the names of eminent persons, the readiness the multitude always display to attribute light morals to grave men, and the infrequency of the cases where a dissolute youth is the prelude to a manhood of strenuous industry and an old age of honor—the cautious reader will require conclusive testimony before he accepts Popham's connection with 'the road' as one of the unassailable facts of history.

The authority for this grave charge against a famous judge is John Aubrey, the antiquary, who was born in 1627, just twenty years after Popham's death. "For severall yeares," this collector says of the Chief Justice, "he addicted himself but little to the studie of the lawes, but profligate company, and was wont to take a purse with them. His wife considered her and his condition, and at last prevailed with him to lead another life and to stick to the studie of the lawe, which, upon her importunity, he did, being then about thirtie yours old." As Popham was born in 1531, he withdrew, according to this account, from the company of gentle highwaymen about the year 1561—more than sixty years before Aubrey's birth, and more than a hundred years before the collector committed the scandalous story to writing. The worth of such testimony is not great. Good stories are often fixed upon eminent men who had no part in the transactions thereby attributed to them. If this writer were to put into a private note-book a pleasant but unauthorized anecdote imputing *kleptomania* to Chief Justice Wiles (who died in 1761), and fifty years hence the note-book should be discovered in a dirty corner of a forgotten closet and published to the world—would readers in the twentieth century be justified in holding that Sir John Willes was an eccentric thief?

But Aubrey tells a still stranger story concerning Popham, when he sets forth the means by which the judge made himself lord of Littlecote Hall in Wiltshire. The case must be given in the narrator's own words.

> "Sir Richard Dayrell of Littlecot in com. Wilts. having got his lady's waiting-woman with child, when her travell came sent a servant with a horse for a midwife, whom he was to bring hoodwinked. She was brought, and layd the woman; but as soon as the child was born, she saw the knight take the child and murther it, and burn it in the fire in the chamber. She having done her business was extraordinarily rewarded for her paines, and went blindfold away. This horrid action did much run in her mind, and she had a desire to discover it, but knew not where 'twas. She considered with herself the time she was riding, and how many miles she might have rode at that rate in that time, and that it must be some great person's house, for the roome was twelve foot high: and she should know the chamber if she sawe it. She went to a justice of peace, and search was made. The very chamber found. The knight was brought to his tryall; and, to be short, this judge had this noble house, park, and manor, and (I think) more, for a bribe to save his life. Sir John Popham gave sentence according to lawe, but being a great person and a favorite, he procured a *nolle prosequi*."

This ghastly tale of crime following upon crime has been reproduced by later writers with various exaggerations and modifications. Dramas and novels have been founded upon it; and a volume might be made of the ballads and songs to which it has given birth. In some versions the corrupt judge does not even go through the form of passing sentence, but secures an acquittal from the jury; according to one account, the mother, instead of the infant, was put to death; according to another, the erring woman was the murderer's daughter, instead of his wife's waiting-woman; another writer, assuming credit as a conscientious narrator of facts, places the crime in the eighteenth instead of the sixteenth century, and transforms the venal judge into a clever barrister.

In a highly seasoned statement of the repulsive tradition communicated by Lord Webb Seymour to Walter Scott, the murder is described with hideous minuteness.

Changing the midwife into 'a Friar of orders grey,' and murdering the mother instead of the baby, Sir Walter Scott revived the story in one of his most popular ballads. But of all the versions of the tradition that have come under this writer's notice, the one that departs most widely from Aubrey's statement is given in Mr. G.L. Rede's 'Anecdotes and Biography,' (1799).

*Chapter 18*

# JUDICIAL SALARIES

For the last three hundred years the law has been a lucrative profession, our great judges during that period having in many instances left behind them large fortunes, earned at the bar or acquired from official emoluments. The rental of Egerton's landed estates was £8,000 per annum—a royal income in the days of Elizabeth and James. Maynard left great wealth to his grand-daughters, Lady Hobart and Mary Countess of Stamford. Lord Mansfield's favorite investment was mortgage; and towards the close of his life the income which he derived for moneys lent on sound mortgages was £30,000 per annum. When Lord Kenyon had lost his eldest son, he observed to Mr. Justice Allan Park—"How delighted George would be to take his poor brother from the earth and restore him to life, although he receives £250,000 by his decease." Lord Eldon is said to have left to his descendants £500,000; and his brother, Lord Stowell, to whom we are indebted for the phrase 'the elegant simplicity of the Three per Cents.,' also acquired property that at the time of his death yielded £12,000 per annum.

Lord Stowell's personalty was sworn under £230,000, and he had invested considerable sums in land. It is noteworthy that this rich lawyer did not learn to be contented with the moderate interest of the Three per Cents. until he had sustained losses from bad speculations. Notable also is it that this rich lawyer—whose notorious satisfaction with three per cent. interest has gained for him a reputation of noble indifference to gain—was inordinately fond of money.

These great fortunes were raised from fees taken in practice at the bar, from judicial salaries or pensions, and from other official gains—such as court dues, perquisites, sinecures, and allowances. Since the Revolution of 1688 these last named irregular or fluctuating sources of judicial income have steadily diminished, and in the present day have come to an end. Eldon's receipts during his tenure of the seals cannot be definitely stated, but more is known about them and his earnings at the bar than he intended the world to discover, when he declared in Parliament "that in no one year, since he had been made Lord Chancellor, had he received the same amount of profit which he enjoyed while at the bar." Whilst he was Attorney General he earned something more than £10,000 a year; and in returns which he himself made to the House of Commons, he admits that in 1810 he received, as Lord Chancellor, a gross income of £22,730, from which sum, after deduction of all expenses, there remained a net income of £17,000 per annum. He was enabled also to enrich the members of his family with presentations to offices, and reversions of places.

Until comparatively recent times, judges were dangerously dependent on the king's favor; for they not only held their offices during the pleasure of the crown, but on dismissal they could not claim a retiring pension. In the seventeenth century, an aged judge, worn out by toil and length of days, was deemed a notable instance of royal generosity, if he obtained a small allowance on relinquishing his place in court. Chief Justice Hale, on his retirement, was signally favored when Charles II graciously promised to continue his salary till the end of his life—which was manifestly near its close. Under the Stuarts, the judges who lost their places for courageous fidelity to law, were wont to resume practice at the bar. To provide against the consequences of ejection from office, great lawyers, before they consented to exchange the gains of advocacy for the uncertain advantages of the woolsack, used to stipulate for special allowance—over and above the ancient emoluments of place. Lord Nottingham had an allowance of £4000 per annum; and Lord Guildford, after a struggle for better times, was constrained, at a cost of mental serenity, to accept the seals, with a special salary of half that sum.[19]

From 1688 down to the present time, the chronicler of changes in the legal profession, has to notice a succession of alterations in the system and scale of judicial payments—all of the innovations having a tendency to raise the dignity of the bench. Under William and Mary, an allowance (still continued), was made to holders of the seal on their appointment, for the cost of outfit and equipages. The amount of this special aid was £2000, but fees reduced it to £1843 13*s*. Mr. Foss observes—"The earliest existing record of this allowance, is dated June 4, 1700, when Sir Nathan Wright was made Lord Keeper, which states it to be the same sum as had been allowed to his predecessor."

At the same period, the salary of a puisne judge was but £1000 a year—a sum that would have been altogether insufficient for his expenses. A considerable part of a puisne's remuneration consisted of fees, perquisites, and presents. Amongst the customary presents to judges at this time, may be mentioned the *white gloves*, which men convicted of manslaughter, presented to the judges when they pleaded the king's pardon; the *sugar loaves*, which the Warden of the Fleet annually sent to the judges of the Common Pleas; and the almanacs yearly distributed amongst the occupants of the bench by the Stationers' Company. From one of these almanacs, in which Judge Rokeby kept his accounts, it appears that in the year 1694, the casual profits of his place amounted to

[19] During the Commonwealth, the people, unwilling to pay their judges liberally, decided that a thousand a year was a sufficient income for a Lord Commissioner of the Great Seal.

£694, 4*s.* 6*d.* Here is the list of his official incomes, (net) for ten years:—in 1689, £1378, 10*s.*; in 1690, £1475, 10*s.* 10*d.*; in 1691, £2063, 18*s.* 4*d.*; in 1692, £1570, 1*s.* 4*d.*; in 1693, £1569, 13*s.* 1*d.*; in 1694, £1629, 4*s.* 6*d.*; in 1695, £1443, 7*s.* 6*d.*; in 1696, £1478, 2*s.* 6*d.*; in 1697, £1498, 11*s.* 11*d.*; in 1698, £1631, 10*s.* 11*d.* The fluctuation of the amounts in this list, is worthy of observation; as it points to one bad consequence of the system of paying judges by fees, gratuities, and uncertain perquisites. A needy judge, whose income in lucky years was over two thousand pounds, must have been sadly pinched in years when he did not receive fifteen hundred.

Under the heading, "The charges of my coming into my judge's place, and the taxes upon it the first yeare and halfe," Judge Rokeby gives the following particulars:

> "1689, May 11. To Mr. Milton, Deputy Clerk of the Crown, as per note, for the patent and swearing privately, £21, 6*s.* 4*d.* May 30. To Mr. English, charges of the patent at the Secretary of State's Office, as per note, said to be a new fee, £6, 10*s.* Inrolling the patent in Exchequer and Treasury, £2, 3*s.* 4*d.* Ju. 27. Wine given as a judge, as per vintner's note, £23, 19*s.* Ju. 24. Cakes, given as a judge, as per vintner's note, £5, 14*s.* 6*d.* Second-hand judge's robes, with some new lining, £31. Charges for my part of the patent for our salarys, to Aaron Smith, £7, 15*s.*, and the dormant warrant £3.—£10, 15*s.*—£101, 8*s.* 2*d.*
>
> "Taxes, £420.
>
> "The charges of my being made a serjeant-at-law, and of removing myselfe and family to London, and a new coach and paire of horses, and of my knighthood (all which were within the first halfe year of my coming from York), upon the best calculation I can make of them, were att least £600."

Concerning the expenses attendant on his removal from the Common Pleas to the King's Bench in 1695—a removal which had an injurious result upon his income—the judge records: Nov. 1. To Mr. Partridge, the Crier of King's Bench, claimed by him as a fee due to the 2 criers, £2. Nov. 12. To Mr. Ralph Hall, in full of the Clerk of the Crown's bill for my patent, and swearing at the Lord Keeper's, and passing it through the offices, £28, 14*s.* 2*d.* Dec. 6. To Mr. Carpenter, the Vintner, for wine and bottles, £22, 10*s.* 6*d.* To Gwin, the Confectioner, for cakes, £5, 3*s.* 6*d.* To Mr. Mand (his clerk), which he paid att the Treasury, and att the pell for my patent, allowed there, £1, 15*s.* Tot. £60, 2*s.* 8*d.* The charges for wine and cakes were consequences of a custom which required a new judge to send biscuits and macaroons, sack and claret, to his brethren of the bench.

In the reign of George I. the salaries of the common law judges were raised—the pensions of the chiefs being doubled, and the *puisnes* receiving fifteen hundred instead of a thousand pounds.

Cowper's incomes during his tenure of the seals varied between something over seven and something under nine thousand per annum: but there is some reason to believe that on accepting office, he stipulated for a handsome yearly salary, in case he should be called upon to relinquish the place. Evelyn, not a very reliable authority, but still a chronicler worthy of notice even on questions of fact, says:—"Oct. 1705. Mr. Cowper made Lord Keeper. Observing how uncertain greate officers are of continuing long in their places, he would not accept it unless £2,000 a yeare were given him in reversion when he was put out, in consideration of his loss of practice. His predecessors, how little time soever they had the seal, usually got £100,000, and made themselves barons." It is doubtful whether this bargain was actually made; but long after Cowper's time, lawyers about to mount the woolsack, insisted on having terms that should compensate them for loss of practice. Lord Macclesfield had a special salary of £4000 per annum, during his occupancy of the marble chair, and obtained a grant of £12,000 from the king;—a tellership in the Exchequer being also bestowed upon his eldest son. Lord King obtained even better terms—a salary of £6000 per annum from the Post Office, and £1200 from the Hanaper Office; this large income being granted to him in consideration of the injury done to the Chancellor's emoluments by the proceedings against Lord Macclesfield—whereby it was declared illegal for chancellors to sell the subordinate offices in the Court of Chancery. This arrangement—giving the Chancellor an increased salary in *lieu* of the sums which he could no longer raise by sales of offices—is conclusive testimony that in the opinion of the crown Lord Macclesfield had a right to sell the masterships. The terms made by Lord Northington, in 1766, on resigning the Seals and becoming President of the Council, illustrate this custom. On quitting the marble chair, he obtained an immediate pension of £2000 per annum; and an agreement that the annual payment should be made £4000 per annum, as soon as he retired from the Presidency: he also obtained a reversionary grant for two lives of the lucrative office of Clerk of the Hanaper in Chancery.

In Lord Chancellor King's time, amongst the fees and perquisites which he wished to regulate and reform were the supplies of stationery, provided by the country for the great law-officers. It may be supposed that the sum thus expended on paper, pens, and wax was an insignificant item in the national expenditure; but such was not the case—for the chief of the courts were accustomed to place their personal friends on the free-list for articles of stationery. The Archbishop of Dublin, a dignitary well able to pay for his own writing materials, wrote to Lord King, April 10, 1733: "My Lord,—Ever since I had the honor of being acquainted with Lord Chancellors, I have lived in England and Ireland upon Chancery paper, pens, and wax. I am not willing to lose an old advantageous custom. If your Lordship hath any to spare me by my servant, you will oblige your very humble servant,

"John Dublin."

So long as judges or subordinate officers were paid by casual perquisites and fees, paid directly to them by suitors, a taint of corruption lingered in the practice of our courts.

Long after judges ceased to sell injustice, they delayed justice from interested motives, and when questions concerning their perquisites were raised, they would sometimes strain a point, for the sake of their own private advantage. Even Lord Ellenborough, whose fame is bright amongst the reputations of honorable men, could not always exercise self-control when attempts were made to lessen his customary profits, "I never," writes Lord Campbell, "saw this feeling at all manifest itself in Lord Ellenborough except once, when a question arose whether money paid into court was liable to poundage. I was counsel in the case, and threw him into a furious passion, by strenuously resisting the demand; the poundage was to go into his own pocket—being payable to the chief clerk—an office held in trust for him. If he was in any degree influenced by this consideration, I make no doubt that he was wholly unconscious of it."

George III's reign witnessed the introduction of changes long required, and frequently demanded in the mode and amounts of judicial payments. In 1779, puisne judges and barons received an additional £400 per annum, and the Chief Baron an increase of £500 a year. Twenty years later, Stat. 39, Geo. III., c. 110, gave the Master of the Rolls, £4000 a year, the Lord Chief Baron £4000 a year, and each of the puisne judges and barons, £3000 per annum. By the same act also, life-pensions of £4000 per annum were secured to retiring holders of the seal, and it was provided that after fifteen years of service, or in case of incurable infirmity, the Chief Justice of the King's Bench could claim, on retirement, £3000 per annum, the Master of the Rolls, Chief of Common Pleas, and Chief Baron £2500 per annum, and each minor judge of those courts or Baron of the coif, £2000 a year. In 1809, (49 Geo. III, c. 127) the Lord Chief Baron's annual salary was raised to £5000; whilst a yearly stipend of £4000 was assigned to each puisne judge or baron. By 53 Geo. III., c. 153, the Chiefs and Master of the Rolls, received on retirement an additional yearly £800, and the puisnes an additional yearly £600. A still more important reform of George III.'s reign was the creation of the first Vice Chancellor in March, 1813. Rank was assigned to the new functionary next after the Master of the Rolls, and his salary was fixed at £5000 per annum.

Until the reign of George IV judges continued to take fees and perquisites; but by 6 Geo. IV. c. 82, 83, 84, it was arranged that the fees should be paid into the Exchequer, and that the undernamed great officers of justice should receive the following salaries and pensions on retirement:—

| | **An. Sal.** | **An. Pension on retirement.** |
|---|---|---|
| Lord Chief Justice of King's Bench | £10,000 | £4000 |
| Lord Chief Justice of Common Pleas | 8000 | 3750 |
| The Master of the Rolls | 7000 | 3750 |
| The Vice Chancellor of England | 6000 | 3750 |
| The Chief Baron of the Exchequer | 7000 | 3750 |
| Each Puisne Baron or Judge | 5500 | 3500 |

Moreover by this Act, the second judge of the King's Bench was entitled, as in the preceding reign, to £40 for giving charge to the grand jury in each term, and pronouncing judgment on malefactors.

The changes with regard to judicial salaries under William IV were comparatively unimportant. By 2 and 3 Will. IV. c. 116, the salaries of puisne judges and barons were reduced to £5000 a year; and by 2 and 3 Will. IV. c. 111, the Chancellor's pension, on retirement, was raised to £5000, the additional £1000 per annum being assigned to him in compensation of loss of patronage occasioned by the abolition of certain offices. These were the most noticeable of William's provisions with regard to the payment of his judges.

The present reign, which has generously given the country two new judges, called Lord Justices, two additional Vice Chancellors, and a swarm of paid justices, in the shape of county court judges and stipendiary magistrates, has exercised economy with regard to judicial salaries. The annual stipends of the two Chief Justices, fixed in 1825 at £10,000 for the Chief of the King's Bench, and £8000 for the Chief of the Common Pleas, have been reduced, in the former case to £8000 per annum, in the latter to £7000 per annum. The Chancellor's salary for his services as Speaker of the House of Lords, has been made part of the £10,000 assigned to his legal office; so that his income is no more than ten thousand a year. The salary of the Master of the Rolls has been reduced from £7000 to £6000 a year; the same stipend, together with a pension on retirement of £3750, being assigned to each of the Lords Justices. The salary of a Vice Chancellor is £5000 per annum; and after fifteen years' service, or in case of incurable sickness, rendering him unable to discharge the functions of his office, he can retire with a pension of £3500.

Thurlow had no pension on retirement; but with much justice Lord Campbell observes: "Although there was no parliamentary retired allowance for ex-Chancellors, they were better off than at present. Thurlow was a Teller of the Exchequer, and had given sinecures to all his relations, for one of which his nephew now receives a commutation of £9000 a year." Lord Loughborough was the first ex-Chancellor who enjoyed, on retirement, a pension of £4000 per annum, under Stat. 39 Geo. III. c. 110. The next claimant for an ex-Chancellor's pension was Eldon, on his ejection from office in 1806; and the third claimant was Erskine, whom the possession of the pension did not preserve from the humiliation of indigence.

Eldon's obstinate tenacity of office, was attended with one good result. It saved the nation much money by keeping down the number of ex-Chancellors entitled to £4000 per annum. The frequency with which Governments have been changed during the last forty years has had a contrary effect, producing such a strong bevy of lawyers—who are pensioners as well as peers—that financial reformers are loudly asking if some scheme cannot be devised for lessening the number of these costly and comparatively useless personages. At the time when this page is written, there are four ex-Chancellors in receipt of pensions—Lords Brougham, St. Leonards, Cranworth, and Westbury; but death has recently diminished the roll of Chancellors by removing Lords Truro and Lyndhurst. Not long since the present writer read a very able, but one-sided article in a liberal newspaper that gave the sum total spent by the country since Lord Eldon's death in ex-Chancellors' pensions; and in simple truth it must be admitted that the bill was a fearful subject for contemplation.

# PART 4. COSTUME AND TOILET

*Chapter 19*

# BRIGHT AND SAD

From the days of the Conqueror's Chancellor, Baldrick, who is reputed to have invented and christened the sword-belt that bears his name, lawyers have been conspicuous amongst the best dressed men of their times. For many generations clerical discipline restrained the members of the bar from garments of lavish costliness and various colors, unless high rank and personal influence placed them above the fear of censure and punishment; but as soon as the law became a lay-profession, its members—especially those who were still young—eagerly seized the newest fashions of costume, and expended so much time and money on personal decoration, that the governors of the Inns deemed it expedient to make rules, with a view to check the inordinate love of gay apparel.

By these enactments, foppish modes of dressing the hair was discountenanced or forbidden, not less than the use of gaudy clothes and bright arms. Some of these regulations have a quaint air to readers of this generation; and as indications of manners in past times, they deserve attention.

From Dugdale's 'Origines Juridiciales,' it appears that in the earlier part of Henry VIII's reign, the students and barristers of the Inns were allowed great licence in settling for themselves minor points of costume; but before that paternal monarch died, this freedom was lessened. Accepting the statements of a previous chronicler, Dugdale observes of the members of the Middle Temple under Henry—"They have no order for their apparell; but every man may go as him listeth, so that his apparell pretend no lightness or wantonness in the wearer; for, even as his apparell doth shew him to be, even so he shall be esteemed among them." But at the period when this licence was permitted in respect of costume, the general discipline of the Inn was scandalously lax; the very next paragraph of the 'Origines' showing that the templars forbore to shut their gates at night, whereby "their chambers were oftentimes robbed, and many other misdemeanors used."

But measures were taken to rectify the abuses and evil manners of the schools. In the thirty-eighth year of Henry VIII an order was made "that the gentlemen of this company" (i.e., the Inner Temple) "should reform themselves in their cut or disguised apparel, and not to have long beards. And that the Treasurer of this society should confer with the other Treasurers of Court for an uniform reformation." The authorities of Lincoln's Inn had already bestirred themselves to reduce the extravagances of dress and toilet which marked their younger and more frivolous fellow-members. "And for decency in Apparel," writes Dugdale, concerning Lincoln's Inn, "at a council held on the day of the Nativity of St. John the Baptist, 23 Hen. VIII. it was ordered that for a continual rule, to be thenceforth kept in this house, no gentleman, being a fellow of this house, should wear any cut or pansid hose, or bryches; or pansid doublet, upon pain of putting out of the house."

Ten years later the authorities of Lincoln's Inn (33 Hen. VIII.) ordered that no member of the society "being in commons, or at his repast, should wear a beard; and whoso did, to pay double commons or repasts in this house during such time as he should have any beard."

By an order of 5 Maii, 1 and 2 Philip and Mary, the gentlemen of the Inner Temple were forbidden to wear long beards, no member of the society being permitted to wear a beard of more than three weeks' growth. Every breach of this law was punished by the heavy fine of twenty shillings. In 4 and 5 of Philip and Mary it was ordered that no member of the Middle Temple "should thenceforth wear any great bryches in their hoses, made after the Dutch, Spanish, or Almon fashion; or lawnde upon their capps; or cut doublets, upon pain of iii$^{s}$ iiii$^{d}$ forfaiture for the first default, and the second time to be expelled the house." At Lincoln's Inn, "in 1 and 2 Philip and Mary, one M$^{r}$ Wyde, of this house, was (by special order made upon Ascension day) fined at five groats, for going in his study gown in Cheapside, on a Sunday, about ten o'clock before noon; and in Westminister Hall, in the Term time, in the forenoon." Mr. Wyde's offence was one of remissness rather than of excessive care for his personal appearance. With regard to beards in the same reign Lincoln's Inn exacted that such members "as had beards should pay 12*d.* for every meal they continued them; and every man" was required "to be shaven upon pain of putting out of commons."

The orders made under Elizabeth with regard to the same or similar matters are even more humorous and diverse. At the Inner Temple "it was ordered in 36 Elizabeth (16 Junii), that if any fellow in commons, or lying in the Louse, did wear either hat or cloak in the Temple Church, hall, buttry, kitchen, or at the buttry-barr, dresser, or in the garden, he should forfeit for every such offence vi$^{s}$ viii$^{d}$. And in 42 Eliz. (8 Febr.) that they go not in cloaks, hatts, bootes, and spurs into the city, but when they ride out of the town." This order was most displeasing to the young men of the legal academies, who were given to swaggering amongst the brave gallants of city ordinaries, and delighted in showing their rich attire at Paul's. The Templar of the Inner Temple who ventured to wear arms (except his dagger) in hall committed a grave offence, and was fined five pounds. "No fellow of this house should come into the hall" it was enacted at the Inner Temple, 38 Eliz. (20 Dec.) "with any weapons, except his dagger, or his knife, upon pain of forfeiting the sum of five pounds." In old time the lawyers often quarrelled and drew swords in hall; and the object of this regulation doubtless was to diminish the number of scandalous affrays. The Middle Temple, in 26 Eliz., made six prohibitory rules with regard to apparel, enacting, "1. That no ruff should be worn. 2. Nor any White color in doublets or hoses. 3. Nor any facing of velvet in gownes, but by such as were of the bench. 4. That no gentleman should walk in the streets in their cloaks, but in gownes. 5. That no hat, or long, or curled hair be worn. 6. Nor any gown, but such as were of a sad color." Of similar orders made at Gray's Inn, during Elizabeth's reign, the following edict of 42 Eliz. (Feb. 11) may be taken as a specimen:—"That no gentleman of this society do come into the hall, to any meal, with their hats, boots, or spurs; but with their caps, decently and orderly, according to the ancient order of this house: upon pain, for every offence, to forfeit iii$^{s}$ 4$^{d}$, and for the third offence expulsion. Likewise, that no gentleman of this society do go into the city, or suburbs, or to walk in the Fields, otherwise than in his gown, according to the ancient usage of the gentlemen of the Inns of Court, upon penalty of iii$^{s}$ iiii$^{d}$ for every offence; and for the third, expulsion and loss of his chamber."

At Lincoln's Inn it was enacted, "in 38 Eliz., that if any Fellow of this House, being a commoner or repaster, should within the precinct of this house wear any cloak, boots and spurs, or long hair, he should pay for every offence five shillings for a fine, and also to be put out of commons." The attempt to put down beards at Lincoln's Inn failed. Dugdale says, in his notes on that Inn, "And in 1 Eliz. it was further ordered, that no fellow of this house should wear any beard above a fortnight's growth; and that whoso transgresses therein should for the first offence forfeit 3*s*. 4d., to be paid and cast with his commons; and for the second time 6*s*. 8d., in like manner to be paid and cast with his commons; and the third time to be banished the house. But the fashion at that time of wearing beards grew then so predominant, as that the very next year following, at a council held at this house, upon the 27$^{th}$ of November, it was agreed and ordered, that all orders before that time touching beards should be void and repealed." In the same year in which the authorities of Lincoln's Inn forbade the wearing of beards, they ordered that no fellow of their society "should wear any sword or buckler; or cause any to be born after him into the town." This was the first of the seven orders made in 1 Eliz. for *all* the Inns of Court; of which orders the sixth runs thus:—"That none should wear any velvet upper cap, neither in the house nor city. And that none after the first day of January then ensuing, should wear any furs, nor any manner of silk in their apparel, otherwise than he could justifie by the stature of apparel, made *an.* 24 H. 8, under the penalty aforesaid." In the eighth year of the following reign it was ordained at Lincoln's Inn "that no rapier should be worn in this house by any of the society."

Other orders made in the reign of James I., and similar enactments passed by the Inns in still more recent periods, can be readily found on reference to Dugdale and later writers upon the usages of lawyers.

On such matters, however, fashion is all-powerful; and however grandly the benchers of an Inn might talk in their council-chamber, they could not prevail on their youngsters to eschew beards when beards were the mode, or to crop the hair of their heads when long tresses were worn by gallants at court. Even in the time of Elizabeth—when authority was most anxious that utter-barristers should in matters of costume maintain that reputation for 'sadness' which is the proverbial characteristic of apprentices of the law—counsellors of various degrees were conspicuous throughout the town for brave attire. If we had no other evidence bearing on the point, knowledge of human nature would make us certain that the bar imitated Lord Chancellor Hatton's costume. At Gray's Inn, Francis Bacon was not singular in loving rich clothes, and running into debt for satin and velvet, jewels and brocade, lace and feathers. Even of that contemner of frivolous men and vain pursuits, Edward Coke, biography assures us, "The jewel of his mind was put into a fair case, a beautiful body with comely countenance; a case which he did wipe and keep clean, delighting in good clothes, well worn; being wont to say that the outward neatness of our bodies might be a monitor of purity to our souls."

The courts of James I. and his son drew some of their most splendid fops from the multitude of young men who were enjoined by the elders of their profession to adhere to a costume that was a compromise between the garb of an Oxford scholar and the guise of a London 'prentice. The same was the case with Charles II.'s London. Students and barristers outshone the brightest idlers at Whitehall, whilst within the walls of their Inns benchers still made a faint show of enforcing old restrictions upon costume. At a time when every Templar in society wore hair—either natural or artificial—long and elaborately dressed, Sir William Dugdale wrote, "To the office of the chief butler" (i.e., of the Middle Temple) "it likewise appertaineth to take the names of those that be absent at the said solemn revells, and to present them to the bench, as also inform the bench of such as wear hats, bootes, *long hair*, or the like (for the which he is commonly out of the young gentlemen's favor)."

*Chapter 20*

# MILLINERY

Saith Sir William Dugdale, in his chapter concerning the personal attire of judges—"That peculiar and decent vestments have, from great antiquity, been used in religious services, we have the authority of God's sacred precept to Moses, '*Thou shall make holy rayments for Aaron and his sons, that are to minister unto me, that they may be for glory and beauty*.'" In this light and flippant age there are men irreverent enough to smile at the habiliments which our judges wear in court, for the glory of God and the seemly embellishment of their own natural beauty.

Like the stuff-gown of the utter-barrister, the robes of English judges are of considerable antiquity; but antiquaries labor in vain to discover all the facts relating to their origin and history. Mr. Foss says that at the Stuart Restoration English judges resumed the robes worn by their predecessors since the time of Edward I.; but though the judicial robes of the present day bear a close resemblance to the vestments worn by that king's judges, the costume of the bench has undergone many variations since the twentieth year of his reign.

In the eleventh year of Richard II a distinction was made between the costumes of the chiefs of the King's Bench and Common Pleas and their assistant justices; and at the same time the Chief Baron's inferiority to the Chief Justices was marked by costume.

Henry VI.'s Chief Justice of the King's Bench, Sir John Fortescue, in his delightful treatise 'De Laudibus Legum Angliæ,' describes the ceremony attending the creation of a justice, and minutely sets forth the chief items of judicial costume in the Bench and Common Pleas during his time. "Howbeit," runs Robert Mulcaster's rendering of the 'De Laudibus,' "the habite of his rayment, hee shall from time to time forwarde, in some pointes change, but not in all the ensignments thereof. For beeing serjeaunt at lawe, hee was clothed in a long robe priestlyke, with a furred cape about his shoulders, and thereupon a hoode with two labels such as Doctours of the Lawes use to weare in certayne universityes, with the above described quoyfe. But being once made a justice, in steede of his hoode, hee shall weare a cloake cloased upon his righte shoulder, all the other ornaments of a serjeant still remayning; sauing that a justyce shall weare no partye coloured vesture as a serjeant may. And his cape is furred with none other than menever, whereas the serjeant's cape is ever furred with whyte lambe."

Judicial costume varied with the fashion of the day or the whim of the sovereign in the fourteenth and fifteenth centuries. Subsequent generations saw the introduction of other changes; and in the time of Charles I. questions relating to the attire of the common law judges were involved in so much doubt, and surrounded with so many contradictory precedents and traditions, that the judges resolved to simplify matters by conference and unanimous action. The result of their deliberation was a decree, dated June 6, 1635, to which Sir John Bramston, Chief of the King's Bench, Sir John Finch, Chief of the Common Pleas, Sir Humphrey Davenport, Chief of the Exchequer, and all the minor judges of the three courts, gave subscription.

*Chapter 21*

# Wigs

The changes effected in judicial costume during the Commonwealth, like the reformation introduced at the same period into the language of the law, were all reversed in 1660, when Charles II's judges resumed the attire and usages of their predecessors in the first Charles's reign. When he had satisfied himself that monarchical principles were sure of an enduring triumph, and that their victory would conduce to his own advantage, great was young Samuel Pepys's delight at seeing the ancient customs of the lawyers restored, one after another. In October, 1660, he had the pleasure of seeing "the Lord Chancellor and all the judges riding on horseback, and going to Westminster Hall, it being the first day of term." In the February of 1663-4 his eyes were gladdened by the revival of another old practice. "28th (Lord's Day). Up and walked to St. Paul's," he writes, "and, by chance, it was an extraordinary day for the Readers of Inns of the Court and all the Students to come to church, it being an old ceremony not used these twenty-five years, upon the first Sunday in Lent. Abundance there was of students, more than there was room to seat but upon forms, and the church mighty full. One Hawkins preached, an Oxford man, a good sermon upon these words, 'But the wisdom from above is first pure, then peaceable.'" Hawkins was no doubt a humorist, and smiled in the sleeve of his Oxford gown as he told the law-students that *peace* characterized the highest sort of *wisdom*.

But, notwithstanding their zeal in reviving old customs, the lawyers of the Restoration introduced certain novelties into legal life. From Paris they imported the wig which still remains one of the distinctive adornments of the English barrister; and from the same centre of civilization they introduced certain refinements of cookery, which had been hitherto unknown in the taverns of Fleet Street and the Strand. In the earlier part of the 'merry monarch's' reign, the eating-house most popular with young barristers and law-students was kept by a French cook named Chattelin, who, besides entertaining his customers with delicate fare and choice wine, enriched our language with the word 'cutlet'—in his day spelt costelet.

In the seventeenth century, until wigs were generally adopted, the common law judges, like their precursors for several past generations, wore in court velvet caps, coifs, and cornered caps. Pictures preserve to us the appearance of justices, with their heads covered by one or two of these articles of dress, the moustache in many instances adorning the lip, and a well-trimmed beard giving point to the judicial chin. The more common head-dress was the coif and coif-cap, of which it is necessary to say a few words.

The coif was a covering for the head, made of white lawn or silk, and common law judges wore it as a sign that they were members of the learned brotherhood of sergeants. Speaking of the sergeants, Fortescue, in his 'De Laudibus,' says—"Wherefore to this state and degree hath no man beene hitherto admitted, except he hath first continued by the space of sixteene years in the said generall studio of the law, and in token or signe, that all justices are thus graduat, every one of them alwaies, while he sitteth in the Kinge's Courts, weareth a white quoyfe of silke; which is the principal and chiefe insignment of habite, wherewith serjeants-at-lawe in their creation are decked. And neither the justice, nor yet the serjeaunt, shall ever put off the quoyfe, no not in the kinge's presence, though he bee in talke with his majestie's highnesse." At times it was no easy matter to take the coif from the head; for the white drapery was fixed to its place with strings, which in the case of one notorious rascal were not untied without difficulty. In Henry III.'s reign, when William de Bossy was charged in open court with corruption and dishonesty, he claimed the benefit of clerical orders, and endeavored to remove his coif in order that he might display his tonsure; but before he could effect his purpose, an officer of the court seized him by the throat and dragged him off to prison. "Voluit," says Matthew Paris, "ligamenta coifæ suæ solvere, ut, palam monstraret se tonsuram habere clericalem; sed non est permissus. Satelles vero eum arripiens, non per coifæ ligamina sed per guttur eum apprehendens, traxit ad carcerem." From which occurrence Spelman drew the untenable, and indeed, ridiculous inference, that the coif was introduced as a veil, beneath which ecclesiastics who wished to practice as judges or counsel in the secular courts, might conceal the personal mark of their order.

The coif-cap is still worn in undiminished proportions by judges when they pass sentence of death, and is generally known as the 'black cap.' In old time the justice, on making ready to pronounce the awful words which consigned a fellow-creature to a horrible death, was wont to draw up the flat, square, dark cap, that sometimes hung at the nape of his neck or the upper part of his shoulder. Having covered the whiteness of his coif, and partially concealed his forehead and brows with the sable cloth, he proceeded to utter the dread sentence with solemn composure and firmness. At present the black cap is assumed to strike terror into the hearts of the vulgar; formerly it was pulled over the eyes, to hide the emotion of the judge.

Shorn of their original size, the coif and the coif-cap may still be seen in the wigs worn by sergeants at the present day. The black blot which marks the crown of a sergeant's wig is generally spoken of as his coif, but this designation is erroneous. The black blot is the coif-cap; and those who wish to see the veritable coif must take a near view of the wig, when they will see that between the black silk and the horsehair there lies a circular piece of white lawn, which is the vestige of that pure raiment so reverentially mentioned by Fortescue. On the general adoption of wigs, the sergeants, like the rest of the bar, followed in the wake of fashion: but at first they wore their old coifs and caps over their false hair. Finding this plan cumbersome, they gradually diminished the size of the ancient covering, until the coif and cap became the absurd thing which resembles a bald place covered with court-plaster quite as much as the rest of the wig resembles human hair.

Whilst the common law judges of the seventeenth century, before the introduction of wigs, wore the undiminished coif and coif-cap, the Lord Chancellor, like the Speaker of the House of Commons, wore a hat. Lord Keeper Williams, the last clerical holder of the seals, used to wear in the Court of Chancery a round, conical hat. Bradshaw, sitting as president of the commissioners who tried Charles I., wore a hat instead of the coif and cap which he donned at other times as a serjeant of law. Kennett tells us that "Mr. Sergeant Bradshaw, the President, was afraid of some tumult upon such new and unprecedented insolence as that of sitting judge upon his king; and therefore, beside other defence, he had a thick big-crowned beaver hat, lined with plated steel, to ward off blows." It is scarcely credible that Bradshaw resorted to such means for securing his own safety, for in the case of a tumult, a hat, however strong, would have been an insignificant protection against popular fury. If conspirators had resolved to take his life, they would have tried to effect their purpose by shooting or stabbing him, not by knocking him on the head. A steel-plated hat would have been but a poor guard against a bludgeon, and a still poorer defence against poignard or pistol. It is far more probable that in laying aside the ordinary head-dress of an English common law judge, and in assuming a high-crowned hat, the usual covering of a Speaker, Bradshaw endeavored to mark the exceptional character of the proceeding, and to remind the public that he acted under parliamentary sanction. Whatever the wearer's object, England was satisfied that he had a notable purpose, and persisted in regarding the act as significant of cowardice or of insolence, of anxiety to keep within the lines of parliamentary privilege or of readiness to set all law at defiance. At the time and long after Bradshaw's death, that hat caused an abundance of discussion; it was a problem which men tried in vain to solve, an enigma that puzzled clever heads, a riddle that was interpreted as an insult, a caution, a protest, a menace, a doubt. Oxford honored it with a Latin inscription, and a place amongst the curiosities of the university, and its memory is preserved to Englishmen of the present day in the familiar lines—

"Where England's monarch once uncovered sat,
And Bradshaw bullied in a broad-brimmed hat."

Judges were by no means unanimous with regard to the adoption of wigs, some of them obstinately refusing to disfigure themselves with false tresses, and others displaying a foppish delight in the new decoration. Sir Matthew Hale, who died in 1676, to the last steadily refused to decorate himself with artificial locks. The likeness of the Chief Justice that forms the frontispiece to Burnet's memoir of the lawyer, represents him in his judicial robes, wearing his SS collar, and having on his head a cap—not the coif-cap, but one of the close-fitting skull-caps worn by judges in the seventeenth century. Such skull-caps, it has been observed in a prior page of this work, were worn by barristers under their wigs, and country gentlemen at home, during the last century. Into such caps readers have seen Sir Francis North put his fees. The portrait of Sir Cresswell Levinz (who returned to the bar on dismissal from the bench in 1686) shows that he wore a full-bottomed wig whilst he was a judge; whereas Sir Thomas Street, who remained a judge till the close of James II.'s reign, wore his own hair and a coif-cap.

When Shaftesbury sat in court as Lord High Chancellor of England he wore a hat, which Roger North is charitable enough to think might have been a black hat. "His lordship," says the 'Examen,' "regarded censure so little, that he did not concern himself to use a decent habit as became a judge of his station; for he sat upon the bench in an ash-colored gown silver-laced, and full-ribboned pantaloons displayed, without any black at all in his garb, unless it were his hat, which, now, I cannot positively say, though I saw him, was so."

Even so late as Queen Anne's reign, which witnessed the introduction of three-cornered hats, a Lord Keeper wore his own hair in court instead of a wig, until he received the sovereign's order to adopt the venerable disguise of a full-bottomed wig. Lady Sarah Cowper recorded of her father, 1705:—"The queen after this was persuaded to trust a Whigg ministry, and in the year 1705, Octr., she made my father Ld. Keeper of the Great Seal, in the 41st year of his age—'tis said the youngest Lord Keeper that ever had been. He looked very young, and wearing his own hair made him appear yet more so, which the queen observing, obliged him to cut it off, telling him the world would say she had given the seals to a boy."

The young Lord Keeper of course obeyed; and when he appeared for the first time at court in a wig, his aspect was so grave and reverend that the queen had to look at him twice before she recognized him. More than half a century later, George II experienced a similar difficulty, when Lord Hardwicke, after the close of his long period of official service, showed himself at court in a plain suit of black velvet, with a bag and sword. Familiar with the appearance of the Chancellor dressed in full-bottomed wig and robes, the king failed to detect his old friend and servant in the elderly gentleman who, in the garb of a private person of quality, advanced and rendered due obeisance. "Sir, it is Lord

Hardwicke," whispered a lord in waiting who stood near His Majesty's person, and saw the cause of the cold reception given to the ex-Chancellor. But unfortunately the king was not more familiar with the ex-Chancellor's title than his appearance, and in a disastrous endeavor to be affable inquired, with an affectation of interest, "How long has your lordship been in town?" The peer's surprise and chagrin were great until the monarch, having received further instruction from the courtly prompter at his elbow, frankly apologized in bad English and with noisy laughter. "Had Lord Hardwicke," says Campbell, "worn such a uniform as that invented by George IV for ex-Chancellors (very much like a Field Marshal's), he could not have been mistaken for a common man."

The judges who at the first introduction of wigs refused to adopt them were prone to express their dissatisfaction with those coxcombical contrivances when exhibited upon the heads of counsel; and for some years prudent juniors, anxious to win the favorable opinion of anti-wig justices, declined to obey the growing fashion. Chief Justice Hale, a notable sloven, conspicuous amongst common law judges for the meanness of his attire, just as Shaftesbury was conspicuous in the Court of Chancery for foppishness, cherished lively animosity for two sorts of legal practitioners—attorneys who wore swords, and young Templars who adorned themselves with periwigs. Bishop Burnet says of Hale: "He was a great encourager of all young persons that he saw followed their books diligently, to whom he used to give directions concerning the method of their study, with a humanity and sweetness that wrought much on all that came near him; and in a smiling, pleasant way he would admonish them, if he saw anything amiss in them; particularly if they went too fine in their clothes, he would tell them it did not become their profession. He was not pleased to see students wear long periwigs, or attorneys go with swords, so that such men as would not be persuaded to part with those vanities, when they went to him laid them aside and went as plain as they could, to avoid the reproof which they knew they might otherwise expect." In England, however, barristers almost universally wore wigs at the close of the seventeenth century; but north of the Tweed advocates wore cocked hats and powdered hair so late as the middle of the eighteenth century. When Alexander Wedderburn joined the Scotch bar in 1754, wigs had not come into vogue with the members of his profession.

Many are the good stories told of judicial wigs, and amongst the best of them, is the anecdote which that malicious talker Samuel Rogers delighted to tell at Edward Law's expense. "Lord Ellenborough," says the 'Table-Talk,' "was once about to go on circuit, when Lady Ellenborough said that she should like to accompany him. He replied that he had no objection provided she did not encumber the carriage with bandboxes, which were his utter abhorrence. During the first day's journey Lord Ellenborough, happening to stretch his legs, struck his foot against something below the seat; he discovered that it was a bandbox. Up went the window, and out went the bandbox. The coachman stopped, and the footman, thinking that the bandbox had tumbled out of the window by some extraordinary chance, was going to pick it up, when Lord Ellenborough furiously called out, 'Drive on!' The bandbox, accordingly, was left by the ditch-side. Having reached the county town where he was to officiate as judge, Lord Ellenborough proceeded to array himself for his appearance in the court-house. 'Now,' said he, 'where's my wig?—where *is* my wig?' 'My lord,' replied his attendant, 'it was thrown out of the carriage window!'"

Changing together with fashion, barristers ceased to wear their wigs in society as soon as the gallants and bucks of the West End began to appear with their natural tresses in theatres and ball rooms; but the conservative genius of the law has hitherto triumphed over the attempts of eminent advocates to throw the wig out of Westminster Hall. When Lord Campbell argued the great Privilege case, he obtained permission to appear without a wig; but this concession to a counsel—who, on that occasion, spoke for sixteen hours—was accompanied with an intimation that "it was not to be drawn into precedent."

Less wise or less fortunate than the bar, the judges of England wore their wigs in society after advocates of all ranks and degrees had agreed to lay aside the professional head-gear during hours of relaxation. Lady Eldon's good taste and care for her husband's comfort, induced Lord Eldon, soon after his elevation to the pillow of the Common Pleas, to beg the king's permission that he might put off his judicial wig on leaving the courts, in which as Chief Justice he would be required to preside. The petition did not meet with a favorable reception. For a minute George III. hesitated; whereupon Eldon supported his prayer by observing, with the fervor of an old-fashioned Tory, that the lawyer's wig was a detestable innovation—unknown in the days of James I. and Charles the Martyr, the judges of which two monarchs would have rejected as an insult any proposal that they should assume a head-dress fit only for madmen at masquerades or mummers at country wakes. "What! what!" cried the king, sharply; and then, smiling mischievously, as he suddenly saw a good answer to the plausible argument, he added—"True, my lord, Charles the First's judges wore no wigs, but they wore beards. You may do the same, if you like. You may please yourself about wearing or not wearing your wig; but mind, if you please yourself by imitating the old judges, as to the head—you must please me by imitating them as to the chin. You may lay aside your wig; but if you do—you must wear a beard." Had he lived in these days, when barristers occasionally wear beards in court, and judges are not less conspicuous than the junior bar for magnitude of nose and whisker, Eldon would have accepted the condition. But the last year of the last century, was the very centre and core of that time which may be called the period of close shavers; and John Scott, the decorous and respectable, would have endured martyrdom rather than have grown a beard, or have allowed his whiskers to exceed the limits of mutton-chop whiskers.

As Chief Justice of the Common Pleas, and subsequently as Chancellor, Eldon wore his wig whenever he appeared in general society; but in the privacy of his own house he gratified Lady Eldon by laying aside the official head-gear. That this was his usage, the gossips of the law-courts knew well; and at Carlton House, when the Prince of Wales was most indignant with the Chancellor, who subsequently became his familiar friend, courtiers were wont to soothe the royal rage with diverting anecdotes of the attention which the odious lawyer lavished on the natural hair that gave his Bessie so much delight. On one occasion, when Eldon was firmly supporting the cause of the Princess of Wales, 'the first gentleman of Europe' forgot common decency so far, that he made a jeering allusion to this instance of the Chancellor's domestic amiability. "I am not the sort of person," growled the prince with an outbreak of peevishness, "to let my hair grow under my wig to please my wife." With becoming dignity Eldon answered—"Your Royal Highness condescends to be personal. I beg leave to withdraw;" and suiting his action to his words, the Chancellor made a low bow to the angry prince, and retired. The prince sneaked out of the position by an untruth, instead of an apology. On the following day he caused a written assurance to be conveyed to the Chancellor, that the offensive speech "was nothing personal, but simply a proverb—a proverbial way of saying a man was governed by his wife." It is needless to say that the expression was not proverbial, but distinctly and grossly personal. Lord Malmesbury's comment on this affair is "Very absurd of Lord Eldon; but explained by his having literally done what the prince said." Lord Eldon's conduct absurd! What was the prince's?

*Chapter 22*

# BANDS AND COLLARS

Bands came into fashion with Englishmen many years before wigs, but like wigs they were worn in general society before they became a recognized and distinctive feature of professional costume. Ladies of rank dyed their hair, and wore false tresses in Elizabethan England; but their example was not extensively followed by the men of their time—although the courtiers of the period sometimes donned 'periwinkes,' to the extreme disgust of the multitude, and the less stormy disapprobation of the polite. The frequency with which bands are mentioned in Elizabethan literature, affords conclusive evidence that they were much worn toward the close of the sixteenth century; and it is also matter of certainty that they were known in England at a still earlier period. Henry VIII. had "4 shirte bands of silver with ruffes to the same, whereof one was perled with golde;" and in 1638 Peacham observed, "King Henry VIII. was the first that ever wore a band about his neck, and that very plain, without lace, and about an inch or two in depth. We may see how the case is altered, he is not a gentleman, or in the fashion, whose band of Italian cutwork standeth him not at the least in three or four pounds; yea, a sempster in Holborn told me there are of threescore pound price apiece." That the fops of Charles I.'s reign were spending money on a fashion originally set by King Henry the Bluff, was the opinion also of Taylor the Water Poet, who in 1630 wrote—

> "Now up alofte I mount unto the ruffe,
> Which into foolish mortals pride doth puffe;
> Yet ruffes' antiquity is here but small—
> Within this eighty years not one at all;
> For the Eighth Henry (so I understand)
> Was the first king that ever wore a band;
> And but a falling-band, plaine with a hem;
> All other people knew no use of them.
> Yet imitation in small time began

To grow, that it the kingdom overran;
The little falling-bands encreased to ruffes,
Ruffes (growing great) were waited on by cuffes,
And though our frailties should awake our care,
We make our ruffes as careless as we are."

In regarding the falling-band as the germ of the ruff, the Water-Poet differs from those writers who, with greater appearance of reason, maintain that the ruff was the parent of the band. Into this question concerning origin of species, there is no occasion to enter on the present occasion. It is enough to state that in the earlier part of the seventeenth century bands or collars—bands stiffened and standing at the backward part, and bands falling upon the shoulder and breast—were articles of costume upon which men of expensive and modish habits spent large sums.

In the days of James I., when standing bands were still the fashion, and falling-bands had not come in, the Inns of Court men were very particular about the stiffness, cut, and texture of their collars. Speaking of the Inns of Court men, Sir Thomas Overbury, (who was poisoned in 1613), says: "He laughs at every man whose band sits not well, or that hath not a fair shoe-type, and is ashamed to be in any man's company who wears not his cloathes well."

If portraits may be trusted, the falling-band of Charles I.'s time, bore considerable resemblance to the falling neck-frill, which twenty years since was very generally worn by quite little boys, and is still sometimes seen on urchins who are about six years of age. The bands worn by the barristers and clergy of our own time are modifications of this antique falling-band, and like the coif cap of the modern sergeant, they bear only a faint likeness to their originals. But though bands—longer than those still worn by clergymen—have come to be a distinctive feature of legal costume, the bar was slow to adopt falling-collars—regarding them as a strange and fanciful innovation. Whitelock's personal narrative furnishes pleasant testimony that the younger gentry of Charles I.'s England adopted the new collar before the working lawyers.

"At the Quarter-Sessions of Oxford," says Whitelock, speaking of the year 1635, when he was only thirty years of age, "I was put into the chair in court, though I was in colored clothes, a sword by my side, and a falling-band, which was unusual for lawyers in those days, and in this garb I gave the charge to the Grand Jury. I took occasion to enlarge on the point of jurisdiction in the temporal courts in matters ecclesiastical, and the antiquity thereof, which I did the rather because the spiritual men began in those days to swell higher than ordinary, and to take it as an injury to the Church that anything savoring of the spirituality, should be within the cognisance of ignorant laymen. The gentlemen and freeholders seemed well pleased with my charge, and the management of the business of the sessions; and said they perceived one might speak as good sense in a falling-band as in a ruff." At this time Whitelock had been about seven years at the bar;

but at the Quarter-Sessions the young Templar was playing the part of country squire, and as his words show, he was dressed in a fashion that directly violated professional usage.

Whitelock's speech seems to have been made shortly before the bar accepted the falling-band as an article of dress admissible in courts of law. Towards the close of Charles's reign, such bands were very generally worn in Westminster Hall by the gentlemen of the long robe; and after the Restoration, a barrister would as soon have thought of appearing at the King's Bench without his gown as without his band. Unlike the bar-bands of the present time—which are lappets of fine lawn, of simple make—the bands worn by Charles II.'s lawyers were dainty and expensive articles, such as those which Peacham exclaimed against in the preceding reign. At that date the Templar in prosperous circumstances had his bands made entirely of point lace, or of fine lawn edged with point lace; and as he wore them in society as well as in court, he was constantly requiring a fresh supply of them. Few accidents were more likely to ruffle a Templar's equanimity than a mishap to his band occurring through his own inadvertence or carelessness on the part of a servant. At table the pieces of delicate lace-work were exposed to many dangers. Continually were they stained with wine or soiled with gravy, and the young lawyer was deemed a marvel of amiability who could see his point lace thus defiled and abstain from swearing. "I remember," observes Roger North, when he is showing the perfect control in which his brother Francis kept his temper, at his table a stupid servant spilt a glass of red wine upon his point band and clothes. "He only wiped his face and clothes with the napkin, and 'Here,' said he, 'take this away;' and no more."

In 'The London Spy,' Ned Ward shows that during Queen Anne's reign legal practitioners of the lowest sort were particular to wear bands. Describing the pettifogger, Ward says, "He always talks with as great assurance as if he understood what he pretends to know; and always wears a band, in which lies his gravity and wisdom." At the same period a brisk trade was carried on in Westminster Hall by the sempstresses who manufactured bands and cuffs, lace ruffles, and lawn kerchiefs for the grave counsellors and young gallants of the Inns of Court. "From thence," says the author of 'The London Spy', "we walked down by the sempstresses, who were very nicely digitising and pleating turnsovers and ruffles for the young students, and coaxing them with amorous looks, obliging cant, and inviting gestures, to give so extravagant a price for what they buy."

From collars of lace and lawn, let us turn to collars of precious metal.

Antiquarians have unanimously rejected the fanciful legend adopted by Dugdale concerning the SS collar, as well as many not less ingenious interpretations of the mystic letters; and at the present time it is almost unanimously settled that the SS collar is the old Lancastrian badge, corresponding to the Yorkist collar of Roses and Suns, and that the S is either the initial of the sentimental word 'Souvenez,' or, as Mr. Beltz maintains, the initial letter of the sentimental motto, 'Souvenez-vous de moi.' In Mr. Foss's valuable work, 'The Judges of England,' at the commencement of the seventh volume, the curious reader may find an excellent summary of all that has been or can be said about the origin of this piece of feudal livery, which, having at one time been very generally assumed by all gentle and fairly prosperous partisans of the House of Lancaster, has for many generations been the distinctive badge of a few official persons. In the second year of Henry IV. an ordinance forbade knights and Esquires to wear the collar, save in the king's presence; and in the reign of Henry VIII., the privilege of wearing the collar was taken away from simple esquires by the 'Acte for Reformacyon of Excesse in Apparayle,' 24 Henry VIII. c. 13, which ordained "That no man oneless he be a knight ... weare any color of Gold, named a color of S." Gradually knights and non-official persons relinquished the decoration; and in our own day the right to bear it is restricted to the two Chief Justices, the Chief Baron, the sergeant-trumpetor, and all the officers of the Heralds' College, pursuivants excepted; "unless," adds Mr. Foss, "the Lord Mayor of London is to be included, whose collar is somewhat similar, and is composed of twenty-eight SS, fourteen roses, thirteen knots; and measures sixty-four inches."

*Chapter 23*

# Bags and Gowns

On the stages of the Caroline theatres the lawyer is found with a green bag in his hand; the same is the case in the literature of Queen Anne's reign; and until a comparatively recent date green bags were generally carried in Westminster Hall and in provincial courts by the great body of legal practitioners. From Wycherley's 'Plain Dealer,' it appears that in the time of Charles II angry clients were accustomed to revile their lawyers as 'green bag-carriers.' When the litigious Widow Blackacre upbraids the barrister who declines to argue for her, she exclaims—"Impertinent again, and ignorant to me! Gadsboddikins! you puny upstart in the law, to use me so, you green-bag carrier, you murderer of unfortunate causes, the clerk's ink is scarce off of your fingers." In the same drama, making much play with the green bag, Wycherley indicates the Widow Blackacre's quarrelsome disposition by decorating her with an enormous green reticule, and makes her son the law-student, stagger about the stage in a gown, and under a heavy burden of green bags.

So also in the time of Queen Anne, to say that a man intended to carry a green bag, was the same as saying that he meant to adopt the law as a profession. In Dr. Arbuthnot's 'History of John Bull,' the prevalence of the phrase is shown by the passage, "I am told, Cousin Diego, you are one of those that have undertaken to manage me, and that you have said you will carry a green bag yourself, rather than we shall make an end of our lawsuit. I'll teach them and you too to manage." It must, however, be borne in mind that in Queen Anne's time, green bags, like white bands, were as generally adopted by solicitors and attorneys, as by members of the bar. In his 'character of a pettifogger' the author of 'The London Spy' observes—"His learning is commonly as little as his honesty, and his conscience much larger than his green bag."

Some years have elapsed since green bags altogether disappeared from our courts of law; but the exact date of their disappearance has hitherto escaped the vigilance and research of Colonel Landman, 'Causidicus,' and other writers who in the pages of that useful and very entertaining publication, *Notes and Queries*, have asked for information on that point and kindred questions. Evidence sets aside the suggestion that the color of the lawyer's bag was changed from green to red because the proceedings at Queen Caroline's trial rendered green bags odious to the public, and even dangerous to their bearers; for it is a matter of certainty that the leaders of the Chancery and Common Law bars carried red bags at a time considerably anterior to the inquiry into the queen's conduct.

In a letter addressed to the editor of *Notes and Queries*, a writer who signs himself 'Causidicus,' observes—"When I entered the profession (about fifty years ago) no junior barrister presumed to carry a bag in the Court of Chancery, unless one had been presented to him by a King's Counsel; who, when a junior was advancing in practice, took an opportunity of complimenting him on his increase of business, and giving him his own bag to carry home his papers. It was then a distinction to carry a bag, and a proof that a junior was rising in his profession. I do not know whether the custom prevailed in other courts." From this it appears that fifty years since the bag was an honorable distinction at the Chancery bar, giving its bearer some such professional status as that which is conferred by 'silk' in these days when Queen's Counsel are numerous.

The same professional usage seems to have prevailed at the Common Law bar more than eighty years ago; for in 1780, when Edward Law joined the Northern Circuit, and forthwith received a large number of briefs, he was complimented by Wallace on his success, and presented with a bag. Lord Campbell asserts that no case had ever before occurred where a junior won the distinction of a bag during the course of his first circuit. There is no record of the date when members of the junior bar received permission to carry bags according to their own pleasure; it is even matter of doubt whether the permission was ever expressly accorded by the leaders of the profession—or whether the old restrictive usage died a gradual and unnoticed death. The present writer, however, is assured that at the Chancery bar, long after *all* juniors were allowed to carry bags, etiquette forbade them to adopt bags of the same color as those carried by their leaders. An eminent Queen's Counsel, who is a member of that bar, remembers that when he first donned a stuff gown, he, like all Chancery jurors, had a purple bag—whereas the wearers of silk at the same period, without exception, carried red bags.

Before a complete and satisfactory account can be given of the use of bags by lawyers, as badges of honor and marks of distinction, answers must be found for several questions which at present remain open to discussion. So late as Queen Anne's reign, lawyers of the lowest standing, whether advocates or attorneys, were permitted to carry bags;—a right which the junior bar appears to have lost when Edward Law joined the Northern Circuit. At what date between Queen Anne's day and 1780 (the year in which Lord Ellenborough made his *début* in the North), was this change effected? Was the change gradual or sudden? To what cause was it due? Again, is it possible that Lord Campbell and Causidicus wrote under a misapprehension, when they gave testimony concerning the usages of the bar with regard to bags, at the close of the last and the beginning of the present century? The memory of the distinguished Queen's Counsel, to whom allusion is made in the preceding paragraph, is quite clear that in his student days Chancery jurors were forbidden by etiquette to carry *red* bags, but were permitted to carry blue bags; and he is strongly of opinion that the restriction, to which Lord Campbell and Causidicus draw attention, did not apply at any time to blue bags, but only concerned red bags, which, so late as thirty years since, unquestionably were the distinguishing marks of men in leading Chancery practice. Perhaps legal readers of this chapter will favor the writer with further information on this not highly important, but still not altogether uninteresting subject.

The liberality which for the last five and-twenty years has marked the distribution of 'silk' to rising members of the bar, and the ease with which all fairly successful advocates may obtain the rank of Queen's Counsel, enable lawyers of the present generation to smile at a rule which defined a man's professional position by the color of his bag, instead of the texture of his gown; but in times when 'silk' was given to comparatively few members of the bar, and when that distinction was most unfairly withheld from the brightest ornaments of their profession, if their political opinions displeased the 'party in power,' it was natural and reasonable in the bar to institute for themselves an 'order of merit'—to which deserving candidates could obtain admission without reference to the prejudices of a Chancellor or the whims of a clique.

At present the sovereign's counsel learned in the law constitute a distinct order of the profession; but until the reign of William IV they were merely a handful of court favorites. In most cases they were sound lawyers in full employment; but the immediate cause of their elevation was almost always some political consideration—and sometimes the lucky wearer of a silk gown had won the right to put K.C. or Q.C. after his name by base compliance with ministerial power. That our earlier King's Counsel were not created from the purest motives or for the most honorable purposes will be readily admitted by the reader who reflects that 'silk gowns' are a legal species, for which the nation is indebted to the Stuarts. For all practical purposes Francis Bacon was a Q.C. during the reign of Queen Elizabeth. He enjoyed peculiar and distinctive *status* as a barrister, being consulted on legal matters by the Queen, although he held no place that in familiar parlance would entitle him to rank with her Crown Lawyers; and his biographers have agreed to call him Elizabeth's counsellor learned in the law. But a Q.C. holding his office by patent—that is to say, a Q.C. as that term is understood at the present time—Francis Bacon never was. On the accession, however, of James I., he received his formal appointment of K.C., the new monarch having seen fit to recognise the lawyer's claim to be regarded as a 'special counsel,' or 'learned counsel extraordinary.' Another barrister of the same period who obtained the same distinction was Sir Henry Montague, who, in a patent granted in 1608 to the two Temples, is styled "one of our counsel learned in the law." Thus planted, the institution of monarch's special counsel was for many generations a tree of slow growth. Until George III.'s reign the number of monarch's counsel, living and practising at the same time, was never large; and throughout the long period of that king's rule the fraternity of K.C. never assumed them agnitude and character of a professional order. It is uncertain what was the greatest number of contemporaneous K.C.'s during the Stuart dynasty; but there is no doubt that from the arrival of James I. to the flight of James II there was no period when the K.C.'s at all approached the sergeants in name and influence. In Rymer's 'F[oe]dera' mention is made of four barristers who were appointed counsellors to Charles I, one of whom, Sir John Finch, in a patent of precedence is designated "King's Counsel;" but it is not improbable that the royal martyr had other special counsellors whose names have not been recorded. At different times of Charles II's reign, there were created some seventeen K.C.'s, and seven times that number of sergeants. James II made ten K.C.'s; William and Mary appointed eleven special counsellors; and the number of Q.C.'s appointed by Anne was ten. The names of George I's learned counsel are not recorded; the list of George II's K.C.'s, together with barristers holding patents of precedence, comprise thirty names; George III throughout his long tenure of the crown, gave 'silk' with or without the title of K.C., to ninety-three barristers; George IV. to twenty-six; whereas the list of William IV's appointments comprised sixty-five names, and the present queen has conferred the rank of Q.C. on about two hundred advocates—the law-list for 1865 mentioning one hundred and thirty-seven barristers who are Q.C.'s, or holders of patents of precedence; and only twenty-eight sergeants-at-law, not sitting as judges in any of the supreme courts. The diminution in the numbers of the sergeants is due partly to the loss of their old monopoly of business in the Common Pleas, and partly—some say chiefly—to the profuseness with which silk gowns, with Q.C. rank attached, have been thrown to the bar since the passing of the Reform Bill.

Under the old system when 'silk' was less bountifully bestowed, eminent barristers not only led their circuits in stuff; but, after holding office as legal advisers to the crown and wearing silk gowns whilst they so acted with their political friends, they sometimes resumed their stuff gowns and places 'outside the bar,' on descending from official eminence. When Charles York in 1763 resigned the post of Attorney General, he returned to his old place in court without the bar, clad in the black bombazine of an ordinary barrister, whereas during his tenure of office he had worn silk and sat within the bar. In the same manner when Dunning resigned the Solicitor Generalship in 1770, he reappeared in the Court of King's Bench, attired in stuff, and took his place without the bar; but as soon as he had made his first motion, he was addressed by Lord Mansfield, who with characteristic courtesy informed him that he should take precedence in that court before all members of the bar, whatever might be their standing, with the exception of King's Counsel, Sergeants, and the Recorder of London. On joining the Northern Circuit in 1780, Edward Law found Wallace and Lee leading in silk, and twenty years later he and Jemmy Park were the K.C.'s of the same district; Of course the circuit was not without wearers of the coif, one of its learned sergeants being Cockell, who, before

Law obtained the leading place, was known as 'the Almighty of the North;' and whose success, achieved in spite of an almost total ignorance of legal science, was long quoted to show that though knowledge is power, power may be won without knowledge.

From pure dislike of the thought that younger men should follow closely or at a distance in his steps to the highest eminences of legal success, Lord Eldon was disgracefully stingy in bestowing honors on rising barristers who belonged to his own party, but his injustice and downright oppression to brilliant advocates in the Whig ranks merit the warmest expressions of disapproval and contempt. The most notorious sufferers from his rancorous intolerance were Henry Brougham and Mr. Denman, who, having worn silk gowns as Queen Caroline's Attorney General and Solicitor General, were reduced to stuff attire on that wretched lady's death.

It is worthy of notice that in old time, when silk gowns were few, their wearers were sometimes very young men. From the days of Francis North, who was made K.C. before he was a barrister for seven full years' standing, down to the days of Eldon, who obtained silk after seven years' service in stuff, instances could be cited of the rapidity with which lucky youngsters rose to the honors of silk, whilst hard-worked veterans were to the last kept outside the bar. Thurlow was called to the bar in November, 1754, and donned silk in December, 1761. Six years had now elapsed since his call to the English bar, when Alexander Wedderburn was entitled to put the initials K.C. after his name, and wrote to his mother in Scotland, "I can't very well explain to you the nature of my preferment, but it is what most people at the bar are very desirous of, and yet most people run a hazard of losing money by it. I can scarcely expect any advantage from it for some time equal to what I give up; and, notwithstanding, I am extremely happy, and esteem myself very fortunate in having obtained it." Erskine's silk was won with even greater speed, for he was invited within the bar, but his silk gown came to him with a patent of precedence, giving him the status without the title of a King's Counsel.

Bar mourning is no longer a feature of legal costume in England. On the death of Charles II. members of the bar donned gowns indicative of their grief for the national loss, and they continued, either universally or in a large number of cases, to wear these woful habiliments till 1697, when Chief Justice Holt ordered all barristers practising in his court to appear "in their proper gowns and not in mourning ones"—an order which, according to Narcissus Luttrell, compelled the bar to spend £15 per man. From this it may be inferred that (regard being had to change in value of money) a bar-gown at the close of the seventeenth century cost about ten times as much as it does at the present time.

*Chapter 24*

# HATS

Not less famous in history than Bradshaw's broad-brimmed hat, nor less graceful than Shaftesbury's jaunty beaver, nor less memorable than the sailor's tarpaulin, under cover of which Jeffreys slunk into the Red Cow, Wapping, nor less striking than the black cap still worn by Justice in her sternest mood, nor less fanciful than the cocked hat which covered Wedderburn's powdered hair when he daily paced the High Street of Edinburgh with his hands in a muff—was the white hat which an illustrious Templar invented at an early date of the eighteenth century. Beau Brummel's original mind taught the human species to starch their white cravats; Richard Nash, having surmounted the invidious bar of plebeian birth and raised himself upon opposing circumstances to the throne of Bath, produced a white hat. To which of these great men society owes the heavier debt of gratitude thoughtful historians cannot agree; but even envious detraction admits that they deserve high rank amongst the benefactors of mankind. Brummel was a soldier; but Law proudly claims as her own the parent of the pale and spotless *chapeau*.

About lawyers' cocked hats a capital volume might be written, that should contain no better story than the one which is told of Ned Thurlow's discomfiture in 1788, when he was playing a trickster's game with his friends and foes. Windsor Castle just then contained three distinct centres of public interest—the mad king in the hands of his keepers; on the one side of the impotent monarch the Prince of Wales waiting impatiently for the Regency; on the other side, the queen with equal impatience longing for her husband's recovery. The prince and his mother both had apartments in the castle, her majesty's quarters being the place of meeting for the Tory ministers, whilst the prince's apartments were thrown open to the select leaders of the Whig expectants. Of course the two coteries kept jealously apart; but Thurlow, who wished to be still Lord Chancellor, "whatever king might reign," was in private communication with the prince's friends. With furtive steps he passed from the queen's room (where he had a minute before been assuring the ministers that he would be faithful to the king's adherents), and made clandestine way to the apartment where Sheridan and Payne were meditating on the advantages of a regency without restriction. On leaving the prince, the wary lawyer used to steal into the king's chamber, and seek guidance or encouragement from the madman's restless eyes. Was the malady curable? If curable, how long a time would elapse before the return of reason? These were the questions which the Chancellor put to himself, as he debated whether he should break with the Tories and go over to the Whigs. Through the action of the patient's disease, the most delicate part of the lawyer's occupation was gone; and having no longer a king's conscience to keep, he did not care, by way of diversion—to keep his own.

For many days ere they received clear demonstration of the Chancellor's deceit, the other members of the cabinet suspected that he was acting disingenuously, and when his double-dealing was brought to their sure knowledge, their indignation was not even qualified with surprise. The story of his exposure is told in various ways; but all versions concur in attributing his detection to an accident. Like the gallant of the French court, whose clandestine intercourse with a great lady was discovered because, in his hurried preparations for flight from her chamber, he appropriated one of her stockings, Thurlow, according to one account, was convicted of perfidy by the prince's hat, which he bore under his arm on entering the closet where the ministers awaited his coming. Another version says that Thurlow had taken his seat at the council-table, when his hat was brought to him by a page, with an explanation that he had left it in the prince's private room. A third, and more probable representation of the affair, instead of laying the scene in the council-chamber, makes the exposure occur in a more public part of the castle. "When a council was to be held at Windsor," said the Right Honorable Thomas Grenville, in his old age recounting the particulars of the mishap, "to determine the course which ministers should pursue, Thurlow had been there some time before any of his colleagues arrived. He was to be brought back to London by one of them, and the moment of departure being come, the Chancellor's hat was nowhere to be found. After a fruitless search in the apartment where the council had been held, a page came with the hat in his hand, saying aloud, and with great *naïveté*, 'My lord, I found it in the closet of his Royal Highness the Prince of Wales.' The other Ministers were still in the Hall, and Thurlow's confusion corroborated the inference which they drew." Cannot an artist be found to place upon canvas this scene, which furnishes the student of human nature with an instructive instance of

> "That combination strange—a lawyer and a blush?"

For some days Thurlow's embarrassment and chagrim were very painful. But a change in the state of the king's health caused a renewal of the lawyer's attachment to Tory principles and to his sovereign.

The lawyers of what may be termed the cocked hat period seldom maintained the happy mean between too little and too great care for personal appearance. For the most part they were either slovenly or foppish. From the days when as a student he used to slip into Nando's in a costume that raised the supercilious astonishment of his contemporaries, Thurlow to the last erred on the side of neglect. Camden roused the satire of an earlier generation by the miserable condition of the tiewig which he wore on the bench of Chancery, and by an undignified and provoking habit of "gartering up his stockings while counsel were the most strenuous in their eloquence." On the other hand Joseph Yates—the puisne judge whom Mansfield's jeers and merciless oppressions drove from the King's Bench to the Common Pleas, where he died within four months of his retreat—was the finest of fine gentlemen. Before he had demonstrated his professional capacity, the habitual costliness and delicacy of his attire roused the distrust of attorneys, and on more than one occasion wrought him injury. An awkward, crusty, hard-featured attorney entered the foppish barrister's chambers with a bundle of papers, and on seeing the young man in a superb and elaborate evening dress, is said to have inquired, "Can you say, sir, when Mr. Yates will return?" "Return, my good sir!" answered the barrister, with an air of surprise, "I am Mr. Yates, and it will give me the greatest pleasure to talk with you about those papers." Having taken a deliberate survey of the young Templar, and made a mental inventory of all the fantastic articles of his apparel, the honest attorney gave an ominous grunt, replaced the papers in one of the deep pockets of his long-skirted coat, twice nodded his head with contemptuous significance, and then, without another word—walked out of the room. It was his first visit to those chambers, and his last. Joseph Yates lost his client, before he could even learn his name; but in no way influenced by the occurrence he maintained his reputation for faultless taste in dress, and when he had raised himself to the bench, he was amongst the judges of his day all that Revell Reynolds was amongst the London physicians of a later date.

Living in the midst of the fierce contentions which distracted Ireland in the days of our grandfathers, John Toler, first Earl of Norbury, would not have escaped odium and evil repute, had he been a merciful man and a scrupulous judge; but in consequence of failings and wicked propensities, which gave countenance to the slanders of his enemies and at the same time earned for him the distrust and aversion of his political coadjutors, he has found countless accusers and not a single vindicator. Resembling George Jeffreys in temper and mental capacity, he resembled him also in posthumous fame. A shrewd, selfish, overbearing man, possessing wit which was exercised with equal promptitude upon friends and foes, he alternately roused the terror and the laughter of his audiences. At the bar and in the Irish House of Commons he was alike notorious as jester and bully; but he was a courageous bully, and to the last was always as ready to fight with bullets as with epigrams, and though his humor was especially suited to the taste and passions of the rabble, it sometimes convulsed with merriment those who were shocked by its coarseness and brutality. Having voted for the abolition of the Irish Parliament, the Right

Honorable John Toler was prepared to justify his conduct with hair-triggers or sarcasms. To the men who questioned his patriotism he was wont to answer, "Name any hour before my court opens to-morrow," but to the patriotic Irish lady who loudly charged him in a crowded drawing-room with having sold his country, he replied, with an affectation of cordial assent, "Certainly, madam, I have sold my country. It was very lucky for me that I had a country to sell—I wish I had another." On the bench he spared neither counsel nor suitors, neither witnesses nor jurors. When Daniel O'Connell, whilst he was conducting a cause in the Irish Court of Common Pleas, observed, "Pardon me, my lord, I am afraid your lordship does not apprehend me;" the Chief Justice (alluding to a scandalous and false report that O'Connell had avoided a duel by surrendering himself to the police) retorted, "Pardon me also; no one is more easily apprehended than Mr. O'Connell"—(a pause—and then with emphatic slowness of utterance)—"whenever he wishes to be apprehended." It is *said* that when this same judge passed sentence of death on Robert Emmett, he paused when he came to the point where it is usual for a judge to add in conclusion, "And may the Lord have mercy on your soul!" and regarded the brave young man with searching eyes. For a minute there was an awful silence in the court; the bar and the assembled crowd supposing that the Chief Justice had paused so that a few seconds of unbroken stillness might add to the solemnity of his last words. The disgust and indignation of the spectators were beyond the power of language, when they saw a smile of brutal sarcasm steal over the face of the Chief Justice as he rose from his seat of judgment without uttering another word.

Whilst the state prosecutions were going forward, Lord Norbury appeared on the bench in a costume that accorded ill with the gravity of his office. The weather was intensely hot; and whilst he was at his morning toilet the Chief Justice selected from his wardrobe the dress which was most suited to the sultriness of the air. The garb thus selected for its coolness was a dress which his lordship had worn at a masquerade ball, and consisted of a green tabinet coat decorated with huge mother-of-pearl buttons, a waistcoat of yellow relieved by black stripes, and buff breeches. When he first entered the court, and throughout all the earlier part of the proceedings against a party of rebels, his judicial robes altogether concealed this grotesque attire; but unfortunately towards the close of the sultry day's work, Lord Norbury—oppressed by the stifling atmosphere of the court, and forgetting all about the levity as well as the lightness of his inner raiment—threw back his judicial robe and displayed the dress which several persons then present had seen him wear at Lady Castlereagh's ball. Ere the spectators recovered from their first surprise, Lord Norbury, quite unconscious of his indecorum, had begun to pass sentence of death on a gang of prisoners, speaking to them in a solemn voice that contrasted painfully with the inappropriateness of his costume.

In the following bright and picturesque sentence, Dr. Dibdin gives a life-like portrait of Erskine, whose personal vanity was only equalled by the egotism which often gave piquancy to his orations, and never lessened their effect:—"Cocked hats and ruffles, with satin small-clothes and silk stockings, at this time constituted the usual evening dress. Erskine, though a good deal shorter than his brethren, somehow always seemed to take the lead both in pace and in discourse, and shouts of laughter would frequently follow his dicta. Among the surrounding promenaders, he and the one-armed Mingay seemed to be the main objects of attraction. Towards evening, it was the fashion for the leading counsel to promenade during the summer in the Temple Gardens, and I usually formed one in the thronging mall of loungers and spectators. I had analysed Blackstone, and wished to publish it under a dedication to Mr. Erskine. Having requested the favor of an interview, he received me graciously at breakfast before nine, attired in the smart dress of the times, a dark green coat, scarlet waistcoat, and silk breeches. He left his coffee, stood the whole time looking at the chart I had cut in copper, and appeared much gratified. On leaving him, a chariot-and-four drew up to wheel him to some provincial town on a special retainer. He was then coining money as fast as his chariot wheels rolled along." Erskine's advocacy was marked by that attention to trifles which has often contributed to the success of distinguished artists. His special retainers frequently took him to parts of the country where he was a stranger, and required him to make eloquent speeches in courts which his voice had never tested. It was his custom on reaching the town where he would have to plead on the following day, to visit the court over-night, and examine its arrangements, so that when the time for action arrived he might address the jury from the most favorable spot in the chamber. He was a theatrical speaker, and omitted no pains to secure theatrical effect. It was noticed that he never appeared within the bar until the *cause célèbre* had been called; and a buzz of excitement and anxious expectation testified the eagerness of the assembled crowd to *see*, as well as to hear, the celebrated advocate. Every article of his bar costume received his especial consideration; artifice could be discerned in the modulations of his voice, the expressions of his countenance, and the movements of his entire body; but the coldest observer did not detect the artifice until it had stirred his heart. Rumor unjustly asserted that he never uttered an impetuous peroration which he had not frequently rehearsed in private before a mirror. About the cut and curls of his wigs, their texture and color, he was very particular: and the hands which he extended in entreaty towards British juries were always cased in lemon-colored kid gloves.

Erskine was not more noticeable for the foppishness of his dress than was Lord Kenyon for a sordid attire. Whilst he was a leading advocate within the bar, Lord Kenyon's ordinary costume would have disgraced a copying clerk; and during his later years, it was a question amongst barristers whether his breeches were made of velvet or leather. The wits maintained that when he kissed hands upon his elevation to the Attorney's place, he went to court in a second-hand suit purchased from Lord Stormont's *valet*. In the letter attributed to him by a clever writer in the 'Rolliad,' he is made to say—"My income has been cruelly estimated at seven, or, as some will have it, eight thousand pounds per annum. I shall save myself the mortification of denying that I am rich, and refer you to the constant habits and whole tenor of my life. The proof to my friends is easy. My tailor's bill for the last fifteen years is a record of the most indisputable authority. Malicious souls may direct you, perhaps, to Lord Stormont's *valet de chambre*, and can vouch the anecdote that on the day when I kissed hands for my appointment to the office of Attorney General, I appeared in a laced waistcoat that once belonged to his master. I bought the waistcoat, but despise the insinuation; nor is this the only instance in which I am obliged to diminish my wants and apportion them to my very limited means. Lady K—— will be my witness that until my last appointment I was an utter stranger to the luxury of a pocket-handkerchief." The pocket-handkerchief which then came into his possession was supposed to have been found in the pocket of the second-hand waistcoat; and Jekyll always maintained that, as it was not considered in the purchase, it remained the valet's property, and did not pass into the lawyer's rightful possession. This was the only handkerchief which Lord Kenyon is said to have ever possessed, and Lord Ellenborough alluded to it when, in a conversation that turned upon the economy which the income-tax would necessitate in all ranks of life, he observed—"Lord Kenyon, who is not very nice, intends to meet the crisis by laying down his handkerchief."

Of his lordship's way of getting through seasons of catarrh without a handkerchief, there are several stories that would scarcely please the fastidious readers of this volume.

Of his two wigs (one considerably less worn than the other), and of his two hats (the better of which would not have greatly disfigured an old clothesman, whilst the worse would have been of service to a professional scarecrow), Lord Kenyon took jealous care. The inferior wig was always worn with the better hat, and the more dilapidated hat with the superior wig; and it was noticed that when he appeared in court with the shabbier wig he never removed his *chapeau*; whereas, on the days when he sat in his more decent wig, he pushed his old cocked hat out of sight. In the privacy of his house and in his carriage, whenever he traveled beyond the limits of town, he used to lay aside wig and hat, and cover his head with an old red night-cap. Concerning his great-coat, the original blackness of which had been tempered by long usage into a fuscous green, capital tales were fabricated. The wits could not spare even his shoes. "Once," Dr. Didbin gravely narrated, "in the case of an action brought for the non-fulfillment of a contract on a large scale for shoes, the question mainly was, whether or not they were well and soundly made, and with the best materials. A number of witnesses were called, one of them, a first-rate character in the gentle craft, being closely questioned, returned contradictory answers, when the Chief Justice observed, pointing to his own shoes, which were regularly bestridden by the broad silver buckle of the day, 'Were the shoes anything like these?' 'No, my lord,' replied the evidence, 'they were a good deal better and more genteeler.'" Dr. Didbin is at needless pains to assure his readers that the shoemaker's answer was followed by uproarious laughter.

# PART 5. MUSIC

*Chapter 25*

# The Piano in Chambers

In the Inns of Court, even more often than in the colleges of Oxford and Cambridge, musical instruments and performances are regarded by severe students with aversion and abhorrence. Mr. Babbage will live in peace and charity with the organ-grinders who are continually doing him an unfriendly turn before the industrious conveyancer on the first floor will pray for the welfare of 'that fellow upstairs' who daily practises the flute or cornopean from 11 A.M. to 3 P.M. The 'Wandering Minstrels' and their achievements are often mentioned with respect in the western drawing-rooms of London; but if the gentlemen who form that distinguished *troupe* of amateur performers wish to sacrifice their present popularity and take a leading position amongst the social nuisances of the period, they should migrate from the district which delights to honor them to chambers in Old Square, Lincoln's Inn, and give morning concerts every day of term time.

Working lawyers feel warmly on this subject, maintaining that no man should be permitted to be an *amateur*-barrister and an *amateur*-musician at the same time, and holding that law-students with a turn for wind-instruments should, like vermin, be hunted down and knocked on the head—without law. Strange stories might be told of the discords and violent deeds to which music has given rise in the four Inns. In the last century many a foolish fellow was 'put up' at ten paces, because he refused to lay down an ophicleide; even as late as George IV.'s time death has followed from an inordinate addiction to the violin; and it was but the other day that the introduction of a piano into a house in Carey Street led to the destruction of three close and warm friendships.

So alive are lawyers to the frightful consequences of a wholesale exhibition of melodious irritants, that a natural love of order and desire for self-preservation has prompted them to raise numerous obstructions to the free development of musical science in their peculiar localities of town. In the Inns of Court and Chancery Lane professional etiquette forbids barristers and solicitors to play upon organs, harmoniums, pianos, violins, or other stringed instruments, drums, trumpets, cymbals, shawms, bassoons, triangles, castanets or any other bony devices for the production of noise, flageolets, hautboys, or any other sort of boys—between the hours of 9 A.M. and 6 P.M. And this rule of etiquette is supported by various special conditions introduced into the leases by which the tenants hold much of the local house property. Under some landlords, a tenant forfeits his lease if he indulges in any pursuit that causes annoyance to his immediate neighbors; under others, every occupant of a set of chambers binds himself not to play any musical instrument therein, save between the hours of 9 A.M. and 12 P.M.; and in more than one clump of chambers, situated within a stone's throw from Chancery Lane, glee-singing is not permitted at any period of the four-and-twenty hours.

That the pursuit of harmony is a dangerous pastime for young lawyers cannot be questioned, although a long list might be given of cases where musical barristers have gained the confidence of many clients, and eventually raised themselves to the bench. A piano is a treacherous companion for the student who can touch, it deftly—dangerous as an idle friend, whose wit is ever brilliant; fascinating as a beautiful woman, whose smile is always fresh; deceptive as the drug which seems to invigorate, whilst in reality it is stealing away the intellectual powers. Every persevering worker knows how large a portion of his hard work has been done 'against the grain,' and in spite of strong inclinations to indolence—in hours when pleasant voices could have seduced him from duty, and any plausible excuse for indulgence would have been promptly accepted. In the piano these pleasant voices are constantly present, and it can always show good reason—why reluctant industry should relax its exertions.

*Chapter 26*

# THE BATTLE OF THE ORGANS

Sir Thomas More and Lord Bacon—the two most illustrious laymen who have held the Great Seal of England—were notable musicians; and many subsequent Keepers and Chancellors are scarcely less famous for love of harmonious sounds than for judicial efficiency. Lord Keeper Guildford was a musical amateur, and notwithstanding his low esteem of literature condescended to write about melody. Lord Jeffreys was a good after-dinner vocalist, and was esteemed a high authority on questions concerning instrumental performance. Lord Camden was an operatic composer; and Lord Thurlow studied thorough-bass, in order that he might direct the musical exercises of his children.

In moments of depression More's favorite solace was the viol; and so greatly did he value musical accomplishments in women, that he not only instructed his first and girlish wife to play on various instruments, but even prevailed on the sour Mistress Alice Middleton "to take lessons on the lute, the cithara, the viol, the monochord, and the flute, which she daily practised to him." But More's love of music was expressed still more forcibly in the zeal with which he encouraged and took part in the choral services of Chelsea Church. Throughout his residence at Chelsea, Sir Thomas was a regular attendant at the church, and during his tenure of the seals he not only delighted to chant the appointed psalms, but used to don a white surplice, and take his place among the choristers. Having invited the Duke of Norfolk to dine with him, the Chancellor prepared himself for the enjoyment of that great peer's society by attending divine service, and he was still occupied with his religious exercises when his Grace of Norfolk entered the church, and to his inexpressible astonishment saw the keeper of the king's conscience in the flowing raiment of a chorister, and heard him give "Glory to God in the highest!" as though he were a hired singer. "God's body! God's body! My Lord Chancellor a parish clerk?—a parish clerk?" was the duke's testy expostulation with the Chancellor. Whereupon More, with gentle gravity, answered, "Nay; your grace may not think that the king—your master and mine—will with me, for serving his Master, be offended, and thereby account his office dishonored." Not only was it More's custom to sing in the church choir, but he used also to bear a cross in religious processions; and on being urged to mount horse when he followed the rood in Rogation week round the parish boundaries, he answered, "It beseemeth not the servant to follow his master prancing on a cock-horse, his master going on foot." Few incidents in Sir Thomas More's remarkable career point more forcibly to the vast difference between the social manners of the sixteenth century and those of the present day. If Lord Chelmsford were to recreate himself with leading the choristers in Margaret Street, and after service were seen walking homewards in an ecclesiastical dress, it is more than probable that public opinion would declare him a fit companion for the lunatics of whose interests he has been made the official guardian. Society felt some surprise as well as gratification when Sir Roundell Palmer recently published his 'Book of Praise;' but if the Attorney General, instead of printing his select hymns had seen fit to exemplify their beauties with his own voice from the stall of a church-singer, the piety of his conduct would have scarcely reconciled Lord Palmerston to its dangerous eccentricity.

Amongst Elizabethan lawyers, Chief Justice Dyer was by no means singular for his love of music, though Whetstone's lines have given exceptional celebrity to his melodious proficiency:—

"For publique good, when care had cloid his minde,
The only joye, for to repose his sprights,
Was musique sweet, which showd him well inclind;
For he doth in musique much delight,
A conscience hath disposed to do most right:
The reason is, her sound within our eare,
A sympathie of heaven we thinke we heare."

Like James Dyer, Francis Bacon found music a pleasant and salutary pastime, when he was fatigued by the noisy contentions of legal practice or by strenuous application to philosophic pursuits. A perfect master of the science of melody, Lord Bacon explained its laws with a clearness which has satisfied competent judges that he was familiar with the practice as well as the theories of harmony; but few passages of his works display more agreeably his personal delight and satisfaction in musical exercise and investigation than that section of the 'Natural History,' wherein he says, "And besides I practice as I do advise; which is, after long inquiry of things immersed in matter, to interpose some subject which is immateriate or less materiate; such as this of sounds: to the end that the intellect may be rectified and become not partial."

A theorist as well as performer, the Lord Keeper Guilford enunciated his views regarding the principles of melody in 'A Philosophical Essay of Musick, Directed to a Friend'—a treatise that was published without the author's name, by Martin, the printer to the Royal Society, in the year 1677, at which time the future keeper was Chief Justice of the Common Pleas. The merits of the tract are not great; but it displays the subtlety and whimsical quaintness of the musical lawyer, who performed on several instruments, was very vain of a feeble voice, and used to attribute much of his professional success to the constant study of music that marked every period of his life. "I have heard him say," Roger records, "that if he had not enabled himself by these studies, and particular his practice of music upon his bass or lyra viol (which he used to touch lute-fashion upon his knee), to divert himself alone, he had never been a lawyer. His mind was so airy and volatile he could not have kept his chamber if he must needs be there, staked down purely to the drudgery of the law, whether in study or practice; and yet upon such a leaden proposition, so painful to brisk spirits, all the success of the profession, regularly pursued, depends." His first acquaintance with melodious art was made at Cambridge, where in his undergraduate days he took lessons on the viol. At this same period he "had the opportunity of practice so much in his grandfather's and father's families, where the entertainment of music in full concert was solemn and frequent, that he outdid all his teachers, and became one of the neatest violinists of his time." Scarcely in consistence with this declaration of the Lord Keeper's proficiency on the violin is a later passage of the biography, where Roger says that his brother "attempted the violin, being ambitious of the prime part in concert, but soon found that he began such a difficult art too late." It is, however, certain that the eminent lawyer in the busiest passages of his laborious life found time for musical practice, and that besides his essay on music, he contributed to his favorite art several compositions which were performed in private concert-rooms.

Sharing in the musical tastes of his family, Roger North, the biographer, was the *friend* who used to touch the harpsichord that stood at the door of the Lord Keeper's bedchamber; and when political changes had extinguished his hopes of preferment, he found consolation in music and literature. Retiring to his seat in Norfolk, Roger fitted up a concert-room with instruments that roused the astonishment of country squires, and an organ that was extolled by critical professors for the sweetness of its tones. In that seclusion, where he lived to extreme old age, the lettered lawyer composed the greater part of those writings which have rendered him familiar to the present generation. Of his 'Memoirs of Musick,' readers are not accustomed to speak so gratefully as of his biographies; but the curious sketch which Dr. Rimbault edited and for the first time published in 1846, is worthy of perusal, and will maintain a place on the shelves of literary collectors by the side of his brother's 'Essay.'

In that treatise Roger alludes to a contest which in the reigns of Charles II and James II agitated the musicians of London, divided the Templars into two hostile parties, and for a considerable time gave rise to quarrels in every quarter of the town. All this disturbance resulted from "a competition for an organ in the Temple church, for which the two competitors, the best artists in Europe, Smith and Harris, were but just not ruined." The struggle thus mentioned in the 'Memoirs of Musick' is so comic an episode in the story of

London life, and has been the occasion of so much error amongst writers, that it claims brief restatement in the present chapter.

In February, 1682, the Benchers of the Temples, wishing to obtain for their church an organ of superlative excellence, invited Father Smith and Renatus Harris to compete for the honor of supplying the instrument. The masters of the benchers pledged themselves that "if each of these excellent artists would set up an organ in one of the halls belonging to either of the societies, they would have erected in their church that which, in the greatest number of excellencies, deserved the preference." For more than twenty years Father Smith had been the first organ-builder in England; and the admirable qualities of his instruments testify to his singular ability. A German artist (in his native country called Bernard Schmidt, but in London known as Father Smith), he had established himself in the English capital as early as the summer of 1660; and gaining the cordial patronage of Charles II., he and his two grand-nephews soon became leaders of their craft. Father Smith built organs for Westminster Abbey, for the Church of St. Giles-in-the-Fields, for St. Margaret's Church, Westminster, for Durham Cathedral, and for other sacred buildings. In St. Paul's Cathedral he placed the organ which Wren disdainfully designated a "box of whistles;" and dying in 1708, he left his son-in-law, Christopher Schreider, to complete the organ which still stands in the chapel of Trinity College, Cambridge. But notwithstanding his greatness, Father Smith had rivals; his first rival being Harris the Elder, who died in 1672, his second being Renatus Harris, or Harris the Younger. The elder Harris never caused Smith much discomfort; but his son, Renatus, was a very clever fellow, and a strong party of fashionable *connoisseurs* declared that he was greatly superior to the German. Such was the position of these two rivals when the benchers made their proposal, which was eagerly accepted by the artificers, each of whom saw in it an opportunity for covering his antagonist with humiliation.

The men went to work: and within fourteen months their instruments were ready for competition. Smith finished work before Harris, and prevailed on the benchers to let him place his organ in the Temple church, well knowing that the powers of the instrument could be much more readily and effectively displayed in the church than in either of the dining-halls. The exact site where he fixed his organ is unknown, but the careful author of 'A Few Notes on the Temple Organ, 1859,' is of opinion that it was put up "on the screen between the round and oblong churches—the position occupied by the organ until the present organ-chamber was built, and the organ removed there during the progress of the complete restoration of the church in the year 1843." No sooner had Harris finished his organ, than, following Father Smith's example, he asked leave of the benchers to erect it within the church. Harris's petition to this effect bears date May 26, 1684; and soon afterwards the organ was "set up in the Church on the south side of the Communion Table."

Both organs being thus stationed under the roof of the church, the committee of benchers appointed to decide on their relative merits declared themselves ready to listen.

The trial began, but many months—ay, some years—elapsed ere it came to an end. On either side the credit of the manufacturer was sustained by execution of the highest order of art. Father Smith's organ was handled alternately by Purcell and Dr. Blow; and Draghi, the queen's organist, did his best to secure a verdict for Renatus Harris. Of course the employment of these eminent musicians greatly increased the number of persons who felt personal interest in the contest. Whilst the pupils and admirers of Purcell and Blow were loud in declaring that Smith's organ ought to win, Draghi's friends were equally sure that the organ touched by his expert fingers ought not to lose. Discussion soon became violent; and in every profession, clique, coterie of the town, supporters of Smith wrangled with supporters of Harris. Like the battle of the Gauges in our time, the battle of the Organs was the grand topic with every class of society, at Court and on 'Change, in coffee-houses and at ordinaries. Again and again the organs were tested in the hearing of dense and fashionable congregations; and as often the judicial committee was unable to come to a decision. The hesitation of the judges put oil upon the fire; for Smith's friends, indignant at the delay, asserted that certain members of the committee were bound to Harris by corrupt considerations—an accusation that was retorted by the other side with equal warmth and want of justice.

After the squabble had been protracted through many months, Harris created a diversion by challenging Father Smith to make additional reed-stops within a given time. The challenge was accepted; and forthwith the Father went to work and made Vox Humana, Cremorne, Double Courtel, or Double Bassoon, and other stops. A day was appointed for the renewal of the contest; but party feeling ran so high, that during the night preceding the appointed day a party of hot-headed Harrissians broke into the Temple Church, and cut Smith's bellows—so that on the following morning his organ was of no more service than an old linen-press. A row ensued; and in the ardor of debate swords were drawn.

In June, 1685, the benchers of the Middle Temple, made a written declaration in favor of Father Smith, and urged that his organ should be forthwith accepted. Strongly and rather discourteously worded, this declaration gave offence to the benchers of the Inner Temple, who regarded it as an attempt at dictation; and on June 22, 1685, they recommended the appointment of another committee with powers to decide the contest. Declining to adopt this suggestion, the Middle Temple benchers reiterated their high opinion of Smith's instrument. On this the Battle of the Organs became a squabble between the two Temples; and the outside public, laughing over the quarrel of the lawyers, expressed a hope that honest men would get their own since the rogues had fallen out.

At length, when the organ-builders had well-nigh ruined each other, and the town had grown weary of the dispute, the Inner Temple yielded somewhere about the beginning of 1688—at an early date of which year Smith received a sum of money in part payment for his organ. On May 27th of the same year, Mr. Pigott was appointed organist. After its rejection by the Temple, Renatus Harris divided his organ into two, and having sent the one part to the cathedral of Christ's Church, Dublin, he set up the other part in the church of St. Andrew, Holborn. Three years after his disappointment, Renatus Harris was tried at the Old Bailey for a political offence, the nature of which may be seen from the following entry in Narcissus Luttrell's Diary:—"April, 1691. The Sessions have been at the Old Bailey, where these persons, Renatus Harris, John Watts, William Rutland, Henry Gandy, and Thomas Tysoe, were tried at the Old Bailey for setting up policies of insurance that Dublin would be in the hands of some other king than their present majesties by Christmas next: the jury found them guilty of a misdemeanor." For this offence Renatus Harris was fined £200, and was required to give security for his good conduct until Christmas.

An erroneous tradition assigns to Lord Jeffreys the honor of bringing the Battle of the Organs to a conclusion, and writers improving upon this tradition, have represented that Jeffreys acted as sole umpire between the contendants. In his 'History of Music,' Dr. Burney, to whom the prevalence of this false impression is mainly due, observes—"At length the decision was left to Lord Chief Justice Jeffries, afterwards King James the Second's pliant Chancellor, who was of that society (the Inner Temple), and he terminated the controversy in favor of Father Smith; so that Harris's organ was taken away without loss of reputation, having so long pleased and puzzled better judges than Jefferies."

Careful inquirers have ascertained that Harris's organ did not go to Wolverhampton, but to Dublin and St. Andrew's Holborn, part of it being sent to the one, and part to the other place. It is certain that Jeffrys was not chosen to act as umpire in 1681, for the benchers did not make their original proposal to the rival builders until February, 1682; and years passed between that date and the termination of the squabble. When Burney wrote:—"At length the decision was left to Lord Chief Justice Jefferies, *afterwards King James II.'s pliant Chancellor*," the musician was unaware that the squabble was still at white heat whilst Jeffreys occupied the woolsack. On his return from the Western Campaign, Jeffreys received the seals in September, 1685, whereas the dispute about the organs did not terminate till the opening of 1688, or at earliest till the close of 1687. There is no authentic record in the archives of the Temples which supports, or in any way countenances, the story that Jeffreys made choice of Smith's instrument; but it is highly probable that the Lord Chancellor exerted his influence with the Inner Temple (of which society he was a member), and induced the benchers, for the sake of peace, to yield to the wishes of the Middle Temple. It is no less probable that his fine musical taste enabled him to see that the Middle Temple benchers were in the right, and gave especial weight to his words when he spoke against Harris's instrument.

Though Jeffreys delighted in music, he does not seem to have held its professors in high esteem. In the time of Charles II. musical artists of the humbler grades liked to be styled 'musitioners;' and on a certain occasion, when he was sitting as Recorder for the

City of London, George Jeffreys was greatly incensed by a witness who, in a pompous voice, called himself a musitioner. With a sneer the Recorder interposed—"A musitioner! I thought you were a fiddler!" "I am a musitioner," the violinist answered, stoutly. "Oh, indeed," croaked Jeffreys. "That is very important—highly important—extremely important! And pray, Mr. Witness, what is the difference between a musitioner and a fiddler?" With fortunate readiness the man answered, "As much, sir, as there is between a pair of bag-pipes and a Recorder."

*Chapter 27*

# A THICKNESS IN THE THROAT

The date is September, 1805, and the room before us is a drawing-room in a pleasant house at Brighton. The hot sun is beating down on cliff and terrace, beach and pier, on the downs behind the town and the sparkling sea in front. The brightness of the blue sky is softened by white vapor that here and there resembles a vast curtain of filmy gauze, but nowhere has gathered into visible masses of hanging cloud. In the distance the sea is murmuring audibly, and through the screened windows, together with the drowsy hum of the languid waves, comes a light breeze that is invigorating, notwithstanding its sensible warmth.

Besides ourselves there are but two people in the room: a gentlewoman who has said farewell to youth, but not to feminine grade and delicacy; and an old man, who is lying on a sofa near one of the open windows, whilst his daughter plays passages of Handel's music on the piano-forte.

The old man wears the dress of an obsolete school of English gentlemen; a large brown wig with three rows of curls, the lowest row resting on the curve of his shoulders; a loose grey coat, notable for the size of its cuffs and the bigness of its heavy buttons; ruffles at his wrists, and frills of fine lace below his roomy cravat. These are the most conspicuous articles of his costume, but not the most striking points of his aspect. Over his huge, pallid, cadaverous, furrowed face there is an air singularly expressive of exhaustion and power, of debility and latent strength—an air that says to sensitive beholders, "This prostrate veteran was once a giant amongst giants; his fires are dying out; but the old magnificent courage and ability will never altogether leave him until the beatings of his heart shall have quite ceased: touch him with foolishness or disrespect, and his rage will be terrible." Standing here we can see his prodigious bushy eyebrows, that are as white as driven snow, and under them we can see the large black eyes, beneath the angry fierceness of which hundreds of proud British peers, assembled in their council-chamber, have trembled like so many whipped schoolboys. There is no lustre in them now, and their habitual expression is one of weariness and profound indifference to the world—a look that is deeply pathetic and depressing, until some transient cause of irritation or the words of a sprightly talker rouse him into animation. But the most noticeable quality of his face is its look of extreme age. Only yesterday a keen observer said of him, "Lord Thurlow is, I believe, only seventy-four; and from his appearance I should think him a hundred years old."

So quiet is the reclining form, that the pianist thinks her father must be sleeping. Turning on the music-stool to get a view of his countenance, and to satisfy herself as to his state, she makes a false note, when, quick as the blunder, the brown wig turns upon the pillow—the furrowed face is presented to her observation, and an electric brightness fills the big black eyes, as the veteran, with deep rolling tones, reproves her carelessness:—"What are you doing?—what are you doing? I had almost forgotten the world. Play that piece again."

Twelve months more—and the lady will be playing Handel's music on that same instrument; but the old man will not be a listener.

From Brighton, in 1805, let readers transport themselves to Canterbury in 1776, and let them enter a barber's shop, hard by Canterbury Cathedral. It is a primitive shop, with the red and white pole over the door, and a modest display of wigs and puff-boxes in the window. A small shop, but, notwithstanding its smallness, the best shop of its kind in Canterbury; and its lean, stiff, exceedingly respectable master is a man of good repute in the cathedral town. His hands have, ere now, powdered the Archbishop's wig, and he is specially retained by the chief clergy of the city and neighborhood to keep their false hair in order, and trim the natural tresses of their children. Not only have the dignitaries of the cathedral taken the worthy barber under their special protection, but they have extended to his little boy Charles, a demure, prim lad, who is at this present time a pupil in the King's School, to which academy clerical interest gained him admission. The lad is in his fourteenth year; and Dr. Osmund Beauvoir, the master of the school, gives him so good a character for industry and dutiful demeanor, that some of the cathedral ecclesiastics have resolved to make the little fellow's fortune—by placing him in the office of a Chorister. There is a vacant place in the cathedral choir; and the boy who is lucky enough to receive the appointment will be provided for munificently. He will forthwith have a maintenance, and in course of time his salary will be £70 per annum.

During the last fortnight the barber has been in great and constant excitement—hoping that his little boy will obtain this valuable piece of preferment; persuading himself that the lad's thickness of voice, concerning which the choir-master speaks with aggravating persistence, is a matter of no real importance; fearing that the friends of another contemporary boy, who is said by the choir-master to have an exceedingly mellifluous voice, may defeat his paternal aspirations. The momentous question agitates many humble homes in Canterbury; and whilst Mr. Abbott, the barber, is encouraged to hope the best for his son, the relatives and supporters of the contemporary boy are urging him not to despair. Party spirit prevails on either side—Mr. Abbott's family associates maintaining that the contemporary boy's higher notes resemble those of a penny whistle; whilst the contemporary boy's father, with much satire and some justice, murmurs that "old Abbott, who is the gossip-monger of the parsons, wants to push his son into a place for which there is a better candidate."

To-day is the eventful day when the election will be made. Even now, whilst Abbott, the barber, is trimming a wig at his shop window, and listening to the hopeful talk of an intimate neighbor, his son Charley is chanting the Old Hundredth before the whole chapter. When Charley has been put through his vocal paces, the contemporary boy is requested to sing. Whereupon that clear-throated competitor, sustained by justifiable self-confidence and a new-laid egg which he had sucked scarcely a minute before he made his bow to their reverences, sings out with such richness and compass that all the auditors recognize his great superiority.

Ere ten more minutes have passed Charley Abbot knows that he has lost the election; and he hastens from the cathedral with quick steps. Running into the shop he gives his father a look that tells the whole story of—failure, and then the little fellow, unable to command his grief, sits down upon the floor and sobs convulsively.

Failure is often the first step to eminence.

Had the boy gained the chorister's place, he would have a cathedral servant all his days.

Having failed to get it, he returned to the King's School, went a poor scholar to Oxford, and fought his way to honor. He became Chief Justice of the King's Bench, and a peer of the realm. Towards the close of his honorable career Lord Tenterden attended service in the Cathedral of Canterbury, accompanied by Mr. Justice Richardson. When the ceremonial was at an end the Chief Justice said to his friend—"Do you see that old man there amongst the choristers? In him, brother Richardson, behold the only being I ever envied: when at school in this town we were candidates together for a chorister's place; he obtained it; and if I had gained my wish he might have been accompanying you as Chief Justice, and pointing me out as his old school-fellow, the singing man."

# PART 6. AMATEUR THEATRICALS

*Chapter 28*

# ACTORS AT THE BAR

Some years since the late Sergeant Wilkins was haranguing a crowd of enlightened electors from the hustings of a provincial borough, when a stentorian voice exclaimed, "Go home, you rope-dancer!" Disdaining to notice the interruption, the orator continued his speech for fifty seconds, when the same voice again cried out, "Go home, you rope-dancer!" A roar of laughter followed the reiteration of the insult; and in less than two minutes thrice fifty unwashed blackguards were roaring with all the force of their lungs, "Ah-h-h—Go home, you rope-dancer!" Not slow to see the moaning of the words, the unabashed lawyer, who in his life had been a dramatic actor, replied with his accustomed readiness and effrontery. A young man unacquainted with mobs would have descanted indignantly and with many theatrical flourishes on the dignity and usefulness of the player's vocation; an ordinary demagogue would have frankly admitted the discourteous impeachment, and pleaded in mitigation that he had always acted in leading parts and for high salaries. Sergeant Wilkins took neither of those courses, for he knew his audience, and was aware that his connection with the stage was an affair about which he had better say as little as possible. Instead of appealing to their generosity, or boasting of his histrionic eminence, he threw himself broadly on their sense of humor. Drawing himself up to his full height, the big, burly man advanced to the marge of the platform, and extending his right hand with an air of authority, requested silence by the movement of his arm. The sign was instantly obeyed; for having enjoyed their laugh, the multitude wished for the rope-dancer's explanation. As soon as the silence was complete, he drew back two paces, put himself in an oratorical *pose*, as though he were about to speak, and then, disappointing the expectations of the assembly, deliberately raised forwards and upwards the skirts of his frock-coat. Having thus arranged his drapery he performed a slow gyration—presenting his huge round shoulders and unwieldy legs to the populace. When his back was turned to the crowd, he stooped and made a low obeisance to his vacant chair, thereby giving the effect of caricature to the outlines of his most protuberant and least honorable part. This pantomime lasted scarcely a minute; and before the spectators could collect themselves to resent so extraordinary an affront, the sergeant once again faced them, and in a clear, rich, jovial tone exclaimed, "*He* called me a rope-dancer!—after what you have seen, do you believe him?"

With the exception of the man who started the cry, every person in the dense multitude was convulsed with laughter; and till the end of the election no turbulent rascal ventured to repeat the allusion to the sergeant's former occupation. At a moment of embarrassment, Mr. Disraeli, in the course of one of his youthful candidatures, created a diversion in his favor by telling a knot of unruly politicians that he *stood on his head*. With less wit, and much less decency, but with equal good fortune, Sergeant Wilkins took up his position on a baser part of his frame.

The electors who respected Mr. Wilkins because he was a successful barrister, whilst they reproached him with having been a stage-player, were unaware how close an alliance exists between the art of the actor and the art of the advocate. To lawyers of every grade and speciality the histrionic faculty is a useful power; but to the advocate who wishes to sway the minds of jurors it is a necessary endowment. Comprising several distinct abilities, it not only enables the orator to rouse the passions and to play on the prejudices of his hearers, but it preserves him from the errors of judgment, tone, emphasis—in short, from manifold blunders of indiscretion and tact by which verdicts are lost quite as often as through defect of evidence and merit. Like the dramatic performer, the court-speaker, especially at the common law bar, has to assume various parts. Not only should he know the facts of his brief, but he should thoroughly identify himself with the client for whom his eloquence is displayed. On the theatrical stage mimetic business is cut up into specialities, men in most cases filling the parts of men, whilst actresses fill the parts of women; the young representing the characteristics of youth, whilst actors with special endowments simulate the qualities of old age; some confining themselves to light and trivial characters, whilst others are never required to strut before the scenes with hurried paces, or to speak in phrases that lack dignity and fine sentiment. But the popular advocate must in turn fill every *rôle*. If childish simplicity be his client's leading characteristic, his intonations will express pliancy and foolish confidence; or if it is desirable that the jury should appreciate his client's honesty of purpose, he speaks with a voice of blunt, bluff, manly frankness. Whatever quality the advocate may wish to represent as the client's distinctive characteristic, it must be suggested to the jury by mimetic artifice of the finest sort. Speaking of a famous counsel, an enthusiastic juryman once said to this writer—"In my time I have heard Sir Alexander in pretty nearly every part: I've heard him as an old man and a young woman; I have heard him when he has been a ship run down at sea, and when he has been an oil-factory in a state of conflagration; once, when I was foreman of a jury, I saw him poison his intimate friend, and another time he did the part of a pious bank director in a fashion that would have skinned the eyelids of Exeter Hall: he ain't bad as a desolate widow with nine children, of which the eldest is under eight years of age; but if ever I have to listen to him again, I should like to see him as a young lady of good connexions who has been seduced by an officer of the Guards." In the days of his forensic triumphs Henry Brougham was remarkable for the mimetic power which enabled him to describe friend or foe by a few subtle turns of the voice. At a later period, long after he had left the bar, in compliance with a request that he would return thanks for the bridesmaids at a wedding breakfast, he observed, that "doubtless he had been selected for the task in consideration of his youth, beauty, and innocence." The laughter that followed this sally was of the sort which in poetic phraseology is called inextinguishable; and one of the wedding guests who heard the joke and the laughter, assures this writer that the storm of mirthful applause was chiefly due to the delicacy and sweetness of the intonations by which the speaker's facile voice, with its old and once familiar art, made the audience realize the charms of youth, beauty and innocence—charms which, so far as the lawyer's wrinkled visage was concerned, were conspicuous by their absence.

Eminent advocates have almost invariably possessed qualities that would have made them successful mimics on the stage. For his mastery of oratorical artifices Alexander Wedderburn was greatly indebted to Sheridan, the lecturer on elocution, and to Macklin, the actor, from both of whom he took lessons; and when he had dismissed his teachers and become a leader of the English bar he adhered to their rules, and daily practised before a looking-glass the facial tricks by which Macklin taught him to simulate surprise or anger, indignation or triumph. Erskine was a perfect master of dramatic effect, and much of his richly-deserved success was due to the theatrical artifices with which he played upon the passions of juries. At the conclusion of a long oration he was accustomed to feign utter physical prostration, so that the twelve gentlemen in the box, in their sympathy for his sufferings and their admiration for his devotion to the interests of his client, might be impelled by generous emotion to return a favorable verdict. Thus when he defended Hardy, hoarseness and fatigue so overpowered him towards the close of his speech, that during the last ten minutes he could not speak above a whisper, and in order that his whispers might be audible to the jury, the exhausted advocate advanced two steps nearer to their box, and then extended his pale face to their eager eyes. The effect of the artifice on the excited jury is said to have been great and enduring, although they were speedily enlightened as to the real nature of his apparent distress. No sooner had the advocate received the first plaudits of his theatre on the determination of his harangue, than the multitude outside the court, taking up the acclamations which were heard within the building, expressed their feelings with such deafening clamor, and with so many signs of riotous intention, that Erskine was entreated to leave the court and soothe the passions of the mob with a few words of exhortation. In compliance with this suggestion he left the court, and forthwith addressed the dense out-door assembly in clear, ringing tones that were audible in Ludgate Hill, at one end of the Old Bailey, and to the billowy sea of human heads that surged round St. Sepulchre's Church at the other extremity of the dismal thoroughfare.

At the subsequent trial of John Horne Tooke, Sir John Scott, unwilling that Erskine should enjoy a monopoly of theatrical artifice, endeavored to create a diversion in favor of the government by a display of those lachrymose powers, which Byron ridiculed in the following century. "I can endure anything but an attack on my good name," exclaimed the Attorney General, in reply to a criticism directed against his mode of conducting the prosecution; "my good name is the little patrimony I have to leave to my children, and, with God's help, gentlemen of the jury, I will leave it to them unimpaired." As he uttered these words tears suffused the eyes which, at a later period of the lawyer's career, used to moisten the woolsack in the House of Lords—

> "Because the Catholics would not rise,
> In spite of his prayers and his prophecies."

For a moment Horne Tooke, who persisted in regarding all the circumstances of his perilous position as farcical, smiled at the lawyer's outburst in silent amusement; but as soon as he saw a sympathetic brightness in the eyes of one of the jury, the dexterous demagogue with characteristic humor and effrontery accused Sir John Mitford, the Solicitor General, of needless sympathy with the sentimental disturbance of his colleague. "Do you know what Sir John Mitford is crying about?" the prisoner inquired of the jury. "He is thinking of the destitute condition of Sir John Scott's children, and the *little patrimony* they are likely to divide among them." The jury and all present were not more tickled by the satire upon the Attorney General than by the indignant surprise which enlivened the face of Sir John Mitford, who was not at all prone to tears, and had certainly manifested no pity for John Scott's forlorn condition.

*Chapter 29*

# "THE PLAY'S THE THING"

Following the example set by the nobility in their castles and civic palaces, the Inns of Court set apart certain days of the year for feasting and revelry, and amongst the diversions with which the lawyers recreated themselves at these periods of rejoicing, the rude Pre-Shakespearian dramas took a prominent place. So far back as A.D. 1431, the Masters of the Lincoln's Inn Bench restricted the number of annual revels to four—"one at the feast of All-Hallown, another at the feast of St. Erkenwald; the third at the feast of the Purification of our Lady; and the 4th at Midsummer." The ceremonials of these holidays were various; but the brief and sometimes unintelligible notices of the chroniclers give us sufficiently vivid and minute pictures of the boisterous jollity that marked the proceedings. Miracle plays and moralities, dancing and music, fantastic processions and mad pranks, spurred on the hours that were not devoted to heavy meals and deep potations. In the merriments of the different Inns there was a pleasant diversity—with regard to the duration and details of the entertainments: and occasionally the members of the four societies acted with so little concert that their festivals, falling at exactly the same time, were productive of rivalry and disappointments. Dugdale thinks that the Christmas revels were not regularly kept in Lincoln's Inn during the reign of Henry VIII.; and draws attention to an order made by the benchers of that house on 27 Nov., 22 H. VIII., the record of which runs thus:—"It is agreed that if the two Temples do kepe Chrystemas, then the Chrystemas to be kept here; and to know this, the Steward of the House ys commanded to get knowledge, and to advertise my masters by the next day at night."

But notwithstanding changes and novelties, the main features of a revel in an Inn of Court were always much the same. Some member of the society conspicuous for rank or wit of style, or for a combination of these qualities, was elected King of the Revel, and until the close of the long frolic he was despot and sole master of the position—so long as he did not disregard a few not vexatious conditions by which, the benchers limited his authority. He surrounded himself with a mock court, exacted homage from barristers and students, made proclamations to his loyal children, sat on a throne at daily banquets, and never appeared in public without a body-guard, and a numerous company of musicians, to protect his person and delight his ear.

The wit and accomplishments of the younger lawyers were signally displayed in the dramatic interludes that usually enlivened these somewhat heavy and sluggish jollifications. Not only did they write the pieces, and put them before the audience with cunning devices for the production of scenic effect, but they were their own actors. It was not long before their 'moralities' were seasoned with political sentiments and allusions to public affairs. For instance, when Wolsey was in the fulness of his power, Sergeant Roo ventured to satirize the Cardinal in a masque with which Gray's Inn entertained Henry VIII and his courtiers. Hall records that, "This plaie was so set furth with riche and costlie apparel; with strange diuises of maskes and morrishes, that it was highly praised of all menne saving the Cardinall, whiche imagined that the plaie had been deuised of him, and in greate furie sent for the said Maister Roo, and toke from hym his coife, and sent him to the Flete, and after he sent for the yoong gentlemen that plaied in the plaie, and them highly rebuked and threatened, and sent one of them, called Thomas Moyle, of Kent, to the Flete; but by means of friendes Master Roo and he wer deliuered at last." The author stoutly denied that he intended to satirize the Cardinal; and the chronicler, believing the sergeant's assertions, observes, "This plaie sore displeased the Cardinal, and yet it was never meant to him." That the presentation of plays was a usual feature of the festivals at Gray's Inn may be inferred from the passage where Dugdale, in his notes on that society, says;—"In 4 Edw. VI. (17 Nov.), it was also ordered that henceforth there should be no comedies called *Interludes* in this House out of Term time, but when the feast of the Nativity of our Lord is solemnly observed. And that when there shall be any such comedies, then all the society at that time in commons to bear the charge of the apparel."

Notwithstanding her anxiety for the maintenance of good discipline in the Inns of Court, Queen Elizabeth encouraged the Societies to celebrate their feasts with costliness and liberal hospitality, and her taste for dramatic entertainments increased the splendor and frequency of theatrical diversions amongst the lawyers. Christopher Hatton's name is connected with the history of the English drama, by the acts which he contributed to 'The Tragedie of Tancred and Gismunda, compiled by the gentlemen of the Inner Temple, and by them presented before her majestie;' and he was one of the chief actors in that ponderous and extravagant mummery with which the Inner Temple kept Christmas in the fourth year of Elizabeth's reign.

The circumstances of that festival merit special notice.

In the third year of Elizabeth's reign the Middle Temple and the Inner Temple were at fierce war, the former society having laid claim to Lyon's Inn, which had been long regarded as a dependency of the Inner Temple. The two Chief Justices, Sir Robert Catlyn and Sir James Dyer, were known to think well of the claimant's title, and the masters of the Inner Temple bench anticipated an adverse decision, when Lord Robert Dudley (afterwards Earl of Leicester) came to their relief with an order from Queen Elizabeth enjoining the Middle Templars no longer to vex their neighbors in the matter. Submission being the only course open to them, the lawyers of the Middle Temple desisted from their claim; and the Masters of the Inner Temple Bench expressed their great gratitude to Lord Robert Dudley, "by ordering and enacting that no person or persons of their society that then were, or thereafter should be, should be retained of councell against him the said Lord Robert, or his heirs; and that the arms of the said Lord Robert should be set up and placed in some convenient place in their Hall as a continual monument of his lordship's favor unto them."

Further honors were paid to this nobleman at the ensuing Christmas, when the Inner Temple held a revel of unusual magnificence and made Lord Robert the ruler of the riot. Whilst the holidays lasted the young lord's title and style were "Pallaphilos, prince of Sophie High Constable Marshal of the Knights Templars, and Patron of the Honorable Order of Pegasus." And he kept a stately court, having for his chief officers—Mr. Onslow (Lord Chancellor), Anthony Stapleton (Lord Treasurer), Robert Kelway (Lord Privy Seal), John Fuller (Chief Justice of the King's Bench), William Pole (Chief Justice of the Common Pleas), Roger Manwood (Chief Baron of the Exchequer), Mr. Bashe (Steward of the Household), Mr. Copley (Marshal of the Household), Mr. Paten (Chief Butler), Christopher Hatton (Master of the Game), Messieurs Blaston, Yorke, Penston, Jervise (Masters of the Revels), Mr. Parker (Lieutenant of the Tower), Mr. Kendall (Carver), Mr. Martyn (Ranger of the Forests), and Mr. Stradling (Sewer). Besides these eighteen Placemen, Pallaphilos had many other mock officers, whose names are not recorded, and he was attended by a body-guard of fourscore members of the Inn.

From the pages of Gerard Leigh and Dugdale, the reader can obtain a sufficiently minute account of the pompous ceremonials and heavy buffooneries of the season. He may learn some of the special services and contributions which Prince Pallaphilos required of his chief courtiers, and take note how Mr. Paten, as Chief Butler, had to provide seven dozen silver and gilt spoons, twelve dozen silver and gilt salt-cellars, twenty silver and gilt candlesticks, twenty fine large table-cloths of damask and diaper, twenty dozen white napkins, three dozen fair large towels, twenty dozen white cups and green pots, to say nothing of carving-knives, carving table, tureens, bread, beer, ale, and wine. The reader also may learn from those chroniclers how the company were placed according to degrees at different tables; how the banquets were served to the sound of drums and fifes; how the boar's head was brought in upon a silver dish; how the gentlemen in gowns, the trumpeters, and other musicians followed the boar's head in stately procession; and how, by a rule somewhat at variance with modern notions concerning old English hospitality, strangers of worth were expected to pay in cash for their entertainment, eightpence per head being the charge for dinner on the day of

Christmas Eve, and twelve-pence being demanded from each stranger for his dinner on the following day.

Ladies were not excluded from all the festivities; though it may be presumed they did not share in all the riotous meals of the period. It is certain that they were invited, together with the young law-students from the Inns of Chancery, to see a play and a masque acted in the hall; that seats were provided for their special accommodation in the hall whilst the sports were going forward; and that at the close of the dramatic performances the gallant dames and pretty girls were entertained by Pallaphilos in the library with a suitable banquet; whilst the mock Lord Chancellor, Mr. Onslow, presided at a feast in the hall, which with all possible speed had been converted from theatrical to more appropriate uses.

But though the fun was rare and the array was splendid to idle folk of the sixteenth century, modern taste would deem such gaiety rude and wearisome, would call the ladies' banquet a disorderly scramble, and think the whole frolic scarce fit for schoolboys. And in many respects those revels of olden time were indecorous, noisy, comfortless affairs. There must have been a sad want of room and fresh air in the Inner Temple dining-hall, when all the members of the inn, the selected students from the subordinate Inns of Chancery, and half a hundred ladies (to say nothing of Mr. Gerard Leigh and illustrious strangers), had crowded into the space set apart for the audience. At the dinners what wrangling and tumult must have arisen through squabbles for place, and the thousand mishaps that always attend an endeavor to entertain five hundred gentlemen at a dinner, in a room barely capacious enough for the proper accommodation of a hundred and fifty persons. Unless this writer greatly errs, spoons and knives were in great request, and table linen was by no means 'fair and spotless' towards the close of the rout.

Superb, on that holyday, was the aspect of Prince Pallaphilos. Wearing a complete suit of elaborately wrought and richly gilt armor, he bore above his helmet a cloud of curiously dyed feathers, and held a gilt pole-axe in his hand. By his side walked the Lieutenant of the Tower (Mr. Parker), clad in white armor, and like Pallaphilos furnished with feathers and a pole-axe.

On entering the hall the prince and his Lieutenant of the Tower were preceded by sixteen trumpeters (at full blare), four drummers (at full drum), and a company of fifers (at full whistle), and followed by four men in white armor, bearing halberds in their hands. Thrice did this procession march round the fire that blazed in the centre of the hall; and when in the course of these three circuits the four halberdiers and the musicians had trodden upon everybody's toes (their own included), and when moreover they had blown themselves out of time and breath, silence was proclaimed; and Prince Pallaphilos, having laid aside his pole-axe and his naked sword and a few other trifles, took his seat at the urgent entreaty of the mock Lord Chancellor.

But Kit Hatton's appearance and part in the proceedings were even more outrageously ridiculous. The future Lord Chancellor of England was then a very elegant and witty young fellow, proud of his quick humor and handsome face, but far prouder of his exquisitely proportioned legs. No sooner had Prince Pallaphilos taken his seat, at the Lord Chancellor's suggestion, than Kit Hatton (as master of the game) entered the hall, dressed in a complete suit of green velvet, and holding a green bow in his left hand. His quiver was supplied with green arrows, and round his neck was slung a hunting-horn. By Kit's side, arrayed in exactly the same style, walked the Ranger of the Forests (Mr. Martyn); and having forced their way into the crowded chamber, the two young men blew three blasts of venery upon their horns, and then paced three times round the fire. After thus parading the hall they paused before the Lord Chancellor, to whom the Master of Game made three curtsies, and then on his knees proclaimed the desire of his heart to serve the mighty Prince Pallaphilos.

Having risen from his kneeling posture Kit Hatton blew his horn, and at the signal his huntsman entered the room, bringing with him a fox, a cat, and ten couples of hounds. Forthwith the fox was released from the pole to which it was bound; and when the luckless creature had crept into a corner under one of the tables, the ten couples of hounds were sent in pursuit. It is a fact that English gentlemen in the sixteenth century thus amused themselves with a fox-hunt in a densely crowded dining-room. Over tables and under tables, up the hall and down the hall, those score hounds went at full cry after a miserable fox, which they eventually ran into and killed in the cinder-pit, or as Dugdale expresses it, "beneath the fire." That work achieved, the cat was turned off, and the hounds sent after her, with much blowing of horns, much cracking of whips, and deafening cries of excitement from the gownsmen, who tumbled over one another in their eagerness to be in at the death.

*Chapter 30*

# THE RIVER AND THE STRAND BY TORCHLIGHT

Scarcely less out of place in the dining-hall than Kit Hatton's hounds, was the mule fairly mounted on which the Prince Pallaphilos made his appearance at the High Table after supper, when he notified to his subjects in what manner they were to disport themselves till bedtime. Thus also when the Prince of Purpoole kept his court at Gray's Inn, A.D. 1594, the prince's champion rode into the dining-hall upon the back of a fiery charger which, like the rider, was clothed in a panoply of steel.

In costliness and riotous excess the Prince of Purpoole's revel at Gray's Inn was not inferior to any similar festivity in the time of Elizabeth. On the 20th of December, St. Thomas's Eve, the Prince (one Master Henry Holmes, a Norfolk gentleman) took up his quarters in the Great Hall of the Inn, and by the 3rd day of January the grandeur and comicality of his proceedings had created so much talk throughout the town that the Lord Treasurer Burghley, the Earls of Cumberland, Essex, Shrewsbury and Westmoreland, the Lords Buckhurst, Windsor, Sheffield, Compton, and a magnificent array of knights and ladies visited Gray's Inn Hall on that day and saw the masque which the revellers put upon the stage. After the masque there was a banquet, which was followed by a ball. On the following day the prince, attended by eighty gentlemen of Gray's Inn and the Temple (each of the eighty wearing a plume on his head), dined in state with the Lord Mayor and aldermen of the city, at Crosby Place. The frolic continued for many days more; the royal Purpoole on one occasion visiting Blackwall with a splendid retinue, on another (Twelfth Night) receiving a gallant assembly of lords, ladies, and Knights, at his court in Gray's Inn, and on a third (Shrovetide) visiting the queen herself at Greenwich, when Her Majesty warmly applauded the masque set before her by the actors who were members of the Prince's court. So delighted was Elizabeth with the entertainment, that she graciously allowed the masquers to kiss her right hand, and loudly extolled Gray's Inn "as an house she was much indebted to, for it did always study for some sports to present unto her;"

whilst to the mock Prince she showed her favor, by placing in his hand the jewel (set with seventeen diamonds and fourteen rubies) which he had won by valor and skill in the tournament which formed part of the Shrovetide sports.

Numerous entries in the records of the inns testify to the importance assigned by the olden lawyers to their periodic feasts; and though in the fluctuations of public opinion with regard to the effects of dramatic amusements, certain benchers, or even all the benchers of a particular inn, may be found at times discountenancing the custom of presenting masques, the revels were usually diversified and heightened by stage plays. Not only were interludes given at the high and grand holidays styled *Solemn Revels*, but also at the minor festivities termed Post Revels they were usually had recourse to for amusement. "Besides those *solemn revels*, or measures aforesaid," says Dugdale, concerning the old usages of the 'Middle Temple,' "they had wont to be entertained with Post Revels performed by the better sort of the young gentlemen of the society, with galliards, corrantoes, and other dances, or else with stage-plays; the first of these feasts being at the beginning, and the other at the latter end of Christmas. But of late years these Post Revels have been disused, both here and in the other Inns of Court."

Besides producing and acting some of our best Pro-Shakespearian dramas, the Elizabethan lawyers put upon the stage at least one of William Shakespeare's plays. From the diary of a barrister (supposed to be John Manningham, of the Middle Temple), it is learnt that the Middle Templar's acted Shakespeare's 'Twelfth Night' at the Readers' feast on Candlemas Day, 1601-2.[20]

In the following reign, the masques of the lawyers in no degree fell off with regard to splendor. Seldom had the Thames presented a more picturesque and exhilarating spectacle than it did on the evening of February 20, 1612, when the gentlemen masquers of Gray's Inn and the Temple, entered the king's royal barge at Winchester House, at seven o'clock, and made the voyage to Whitehall, attended by hundreds of barges and boats, each vessel being so brilliantly illuminated that the lights reflected upon the ripples of the river, seemed to be countless. As though the hum and huzzas of the vast multitude on the water were insufficient to announce the approach of the dazzling pageant, guns marked the progress of the revellers, and as they drew near the palace, all the attendant bands of musicians played the same stirring tune with uniform time. It is on record that the king received the amateur actors with an excess of condescension, and was delighted with the masque which Master Beaumont of the Inner Temple, and his friend, Master Fletcher, had written and dedicated "to the worthy Sir Francis Bacon, his Majesty's Solicitor-General, and the grave and learned bench of the anciently-called houses of Grayes Inn and the Inner Temple, and the Inner Temple and Grayes Inn." The cost of this

[20] The propensity of lawyers for the stage, lingered amongst barristers on Circuit, to a comparatively recent date. 'Old stagers' of the Home and Western Circuits, can recall how the juniors of their briefless and bagless days used to entertain the natives of Guildford and Exeter with Shakspearian performances. The Northern Circuit also was at one time famous for the histrionic ability of its bar, but toward the close of the last century, the dramatic recreations of its junior members were discountenanced by the Grand Court.

entertainment was defrayed by the members of the two inns—each reader paying £4, each ancient, £2 10*s*.; each barrister, £2, and each student, 20*s*.

The Inner Temple and Gray's Inn having thus testified their loyalty and dramatic taste, in the following year on Shrove-Monday night (Feb. 15, 1613), Lincoln's Inn and the Middle Temple, with no less splendor and *éclat*, enacted at Whitehall a masque written by George Chapman. For this entertainment, Inigo Jones designed and perfected the theatrical decorations in a style worthy of an exhibition that formed part of the gaieties with which the marriage of the Palsgrave with the Princess Elizabeth was celebrated. And though the masquers went to Whitehall by land, their progress was not less pompous than the procession which had passed up the Thames in the February of the preceding year. Having mustered in Chancery Lane, at the official residence of the Master of the Rolls, the actors and their friends delighted the town with a gallant spectacle. Mounted on richly-caparisoned and mettlesome horses, they rode from Fleet Street up the Strand, and by Charing Cross to Whitehall, through a tempest of enthusiasm. Every house was illuminated, every window was crowded with faces, on every roof men stood in rows, from every balcony bright eyes looked down upon the gay scene, and from basement to garret, from kennel to roof-top throughout the long way, deafening cheers testified, whilst they increased the delight of the multitude. Such a pageant would, even in these sober days, rouse London from her cold propriety. Having thrown aside his academic robe, each masquer had donned a fantastic dress of silver cloth embroidered with gold lace, gold plate, and ostrich plumes. He wore across his breast a gold baldrick, round his neck a ruff of white feathers brightened with pearls and silver lace, and on his head a coronal of snowy plumes. Before each mounted masquer rode a torch-bearer, whose right hand waved a scourge of flame, instead of a leathern thong. In a gorgeous chariot, preceded by a long train of heralds, were exhibited the Dramatis Personæ—Honor, Plutus, Eunomia, Phemeis, Capriccio—arrayed in their appointed costumes; and it was rumored that the golden canopy of their coach had been bought for an enormous sum. Two other triumphal cars conveyed the twelve chief musicians of the kingdom, and these masters of melody were guarded by torch-bearers, marching two deep before and behind, and on either side of the glittering carriages. Preceding the musicians, rode a troop of ludicrous objects, who roused the derision of the mob, and made fat burghers laugh till tears ran down their cheeks. They were the mock masque, each resembling an ape, each wearing a fantastic dress that heightened the hideous absurdity of his monkey's visage, each riding upon an ass, or small pony, and each of them throwing shells upon the crowd by way of a largess. In the front of the mock masque, forming the vanguard of the entire spectacle, rode fifty gentlemen of the Inns of Court, reining high-bred horses, and followed by their running footmen, whose liveries added to the gorgeous magnificence of the display.

Besides the expenses which fell upon individuals taking part in the play, or procession, this entertainment cost the two inns £1086 8*s*. 11*d*. About the same time

Gray's Inn, at the instigation of Attorney General Sir Francis Bacon, performed 'The Masque of Flowers' before the lords and ladies of the court, in the Banqueting-house, Whitehall; and six years later Thomas Middleton's Inner Temple Masque, or Masque of Heroes' was presented before a goodly company of grand ladies by the Inner Templars.

*Chapter 31*

# ANTI-PRYNNE

Of all the masques mentioned in the records of the Inns of Court, the most magnificent and costly was the famous Anti-Prynne demonstration, by which the lawyers endeavored to show their contemptuous disapproval of a work that inveighed against the licentiousness of the stage, and preferred a charge of wanton levity against those who encouraged theatrical performances.

Whilst the 'Histriomastix' rendered the author ridiculous to mere men of pleasure, it roused fierce animosities by the truth and fearless completeness of its assertions; but to no order of society was the famous attack on the stage more offensive than to the lawyers; and of lawyers the members of Lincoln's Inn were the most vehement in their displeasure. The actors writhed under the attack; the lawyers were literally furious with rage—for whilst rating them soundly for their love of theatrical amusements, Prynne almost contrived to make it seem that his views were acceptable to the wisest and most reverend members of the legal profession. Himself a barrister of Lincoln's Inn, he with equal craft and audacity complimented the benchers of that society on the firmness with which they had forbidden professional actors to take part in the periodic revels of the inn, and on their inclination to govern the society in accordance with Puritanical principles. Addressing his "Much Honored Friends, the Right Worshipful Masters of the Bench of the Honorable Flourishing Law Society of Lincoln's Inne," the utter-barrister said: "For whereas other Innes of Court (I know not by what evil custom, and worse example) admit of common actors and interludes upon their two grand festivalls, to recreate themselves withall, notwithstanding the statutes of our Kingdome (of which lawyers, of all others, should be most observant), have branded all professed stage-players for infamous rogues, and stage-playes for unlawful pastimes, especially on Lord's-dayes and other solemn holidayes, on which these grand dayes ever fall; yet such hath been your pious tender care, not only of this societie's honor, but also of the young students' good (for the advancing of whose piety and studies you have of late erected a magnificent chapel, and since that a library), that as you have prohibited by late publicke orders, all disorderly Bacchanalian Grand-Christmasses (more fit for pagans than Christians; for the deboisest roarers than grave civill students, who should be patternes of sobriety unto others), together with all publicke dice-play in the Hall (a most pernicious, infamous game; condemned in all ages, all places, not onely by councels, fathers, divines, civilians, canonists, politicians, and other Christian writers; by divers Pagan authors of all sorts, and by Mahomet himselfe; but likewise by sundry heathen, yea, Christian Magistrates' edicts)."

Concerning the London theatres he observes that the "two old play houses" (i.e., the Fortune and the Red Bull), the "new theatre" (i.e., Whitefriars play-house), and two other established theatres, being found inadequate to the wants of the play-going public, a sixth theatre had recently been opened. "The multitude of our London play-haunters being so augmented now, that all the ancient Divvel's Chappels (for so the fathers style all play-houses) being five in number, are not sufficient to containe their troops, whence we see a sixth now added to them, whereas even in vitious Nero his raigne there were but three standing theatres in Pagan Rome (though far more splendid than Christian London), and those three too many." Having thus enumerated some of the saddest features of his age, the author of the 'Player's Scourge' again commends the piety and decorum of the Lincoln's Inn Benchers, saying, "So likewise in imitation of the ancient Lacedæmonians and Massilienses, or rather of primitive zealous Christians, you have always from my first admission into your society, and long before, excluded all common players with their ungodly interludes, from all your solemn festivals."

If the benchers of one Inn winced under Prynne's 'expressions of approval,' the students of all the Inns of Court were even more displeased with the author who, in a dedicatory letter "to the right Christian, Generous Young Gentlemen-Students of the four Innes of Court, and especially those of Lincolne's Inne," urged them to "at last falsifie that ignominious censure which some English writers in their printed works have passed upon Innes of Court Students, of whom they record:—That Innes of Court men were undone but for players, that they are their chiefest guests and imployment, and the sole business that makes them afternoon's men; that is one of the first things they learne as soon as they are admitted, to see stage-playes, and take smoke at a play-house, which they commonly make their studie; where they quickly learne to follow all fashions, to drinke all healths, to wear favours and good cloathes, to consort with ruffianly companions, to swear the biggest oaths, to quarrel easily, fight desperately, quarrel inordinately, to spend their patrimony ere it fall, to use gracefully some gestures of apish compliment, to talk irreligiously, to dally with a mistresse, and hunt after harlots, to prove altogether lawless in steed of lawyers, and to forget that little learning, grace, and vertue which they had before; so much that they grow at last past hopes of ever doing good, either to the church, their country, their owne or others' souls."

The storm of indignation which followed the appearance of the 'Histriomastix' was directed by the members of the Four Inns, who felt themselves bound by honor no less than by interest, to disavow all connexion with, or leaning towards, the unpopular author.

On the suggestion of Lincoln's Inn, the four societies combined their forces, and at a cost of more than twenty thousand pounds, in addition to sums spent by individuals, entertained the Court with that splendid masque which Whitelock has described in his 'Memoirs' with elaborate prolixity. The piece entitled 'The Triumph of Peace,' was written by Shirley, and it was produced with a pomp and lavish expenditure that were without precedent. The organization and guidance of the undertaking were entrusted to a committee of eight barristers, two from each inn; and this select body comprised men who were alike remarkable for talents, accomplishments, and ambition, and some of whom were destined to play strangely diverse parts in the drama of their epoch. It comprised Edward Hyde, then in his twenty-sixth year; young Bulstrode Whitelock, who had not yet astonished the more decorous magnates of his country by wearing a falling-band at the Oxford Quarter Sessions; Edward Herbert, the most unfortunate of Cavalier lawyers; John Selden, already a middle-aged man; John Finch, born in the same year as Selden, and already far advanced in his eager course to a not honorable notoriety. Attorney General Noy was also of the party, but his disastrous career was already near its close.

The committee of management had their quarters at Ely House, Holborn; and from that historic palace the masquers started for Whitehall on the eve of Candlemas Day, 1633-4. It was a superb procession. First marched twenty tall footmen, blazing in liveries of scarlet cloth trimmed with lace, each of them holding a baton in his right hand, and in his left a flaring torch that covered his face with light, and made the steel and silver of his sword-scabbard shine brilliantly. A company of the marshal's men marched next with firm and even steps, clearing the way for their master. A burst of deafening applause came from the multitude as the marshal rode through the gateway of Ely House, and caracoled over the Holborn way on the finest charger that the king's stables could furnish. A perfect horseman and the handsomest man then in town, Mr. Darrel of Lincoln's Inn, had been elected to the office of marshal in deference to his wealth, his noble aspect, his fine nature, and his perfect mastery of all manly sports. On either side of Mr. Darrel's horse marched a lacquey bearing a flambeau, and the marshal's page was in attendance with his master's cloak. An interval of some twenty paces, and then came the marshal's body-guard, composed of one hundred mounted gentlemen of the Inns of Court—twenty-five from each house; showing in their faces the signs of gentle birth and honorable nurture; and with strong hands reining mettlesome chargers that had been furnished for their use by the greatest nobles of the land. This flood of flashing chivalry was succeeded by an anti-masque of beggars and cripples, mounted on the lamest and most unsightly of rat-tailed srews and spavined ponies, and wearing dresses that threw derision on legal vestments and decorations. Another anti-masque satirized the wild projects of crazy speculators and inventors; and as it moved along the spectators laughed aloud at the "fish-call, or looking-glass for fishes in the sea, very useful for fishermen to call all kinds of fish to their nets;" the newly-invented wind-mate for raising a breeze over becalmed seas, the "movable hydraulic" which should give sleep to patients suffering under fever.

Chariots and horsemen, torch-bearers and lacqueys, followed in order. "Then came the first chariot of the grand masquers, which was not so large as those that went before, but most curiously framed, carved, and painted with exquisite art, and purposely for this service and occasion. The form of it was after that of the Roman triumphant chariots. The seats in it were made of oval form in the back end of the chariot, so that there was no precedence in them, and the faces of all that sat in it might be seen together. The colors of the first chariot were silver and crimson, given by the lot to Gray's Inn: the chariot was drawn with four horses all abreast, and they were covered to their heels all over with cloth of tissue, of the colors of crimson and silver, huge plumes of white and red feathers on their heads; the coachman's cap and feather, his long coat, and his very whip and cushion of the same stuff and color. In this chariot sat the four grand masquers of Gray's Inn, their habits, doublets, trunk-hose, and caps of most rich cloth of tissue, and wrought as thick with silver spangles as they could be placed; large white stockings up to their trunk-hose, and rich sprigs in their cap, themselves proper and beautiful young gentlemen. On each side of the chariot were four footmen in liveries of the color of the chariot, carrying huge flamboys in their hands, which, with the torches, gave such a lustre to the paintings, spangles, and habits that hardly anything could be invented to appear more glorious."

Six musicians followed the state-chariot of Gray's Inn, playing as they went; and then came the triumphal cars of the Middle Templars, the Inner Templars, and the Lincoln's Inn men—each car being drawn by four horses and attended by torch-bearers, flambeau-bearers, and musicians. In shape these four cars were alike, but they differed in the color of their fittings. Whilst Gray's Inn used scarlet and silver, the Middle Templars chose blue and silver decorations, and each of the other two houses adopted a distinctive color for the housings of their horses and the liveries of their servants. It is noteworthy that the inns (equal as to considerations of dignity) took their places in the pageant by lot; and that the four grand masquers of each inn were seated in their chariot on seats so constructed that none of the four took precedence of the others. The inns, in days when questions of precedence received much attention, were very particular in asserting their equality, whenever two or more of them acted in co-operation. To mark this equality, the masque written by Beaumont and Fletcher in 1612 was described "The Masque of the Inner Temple and Grayes Inn; Grayes Inn and the Inner Temple:" and the dedication of the piece to Francis Bacon, reversing this transposition, mentions "the allied houses of Grayes Inn and the Inner Temple, and the Inner Temple and Grayes Inn," these changes being made to point the equal rank of the two fraternities.

Through the illuminated streets this pageant marched to the sound of trumpets and drums, cymbals and fifes, amidst the deafening acclamations of the delighted town; and when the lawyers reached Whitehall, the king and queen were so delighted with the spectacle, that the procession was ordered to make the circuit of the tilt-yard for the gratification of their Majesties, who would fain see the sight once again from the windows of their palace. Is there need to speak of the manner in which the masque was acted, of the music and dances, of the properties and scenes, of the stately banquet after the play and the grand ball which began at a still later hour, of the king's urbanity and the graciousness of Henrietta, who "did the honor to some of the masquers to dance with them herself, and to judge them as good dancers as she ever saw!"

Notwithstanding a few untoward broils and accidents, the entertainment passed off so satisfactorily that 'The Triumph of Peace' was acted for a second time in the presence of the king and queen, in the Merchant Taylors' Hall. Other diversions of the same kind followed with scarcely less *éclat*. At Whitehall the king himself and some of the choicest nobles of the land turned actors, and performed a grand masque, on which occasion the Templars were present as spectators in seats of honor.

During the Shrovetide rejoicings of 1635, Henrietta even condescended to witness the performance of Davenant's 'Triumphs of the Prince d'Amour,' in the hall of the Middle Temple. Laying aside the garb of royalty, she went to the Temple, attended by a party of lords and ladies, and fine gentlemen who, like herself, assumed for the evening dresses suitable to persons of private station. The Marquis of Hamilton, the Countess of Denbigh, the Countess of Holland, and Lady Elizabeth Fielding were her companions; whilst the official attendants on her person were the Earl of Holland, Lord Goring, Mr. Percy, and Mr. Jermyn. Led to her place by "Mrs. Basse, the law-woman," Henrietta took a seat upon a scaffold fixed along the northern side of the hall, and amidst a crush of benchers' wives and daughters saw the play and heartily enjoyed it.

Says Whitelock, at the conclusion of his account of the grand masque given by the four inns, "Thus these dreams past, and these pomps vanished." Scarcely had the frolic terminated when death laid a chill hand on the time-serving Noy, who in the consequences of his dishonest counsels left a cruel legacy to the master and the country whom he alike betrayed. A few more years—and John Finch, having lost the Great Seal, was an exile in a foreign land, destined to die in penury, without again setting foot on his native soil. The graceful Herbert, whose smooth cheek had flushed with joy at Henrietta's musical courtesies, became for a brief day the mock Lord Keeper of Charles II.'s mock court at Paris, and then, dishonored and disowned by his capricious master, he languished in poverty and disease, until he found an obscure grave in the French capital. More fortunate than his early rival, Edward Hyde outlived Charles Stuart's days of adverse fortune, and rose to a grievous greatness; but like that early rival, he, too, died in exile in France. Perhaps of all the managers of the grand masque the scholarly pedant, John Selden, had the greatest share of earthly satisfaction. Not the least fortunate of the party was the historian of "the pomp and glory, if not the vanity of the show," who having survived the Commonwealth and witnessed the Restoration, was permitted to retain his paternal estate, and in his last days could tell his numerous descendants how his old chum, Edward Hyde, had risen, fallen, and—passed to another world.

*Chapter 32*

# AN EMPTY GRATE

With the revival of gaiety which attended and followed the Restoration, revels and masques came once more into vogue at the Inns of Court, where, throughout the Commonwealth, plays had been prohibited, and festivals had been either abolished or deprived of their ancient hilarity. The caterers of amusement for the new king were not slow to suggest that he should honor the lawyers with a visit; and in accordance with their counsel, His Majesty took water on August 15, 1661, and went in the royal barge from Whitehall to the Temple to dine at the Reader's feast.

Heneage Finch had been chosen Autumn Reader of that inn, and in accordance with ancient usage he demonstrated his ability to instruct young gentlemen in the principles of English law, by giving a series of costly banquets. From the days of the Tudors to the rise of Oliver Cromwell, the Reader's feasts had been amongst the most sumptuous and ostentatious entertainments of the town—the Sergeant's feasts scarcely surpassing them in splendor, the inaugural dinners of lord mayors often lagging behind them in expense. But Heneage Finch's lavish hospitality outstripped the doings of all previous Readers. His revel was protracted throughout six days, and on each of these days he received at his table the representative members of some high social order or learned body. Beginning with a dinner to the nobility and Privy Councillors, he finished with a banquet to the king; and on the intervening days he entertained the civic authorities, the College of Physicians, the civil lawyers, and the dignitaries of the Church.

The king's visit was attended with imposing ceremony, and wanted no circumstance that could have rendered the occasion more honorable to the host or to the society of which he was a member. All the highest officers of the court accompanied the monarch, and when he stepped from his barge at the Temple Stairs, he spoke with jovial urbanity to his entertainer and the Lord Chief Justice of the Common Pleas, who received him with tokens of loyal deference and attachment. "On each side," says Dugdale, "as His Majesty passed, stood the Reader's servants in scarlet cloaks and white tabba doublets; there being a way made through the wall into the Temple Gardens; and above them on each side the benchers, barristers, and other gentlemen of the society, all in their gowns and formalities, the loud music playing from the time of his landing till he entered the hall; where he was received with xx violins, which continued as long as his majesty stayed." Fifty chosen gentlemen of the inn, wearing their academic gowns, placed dinner on the table, and waited on the feasters—no other servants being permitted to enter the hall during the progress of the banquet. On the dais at the top of the hall, under a canopy of state, the king and his brother James sat apart from men of lower degree, whilst the nobles of Whitehall occupied one long table, under the presidency of the Lord Chancellor, and the chief personages of the inn dined at a corresponding long table, having the reader for their chairman.

In the following January, Charles II and the Duke of York honored Lincoln's Inn with a visit, whilst the mock Prince de la Grange held his court within the walls of that society. Nine years later—in the February of 1671—King Charles and his brother James again visited Lincoln's Inn, on which occasion they were entertained by Sir Francis Goodericke, Knt., the reader of the inn, who seems almost to have gone beyond Heneage Finch in sumptuous profusion of hospitality. Of this royal visit a particular account is to be seen in the Admittance Book of the Honorable Society, from which it appears that the royal brothers were attended by the Dukes of Monmouth and Richmond; the Earls of Manchester, Bath, and Anglesea; Viscount Halifax, the Bishop of Ely, Lord Newport, Lord Henry Howard, and "divers others of great qualitie."

The entertainment in most respects was a repetition of Sir Heneage Finch's feast—the king, the Duke of York, and Prince Rupert dining on the dais at the top of the hall, whilst the persons of inferior though high quality were regaled at two long tables, set down the hall; and the gentlemen of the inn condescending to act as menial servants. The reader himself, dropping on his knee when he performed the servile office, proffered the towel with which the king prepared himself for the repast; and barristers of ancient lineage and professional eminence contended for the honor of serving His Majesty with surloin and cheesecake upon the knee, and hastened with the alacrity of well-trained lacqueys to do the bidding of "the lords att their table." Having eaten and drunk to his lively satisfaction, Charles called for the Admittance Book of the Inn, and placed his name on the roll of members, thereby conferring on the society an honor for which no previous king of England had furnished a precedent. Following their chief's example, the Duke of York and Prince Rupert and other nobles forthwith joined the fraternity of lawyers; and hastily donning students' gowns, they mingled with the troop of gowned servitors, and humbly waited on their liege lord.

In like manner, twenty-one years since (July 29, 1845) when Queen Victoria and her lamented consort visited Lincoln's Inn, on the opening of the new hall, they condescended to enter their names in the Admission Book of the Inn, thereby making themselves students of the society. Her Majesty has not been called to the bar; but Prince

Albert in due course became a barrister and bencher. Repeating the action of Charles II.'s courtiers, the great Duke of Wellington and the bevy of great nobles present at the celebration became fellow-students with the queen; and on leaving the table the prince walked down the hall, wearing a student's stuff gown (by no means the most picturesque of academic robes), over his field-marshal's uniform. Her Majesty forbore to disarrange her toilet—which consisted of a blue bonnet with blue feathers, a dress of Limerick lace, and a scarlet shawl, with a deep gold edging—by putting her arms through the sleeveless arm-holes of a bombazine frock.

Grateful to the lawyers for the cordiality with which they welcomed him to the country, William III accepted an invitation to the Middle Temple, and was entertained by that society with a banquet and a masque, of which notice has been taken in another chapter of this work; and in 1697-8 Peter the Great was a guest at the Christmas revels of the Templars. On that occasion the Czar enjoyed a favorable opportunity for gratifying his love of strong drink, and for witnessing the ease with which our ancestors drank wine by the magnum and punch by the gallon, when they were bent on enjoyment.

In the greater refinement and increasing delicacy of the eighteenth century, the Inns of Court revels, which had for so many generations been conspicuous amongst the gaieties of the town, became less and less magnificent; and they altogether died out under the second of those Georges who are thought by some persons to have corrupted public morals and lowered the tastes of society. In 1733-4, when Lord Chancellor Talbot's elevation to the woolsack was celebrated by a revel in the Inner Temple Hall, the dulness and disorder of the celebration convinced the lawyers that they had not acted wisely in attempting to revive usages that had fallen into desuetude because they were inconvenient to new arrangements or repugnant to modern taste. No attempt was made to prolong the festivity over a succession of days. It was a revel of one day; and no one wished to add another to the period of riot. At two o'clock on Feb. 2, 1733-4, the new Chancellor, the master of the revels, the benchers of the inns, and the guests (who were for the most part lawyers), sat down to dinner in the hall. The barristers and students had their ordinary fare, with the addition of a flask of claret to each mess; but a superior repast was served at the High Table where fourteen students (of whom the Chancellor's eldest son was one), served as waiters. Whilst the banquet was in progress, musicians stationed in the gallery at the upper end of the hall filled the room with deafening noise, and ladies looked down upon the feasters from a large gallery which had been fitted up for their reception over the screen. After dinner, as soon as the hall could be cleared of dishes and decanters, the company were entertained with 'Love for Love,' and 'The Devil to Pay,' performed by professional actors who "all came from the Haymarket in chairs, ready dressed, and (as it was said), refused any gratuity for their trouble, looking upon the honor of distinguishing themselves on this occasion as sufficient." The players having withdrawn, the judges, sergeants, benchers, and other dignitaries, danced 'round about the coal fire;' that is to say, they danced round about a stove in which there was not a single spark of fire. The congregation of many hundreds of persons, in a hall which had not comfortable room for half the number, rendered the air so oppressively hot that the master of the revels wisely resolved to lead his troop of revellers round an empty grate. The chronicler of this ridiculous mummery observes: "And all the time of the dance the ancient song, accompanied by music, was sung by one Toby Aston, dressed in a bar-gown, whose father had formerly been Master of the Plea Office in the King's Bench. When this was over, the ladies came down from the gallery, went into the parliament chamber, and stayed about a quarter of an hour, while the hall was being put in order. They then went into the hall and danced a few minuets. Country dances began at ten, and at twelve a Very fine cold collation was provided for the whole company, from which they returned to dancing, which they continued as long as they pleased, and the whole day's entertainment was generally thought to be very genteelly and liberally conducted. The Prince of Wales honored the performance with his company part of the time; he came into the music *incog.* about the middle of the play, and went away as soon as the farce of 'walking round the coal fire' was over."

With this notable dance of lawyers round an empty grate, the old revels disappeared. In their Grand Days, equivalent to the gaudy days, or feast days, or audit days of the colleges at Oxford and Cambridge, the Inns of Court still retain the last vestiges of their ancient jollifications, but the uproarious riot of the obsolete festivities is but faintly echoed by the songs and laughter of the junior barristers and students who in these degenerate times gladden their hearts and loosen their tongues with an extra glass of wine after grand dinners, and then hasten back to chambers for tobacco and tea.

On the discontinuance of the revels the Inns of Court lost their chief attractions for the courtly pleasure-seekers of the town, and many a day passed before another royal visit was paid to any one of the societies. In 1734 George III.'s father stood amongst the musicians in the Inner Temple Hall; and after the lapse of one century and eleven years the present queen accepted the hospitality of Lincoln's Inn. No record exists of a royal visit made to an Inn of Court between those events. Only the other day, however, the Prince of Wales went eastwards and partook of a banquet in the hall of Middle Temple, of which society he is a barrister and a bencher.

# PART 7. LEGAL EDUCATION

*Chapter 33*

# INNS OF COURT AND INNS OF CHANCERY

Schools for the study of the Common Law, existed within the bounds of the city of London, at the commencement of the thirteenth century. No sooner had a permanent home been assigned to the Court of Common Pleas, than legal practitioners fixed themselves in the neighborhood of Westminster, or within the walls of London. A legal society speedily grew up in the city; and some of the older and more learned professors of the Common Law, devoting a portion of their time and energies to the labors of instruction, opened academies for the reception of students. Dugdale notices a tradition that in ancient times a law-school, called Johnson's Inn, stood in Dowgate, that another existed in Pewter Lane, and that Paternoster Row contained a third; and it is generally thought that these three inns were amongst the academies which sprung up as soon as the Common Pleas obtained a permanent abode.

The schools thus established in the opening years of the thirteenth century, were not allowed to flourish for any great length of time; for in the nineteenth year of his reign, Henry III suppressed them by a mandate addressed to the mayor and sheriffs of the city. But though this king broke up the schools, the scholars persevered in their study; and if the king's mandate aimed at a complete discontinuance of legal instruction, his policy was signally defeated.

Successive writers have credited Edward III's reign with the establishment of Inns of Court; and it has been erroneously inferred that the study of the Common Law not only languished, but was altogether extinct during the period of nearly one hundred years that intervened between Henry III's dissolution of the city schools and Edward III's accession. Abundant evidence, however, exists that this was not the case. Edward I, in the twentieth year of his reign, ordered his judges of the Common Pleas to "provide and ordain, from every county, certain attorneys and lawyers" (in the original "atturnatus et *apprenticiis*") "of the best and most apt for their learning and skill, who might do service to his court and people; and those so chosen, and no other should follow his court, and transact affairs therein; the words of which order make it clear that the country contained a considerable body of persons who devoted themselves to the study and practice of the law." So also in the Year-book, 1 Ed. III., the words, "et puis une apprentise demand," show that lawyers holding legal degrees existed in the very first year of Edward III's reign; a fact which justifies the inference that in the previous reign England contained Common Law schools capable of granting the legal degree of apprentice. Again Dugdale remarks, "In 20 Ed. III., in a *quod ei deforciat* to an exception taken, it was answered by Sir Richard de Willoughby (then a learned justice of the *Common Pleas*) and William Skipwith, (afterwards also one of the justices of that court), that the same was no exception amongst the *Apprentices in Hostells or Inns*." Whence it is manifest that Inns of Court were institutions in full vigor at the time when they have been sometimes represented as originally established.

But after their expulsion from the city, there is reason to think that the common lawyers made no attempt to reside in colleges within its boundaries. They preferred to establish themselves on spots where they could enjoy pure air and rural quietude, could surround themselves with trees and lawns, or refresh their eyes with the sight of the silver Thames. In the earliest part of the fourteenth century, they took possession of a great palace that stood on the western outskirt of the town, and looked westwards upon green fields, whilst its eastern wall abutted on New Street—a thoroughfare that was subsequently called Chancellor's Lane, and has for many years been known as Chancery Lane. This palace had been the residence of Henry Lacy, Earl of Lincoln, who conferred upon the building the name which it still bears. The earl died in 1310, some seventeen years before Edward III's accession; and Thynne, the antiquary, was of opinion that no considerable period intervened between Henry Lacy's death and the entry of the lawyers. In the same century, the lawyers took possession of the Temple. The exact date of their entry is unknown; but Chaucer's verse enables the student to fix, with sufficient preciseness, the period when the more noble apprentices of the law first occupied the Temple as tenants of the Knight's Hospitallers of St. John of Jerusalem, who obtained a grant of the place from Edward III.[21] The absence of fuller particulars concerning the

---

[21] Chaucer mentions the Temple thus:—

"A manciple there was of the Temple,
Of which all catours might take ensemple
For to be wise in buying of vitaile;
For whether he pay'd or took by taile,
Algate he wayted so in his ashate,
That he was aye before in good estate.
Now is not that of God a full faire grace,
That such a leude man's wit shall pace
The wisdome of an heape of learned men?
Of masters had he more than thrice ten,
That were of law expert and curious,
Of which there was a dozen in that house,
Worthy to been stewards of rent and land

early history of the legal Templars, is ordinarily and with good reason attributed to Wat Tyler's rebels, who destroyed the records of the fraternity by fire. From roof to basement, beginning with the tiles, and working downwards, the mob destroyed the principal houses of the college; and when they had burnt all the archives on which they could lay hands, they went off and expended their remaining fury on other buildings, of which the Knights of St. John were proprietors.

The same men who saw the lawyers take possession of the Temple on the northern banks of the Thames, and of the Earl of Lincoln's palace in New Street, saw them also make a third grand settlement. The manor of Portepoole, or Purpoole, became the property of the Grays of Wilton, in the twenty-second year of Edward I.; and on its green fields, lying north of Holborn, a society of lawyers established a college which still retains the name of the ancient proprietors of the soil. Concerning the exact date of its institution, the uncertainty is even greater than that which obscures the foundation of the Temple and Lincoln's Inn; but antiquaries have agreed to assign the creation of Gray's Inn, as an hospicium for the entertainment of lawyers, to the time of Edward III.

The date at which the Temple lawyers split up into two separate societies, is also unknown; but assigning the division to some period posterior to Wat Tyler's insurrection, Dugdale says, "But, notwithstanding, this spoil by the rebels, those students so increased here, that at length they divided themselves into two bodies; the one commonly known by the Society of the Inner Temple, and the other of the Middle Temple, holding this mansion as tenants." But as both societies had a common origin in the migration of lawyers from Thavies Inn, Holborn, in the time of Edward III, it is usual to speak of the two Temples as instituted in that reign, and to regard all four Inns of Court as the work of the fourteenth century.

The Inns of Chancery for many generations maintained towards the Inns of Court a position similar to that which Eton School maintains towards King's at Cambridge, or that which Winchester School holds to New College at Oxford. They were seminaries in which lads underwent preparation for the superior discipline and greater freedom of the four colleges. Each Inn of Court had its own Inns of Chancery, yearly receiving from them the pupils who had qualified themselves for promotion to the status of Inns-of-Court men. In course of time, students after receiving the preliminary education in an Inn of Chancery were permitted to enter an Inn of Court on which their Inn of Chancery was not dependent; but at every Inn of Court higher admission fees were charged to students coming from Inns of Chancery over which it had no control, than to students who came from its own primary schools. If the reader bears in mind the difference in respect to age,

---

Of any lord that is in England;
To maken him live by his proper good
In honour debtless, but if he were wood;
Or live as scarcely as him list desire,
And able to helpen all a shire,
In any case that might have fallen or hap,
And yet the manciple set all her capp."

learning, and privileges between our modern public schoolboys and university undergraduates, he will realize with sufficient nearness to truth the differences which existed between the Inns of Chancery students and the Inns of Court students in the fifteenth century; and in the students, utter-barristers, and benchers of the Inns of Court at the same period he may see three distinct orders of academic persons closely resembling the undergraduates, bachelors of arts, and masters of arts in our universities.

In the 'De Laudibus Legum Angliæ,'[22] written in the latter part of the fifteenth century, Sir John Fortescue says—"But to the intent, most excellent Prince, yee may conceive a forme and an image of this study, as I am able, I wil describe it unto you. For there be in it ten lesser houses or innes, and sometimes moe, which are called Innes of the Chaunceryye. And to every one of them belongeth an hundred students at least, and to some of them a much greater number, though they be not ever all together in the same."

In Charles II's time there were eight Inns of Chancery; and of them three were subsidiary to the Inner Temple—viz., Clifford's Inn, Clement's Inn, and Lyon's Inn. Clifford's Inn (originally the town residence of the Barons Clifford) was first inhabited by law-students in the eighteenth year of Edward III. Clement's Inn (taking its name from the adjacent St. Clement's Well) was certainly inhabited by law-students as early as the nineteenth year of Edward IV. Lyon's Inn was an Inn of Chancery in the time of Henry V.

One alone (New Inn) was attached to the Middle Temple. In the previous century, the Middle Temple had possessed another Inn of Chancery called Strand Inn; but in the third year of Edward VI this nursery was pulled down by the Duke of Somerset, who required the ground on which it stood for the site of Somerset House.

Lincoln's Inn had for dependent schools Furnival's Inn and Thavies Inn—the latter of which hostels was inhabited by law-students in Edward III.'s time. Of Furnival's Inn (originally Lord Furnival's town mansion, and converted into a law-school in Edward VI's reign) Dugdale says: "After which time the Principall and Fellows of this Inne have paid to the society of Lincoln's Inne the rent of iii$^{l}$ vi$^{s}$ iii$^{d}$ as an yearly rent for the same, as may appear by the accompts of that house; and by speciall order there made, have had these following priviledges: first (viz. 10 Eliz.), that the utter-barristers of Furnivall's Inne, of a yeares continuance, and so certified and allowed by the Benchers of Lincoln's Inne, shall pay no more than four marks apiece for their admittance into that society. Next (viz. in Eliz.) that every fellow of this inne, who hath been allowed an utter-barrister here, and that hath mooted here two vacations at the Utter Bar, shall pay no more for their admission into the Society of Lincoln's Inne, than xiii$^{s}$ iiii$^{d}$, though all utter-barristers of any other Inne of Chancery (excepting Thavyes Inne) should pay xx$^{s}$, and that every inner-barrister of this house, who hath mooted here one vacation at the Inner Bar, should pay for his admission into this House but xx$^{s}$, those of other houses (excepting Thavyes Inne) paying xxvi$^{s}$ viii$^{d}$."

[22] The 'De Laudibus' was written in Latin; but for the convenience of readers not familiar with that classic tongue, the quotations from the treatise are given from Robert Mulcaster's English version.

The subordinate seminaries of Gray's Inn, in Dugdale's time, were Staple Inn and Barnard's Inn. Originally the Exchange of the London woolen merchants, Staple Inn was a law-school as early as Henry V's time. It is probable that Bernard's Inn became an academy for law-students in the reign of Henry VI.

*Chapter 34*

# LAWYERS AND GENTLEMEN

Thus planted in the fourteenth century beyond the confines of the city, and within easy access of Westminster Hall, the Inns of Court and Chancery formed an university, which soon became almost as powerful and famous as either Oxford or Cambridge. For generations they were spoken of collectively as the law-university, and though they were voluntary societies—in their nature akin to the club-houses of modern London—they adopted common rules of discipline, and an uniform system of instruction. Students flocked to them in abundance; and whereas the students of Oxford and Cambridge were drawn from the plebeian ranks of society, the scholars of the law-university were almost invariably the sons of wealthy men and had usually sprung from gentle families. To be a law-student was to be a stripling of quality. The law university enjoyed the same patrician *prestige* and *éclat* that now belong to the more aristocratic houses of the old universities.

Noblemen sent their sons to it in order that they might acquire the style and learning and accomplishments of polite society. A proportion of the students were encouraged to devote themselves to the study of the law and to attend sedulously the sittings of Judges in Westminster Hall; but the majority of well-descended boys who inhabited the Inns of Chancery were heirs to good estates, and were trained to become their wealth rather than to increase it—to perfect themselves in graceful arts, rather than to qualify themselves to hold briefs. The same was the case in the Inns of Court, which were so designated—not because they prepared young men to rise in courts of law, but because they taught them to shine in the palaces of kings. It is a mistake to suppose that the Inns of Court contain at the present time a larger proportion of idle members, who have no intention to practise at the bar, than they contained under the Plantagenets and Tudors. On the contrary, in the fourteenth and fifteenth centuries, the number of Templars who merely played at being lawyers, or were lawyers only in name, was actually as well as relatively greater than the merely *nominal* lawyers of the Temple at the present time. For several generations, and for two centuries after Sir John Fortescue wrote the 'De Laudibus,' the Inns-of-Court man was more busied in learning to sing than in learning to argue a law cause, more desirous to fence with a sword than to fence with logic.

"Notwithstanding," runs Mulcaster's translation of the 'De Laudibus,'[23] "the same lawes are taught and learned, in a certaine place of publique or common studie, more convenient and apt for attayninge to the knowledge of them, than any other university. For theyr place of studie is situate nigh to the Kinges Courts, where the same lawes are pleaded and argued, and judgements by the same given by judges, men of gravitie, auncient in yeares, perfit and graduate in the same lawes. Wherefore, euerie day in court, the students in those lawes resorte by great numbers into those courts wherein the same lawes are read and taught, as it were in common schooles. This place of studie is far betweene the place of the said courts and the cittie of London, which of all thinges necessarie is the plentifullest of all cities and townes of the realme. So that the said place of studie is not situate within the cittie, where the confluence of people might disturb the quietnes of the studentes, but somewhat severall in the suburbes of the same cittie, and nigher to the saide courts, that the studentes may dayelye at their pleasure have accesse and recourse thither without weariness."

Setting forth the condition and pursuits of law-students in his day, Sir John Fortesque continues; "For in these greater inns, there can no student bee mayntayned for lesse expenses by the yeare than twentye markes. And if hee have a servaunt to wait uppon him, as most of them have, then so much the greater will his charges bee. Nowe, by reason of this charge, the children onely of noblemenne doo studye the lawes in those innes. For the poore and common sorte of the people are not able to bear so great charges for the exhibytion of theyr chyldren. And Marchaunt menne can seldome finde in theyr heartes to hynder theyr merchaundise with so greate yearly expenses. And it thus falleth out that there is scant anye man founde within the realme skilfull and cunning in the lawes, except he be a gentleman borne, and come of noble stocke. Wherefore they more than any other kinde of men have a speciall regarde to their nobility, and to the preservation of their honor and fame. And to speake upryghtlye, there is in these greater innes, yea, and in the lesser too, beside the studie of the lawes, as it were an university or schoole of all commendable qualities requisite for noble men. There they learn to sing, and to exercise themselves in all kinde of harmonye. There also they practice daunsing, and other noblemen's pastimes, as they use to do, which are brought up in the king's house. On the working dayes, the most of them apply themselves to the studye of the lawe, and on the holye dayes to the studye of holye Scripture;[24] and out of the tyme of divine service, to the reading of Chronicles. For there indeede are vertues studied, and vices exiled. So that, for the endowment of vertue, and abandoning of vice, Knights and

---

[23] This charming book was written during the author's exile, which began in 1463.

[24] This passage is one of several passages in Pre-reformation English literature which certify that the Bible was much more widely and carefully read by lettered and studious layman, in times prior to the rupture between England and Rome, than many persons are aware, and some violent writers like to acknowledge.

Barrons, with other states and noblemen of the realme, place their children in those innes, though they desire not to have them learned in the lawes, nor to lieue by the practice thereof, but onely uppon their father's allowance. Scant at anye tyme is there heard among them any sedition, chyding, or grudging, and yet the offenders are punished with none other payne, but onely to bee amooved from the compayne of their fellowshippe. Which punishment they doo more feare than other criminall offendours doo feare imprisonment and yrons: For hee that is once expelled from anye of those fellowshippes is never received to bee a felowe in any of the other fellowshippes. And so by this means there is continuall peace; and their demeanor is lyke the behaviour of such as are coupled together in perfect amytie."

Any person familiar with the Inns of Court at the present time will see how closely the law-colleges of Victoria's London resemble in many important particulars the law-colleges of Fortescue's period. After the fashion of four centuries since young men are still induced to enter them for the sake of honorable companionship, good society, and social prestige, rather than for the sake of legal education. After the remarks already made with regard to musical lawyers in a previous section of this work, it is needless to say that Inns of Court men are not remarkable for their application to vocal harmony; but the younger members are still remarkable for the zeal with which they endeavor to master the accomplishments which distinguish men of fashion and tone. If the nominal (sometimes they are called 'ornamental') barristers of the fifteenth century liked to read the Holy Scriptures, the young lawyers of the nineteenth century are no less disposed to read their Bibles critically, and argue as to the merits of Bishop Colenso and his opponents. Moreover, the discipline described by Fortescue is still found sufficient to maintain order in the inns.

Writing more than a century after Fortescue, Sir John Ferne, in his 'Blazon of Gentrie, the Glory of Generosity, and the Lacy's Nobility,' observes: "Nobleness of blood, joyned with virtue, compteth the person as most meet to the enterprize of any public service; and for that cause it was not for nought that our antient governors in this land, did with a special foresight and wisdom provide, that none should be admitted into the Houses of Court, being seminaries sending forth men apt to the government of justice, except he were a gentleman of blood. And that this may seem a truth, I myself have seen a kalendar of all those which were together in the society of one of the same houses, about the last year of King Henry the Fifth, with the armes of their House and family marshalled by their names; and I assure you, the self same monument doth both approve them all to be gentlemen of perfect descents and also the number of them much less than now it is, being at that time in one house scarcely three score."[25]

[25] Pathetically deploring the change wrought by time, Ferne also observes of the Inns of Court,—"Pity to see the same places, through the malignity of the times, and the negligence of those which should have had care to the same, been altered quite from their first institution."

This passage from an author who delighted to magnify the advantages of generous descent, has contributed to the very general and erroneous impression that until comparatively recent times the members of the English bar were necessarily drawn from the highest ranks of society; and several excellent writers on the antiquities of the law have laid aside their customary caution and strengthened Ferne's words with inaccurate comment.

Thus Pearce says of the author of the 'Glory of Generositie'—"He was one of the advocates for excluding from the Inns of Court all who were not 'a gentleman by blood,' according to the ancient rule mentioned by Fortescue, which seems to have been disregarded in Elizabeth's time." Fortescue nowhere mentions any such rule, but attributes the aristocratic character of the law-colleges to the high cost of membership. Far from implying that men of mean extraction were excluded by an express prohibition, his words justify the inference that no such rule existed in his time.

Though Inns-of-Court men were for many generations gentlemen by birth almost without a single exception, it yet remains to be proved that plebeian birth at any period disqualified persons for admission to the law-colleges. If such a restriction ever existed it had disappeared before the close of the fifteenth century—a period not favorable to the views of those who were most anxious to remove the barriers placed by feudal society between the gentle and the vulgar. Sir John More (the father of the famous Sir Thomas) was a Judge in the King's Bench, although his parentage was obscure; and it is worthy of notice that he was a successful lawyer of Fortescue's period. Lord Chancellor Audley was not entitled to bear arms by birth, but was merely the son of a prosperous yeoman. The lowliness of his extraction cannot have been any serious impediment to him, for before the end of his thirty-sixth year he was a sergeant. In the following century the inns received a steadily increasing number of students, who either lacked generous lineage or were the offspring of shameful love. For instance, Chief Justice Wray's birth was scandalous; and if Lord Ellesmere in his youth reflected with pride on the dignity of his father, Sir Richard Egerton, he had reason to blush for his mother. Ferne's lament over the loss of heraldric virtue and splendor, which the inns had sustained in his time, testifies to the presence of a considerable plebeian element amongst the members of the law-university. But that which was marked in the sixteenth was far more apparent in the seventeenth century. Scroggs's enemies were wrong in stigmatizing him as a butcher's son, for the odious chief justice was born and bred a gentleman, and Jeffreys could boast a decent extraction; but there is abundance of evidence that throughout the reigns of the Stuarts the inns swarmed with low-born adventurers. The career of Chief Justice Saunders, who, beginning as a "poor beggar boy," of unknown parentage, raised himself to the Chiefship of the King's Bench, shows how low an origin a judge might have in the seventeenth century. To mention the names of such men as Parker, King, Yorke, Ryder, and the Scotts, without placing beside them the names of such men as Henley, Harcourt, Bathurst, Talbot, Murray, and Erskine, would tend to create an erroneous impression that in the eighteenth century the bar ceased to comprise amongst its industrious members a large aristocratic element.

The number of barristers, however, who in that period brought themselves by talent and honorable perseverance into the foremost rank of the legal profession in spite of humble birth, unquestionably shows that ambitious men from the obscure middle classes were more frequently than in any previous century found pushing their fortunes in Westminster Hall. Lord Macclesfield was the son of an attorney whose parents were of lowly origin, and whose worldly means were even lower than their ancestral condition. Lord Chancellor King's father was a grocer and salter who carried on a retail business at Exeter; and in his youth the Chancellor himself had acted as his father's apprentice—standing behind the counter and wearing the apron and sleeves of a grocer's servitor. Philip Yorke was the son of a country attorney who could boast neither wealth nor gentle descent. Chief Justice Ryder was the son of a mercer whose shop stood in West Smithfield, and grandson of a dissenting minister, who, though he bore the name, is not known to have inherited the blood of the Yorkshire Ryders. Sir William Blackstone was the fourth son of a silkman and citizen of London. Lords Stowell and Eldon were the children of a provincial tradesman. The learned and good Sir Samuel Romilly's father was Peter Romilly, jeweller, of Frith Street, Soho. Such were the origins of some of the men who won the prizes of the law in comparatively recent times. The present century has produced an even greater number of barristers who have achieved eminence, and are able to say with honest pride that they are the *first* gentlemen mentioned in their pedigrees; and so thoroughly has the bar become an open profession, accessible to all persons[26] who have the means of gentlemen, that no barrister at the present time would have the bad taste or foolish hardihood to express openly his regret that the members of a liberal profession should no longer pay a hurtful attention to illiberal distinctions.

According to Fortescue, the law-students belonging at the same time to the Inns of Court and Chancery numbered *at least* one thousand eight hundred in the fifteenth century; and it may be fairly inferred from his words that their number considerably exceeded two thousand. To each of the ten Inns of Chancery the author of the 'De Laudibus' assigns "an hundred students at the least, and to some of them a much greater number;" and he says that the least populous of the four Inns of Court contained "two hundred students or thereabouts." At the present time the number of barristers—together with Fellows of the College of Advocates, and certificated special pleaders and conveyancers not at the bar—is shown by the Law List for 1866 to be somewhat more

---

[26] It is not unusual now-a-days to see on the screened list of students about to be called to the bar the names of gentlemen who have caused themselves to be described in the quasi-public lists as the sons of tradesmen. Some few years since a gentleman who has already made his name known amongst juniors, was thus 'screened'in the four halls as the son of a petty tradesman in an obscure quarter of London; and assuming that his conduct was due to self-respect and affectionate regard for his parent, it seemed to most observers that the young lawyer, in thus frankly stating his lowly origin, acted with spirit and dignity. It may be that years hence this highly-accomplished gentleman will, like Lord Tenterden and Lord St. Leonards (both of whom were the sons of honest but humble tradesmen), see his name placed upon the roll of England's hereditary noblesse.

than 4800.[27] Even when it is borne in mind how much the legal business of the whole nation has necessarily increased with the growth of our commercial prosperity—it being at the same time remembered, upon the other hand, how many times the population of the country has doubled itself since the wars of the Roses—few persons will be of opinion that the legal profession, either by the number of its practitioners or its command of employment, is a more conspicuous and prosperous power at the present time than it was in the fifteenth century.

Ferne was by no means the only gentleman of Elizabethan London to deplore the rapid increase in the number of lawyers, and to regret the growing liberality which encouraged—or rather the national prosperity which enabled—men of inferior parentage to adopt the law as a profession. In his address on Mr. Clerke's elevation to the dignity of a sergeant, Lord Chancellor Hatton, echoing the common complaint concerning the degradation of the law through the swarms of plebeian students and practitioners, observed—"Let not the dignitie of the lawe be geven to men unmeete. And I do exhorte you all that are heare present not to call men to the barre or the benches that are so unmeete. I finde that there are now more at the barre in one house than there was in all the Innes of Court when I was a younge man." Notwithstanding the Chancellor's earnest statement of his personal recollection of the state of things when he was a young man, there is reason to think that he was quite in error in thinking that lawyers had increased so greatly in number. From a MS. in Lord Burleigh's collection, it appears that in 1586 the number of law-students, resident during term, was only 1703—a smaller number than that which Fortescue computed the entire population of the London law-students, at a time when civil war had cruelly diminished the number of men likely to join an aristocratic university. Sir Edward Coke estimated the roll of Elizabethan law-students at one thousand, half their number in Fortescue's time. Coke, however, confined his attention in this matter to the Students of Inns of Court, and paid no attention to Inns of Chancery. Either Hatton greatly exaggerated the increase of the legal working profession; or in previous times the proportion of law-students who never became barristers greatly exceeded those who were ultimately called to the bar.

Something more than a hundred years later, the old cry against the low-born adventurers, who, to the injury of the public and the degradation of the law, were said to overwhelm counsellors and solicitors of superior tone and pedigree, was still frequently heard in the coteries of disappointed candidates for employment in Westminster Hall, and on the lips of men whose hopes of achieving social distinction were likely to be frustrated so long as plebeian learning and energy were permitted to have free action. In his 'History of Hertfordshire' (published in 1700), Sir Henry Chauncey, Sergeant-at-Law, exclaims: "But now these mechanicks, ambitious of rule and government, often educate their sons

[27] Of this number about 2500 reside in or near London and maintain some apparent connexion with the Inns of Court. Of the remainder, some reside in Scotland, some in Ireland, some in the English provinces, some in the colonies; whilst some of them, although their names are still on the Law List, have ceased to regard themselves as members of the legal profession.

in these seminaries of law, whereby they overstock the profession, and so make it contemptible; whilst the gentry, not sensible of the mischief they draw upon themselves, but also upon the nation, prefer them in their business before their own children, whom they bereave of their employment, formerly designed for their support; qualifying their servants, by the profit of this profession, to purchase their estates, and by this means make them their lords and masters, whilst they lessen the trade of the kingdom, and cause a scarcity of husbandmen, workmen, artificers, and servants in the nation."

That the Inns of Court became less and less aristocratic throughout the seventeenth and eighteenth centuries there is no reason to doubt; but it may be questioned whether it was so overstocked with competent working members, as poor Sir Henry Chauncey imagined it. Describing the state of the inns some two generations later, Blackstone computed the number of law-students at about a thousand, perhaps slightly more; and he observes that in his time the merely *nominal* law-students were comparatively few. "Wherefore," he says, "few gentlemen now resort to the Inns of Court, but such for whom the knowledge of practice is absolutely necessary; such, I mean, as are intended for the profession; the rest of our gentry, (not to say our nobility also) having usually retired to their estates, or visited foreign kingdoms, or entered upon public life, without any instruction in the laws of the land, and indeed with hardly any opportunity of gaining instruction, unless it can be afforded to them in the universities."

The folly of those who lamented that men of plebeian rank were allowed to adopt the legal profession as a means of livelihood, was however exceeded by the folly of men of another sort, who endeavored to hide the humble extractions of eminent lawyers, under the ingenious falsehoods of fictitious pedigrees. In the last century, no sooner had a lawyer of humble birth risen to distinction, than he was pestered by fabricators of false genealogies, who implored him to accept their silly romances about his ancestry. In most cases, these ridiculous applicants hoped to receive money for their dishonest representations; but not seldom it happened that they were actuated by a sincere desire to protect the heraldic honor of the law from the aspersions of those who maintained that a man might fight his way to the woolsack, although his father had been a tender of swine. Sometimes these imaginative chroniclers, not content with fabricating a genealogical chart for a *parvenu* Lord Chancellor, insisted that he should permit them to write their lives in such a fashion, that their earlier experiences should seem to be in harmony with their later fortunes. Lord Macclesfield (the son of a poor and ill-descended country attorney), was traced by officious adulators to Reginald Le Parker, who accompanied Edward I., while Prince of Wales, to the Holy Land. In like manner a manufacturer of genealogies traced Lord Eldon to Sir Michael Scott of Balwearie. When one of this servile school of worshippers approached Lord Thurlow with an assurance that he was of kin with Cromwell's secretary Thurloe, the Chancellor, with bluff honesty, responded, "Sir, as Mr. Secretary Thurloe was, like myself, a Suffolk man, you have an excuse for your mistake. In the seventeenth century two Thurlows, who were in no way related to each other, flourished in Suffolk. One was Cromwell's secretary Thurloe, the other was Thurlow, the Suffolk carrier. I am descended from the carrier." Notwithstanding Lord Thurlow's frequent and consistent disavowals of pretension to any heraldic pedigree, his collateral descendants are credited in the 'Peerages' with a descent from an ancient family.

*Chapter 35*

# LAW-FRENCH AND LAW-LATIN

No circumstances of the Norman Conquest more forcibly illustrate the humiliation of the conquered people, than the measures by which the invaders imposed their language on the public courts of the country, and endeavored to make it permanently usurp the place of the mother-tongue of the despised multitude; and no fact more signally displays our conservative temper than the general reluctance of English society to relinquish the use of the French words and phrases which still tincture the language of parliament, and the procedures of Westminster Hall, recalling to our minds the insolent domination of a few powerful families who occupied our country by force, and ruled our forefathers with vigorous injustice.

Frenchmen by birth, education, sympathy, William's barons did their utmost to make England a new France: and for several generations the descendants of the successful invaders were no less eager to abolish every usage which could remind the vanquished race of their lost supremacy. French became the language of parliament and the council-chamber. It was spoken by the judges who dispensed justice in the name of a French king, and by the lawyers who followed the royal court in the train of the French-speaking judges. In the hunting-field and the lists no gentleman entitled to bear coat-armour deigned to utter a word of English: it was the same in Fives' Court and at the gambling-table. Schoolmasters were ordered to teach their pupils to construe from Latin into French, instead of into English; and young men of Anglo-Saxon extraction, bent on rising in the world by native talent and Norman patronage, labored to acquire the language of the ruling class and forget the accents of their ancestors. The language and usages of modern England abound with traces of the French of this period. To every act that obtained the royal assent during last session of parliament, the queen said "La reyne le veult." Every bill which is sent up from the Commons to the Lords, an officer of the lower house endorses with "Soit bailé aux Seigneurs;" and no bill is ever sent down from the Lords to the Commons until a corresponding officer of the upper house has written on its back, "Soit bailé aux Communes."

In like manner our parochial usages, local sports, and domestic games continually remind us of the obstinate tenacity with which the Anglo-Saxon race has preserved, and still preserves, the vestiges of its ancient subjection to a foreign yoke. The crier of a country town, in any of England's fertile provinces, never proclaims the loss of a yeoman's sporting-dog, the auction of a bankrupt dealer's stock-in-trade, or the impounding of a strayed cow, until he has commanded, in Norman-French, the attention of the sleepy rustics. The language of the stable and the kennel is rich in traces of Norman influence; and in backgammon, as played by orthodox players, we have a suggestive memorial of those Norman nobles, of whom Fortescue, in the 'De Laudibus' observes: "Neither had they delyght to hunt, and to exercise other sportes and pastimes, as dyce-play and the hand-ball, but in their own proper tongue."

In behalf of the Norman *noblesse* it should be borne in mind that their policy in this matter was less intentionally vexatious and insolent than it has appeared to superficial observers. In the great majority of causes the suitors were Frenchmen; and it was just as reasonable that they should like to understand the arguments of their counsel and judges, as it is reasonable for suitors in the present day to require the proceedings in Westminster Hall to be clothed in the language most familiar to the majority of persons seeking justice in its courts. If the use of French pleadings was hard on the one Anglo-Saxon suitor who demanded justice in Henry I.'s time, the use of English pleadings would have been equally annoying to the nine French gentlemen who appeared for the same purpose in the king's court. It was greatly to be desired that the two races should have one common language; and common sense ordained that the tongue of the one or the other race should be adopted as the national language. Which side therefore was to be at the pains to learn a new tongue? Should the conquerors labor to acquire Anglo-Saxon? or should the conquered be required to learn French? In these days the cultivated Englishmen who hold India by military force, even as the Norman invaders held England, by the right of might, settle a similar question by taking upon themselves the trouble of learning as much of the Asiatic dialects as is necessary for purposes of business. But the Norman barons were not cultivated; and for many generations ignorance was with them an affair of pride no less than of constitutional inclination.

Soon ambitious Englishmen acquired the new language, in order to use it as an instrument for personal advancement. The Saxon stripling who could keep accounts in Norman fashion, and speak French as fluently as his mother tongue, might hope to sell his knowledge in a good market. As the steward of a Norman baron he might negotiate between my lord and my lord's tenants, letting my lord know as much of his tenant's wishes, and revealing to the tenants as much of their lord's intentions as suited his purpose. Uniting in his own person the powers of interpreter, arbitrator, and steward, he possessed enviable opportunities and facilities for acquiring wealth. Not seldom, when he had grown rich, or whilst his fortunes were in the ascendant, he assumed a French name as well as a French accent; and having persuaded himself and his younger neighbors that he was a Frenchman, he in some cases bequeathed to his children an ample estate and a Norman pedigree. In certain causes in the law courts the agent (by whatever title known) who was a perfect master of the three languages (French, Latin, and English) had greatly the advantage over an opposing agent who could speak only French and Latin.

From the Conquest till the latter half of the fourteenth century the pleadings in courts of justice were in Norman-French; but in the 36 Ed. III., it was ordained by the king "that all plees, which be to be pleded in any of his courts, before any of his justices; or in his other places; or before any of his other ministers; or in the courts and places of any other lords within the realm, shall be pleded, shewed, and defended, answered, debated, and judged in the English tongue, and that they be entred and enrolled in Latine. And that the laws and customs of the same realm, termes, and processes, be holden and kept as they be, and have been before this time; and that by the antient termes and forms of the declarations no man be prejudiced; so that the matter of the action be fully shewed in the demonstration and in the writ." Long before this wise measure of reform was obtained by the urgent wishes of the nation, the French of the law courts had become so corrupt and unlike the language of the invaders, that it was scarcely more intelligible to educated natives of France than to most Englishmen of the highest rank. A jargon compounded of French and Latin, none save professional lawyers could translate it with readiness or accuracy; and whilst it unquestionably kept suitors in ignorance of their own affairs, there is reason to believe that it often perplexed the most skilful of those official interpreters who were never weary of extolling his lucidity and precision.

But though English lawyers were thus expressly forbidden in 1362 to plead in Law-French, they persisted in using the hybrid jargon for reports and treatises so late as George II.'s reign; and for an equal length of time they seized every occasion to introduce scraps of Law-French into their speeches at the bars of the different courts. It should be observed that these antiquarian advocates were enabled thus to display their useless erudition by the provisions of King Edward's act, which, while it forbade French *pleadings*, specially ordained the retention of French terms.

Roger North's essay 'On the study of the Laws' contains amusing testimony to the affection with which the lawyers of his day regarded their Law-French, and also shows how largely it was used till the close of the seventeenth century by the orators of Westminster Hall. "Here I must stay to observe," says the author, enthusiastically, "the necessity of a student's early application to learn the old Law-French, for these books, and most others of considerable authority, are delivered in it. Some may think that because the Law-French is no better than the old Norman corrupted, and now a deformed hotch-potch of the English and Latin mixed together, it is not fit for a polite spark to foul himself with; but this nicety is so desperate a mistake, that lawyer and Law-French are coincident; one will not stand without the other." So enamored was he of the grace and excellence of law-reporters' French, that he regarded it as a delightful study for a man of fashion, and maintained that no barrister would do justice to the law and the interests of his clients who did not season his sentences with Norman verbiage. "The law," he held, "is scarcely expressible properly in English, and when it is done, it must be *Françoise*, or very uncouth."

Edward III.'s measure prohibitory of French pleadings had therefore comparatively little influence on the educational course of law-students. The published reports of trials, known by the name of Year-Books, were composed in French, until the series terminated in the time of Henry VIII.; and so late as George II.'s reign, Chief Baron Comyn preferred such words as 'chemin,' 'dismes,' and 'baron and feme,' to such words as 'highway,' 'tithes,' 'husband and wife.' More liberal than the majority of his legal brethren, even as his enlightenment with regard to public affairs exceeded that of ordinary politicians of his time, Sir Edward Coke wrote his commentaries in English, but when he published them, he felt it right to soothe the alarm of lawyers by assuring them that his departure from ancient usage could have no disastrous consequences. "I cannot conjecture," he apologetically observes in his preface, "that the general communicating these laws in the English tongue can work any inconvenience."

Some of the primary text-books of legal lore had been rendered into English, and some most valuable treatises had been written and published in the mother tongue of the country; but in the seventeenth century no Inns-of-Court man could acquire an adequate acquaintance with the usages and rules of our courts and the decisions of past judges, until he was able to study the Year-Books and read Littleton in the original. To acquire this singular language—a *dead* tongue that cannot be said to have ever lived—was the first object of the law-student. He worked at it in his chamber, and with faltering and uncertain accents essayed to speak it at the periodic mootings in which he was required to take part before he could be called to the bar, and also after he had become an utter-barrister. In his 'Autobiography,' Sir Simonds D'Ewes makes mention in several places of his Law-French exercises (*temp.* James I.), and in one place of his personal story he observes, "I had twice mooted in Law-French before I was called to the bar, and several times after I was made an utter-barrister, in our open hall. Thrice also before I was of the bar, I argued the reader's cases at the Inns of Chancery publicly, and six times afterwards. And then also, being an utter-barrister, I had twice argued our Middle-Temple reader's case at the cupboard, and sat nine times in our hall at the bench, and argued such cases in English as had before been argued by young gentlemen or utter-barristers in Law-French bareheaded."

Amongst the excellent changes by which the more enlightened of the Commonwealth lawyers sought to lessen the public clamor of law-reform was the resolution that all legal records should be kept, and all writs composed, in the language of the country. Hitherto the law records had been kept in a Latin that was quite as barbarous as the French used by the reporters; and the determination to abolish a custom which served only to obscure the operations of justice and to confound the illiterate was hailed by the more intelligent purchasers of law as a notable step in the right direction. But the reform was by no means acceptable to the majority of the bar, who did not hesitate to stigmatize the measure as a dangerous innovation—which would prove injurious to learned lawyers and peace-loving citizens, although it might possibly serve the purposes of ignorant counsel and litigious 'lay gents.'[28] The legal literature of three generations following Charles I.'s execution abounds with contemptuous allusions to the 'English times' of Cromwell; the old-fashioned reporters, hugging their Norman-French and looking with suspicion on popular intelligence, were vehement in expressing their contempt for the prevalent misuse of the mother tongue. "I have," observes Styles, in the preface to his reports, "made these reports speak English; not that I believe that they will be thereby more generally useful, for I have always been and yet am of opinion, that that part of the Common Law which is in the English hath only occasioned the making of unquiet spirits contentiously knowing, and more apt to offend others than to defend themselves; but I have done it in obedience to authority, and to stop the mouths of such of this English age, who, though they be confessedly different in their minds and judgments, as the builders of Babel were in their language, yet do think it vain, if not impious, to speak or understand more than their own mother tongue." In like manner, Whitelock's uncle Bulstrode, the celebrated reporter, says of the second part of his reports, "that he had manny years since perfected the words in French, in which language he had desired it might have seen the light, being most proper for it, and most convenient for the professors of the law."

The restorers who raised Charles II to his father's throne, lost no time in recalling Latin to the records and writs; and so gladly did the reporters and the practising counsel avail themselves of the reaction in favor of discarded usages, that more Law-French was written and talked in Westminster Hall during the time of the restored king, than had been penned and spoken throughout the first fifty years of the seventeenth century.

The vexatious and indescribably absurd use of Law-Latin in records, writs, and written pleadings, was finally put an end to by statute 4 George II. c. 26; but this bill, which discarded for legal processes a cumbrous and harsh language, that was alike unmusical and inexact, and would have been utterly unintelligible to a Roman gentleman of the Augustan period, did not become law without much opposition from some of the authorities of Westminster Hall. Lord Raymond, Chief Justice of the King's Bench, spoke in accordance with opinions that had many supporters on the bench and at the bar, when he expressed his warm disapprobation of the proposed measure, and sarcastically observed "that if the bill paused, the law might likewise be translated into Welsh, since many in Wales understood not English." In the same spirit Sir Willian Blackstone and more recent authorities have lamented the loss of Law-Latin. Lord Campbell, in the

[28] In the seventeenth century, lawyers usually called their clients and the non-legal public 'Lay Gents.'

'Chancellors,' records that he "heard the late Lord Ellenborough from the bench regret the change, on the ground that it had had the tendency to make attorneys illiterate."

The sneer by which Lord Raymond endeavored to cast discredit on the proposal to abolish Law-Latin, was recalled after the lapse of many years by Sergeant Heywood, who forthwith acted upon it as though it originated in serious thought. Whilst acting as Chief Justice of the Carmarthen Circuit, the sergeant was presiding over a trial of murder, when it was discovered that neither the prisoner, nor any member of the jury, could understand a word of English; under these circumstances it was suggested that the evidence and the charge should be explained *verbatim*, to the prisoner and his twelve triers by an interpreter. To this reasonable petition that the testimony should be presented in a Welsh dress, the judge replied that, "to accede to the request would be to repeal the act of parliament, which required that all proceedings in courts of justice should be in the English tongue, and that the case of a trial in Wales, in which the prisoner and jury should not understand English, was a case not provided for, although the attention of the legislature had been called to it by that great judge Lord Raymond." The judge having thus decided, the inquiry proceeded—without the help of an interpreter—the counsel for the prosecution favoring the jury with an eloquent harangue, no single sentence of which was intelligible to them; a series of witnesses proving to English auditors, beyond reach of doubt, that the prisoner had deliberately murdered his wife; and finally the judge instructing the jury, in language which was as insignificant to their minds as the same quantity of obsolete Law-French would have been, that it was their duty to return a verdict of 'Guilty.' Throwing themselves into the humor of the business, the Welsh jurymen, although they were quite familiar with the facts of the case, acquitted the murderer, much to the encouragement of many wretched Welsh husbands anxious for a termination of their matrimonial sufferings.

*Chapter 36*

# STUDENT LIFE IN OLD TIME

From statements made in previous chapters, it may be seen that in ancient times the Law University was a far more conspicuous feature of the metropolis than it has been in more modern generations. In the fifteenth century the law students of the town numbered about two thousand; in Elizabethan London their number fluctuated between one thousand and two thousand; towards the close of Charles II.'s reign they were probably much less than fifteen hundred; in the middle of the eighteenth century they do not seem to have much exceeded one thousand. Thus at a time when the entire population of the capital was considerably less than the population of a third-rate provincial town of modern England, the Inns of Court and Chancery contained more undergraduates than would be found on the books of the Oxford Colleges at the present time.

Henry VIII's London looked to the University for mirth, news, trade. During vacations there was but little stir in the taverns and shops of Fleet Street; haberdashers and vintners sate idle; musicians starved; and the streets of the capital were comparatively empty when the students had withdrawn to spend their holidays in the country. As soon as the gentlemen of the robe returned to town all was brisk and merry again. As the town grew in extent and population, the social influence of the university gradually decreased; but in Elizabethan London the *éclat* of the inns was at its brightest, and during the reigns of Elizabeth's two nearest successors London submitted to the Inns-of-Court men as arbiters of all matters pertaining to taste—copying their dress, slang, amusements, and vices. The same may be said, with less emphasis, of Charles II.'s London. Under the 'Merry Monarch' theatrical managers were especially anxious to please the inns, for they knew that no play would succeed which the lawyers had resolved to damn—that no actor could achieve popularity if the gallants of the Temple combined to laugh him down—that no company of performers could retain public favor when they had lost the countenance of law-colleges. Something of this power the young lawyers retained beyond the middle of the last century. Fielding and Addison caught with nervous eagerness the critical gossip of the Temple and Chancery Lane, just as Congreve and Wycherly, Dryden and Cowley had caught it in previous generations. Fashionable tradesmen and caterers for the amusement of the public made their engagements and speculations with reference to the opening of term. New plays, new books, new toys were never offered for the first time to London purchasers when the lawyers were away. All that the 'season' is to modern London, the 'term' was to old London, from the accession of Henry VIII to the death of George II, and many of the existing commercial and fashionable arrangements of a London 'season' maybe traced to the old-world 'term.'

In olden time the influence of the law-colleges was as great upon politics as upon fashion. Sheltering members of every powerful family in the country they were centres of political agitation, and places for the secret discussion of public affairs. Whatever plot was in course of incubation, the inns invariably harbored persons who were cognisant of the conspiracy. When faction decided on open rebellion or hidden treason, the agents of the malcontent leaders gathered together in the inns, where, so long as they did not rouse the suspicions of the authorities and maintained the bearing of studious men, they could hire assassins, plan risings, hold interviews with fellow-conspirators, and nurse their nefarious projects into achievement. At periods of danger therefore spies were set to watch the gates of the hostels, and mark who entered them. Governments took great pains to ascertain the secret life of the collegians. A succession of royal directions for the discipline of the inns under the Tudors and Stuarts points to the jealousy and constant apprehensions with which the sovereigns of England long regarded those convenient lurking-places for restless spirits and dangerous adversaries. Just as the Student-quarter of Paris is still watched by a vigilant police, so the Inns of Court were closely watched by the agents of Wolsey and Thomas Cromwell, of Burleigh and Buckingham. During the troubles and contentions of Elizabeth's reign Lord Burleigh was regularly informed concerning the life of the inns, the number of students in and out of town, the parentage and demeanor of new members, the gossip of the halls, and the rumors of the cloisters. In proportion as the political temper and action of the lawyers were deemed matters of high importance, their political indiscretions and misdemeanors were promptly and sometimes ferociously punished. An idle joke over a pot of wine sometimes cost a witty barrister his social rank and his ears. To promote a wholesome fear of authority in the colleges, government every now and then flogged a student at the cart's tail in Holborn, or pilloried a sad apprentice of the law in Chancery Lane, or hung an ancient on a gibbet at the entrance of his inn.

The anecdote-books abound with good stories that illustrate the political excitability of the inns in past times, and the energy with which ministers were wont to repress the first manifestations of insubordination. Rushworth records the adventure of four young men of Lincoln's Inn who throw aside prudence and sobriety in a tavern hard by their inn, and drank to "the confusion of the Archbishop of Canterbury." The next day, full of penitence and head-ache, the offenders were brought before the council, and called to account for their scandalous conduct; when they would have fared ill had not the Earl of Dorset done them good service, and privately instructed them to say in their defence, that they had not drunk confusion to the archbishop but to the archbishop's *foes*. On this ingenious representation, the council supposed that the drawer—on whose information the proceedings were taken—had failed to catch the last word of the toast; and consequently the young gentlemen were dismissed with a 'light admonition,' much to their own surprise and the informer's chagrin.

Of the political explosiveness of the inns in Charles II.'s time Narcissus Luttrell gives the following illustration in his diary, under date June 15 and 16, 1681:—"The 15th was a project sett on foot in Grayes Inn for the carrying on an addresse for thankes to his majestie for his late declaration; and was moved that day in the hall by some at dinner, and being (as is usual) sent to the barre messe to be by them recommended to the bench, but was rejected both by bench and barr; but the other side seeing they could doe no good this way, they gott about forty together and went to the tavern, and there subscribed the said addresse in the name of the truelye loyall gentlemen of Grayes Inn. The chief sticklers for the said addition were Sir William Seroggs, Jun., Robert Fairebeard, Capt. Stowe, Capt. Radcliffe, one Yalden, with others, to the number of 40 or thereabouts; many of them sharpers about town, with clerks not out of their time, and young men newly come from the university. And some of them went the 17th to Windsor, and presented the said addresse to his majesty: who was pleasd to give them his thanks and confer (it is said) knighthood on the said Mr. Fairebeard; this proves a mistake since. The 16th was much such another addresse carried on in the Middle Temple, where several Templars, meeting about one or two that afternoon in the hall for that purpose, they began to debate it, but they were opposed till the hall began to fill; and then the addressers called for Mr. Montague to take the chaire; on which a poll was demanded, but the addressers refused it, and carried Mr. Montague and sett him in the chaire, and the other part pulled him out, on which high words grew, and some blows were given; but the addressers seeing they could doe no good with it in the hall, adjourned to the Divill Tavern, and there signed the addresse; the other party kept in the hall, and fell to protesting against such illegall and arbitrary proceedings, subscribing their names to a greater number than the addressers were, and presented the same to the bench as a grievance."

Like the King's Head Tavern, which stood in Chancery Lane, the Devil Tavern, in Fleet Street, was a favorite house with the Caroline Lawyers. Its proximity to the Temple secured the special patronage of the templars, whereas the King's Head was more frequented by Lincoln's-Inn men; and in the tavern-haunting days of the seventeenth century those two places of entertainment saw many a wild and dissolute scene. Unlike Chattelin, who endeavored to satisfy his guests with delicate repasts and light wines, the hosts of the Devil and the King's Head provided the more substantial fare of old England, and laid themselves out to please roysterers who liked pots of ale in the morning, and were wont to drink brandy by the pint as the clocks struck midnight. Nando's, the house where Thurlow in his student-period used to hold nightly disputations with all comers of suitable social rank, was an orderly place in comparison with these more venerable hostelries; and though the Mitre, Cock, and Rainbow have witnessed a good deal of deep drinking, it may be questioned if they, or any other ancient taverns of the legal quarter, encouraged a more boisterous and reckless revelry than that which constituted the ordinary course of business at the King's Head and the Devil.

In his notes for Jan. 1681-2, Mr. Narcissus Luttrell observes—"The 13th, at night, some young gentlemen of the Temple went to the King's Head Tavern, Chancery Lane, committing strange outrages there, breaking windowes, &c., which the watch hearing of came to disperse them; but they sending for severall of the watermen with halberts that attend their comptroller of the revells, were engaged in a desperate riott, in which one of the watchmen was run into the body and lies very ill; but the watchmen secured one or two of the watermen." Eleven years later the diarist records: "Jan. 5. One Batsill, a young gentleman of the Temple, was committed to Newgate for wounding a captain at the Devil Tavern in Fleet Street on Saturday last." Such ebullitions of manly spirit—ebullitions pleasant enough to the humorist, but occasionally productive of very disagreeable and embarrassing consequences—were not uncommon in the neighborhood of the Inns of Court whilst the Christmas revels were in progress.

A tempestuous, hot-blooded, irascible set were these gentlemen of the law-colleges, more zealous for their own honor than careful for the feelings of their neighbors. Alternately warring with sharp tongues, sharp pens, and sharp swords they went on losing their tempers, friends, and lives in the most gallant and picturesque manner imaginable. Here is a nice little row which occurred in the Middle Temple Hall during the days of good Queen Bess! "The records of the society," says Mr. Foss, "preserve an account of the expulsion of a member, which is rendered peculiarly interesting in consequence of the eminence to which the delinquent afterwards attained as a statesman, a poet, and a lawyer. Whilst the masters of the bench and other members of the society were sitting quietly at dinner on February 9, 1597-8, John Davis came into the hall with his hat on his head, and attended by two persons armed with swords, and going up to the barrister's table, where Richard Martin was sitting, he pulled out from under his gown a cudgel 'quem vulgariter vocant a bastinado,' and struck him over the head repeatedly, and with so much violence that the bastinado was shivered into many pieces. Then retiring to the bottom of the hall, he drew one of his attendants' swords and flourished it over his head, turning his face towards Martin, and then turning away down the water steps of the Temple, threw himself into a boat. For this outrageous act he was immediately disbarred and expelled the house, and deprived forever of all authority to speak or consult in law. After nearly four years' retirement he petitioned the benchers for his restoration, which they accorded on October 30, 1601, upon his making a public submission in the hall, and asking pardon of Mr. Martin, who at once generously forgave him." Both the principals in this scandalous outbreak and subsequent reconciliation became honorably known in their profession—Martin rising to be a Recorder of London and a member of parliament; and Davies acting as Attorney General of Ireland and Speaker of the Irish parliament, and achieving such a status in politics and law that he was appointed to the Chief Justiceship of England, an office, however, which sudden death prevented him from filling.

Nor must it be imagined that gay manners and lax morals were less general amongst the veterans than amongst the youngsters of the bar. Judges and sergeants were quite as prone to levity and godless riot as students about to be called; and such was the freedom permitted by professional decorum that leading advocates habitually met their clients in taverns, and having talked themselves dry at the bars of Westminster Hall, drank themselves speechless at the bars of Strand taverns—ere they reeled again into their chambers. The same habits of uproarious self-indulgence were in vogue with the benchers of the inns, and the Doctors of Doctors' Commons. Hale's austerity was the exceptional demeanor of a pious man protesting against the wickedness of an impious age. Had it not been for the shortness of time that had elapsed since Algernon Sidney's trial and sentence, John Evelyn would have seen no reason for censuring the loud hilarity and drunkenness of Jeffreys and Withings at Mrs. Castle's wedding.

In some respects, however, the social atmosphere of the inns was far more wholesome in the days of Elizabeth, and for the hundred years following her reign, than it is at present. Sprung in most cases from legal families, the students who were educated to be working members of the bar lived much more under the observation of their older relations, and in closer intercourse with their mothers and sisters than they do at present. Now-a-days young Templars, fresh from the universities, would be uneasy and irritable under strict domestic control; and as men with beards and five-and-twenty years' knowledge of the world, they would resent any attempt to draw them within the lines of domestic control. But in Elizabethan and also in Stuart London, law-students were considerably younger than they are under Victoria.

Moreover, the usage of the period trained young men to submit with cheerfulness to a parental discipline that would be deemed intolerable by our own youngsters. During the first terms of their eight, seven, or at least six years of pupilage, until they could secure quarters within college walls, students frequently lodged in the houses or chambers of near relations who were established in the immediate vicinity of the inns. A judge with a house in Fleet Street, an eminent counsel with a family mansion in Holborn, or an office-holder with commodious chambers in Chancery Lane, usually numbered amongst the members of his family a son, or nephew, or cousin who was keeping terms for the bar. Thus placed under the immediate superintendence of an elder whom he regarded with affection and pride, and surrounded by the wholesome interests of a refined domestic circle, the raw student was preserved from much folly and ill-doing into which he would have fallen had he been thrown entirely on his own resources for amusement.

The pecuniary means of Inns-of-Court students have not varied much throughout the last twelve generations. In days when money was scarce and very precious they of course lived on a smaller number of coins than they require in these days when gold and silver are comparatively abundant and cheap; but it is reasonable to suppose that in every period the allowances, on which the less affluent of them subsisted, represent the amounts on which young men of their respective times were just able to maintain the figure and style of independent gentlemen. The costly pageants and feasts of the inns in old days must not be taken as indicative of the pecuniary resources of the common run of students; for the splendor of those entertainments was mainly due to the munificence of those more wealthy members who by a liberal and even profuse expenditure purchased a right to control the diversions of the colleges. Fortescue, speaking of his own time, says: "There can no student bee mayntayned for lesse expenses by the yeare than twentye markes. And if hee haue a seruant to waite uppon him, as most of them haue, then so much the greater will his charges bee." Hence it appears that during the most patrician period of the law university, when wealthy persons were accustomed to maintain ostentatious retinues of servants, a law-student often had no private personal attendant. An ordinance shows that in Elizabethan London the Inns-of-Court men were waited upon by laundresses or bedmakers who served and took wages from several masters at the same time. It would be interesting to ascertain the exact time when the "laundress" was first introduced into the Temple. She certainly flourished in the days of Queen Bess; and Roger North's piquant description of his brother's laundress is applicable to many of her successors who are looking after their perquisites at the present date. "The housekeeper," says Roger, "had been formerly his lordship's laundress at the Temple, and knew well her master's brother so early as when he was at the writing-school. She *was a phthisical old woman, and could scarce crawl upstairs once a day*." This general employment of servants who were common to several masters would alone prove that the Inns-of-Court men in the seventeenth century felt it convenient to husband their resources, and exercise economy. Throughout that century sixty pounds was deemed a sufficient income for a Temple student; and though it was a scant allowance, some young fellows managed to push on with a still more modest revenue. Simonds D'Ewes had £60 per annum during his student course, and £100 a year on becoming an utter-barrister. "It pleased God also in mercy," he writes, "after this to ease me of that continual want or short stipend I had for about five years last past groaned under; for my father, immediately on my call to the bar, enlarged my former allowance with forty pounds more annually; so as, after this plentiful annuity of one hundred pounds was duly and quarterly paid me by him, I found myself easyd of so many cares and discontents as I may well account that the 27th day of June foregoing the first day of my outward happiness since the decease of my dearest mother." All things considered, a bachelor in James I.'s London with a clear income of £100 per annum was on the whole as well off for his time as a young barrister of the present day would be with an annual allowance of £250 or £300. Francis North, when a student, was allowed only

£60 per annum; and as soon as he was called and began to earn a little money, his parsimonious father reduced the stipend by £10; but, adds Roger North, "to do right to his good father, he paid him that fifty pounds a year as long as he lived, saying he would not discourage industry by rewarding it, when successful, with less." George Jeffreys, in his student-days, smarted under a still more galling penury, for he was allowed only £50 a year, £10 being for his clothes, and £40 for the rest of his expenditure. In the following century the nominal incomes of law-students rose in proportion as the wealth of the country increased and the currency fell in value. In George II.'s time a young Templar expected his father to allow him £150 a year, and on encouragement would spend twice that amount in the same time. Henry Fielding's allowance from General Fielding was £200 per annum; but as he said, with a laugh, he had too feeling and dutiful a nature to press an affectionate father for money which he was totally unable to pay. At the present time £150 per annum is about the smallest sum on which a law-student can live with outward decency; and £250 per annum the lowest amount on which a chamber barrister can live with suitable dignity and comfort. If he has to maintain the expenses of a distant circuit Mr. Briefless requires from £100 to £200 more. Alas! how many of Mr. Briefless's meritorious and most ornamental kind are compelled to shift on far less ample means! How many of them periodically repeat the jest of poor A——, who made this brief and suggestive official return to the Income Tax Commissioners—"I am totally dependent on my father, who allows me—nothing!"

*Chapter 37*

# READERS AND MOOTMEN

Romantic eulogists of the Inns of Court maintain that, as an instrument of education, the law-university was nearly perfect for many generations after its consolidation. That in modern time abuses have impaired its faculties and diminished its usefulness they admit. Some of them are candid enough to allow that, as a school for the systematic study of law, it is under existing circumstances a deplorably deficient machine; but they unite in declaring that there *was* a time when the system of the combined Colleges was complete and thoroughly efficacious. The more cautious of these eulogists decline to state the exact limits of the period when the actual condition of the university merited their cordial approval, but they concur in pointing to the years between the accession of Henry VII and the death of James I., as comprising the brightest days of its academical vigor and renown.

It is however worthy of observation that throughout the times when the legal learning and discipline of the colleges are described to have been admirable, the system and the students by no means won the approbation of those critical authorities who were best able to see their failings and merits. Wolsey was so strongly impressed by the faulty education of the barristers who practised before him, and more especially by their total ignorance of the principles of jurisprudence, that he prepared a plan for a new university which should be established in London, and should impart a liberal and exact knowledge of law. Had he lived to carry out his scheme it is most probable that the Inns of Court and Chancery would have become subsidiary and subordinate establishments to the new foundation. In this matter, sympathizing with the more enlightened minds of his age, Sir Nicholas Bacon was no less desirous than the great cardinal that a new law university should be planted in town, and he urged on Henry VIII the propriety of devoting a certain portion of the confiscated church property to the foundation and endowment of such an institution.

On paper the scheme of the old exercises and degrees looks very imposing, and those who delight in painting fancy pictures may infer from them that the scholastic order of the colleges was perfect. Before a young man could be called to the bar, he had under ordinary circumstances to spend seven or eight years in arguing cases at the Inns of Chancery, in proving his knowledge of law and Law-French at moots, in sharpening his wits at case-putting, in patient study of the Year-Books, and in watching the trials of Westminster Hall. After his call he was required to spend another period in study and academic exercise before he presumed to raise his voice at the bar; and in his progress to the highest rank of his profession he was expected to labor in educating the students of his house as assistant-reader, single-reader, double-reader. The gravest lawyers of every inn were bound to aid in the task of teaching the mysteries of the law to the rising generation.

The old ordinances assumed that the law-student was thirsting for a knowledge of law, and that the veterans were no less eager to impart it. During term law was talked in hall at dinner and supper, and after these meals the collegians argued points. "The cases were put" after the earlier repast, and twice or thrice a week moots were "brought in" after the later meal. The students were also encouraged to assemble towards the close of each day and practise 'case-putting' in their gardens and in the cloisters of the Temple or Lincoln's Inn. The 'great fire' of 1678-9 having destroyed the Temple Cloisters, some of the benchers proposed to erect chambers on the ground, to and fro upon which law-students had for generations walked whilst they wrangled aloud; but the Earl of Nottingham, recalling the days when young Heneage Finch used to put cases with his contemporary students, strangled the proposal at its birth, and Sir Christopher Wren subsequently built the Cloisters which may be seen at the present day.

But there is reason to fear that at a very early period in their history the Inns of Court began to pay more attention to certain outward forms of instruction than to instruction itself. The unbiassed inquirer is driven to suspect that 'case-putting' soon became an idle ceremony, and 'mooting' a mere pastime. Gentlemen ate heartily in the sixteenth and seventeenth centuries; and it is not easy to believe that immediately after a twelve o'clock dinner benchers were in the best possible mood to teach, or students in the fittest condition for learning. It is credible that these post-prandial exercitations were often enlivened by sparkling quips and droll occurrences; but it is less easy to believe that they were characterised by severe thought and logical exactness. So also with the after-supper exercises. The six o'clock suppers of the lawyers were no light repasts, but hearty meals of meat and bread, washed down by '*green pots*' of ale and wine. When 'the horn' sounded for supper, the student was in most cases better able to see the truth of knotty points than when in compliance with etiquette he bowed to the benchers, and asked if it was their pleasure to hear a moot. It seems probable that long before 'case-puttings' and 'mootings' were altogether disused, the old benchers were wont to wink mischievously at each other when they prepared to teach the boys, and that sometimes they would turn away from the proceedings of a moot with an air of disdain or indifference. The inquirer is not induced to rate more highly the intellectual effort of such exercises because the teachers refreshed their exhausted powers with bread and beer as soon as the arguments were closed.

When such men as Coke and Francis Bacon were the readers, the students were entertained with lectures of surpassing excellence; but it was seldom that such readers could be found. It seems also that at an early period men became readers, not because they had any especial aptitude for offices of instruction, or because they had some especial fund of information—but simply because it was their turn to read. Routine placed them in the pulpit for a certain number of weeks; and when they had done all that routine required of them, and had thereby qualified themselves for promotion to the rank of sergeant, they took their seats amongst the benchers and ancients with the resolution not to trouble themselves again about the intellectual progress of the boys.

Soon also the chief teacher of an Inn of Court became its chief feaster and principal entertainer; and in like manner his subordinates in office, such as assistant readers and readers elect, were required to put their hands into their pockets, and feed their pupils with venison and wine as well as with law and equity. It is amusing to observe how little Dugdale has to say about the professional duties of readers—and how much about their hospitable functions and responsibilities. Philip and Mary ordered that no reader of the Middle Temple should give away more than fifteen bucks during his readings; but so greatly did the cost of readers' entertainments increase in the following century, that Dugdale observes—"But the times are altered; there being few summer readers who, in half the time that heretofore a reading was wont to continue, spent so little as threescore bucks, besides red deer; some have spent fourscore, some an hundred."

Just as readers were required to spend more in hospitality, they were required to display less learning. Sound lawyers avoided election to the readers' chairs, leaving them to be filled by rich men who could afford to feast the nobility and gentry, or at least by men who were willing to purchase social *éclat* with a lavish outlay of money. Under Charles II the 'readings' were too often nothing better than scandalous exhibitions of mental incapacity: and having sunk into disrepute, they died out before the accession of James II.

The scandalous and beastly disorder of the Grand Day Feasts at the Middle Temple, during Francis North's tenure of the reader's office, was one of the causes that led to the discontinuance of Reader's Banquets at that house; and the other inns gladly followed the example of the Middle Temple in putting an end to a custom which had ceased to promote the dignity of the law. Of this feast, and his brother's part in it, Roger North says: "He (i.e., Francis North) sent out the officers with white staves (for so the way was) and a long list to invite; but he went himself to wait upon the Archbishop of Canterbury, Sheldon; for so also the ceremony required. The archbishop received him very honorably and would not part with him at the stairshead, as usually had been done; but, telling him he was no ordinary reader, went down, and did not part till he saw him past at his outward gate I cannot much commend the extravagance of the feasting used at these readings; and that of his lordship's was so terrible an example, that I think none hath ventured since to read publicly; but the exercise is turned into a revenue, and a composition is paid into the treasury of the society. Therefore one may say, as was said of Cleomenes, that, in this respect, his lordship was *ultimus herorum*, the last of the heroes. And the profusion of the best provisions, and wine, was to the worst of purposes—debauchery, disorder, tumult, and waste. I will give but one instance; upon the grand day, as it was called, a banquet was provided to be set upon the table, composed of pyramids, and smaller services in form. The first pyramid was at least four feet high, with stages one above another. The conveying this up to the table, through a crowd, that were in full purpose to overturn it, was no small work: but, with the friendly assistance of the gentlemen, it was set whole upon the table. But, after it was looked upon a little, all went, hand over hand, among the rout in the hall, and for the most part was trod under foot. The entertainment the nobility had out of this was, after they had tossed away the dishes, a view of the crowd in confusion, wallowing one over another, and contending for a dirty share of it."

It would, however, be unfair to the ancient exercises of 'case-putting' and 'mooting' not to bear in mind that by habituating successful barristers to take personal interest in the professional capabilities of students, they helped to maintain a salutary intercourse betwixt the younger and older members of the profession. So long as 'moots' lasted, it was the fashion with eminent counsel to accost students in Westminster Hall, and gossip with them about legal matters. In Charles II.'s time, such eminent barristers as Sir Geoffrey Palmer daily gave practical hints and valuable suggestions to students who courted their favor; find accurate legal scholars, such as old 'Index Waller,' would, under judicious treatment, exhibit their learning to boys ambitious of following in their steps. Chief Justice Saunders, during the days of his pre-eminence at the bar, never walked through Westminster Hall without a train of lads at his heels. "I have seen him," says Roger North, "for hours and half-hours together, before the court sat, stand at the bar, with an audience of students over against him, putting of cases, and debating so as suited their capacities, and encouraged their industry. And so in the Temple, he seldom moved without a parcel of youths hanging about him, and he merry and jesting with them."

Long after 'moots' had fallen into disuse, their influence in this respect was visible in the readiness of wigged veterans to extend a kindly and useful patronage to students. Even so late as the close of the last century, great black-letter lawyers used to accost students in Westminster Hall, and give them fair words, in a manner that would be misunderstood in the present day. Sergeant Hill—whose reputation for recondite legal erudition, resembled that of '*Index* Waller,' or Maynard, in the seventeenth century—once accosted John Scott, as the latter, in his student days, was crossing Westminster Hall. "Pray, young gentleman," said the black-letter lawyer, "do you think herbage and pannage rateable to the poor's rate?" "Sir," answered the future Lord Eldon, with a courteous bow to the lawyer, whom he knew only by sight, "I cannot presume to give any opinion, inexperienced and unlearned as I am, to a person of your great knowledge, and high character in the profession." "Upon my word," replied the sergeant, eyeing the young man with unaffected delight, "you are a pretty sensible young gentleman; I don't often meet with such. If I had asked Mr. Burgess, a young man upon our circuit, the question, he would have told me that I was an old fool. You are an extraordinary sensible young gentleman."

The period when 'readings,' 'mooting,' and 'case-putting' fell into disuse or contempt, is known with sufficient accuracy. Having noticed the decay of readings, Sir John Bramston writes, in Charles II.'s reign, "At this tyme readings are totally in all the Inns of Court layd aside; and to speak truth, with great reason, for it was a step at once to the dignity of a sergeant, but not soe now." Marking the time when moots became farcical forms, Roger North having stated that his brother Francis, when a student, was "an attendant (as well as exerciser) at the ordinary moots in the Middle Temple and at New Inn," goes on to say, "In those days, the moots were carefully performed, and it is hard to give a good reason (bad ones are prompt enough) why they are not so now." But it should be observed, that though for all practical purposes 'moots' and 'case-puttings' ceased in Charles II.'s time, they were not formally abolished. Indeed, they lingered on throughout the eighteenth century, and to the present time—when vestiges of them may still be observed in the usages and discipline of the Inns. Before the writer of this page was called to the bar by the Masters of the Society of Lincoln's Inn, he, like all other students of his time, had to go through the form of putting a case on certain days in the hall after dinner. The ceremony appeared to him alike ludicrous and interesting. To put his case, he was conducted by the steward of the inn to the top of the senior bar table, when the steward placed an open MS. book before him, and said, "Read that, sir;" whereupon this deponent read aloud something about "a femme sole," or some such thing, and was still reading the rest of the MS., kindly opened under his nose by the steward, when that worthy officer checked him suddenly, saying, "That will do, sir; you have *put* your case—and can sign the book." The book duly signed, this deponent bowed to the assembled barristers, and walked out of the hall, smiling as he thought how, by an ingenious fiction, he was credited with having put an elaborate case to a college of profound jurists, with having argued it before an attentive audience, and with having borne away the laurels of triumph. Recently this pleasant mockery of case-putting has been swept away.

In Roger North's 'Discourse on the Study of the Laws,' and 'Life of the Lord Keeper Guildford,' the reader may see with clearness the course of an industrious law-student during the latter half of the seventeenth century, and it differs less from the ordinary career of an industrious Temple-student in our time, than many recent writers on the subject think.

Under Charles II, James II, and William III the law-student was compelled to muster the barbarous Law-French; but the books which he was required to read were few in comparison with those of a modern Inns-of-Court man. Roger North mentions between twenty and thirty authors, which the student should read in addition to Year-Books and more recent reports; and it is clear that the man who knew with any degree of familiarity such a body of legal literature was a very erudite lawyer two hundred years since. But the student was advised to read this small library again and again, "common-placing" the contents of its volumes, and also "common-placing" all new legal facts. The utility and convenience of common-place books were more apparent two centuries since, than in our time, when books of reference are always published with good tables of contents and alphabetical indexes. Roger North held that no man could become a good lawyer who did not keep a common-place book. He instructs the student to buy for a common-place register "a good large paper book, as big as a church bible;" he instructs him how to classify the facts which should be entered in the work; and for a model of a lucid and thoroughly lawyer-like common-place book he refers "to Lincoln's Inn library, where the Lord Hale's common-place book is conserved, and that may be a pattern, *instar omnium*."

*Chapter 38*

# PUPILS IN CHAMBERS

But the most important part of an industrious law-student's labors in olden time, was the work of watching the practice of Westminster Hall. In the seventeenth century, the constant succession of political trials made the King's Bench Court especially attractive to students who were more eager for gossip than advancement of learning; but it was always held that the student, who was desirous to learn the law rather than to catch exciting news or hear exciting speeches, ought to frequent the Common Pleas, in which court the common law was said to be at home. At the Common Pleas, a student might find a seat vacant in the students' benches so late as ten o'clock; but it was not unusual for every place devoted to the accommodation of students in the Court of King's Bench, to be occupied by six o'clock, A.M. By dawn, and even before the sun had begun to break, students bent on getting good seats at the hearing of an important cause would assemble, and patiently wait in court till the judges made their appearance.

One prominent feature in the advocate's education must always be elocutionary practice. "Talk; if you can, to the point, but anyhow talk," has been the motto of Advocacy from time immemorial. Heneage Finch, who, like every member of his silver-tongued family, was an authority on matters pertaining to eloquence, is said to have advised a young student "to study all the morning and talk all the afternoon." Sergeant Maynard used to express his opinion of the importance of eloquence to a lawyer by calling law the "ars bablativa." Roger North observes—"He whose trade is speaking must not, whatever comes out, fail to speak, for that is a fault in the main much worse than impertinence." And at a recent address to the students of the London University, Lord Brougham urged those of his auditors, who intended to adopt the profession of the bar, to habituate themselves to talk about everything.

In past times law-students were proverbial for their talkativeness; and though the present writer has never seen any records of a Carolinian law-debating society, it is matter of certainty that in the seventeenth century the young students and barristers formed themselves into coteries, or clubs, for the practice of elocution and for legal discussions. The continual debates on 'mootable days,' and the incessant wranglings of the Temple cloisters, encouraged them to pay especial attention to such exercises. In Charles II.'s reign Pool's company, was a coterie of students and young barristers, who used to meet periodically for congenial conversation and debate. "There is seldom a time," says Roger North, speaking of this coterie, "but in every Inn of Court there is a studious, sober company that are select to each other, and keep company at meals and refreshments. Such a company did Mr. Pool find out, whereof Sergeant Wild was one, and every one of them proved eminent, and most of them are now preferred in the law; and Mr. Pool, at the latter end of his life, took such a pride in his company that he affected to furnish his chambers with their pictures." Amongst the benefits to be derived from such a club as that of which Mr. Pool was president, Roger North mentions "Aptness to speak;" adding: "for a man may be possessed of a book-case, and think he has it *ad unguem* throughout, and when he offers at it shall find himself at a loss, and his words will not be right and proper, or perhaps too many, and his expressions confused: *when he has once talked his case over, and, his company have tossed it a little to and fro, then he shall utter it more readily, with fewer words and much more force*."

These words make it clear that Mr. Pool's 'company' was a select 'law-debating society.' Far smaller as to number of members, something more festive in its arrangements, but not less bent on furthering the professional progress of its members, it was, some two hundred years since, all that the 'Hardwicke' and other similar associations are at the present.[29]

To such fraternities—of which the Inns of Court had several in the last century—Murray and Thurlow, Law and Erskine had recourse: and besides attending strictly professional clubs, it was usual for the students, of their respective times, to practise elocution at the coffee-houses and public spouting-rooms of the town. Murray used to argue as well as 'drink champagne' with the wits; Thurlow was the irrepressible talker of Nando's; Erskine used to carry his scarlet uniform from Lincoln's Inn Hall, to the smoke-laden atmosphere of Coachmakers' Hall, at which memorable 'discussion forum' Edward Law is known to have spoken in the presence of a closely packed assembly of politicians,

---

[29] The mention of 'the Hardwicke' brings a droll story to the writer's mind. Some few years since the members of that learned fraternity assembled at their customary plate of meeting—a large room in Anderton's Hotel, Fleet Street—to discuss a knotty point of law about anent Uses. The master of young men was strong; and amongst them—conspicuous for his advanced years, jovial visage, red nose, and air of perplexity—sate an old gentleman who was evidently a stranger to every lawyer present. Who was he? Who brought him? Was there any one in the room who knew him? Such were the whispers that floated about, concerning the portly old man, arrayed in blue coat and drab breeches and gaiters, who took his snuff in silence, and watched the proceedings with evident surprise and dissatisfaction. After listening to three speeches this antique, jolly stranger rose, and with much embarrassment addressed the chair. "Mr. President," he said—"excuse me; but may I ask,—is this 'The Convivial Rabbits?'" A roar of laughter followed this enquiry from a 'convivial rabbit,' who having mistaken the evening of the week, had wandered into the room in which his convivial fellow-clubsters had held a meeting on the previous evening. On receiving the President's assurance that the learned members of a law-debating society were not 'convivial rabbits,' the elderly stranger buttoned his blue coat and beat a speedy retreat.

idlers upon town, shop-men, and drunkards. Thither also Horne Tooke and Dunning used to adjourn after dining with Taffy Kenyon at the Chancery Lane eating-house, where the three friends were wont to stay their hunger for sevenpence halfpenny each. "Dunning and myself," Horne Tooke said boastfully, when he recalled these economical repasts, "were generous, for we gave the girl who waited on us a penny apiece; but Kenyon, who always knew the value of money, rewarded her with a halfpenny, and sometimes with a *promise*."

Notwithstanding the recent revival of lectures and the institution of examinations, the actual course of the law-student has changed little since the author of the 'Pleader's Guide,' in 1706, described the career of John Surrebutter, Esq., Special Pleader and Barrister-at-Law. The labors of 'pupils in chambers, are thus noticed by Mr. Surrebutter:—

> "And, better to improve your taste,
> Are by your parents' fondness plac'd
> Amongst the blest, the chosen few
> (Blest, if their happiness they knew),
> Who for three hundred guineas paid
> To some great master of the trade,
> Have at his rooms by *special* favor
> His leave to use their best endeavor,
> By drawing pleas from nine till four,
> To earn him twice three hundred more;
> And after dinner may repair
> To 'foresaid rooms, and then and there
> Have 'foresaid leave from five till ten,
> To draw th' aforesaid pleas again."

Continuing to describe his professional career, Mr. Surrebutter mentions certain facts which show that so late as the close of last century professional etiquette did not forbid special pleaders and barristers to curry favor with solicitors and solicitors' clerks by attentions which would now-a-days be deemed reprehensible. He says:—

> "Whoe'er has drawn a special plea
> Has heard of old Tom Tewkesbury,
> Deaf as a post, and thick as mustard,
> He aim'd at wit, and bawl'd and bluster'd
> And died a Nisi Prius leader—
> That genius was my special pleader—
> That great man's office I attended,
> By Hawk and Buzzard recommended
> Attorneys both of wondrous skill,

To pluck the goose and drive the quill.
Three years I sat his smoky room in,
Pens, paper, ink, and pounce consuming;
The fourth, when Epsom Day begun,
Joyful I hailed th' auspicious sun,
Bade Tewkesbury and Clerk adieu;
(Purification, eighty-two)
Of both I wash'd my hands; and though
With nothing for my cash to show,
But precedents so scrawl'd and blurr'd,
I scarce could read a single word,
Nor in my books of common-place
One feature, of the law could trace,
Save Buzzard's nose and visage thin,
And Hawk's deficiency of chin,
Which I while lolling at my ease
Was wont to draw instead of pleas.
My chambers I equipt complete,
Made friends, hired books, and gave to eat;
If haply to regale my friends on,
My mother sent a haunch of ven'son,
I most respectfully entreated
The choicest company to eat it;
*To wit*, old Buzzard, Hawk, and Crow;
*Item*, Tom Thornback, Shark, and Co.
Attorneys all as keen and staunch
As e'er devoured a client's haunch.
And did I not their clerks invite
To taste said ven'son hash'd at night?
For well I knew that hopeful fry
My rising merit would descry,
The same litigious course pursue,
And when to fish of prey they grew,
By love of food and contest led,
Would haunt the spot where once they fed.
Thus having with due circumspection
Formed my professional connexion,
My desks with precedents I strew'd,
Turned critic, danc'd, or penn'd an ode,
Suited the *ton*, became a free
And easy man of gallantry;
But if while capering at my glass,
Or toying with a favorite lass,
I heard the aforesaid Hawk a-coming,

Or Buzzard on the staircase humming,
At once the fair angelic maid
Into my coal-hole I convey'd;
At once with serious look profound,
Mine eyes commencing with the ground,
I seem'd like one estranged to sleep,
'And fixed in cogitation deep,'
Sat motionless, and in my hand I
Held my 'Doctrina Placitandi,'
And though I never read a page in't,
Thanks to that shrewd, well-judging agent,
My sister's husband, Mr. Shark,
Soon got six pupils and a clerk.
Five pupils were my stint, the other
I took to compliment his mother."

Having fleeced pupils, and worked as a special pleader for a time, Mr. Surrebutter is called to the bar; after which ceremony his action towards 'the inferior branch' of the profession is not more dignified than it was whilst he practised as a Special Pleader.

It appears that in Mr. Surrebutter's time (*circa* 1780) it was usual for a student to spend three whole years in the same pleader's chambers, paying three hundred guineas for the course of study. Not many years passed before students saw it was not to their advantage to spend so long a period with the same instructor, and by the end of the century the industrious student who could command the fees wherewith to pay for such special tuition, usually spent a year or two in a pleader's chambers, and another year or two in the chambers of an equity draughtsman, or conveyancer. Lord Campbell, at the opening of the present century, spent three years in the chambers of the eminent Special Pleader, Mr. Tidd, of whose learning and generosity the biographer of the Chancellors makes cordial and grateful acknowledgment. Finding that Campbell could not afford to pay a second hundred guineas for a second year's instruction, Tidd not only offered him the run of his chambers without payment, but made the young Scotchman take back the £105 which he had paid for the first twelve months.

In his later years Lord Campbell delighted to trace his legal pedigree to the great pleader and 'pupillizer' of the last century, Tom Warren. The chart ran thus: "Tom Warren had for pupil Sergeant Runnington, who instructed in the mysteries of special pleading the learned Tidd, who was the teacher of John Campbell." With honest pride and pleasant vanity the literary Chancellor maintained that he had given the genealogical tree another generation of forensic honor, as Solicitor General Dundas and Vaughan Williams, of the Common Pleas Bench, were his pupils.

Though Campbell speaks of *Tom Warren* as "the greater founder of the special pleading race," and maintains that "the voluntary discipline of the special pleader's office" was unknown before the middle of the last century, it is certain that the voluntary discipline of a legal instructor's office or chambers was an affair of frequent occurrence long before Warren's rise. Roger North, in his 'Discourse on the Study of the Laws,' makes no allusion to any such voluntary discipline as an ordinary feature of a law-student's career; but in his 'Life of Lord Keeper Guildford' he expressly informs us that he was a pupil in his brother's chambers. "His lordship," writes the biographer, "having taken that advanced post, and designing to benefit a relation (the Honorable Roger North), who was a student in the law, and kept him company, caused his clerk to put into his hands all his draughts, such as he himself had corrected, and after which conveyances had been engrossed, that, by a perusal of them, he might get some light into the formal skill of conveyancing. And that young gentleman instantly went to work, and first numbered the draughts, and then made an index of all the clauses, referring to that number and folio; so that, in this strict perusal and digestion of the various matters, he acquired, not only a formal style, but also apt precedents, and a competent notion of instruments of all kinds. And to this great condescension was owing that little progress he made, which afterwards served to prepare some matters for his lordship's own perusal and settlement." Here then is a case of a pupil in a barrister's chambers in Charles II.'s reign; and it is a case that suffers nothing from the fact that the teacher took no fee.

In like manner, John Trevor (subsequently Master of the Rolls and Speaker of the Commons) about the same time was "bred a sort of clerk in old Arthur Trevor's chamber, an eminent and worthy professor of the law in the Inner Temple." On being asked what might be the name of the boy with such a hideous squint who sate at a clerk's desk in the outer room, Arthur Trevor answered, "A kinsman of mine that I have allowed to sit here, to learn the knavish part of the law." It must be observed that John Trevor was not a clerk, but merely a "sort of a clerk" in his kinsman's chamber.

In the latter half of the seventeenth century, and in the earlier half of the eighteenth century, students who wished to learn the practice of the law usually entered the offices of attorneys in large practice. At that period, the division between the two branches of the profession was much less wide than it subsequently became; and no rule or maxim of professional etiquette forbade Inns-of-Court men to act as the subordinates of attorneys and solicitors. Thus Philip Yorke (Lord Hardwicke) in Queen Anne's reign acted as clerk in the office of Mr. Salkeld, an attorney residing in Brook Street, Holborn, whilst he kept his terms at the Temple; and nearly fifty years later, Ned Thurlow (Lord Thurlow), on leaving Cambridge, and taking up his residence in the Temple, became a pupil in the office of Mr. Chapman, a solicitor, whose place of business was in Lincoln's Inn. There is no doubt that it was customary for young men destined the bar thus to work in attorneys' offices; and they continued to do so without any sense of humiliation or thought of condescension, until the special pleaders superseded the attorneys as instructors.

# PART 8. MIRTH

*Chapter 39*

# WIT OF LAWYERS

No lawyer has given better witticisms to the jest-books than Sir Thomas More. Like all legal wits, he enjoyed a pun, as Sir Thomas Manners, the mushroom Earl of Rutland discovered, when he winced under the cutting reproof of his insolence, conveyed in the translation of 'Honores mutant mores'—*Honors change manners*. But though he would condescend to play with words as a child plays with shells on a sea-beach, he could at will command the laughter of his readers without having recourse to mere verbal antics. He delighted in what may be termed humorous mystification. Entering Bruges at a time when his leaving had gained European notoriety, he was met by the challenge of a noisy fellow who proclaimed himself ready to dispute with the whole world—or any other man—"in omni scibili et de quolibet ente." Accepting the invitation, and entering the lists in the presence of all the scholastic magnates of Bruges, More gravely inquired, "An averia carucæ capta in vetitonamio sint irreplegibilia?" Not versed in the principles and terminology of the common law of England, the challenger could only stammer and blush—whilst More's eye twinkled maliciously, and his auditors were convulsed with laughter.

Much of his humor was of the sort that is ordinarily called *quiet* humor, because its effect does not pass off in shouts of merriment. Of this kind of pleasantry he gave the Lieutenant of the Tower a specimen, when he said, with as much courtesy as irony, "Assure yourself I do not dislike my cheer; but whenever I do, then spare not to thrust me out of your doors!" Of the same sort were the pleasantries with which, on the morning of his execution, he with fine consideration for others strove to divert attention from the cruelty of his doom. "I see no danger," he observed, with a smile, to his friend Sir Thomas Pope, shaking his water-bottle as he spoke, "but that this man may live longer if it please the king." Finding in the craziness of the scaffold a good pretext for leaning in friendly fashion on his gaoler's arm, he extended his hand to Sir William Kingston, saying, "Master Lieutenant, I pray you see me safe up; for my coming down let me shift for myself." Even to the headsman he gave a gentle pleasantry and a smile from the block itself, as he put aside his beard so that the keen blade should not touch it. "Wait, my good friend, till I have removed my beard," he said, turning his eyes upwards to the official, "for it has never offended his highness."

His wit was not less ready than brilliant, and on one occasion its readiness saved him from a sudden and horrible death. Sitting on the roof of his high gate-house at Chelsea, he was enjoying the beauties of the Thames and the sunny richness of the landscape, when his solitude was broken by the unlooked-for arrival of a wandering maniac. Wearing the horn and badge of a Bedlamite, the unfortunate creature showed the signs of his malady in his equipment as well as his countenance. Having cast his eye downwards from the parapet to the foot of the tower, he conceived a mad desire to hurl the Chancellor from the flat roof. "Leap, Tom! leap!" screamed the athletic fellow, laying a firm hand on More's shoulder. Fixing his attention with a steady look, More said, coolly, "Let us first throw my little dog down, and see what sport that will be." In a trice the dog was thrown into the air. "Good!" said More, feigning delight at the experiment: "now run down, fetch the dog, and we'll throw him off again." Obeying the command, the dangerous intruder left More free to secure himself by a bar, and to summon assistance with his voice.

For a good end this wise and mirth-loving lawyer would play the part of a practical joker; and it is recorded that by a jest of the practical sort he gave a wholesome lesson to an old civic magistrate, who, at the Sessions of the Old Bailey, was continually telling the victims of cut-purses that they had only themselves to thank for their losses—that purses would never be cut if their wearers took proper care to retain them in their possession. These orations always terminated with, "I never lose *my* purse; cut-purses never take *my* purse; no, i'faith, because I take proper care of it." To teach his worship wisdom, and cure him of his self-sufficiency, More engaged a cut-purse to relieve the magistrate of his money-bag whilst he sat upon the bench. A story is recorded of another Old Bailey judge who became the victim of a thief under very ridiculous circumstances. Whilst he was presiding at the trial of a thief in the Old Bailey, Sir John Sylvester, Recorder of London, said incidentally that he had left his watch at home. The trial ended in an acquittal, the prisoner had no sooner gained his liberty than he hastened to the recorder's house, and sent in word to Lady Sylvester that he was a constable and had been sent from the Old Bailey to fetch her husband's watch. When the recorder returned home and found he had lost his watch, it is to be feared that Lady Sylvester lost her usual equanimity. *Apropos* of these stories Lord Campbell tells—how, at the opening period of his professional career, soon after the publication of his 'Nisi Prius Reports,' he on circuit successfully defended a prisoner charged with a criminal offence; and how, whilst the success of his advocacy was still quickening his pulses, he discovered that his late client, with whom he held a confidential conversation, had contrived to relieve him of his pocket-book, full of bank-notes. As soon as the presiding judge, Lord Chief Baron Macdonald, heard of the mishap of the reporting barrister, he exclaimed, "What! does Mr. Campbell think that no one is entitled to *take notes* in court except himself?"

By the urbane placidity which marked the utterance of his happiest speeches, Sir Nicholas Bacon often recalled to his hearers the courteous easiness of More's *repartees*. Keeping his own pace in society, as well as in the Court of Chancery, neither satire nor importunity could ruffle or confuse him. When Elizabeth, looking disdainfully at his modest country mansion, told him that the place was too small, he answered with the flattery of gratitude, "Not so, madam, your highness has made me too great for my house." Leicester having suddenly asked him his opinion of two aspirants for court favor, he responded on the spur of the moment, "By my troth, my lord, the one is a grave councillor: the other is a proper young man, and so he will be as long as he lives." To the queen, who pressed him for his sentiments respecting the effect of monopolies—a delicate question for a subject to speak his mind upon—he answered, with conciliatory lightness, "Madam, will you have me speak the truth? *Licentiâ* omnes deteriores sumus." In court he used to say, "Let us stay a little, that we may have done the sooner." But notwithstanding his deliberation and the stutter that hindered his utterances, he could be quicker than the quickest, and sharper than the most acrid, as the loquacious barrister discovered who was suddenly checked in a course of pert talkativeness by this tart remark from the stammering Lord Keeper: "There is a difference between you and me,—for me it is a pain to s-speak, for you a pain to hold your tongue." That the familiar story of his fatal attack of cold is altogether true one cannot well believe, for it seems highly improbable that the Lord Keeper, in his seventieth year, would have sat down to be shaved near an open window in the month of February. But though the anecdote may not be historically exact, it may be accepted as a faithful portraiture of his more stately and severely courteous humor. "Why did you suffer me to sleep thus exposed?" asked the Lord Keeper, waking in a fit of shivering from slumber into which his servant had allowed him to drop, as he sat to be shaved in a place where there was a sharp current of air. "Sir, I durst not disturb you," answered the punctilious valet, with a lowly obeisance. Having eyed him for a few seconds, Sir Nicholas rose and said, "By your civility I lose my life." Whereupon the Lord Keeper retired to the bed from which he never rose.

Amongst Elizabethan Judges who aimed at sprightliness on the Bench, Hatton merits a place; but there is reason to think that the idlers, who crowded his court to admire the foppishness of his judicial costume, did not get one really good *mot* from his lips to every ten bright sayings that came from the clever barristers practising before him. One of the best things attributed to him is a pun. In a case concerning the limits of certain land, the counsel on one side having remarked with explanatory emphasis, "We lie on this side, my Lord;" and the counsel on the other side having interposed with equal vehemence, "We lie on this side, my Lord,"—the Lord Chancellor leaned backwards, and dryly observed, "If you lie on both sides, whom am I to believe?" In Elizabethan England the pun was as great a power in the jocularity of the law-courts as it is at present; the few surviving witticisms that are supposed to exemplify Egerton's lighter mood on the bench, being for the most part feeble attempts at punning. For instance, when he was asked, during his tenure of the Mastership of the Rolls, to *commit* a cause, i.e., to refer it to a Master in Chancery, he used to answer, "What has the cause done that it should be committed?" It is also recorded of him that, when he was asked for his signature to a petition of which he disapproved, he would tear it in pieces with both hands, saying, "You want my hand to this? You shall have it; aye, and both my hands, too."

Of Egerton's student days a story is extant, which has merits, independent of its truth or want of truth. The hostess of a Smithfield tavern had received a sum of money from three graziers, in trust for them, and on engagement to restore it to them on their joint demand. Soon after this transfer, one of the co-depositors, fraudulently representing himself to be acting as the agent of the other two, induced the old lady to give him possession of the whole of the money—and thereupon absconded. Forthwith the other two depositors brought an action against the landlady, and were on the point of gaining a decision in their favor, when young Egerton, who had been taking notes of the trial, rose as *amicus curiæ*, and argued, "This money, by the contract, was to be returned to *three*, but *two* only sue;—where is the *third*? let him appear with the others; till then the money cannot be demanded from her." Nonsuit for the plaintiffs—for the young student a hum of commendation.

Many of the pungent sayings current in Westminster Hall at the present time, and attributed to eminent advocates who either are still upon the forensic stage, or have recently withdrawn from it, were common jests amongst the lawyers of the seventeenth century. What law-student now eating dinners at the Temple has not heard the story of Sergeant Wilkins, who, on drinking a pot of stout in the middle of the day, explained that, as he was about to appear in court, he thought it right to fuddle his brain down to the intellectual standard of a British jury. This merry thought, two hundred and fifty years since, was currently attributed to Sir John Millicent, of Cambridgeshire, of whom it is recorded—"being asked how he did conforme himselfe to the grave justices his brothers, when they met, 'Why, in faithe,' sayes he, 'I have no way but to drinke myself downe to the capacitie of the Bench.'"

Another witticism, currently attributed to various recent celebrities, but usually fathered upon Richard Brinsley Sheridan—on whose reputation have been heaped the brilliant *mots* of many a speaker whom he never heard, and the indiscretions of many a sinner whom he never knew—is certainly as old as Shaftesbury's bright and unprincipled career. When Charles II exclaimed, "Shaftesbury, you are the most profligate man in my dominions," the reckless Chancellor answered, "Of a subject, sir, I believe I am." It is likely enough that Shaftesbury merely repeated the witticism of a previous courtier; but it is certain that Sheridan was not the first to strike out the pun.

In this place let a contradiction be given to a baseless story, which exalts Sir William Follett's reputation for intellectual readiness and argumentative ability. The story runs, that early in the January of 1845, whilst George Stephenson, Dean Buckland, and Sir William Follett were Sir Robert Peel's guests at Drayton Manor, Dean Buckland vanquished the engineer in a discussion on a geological question. The next morning, George Stephenson was walking in the gardens of Drayton Manor before breakfast, when Sir William Follett accosted him, and sitting down in an arbor asked for the facts of the argument. Having quickly 'picked up the case,' the lawyer joined Sir Robert Peel's guests at breakfast, and amused them by leading the dean back to the dispute of the previous day, and overthrowing his fallacies by a skilful use of the same arguments which the self-taught engineer had employed with such ill effect. "What do you say, Mr. Stephenson?" asked Sir Robert Peel, enjoying the dean's discomfiture. "Why," returned George Stephenson, "I only say this, that of all the powers above and under earth, there seems to me no power so great as the gift of the gab." This is the story. But there are facts which contradict it. The only visit paid by George Stephenson to Drayton Manor was made in the December of 1844, not the January of 1845. The guests (invited for Dec. 14, 1844), were Lord Talbot, Lord Aylesford, the Bishop of Lichfield, Dr. Buckland, Dr. Lyon Playfair, Professor Owen, George Stephenson, Mr. Smith of Deanston, and Professor Wheatstone. Sir William Follett was not of the party, and did not set foot within Drayton Manor during George Stephenson's visit there. Of this, Professor Wheatstone (who furnished the present writer with these particulars), is certain. Moreover, it is not to be believed that Sir William Follett, an overworked invalid (who died in the June of 1845 of the pulmonary disease under which he had suffered for years), would sit in an arbor before breakfast on a winter's morning to hold debate with a companion on any subject. The story is a revival of an anecdote first told long before George Stephenson was born.

In lists of legal *facetiæ* the habit of punning is not more noticeable than the prevalent unamiability of the jests. Advocates are intellectual gladiators, using their tongues as soldiers of fortune use their swords; and when they speak, it is to vanquish an adversary. Antagonism is an unavoidable condition of their existence; and this incessant warfare gives a merciless asperity to their language, even when it does not infuse their hearts with bitterness. Duty enjoins the barrister to leave no word unsaid that can help his client, and encourages him to perplex by satire, baffle by ridicule, or silence by sarcasm, all who may oppose him with statements that cannot be disproved, or arguments that cannot be upset by reason. That which duty bids him do, practice enables him to do with terrible precision and completeness; and in many a case the caustic tone, assumed at the outset as a professional weapon, becomes habitual, and, without the speaker's knowledge, gives more pain within his home than in Westminster Hall.

Some of the well-known witticisms attributed to great lawyers are so brutally personal and malignant, that no man possessing any respect for human nature can read them without endeavoring to regard them as mere biographic fabrications. It is recorded of Charles Yorke that, after his election to serve as member for the University of Cambridge, he, in accordance with etiquette, made a round of calls on members of senate, giving them personal thanks for their votes; and that on coming to the presence of a supporter—an old 'fellow' known as the ugliest man in Cambridge—he addressed him thus, after smiling 'an aside' to a knot of bystanders—"Sir, I have reason to be thankful to my friends in general; but I confess myself under particular obligation to you for the very *remarkable countenance* you have shown me on this occasion." There is no doubt that Charles Yorke could make himself unendurably offensive; it is just credible that without a thought of their double meaning he uttered the words attributed to him; but it is not to be believed that he—an English gentleman—thus intentionally insulted a man who had rendered him a service.

A story far less offensive than the preceding anecdote, but in one point similar to it, is told of Judge Fortescue-Aland (subsequently Lord Fortescue), and a counsel. Sir John Fortescue-Aland was disfigured by a nose which was purple, and hideously misshapen by morbid growth. Having checked a ready counsel with the needlessly harsh observation, "Brother, brother, you are handling the case in a very lame manner," the angry advocate gave vent to his annoyance by saying, with a perfect appearance of *sang-froid*, "Pardon me, my lord; have patience with me, and I will do my best to make the case as plain as—as—the nose on your lordship's face." In this case the personality was uttered in hot blood, by a man who deemed himself to be striking the enemy of his professional reputation.

If they were not supported by incontrovertible testimony, the admirers of the great Sir Edward Coke would reject as spurious many of the overbearing rejoinders which escaped his lips in courts of justice. His tone in his memorable altercation with Bacon at the bar of the Court of Exchequer speaks ill for the courtesy of English advocates in Elizabeth's reign; and to any student who can appreciate the dignified formality and punctilious politeness that characterized English gentlemen in the old time, it is matter of perplexity how a man of Coke's learning, capacity, and standing, could have marked his contempt for 'Cowells Interpreter,' by designating the author in open court Dr. Cowheel. Scarcely in better taste were the coarse personalities with which, as Attorney General, he deluged Garnet the Jesuit, whom he described as "a Doctor of Jesuits; that is, a Doctor of six D's—as Dissimulation, Deposing of princes, Disposing of kingdoms, Daunting and Deterring of Subjects, and Destruction."

In comparatively recent times few judges surpassed Thurlow in overbearing insolence to the bar. To a few favorites, such as John Scott and Kenyon, he could be consistently indulgent, although even to them his patronage was often disagreeably contemptuous; but to those who provoked his displeasure by a perfectly independent and fearless bearing he was a malignant persecutor. For instance, in his animosity to Richard Pepper Arden (Lord Alvanley), he often forgot his duty as a judge and his manners as a gentleman. John Scott, on one occasion, rising in the Court of Chancery to address the court after Arden, who was his leader in the cause, and had made an unusually able speech, Lord Thurlow had the indecency to say, "Mr. Scott, I am glad to find that you are engaged in the cause, for I now stand some chance of knowing something about the matter." To the Chancellor's habitual incivility and insolence it is allowed that Arden always responded with dignity and self-command, humiliating his powerful and ungenerous adversary by invariable good-breeding. Once, through inadvertence, he showed disrespect to the surly Chancellor, and then he instantly gave utterance to a cordial apology, which Thurlow was not generous enough to accept with appropriate courtesy. In the excitement of professional altercation with counsel respecting the ages of certain persons concerned in a suit, he committed the indecorum of saying aloud, "I'll lay you a bottle of wine." Ever on the alert to catch his enemy tripping, Thurlow's eye brightened as his ear caught the careless words; and in another instant he assumed a look of indignant disgust. But before the irate judge could speak, Arden exclaimed, "My lord, I beg your lordship's pardon; I really forgot where I was." Had Thurlow bowed a grave acceptance of the apology, Arden would have suffered somewhat from the misadventure; but unable to keep his abusive tongue quiet, the 'Great Bear' growled out, in allusion to the offender's Welsh judgeship, "You thought you were in your own court, I presume."

More laughable, but not more courteous, was the same Chancellor's speech to a solicitor who had made a series of statements in a vain endeavor to convince his lordship of a certain person's death. "Really, my lord," at last the solicitor exclaimed, goaded into a fury by Thurlow's repeated ejaculations of "That's no proof of the man's death;" "Really, my lord, it is very hard, and it is not right that you won't believe me. I saw the man dead in his coffin. My lord, I tell you he was my client, and he is dead." "No wonder," retorted Thurlow, with a grunt and a sneer, "*since he was your client*. Why did you not tell me that sooner? It would kill me to have such a fellow as you for my attorney." That this great lawyer could thus address a respectable gentleman is less astonishing when it is remembered, that he once horrified a party of aristocratic visitors at a country-house by replying to a lady who pressed him to take some grapes, "Grapes, madam, grapes! Did not I say a minute ago that I had the *gripes*!" Once this ungentle lawyer was fairly worsted in a verbal conflict by an Irish pavier. On crossing the threshold of his Ormond Street house one morning, the Chancellor was incensed at seeing a load of paving-stones placed before his door. Singling out the tallest of a score of Irish workmen who were repairing the thoroughfare, he poured upon him one of those torrents of curses with which his most insolent speeches were usually preluded, and then told the man to move the stones away instantly. "Where shall I take them to, your honor?" the pavier inquired. From the Chancellor another volley of blasphemous abuse, ending with, "You lousy scoundrel, take them to hell!—do you hear me?" "Have a care, your honor," answered the workman, with quiet drollery, "don't you think now that if I took 'em to the other place your honor would be less likely to fall over them?"

Thurlow's incivility to the solicitor reminds us of the cruel answer given by another great lawyer to a country attorney, who, through fussy anxiety for a client's interests, committed a grave breach of professional etiquette. Let this attorney be called Mr. Smith, and let it be known that Mr. Smith, having come up to London from a secluded district of a remote country, was present at a consultation of counsellors learned in the law upon his client's cause. At this interview, the leading counsel in the cause, the Attorney General of the time, was present and delivered his final opinion with characteristic clearness and precision. The consultation over, the country attorney retreated to the Hummums Hotel, Covent Garden, and, instead of sleeping over the statements made at the conference, passed a wretched and wakeful night, harassed by distressing fears, and agitated by a conviction that the Attorney General had overlooked the most important point of the case. Early next day, Mr. Smith, without appointment, was at the great counsellor's chambers, and by vehement importunity, as well as a liberal donation to the clerk, succeeded in forcing his way to the advocate's presence. "Well, Mis-ter Smith," observed the Attorney General to his visitor, turning away from one of his devilling juniors, who chanced to be closeted with him at the moment of the intrusion, "what may you want to say? Be quick, for I am pressed for time." Notwithstanding the urgency of his engagements, he spoke with a slowness which, no less than the suspicious rattle of his voice, indicated the fervor of displeasure. "Sir Causticus Witherett, I trust you will excuse my troubling you; but, sir, after our yesterday's interview, I went to my hotel, the Hummums, in Covent Garden, and have spent the evening and all night turning over my client's case in my mind, and the more I turn the matter over in my mind, the more reason I see to fear that you have not given one point due consideration." A pause, during which Sir Causticus steadily eyed his visitor, who began to feel strangely embarrassed under the searching scrutiny: and then—"State the point, Mis-ter Smith, but be brief." Having heard the point stated, Sir Causticus Witherett inquired, "Is that all you wish to say?" "All, sir—all," replied Mr. Smith; adding nervously, "And I trust you will excuse me for troubling you about the matter; but, sir, I could not sleep a wink last night; all through the night I was turning this matter over in my mind." A glimpse of silence. Sir Causticus rose and standing over his victim made his final speech—"Mis-ter Smith, if you take my advice, given with sincere commiseration for your state, you will without delay return to the tranquil village in which you habitually reside. In the quietude of your accustomed scenes you will have leisure to *turn this matter over in what you are pleased to call your mind.* And I am willing to hope that *your mind* will recover its usual serenity. Mr. Smith, I wish you a very good morning."

Legal biography abounds with ghastly stories that illustrate the insensibility with which the hanging judges in past generations used to don the black cap jauntily, and smile at the wretched beings whom they sentenced to death. Perhaps of all such anecdotes the most thoroughly sickening is that which describes the conduct of Jeffreys, when, as Recorder of London, he passed sentence of death on his old and familiar friend, Richard Langhorn, the Catholic barrister—one of the victims of the Popish Plot phrensy. It is recorded that Jeffreys, not content with consigning his friend to a traitor's doom, malignantly reminded him of their former intercourse, and with devilish ridicule admonished him to prepare his soul for the next world. The authority which gives us this story adds, that by thus insulting a wretched gentleman and personal associate, Jeffreys, instead of rousing the disgust of his auditors, elicited their enthusiastic applause.

In a note to a passage in one of the Waverley Novels, Scott tells a story of an old Scotch judge, who, as an enthusiastic chess-player, was much mortified by the success of an ancient friend, who invariably beat him when they tried their powers at the beloved game. After a time the humiliated chess-player had his day of triumph. His conqueror happened to commit murder, and it became the judge's not altogether painful duty to pass upon him the sentence of the law. Having in due form and with suitable solemnity commended his soul to the divine mercy, he, after a brief pause, assumed his ordinary colloquial tone of voice, and nodding humorously to his old friend, observed—"And noo, Jammie, I think ye'll alloo that I hae checkmated you for ance."

Of all the bloodthirsty wearers of the ermine, no one, since the opening of the eighteenth century, has fared worse than Sir Francis Page—the virulence of whose tongue and the cruelty of whose nature were marks for successive satirists. In one of his Imitations of Horace, Pope says—

> "Slanderer, poison dread from Delia's rage,
> Hard words or hanging, if your judge be Page."

In the same spirit the poet penned the lines of the 'Dunciad'—

> "Mortality, by her false guardians drawn,
> Chicane in furs, and Casuistry in lawn,
> Gasps, as they straighten at each end the cord,
> And dies, when Dulness gives her——the Sword."

Powerless to feign insensibility to the blow, Sir Francis openly fitted this *black* cap to his dishonored head by sending his clerk to expostulate with the poet. The ill-chosen ambassador performed his mission by showing that, in Sir Francis's opinion, the whole passage would be sheer nonsense, unless 'Page' were inserted in the vacant place. Johnson and Savage took vengeance on the judge for the judicial misconduct which branded the latter poet a murderer; and Fielding, in 'Tom Jones,' illustrating by a current story the offensive levity of the judge's demeanor at capital trials, makes him thus retort on a horse-stealer: "Ay! thou art a lucky fellow; I have traveled the circuit these forty years, and never found a horse in my life; but I'll tell thee what, friend, thou wast more lucky than thou didst know of; for thou didst not only find a horse, but a halter too, I promise thee." This scandal to his professional order was permitted to insult the humane sentiments of the nation for a long period. Born in 1661, he died in 1741, whilst he was still occupying a judicial place; and it is said of him, that in his last year he pointed the ignominious story of his existence by a speech that soon ran the round of the courts. In answer to an inquiry for his health, the octogenarian judge observed, "My dear sir—you see how it fares with me; I just manage to keep *hanging on, hanging on.*" This story is ordinarily told as though the old man did not see the unfavorable significance of his words; but it is probable that, he uttered them wittingly and with, a sneer—in the cynicism and shamelessness of old age.

A man of finer stuff and of various merits, but still famous as a 'hanging judge,' was Sir Francis Buller, who also made himself odious to the gentler sex by maintaining that husbands might flog their wives, if the chastisement were administered with a stick not thicker than the operator's thumb. But the severity to criminals, which gave him a place amongst hanging judges, was not a consequence of natural cruelty. Inability to devise a satisfactory system of secondary punishments, and a genuine conviction that ninety-nine out of every hundred culprits were incorrigible, caused him to maintain that the gallows-tree was the most efficacious as well as the cheapest instrument that could be invented for protecting society against malefactors. Another of his stern *dicta* was, that previous good character was a reason for increasing rather than a reason for lessening a culprit's punishment; "For," he argued, "the longer a prisoner has enjoyed the good opinion of the world, the less are the excuses for his misdeeds, and the more injurious is his conduct to public morality."

In contrast to these odious stories of hanging judges are some anecdotes of great men, who abhorred the atrocities of our penal system, long before the worst of them were swept away by reform. Lord Mansfield has never been credited with lively sensibilities, but his humanity was so shocked by the bare thought of killing a man for committing a trifling theft, that he on one occasion ordered a jury to find that a stolen trinket was of less value than forty shillings—in order that the thief might escape the capital sentence. The prosecutor, a dealer in jewelry, was so mortified by the judge's leniency, that he exclaimed, "What, my lord, my golden trinket not worth forty shillings? Why, the fashion alone cost me twice the money!" Removing his glance from the vindictive tradesman, Lord Mansfield turned towards the jury, and said, with solemn gravity, "As we stand in need of God's mercy, gentlemen, let us not hang a man for fashion's sake."

Tenderness of heart was even less notable in Kenyon than in Murray; but Lord Mansfield's successor was at least on one occasion stirred by apathetic consequence of the bloody law against persons found guilty of trivial theft. On the Home Circuit, having passed sentence of death on a poor woman who had stolen property to the value of forty shillings in a dwelling-house, Lord Kenyon saw the prisoner drop lifeless in the dock, just as he ceased to speak. Instantly the Chief Justice sprang to his feet, and screamed in a shrill tone, "I don't mean to hang you—do you hear!—don't you hear?—Good——will nobody tell her that I don't mean to hang her?"

One of the humorous aspects of a repulsive subject is seen in the curiosity and fastidiousness of prisoners on trial for capital offences with regard to the professional *status* of the judges who try them. A sheep-stealer of the old bloody days liked that sentence should be passed upon him by a Chief Justice; and in our own time murderers awaiting execution, sometimes grumble at the unfairness of their trials, because they have been tried by judges of inferior degree. Lord Campbell mentions the case of a sergeant, who, whilst acting as Chief Justice Abbott's deputy, on the Oxford circuit, was reminded that he was 'merely a temporary' by the prisoner in the dock. Being asked in the usual way if he had aught to say why sentence of death should not be passed upon him, the prisoner answered—"*Yes; I have been tried before a journeyman judge.*"

*Chapter 40*

# HUMOROUS STORIES

Alike commendable for its subtlety and inoffensive humor was the pleasantry with which young Philip Yorke (afterwards Lord Hardwicke), answered Sir Lyttleton Powys's banter on the Western Circuit. An amiable and upright, but far from brilliant judge, Sir Lyttleton had a few pet phrases—-amongst them, "I humbly conceive," and "Look, do you see"—which he sprinkled over his judgments and colloquial talk with ridiculous profuseness. Surprised at Yorke's sudden rise into lucrative practice, this most gentlemanlike worthy was pleased to account for the unusual success by maintaining that young Mr. Yorke must have written a law-book, which had brought him early into favor with the inferior branch of the profession. "Mr. Yorke," said the venerable justice, whilst the barristers were sitting over their wine at a 'judges' dinner,' "I cannot well account for your having so much business, considering how short a time you have been at the bar: I humbly conceive you must have published something; for look you, do you see, there is scarcely a cause in court but you are employed in it on one side or the other. I should therefore be glad to know, Mr. Yorke, do you see, whether this be the case." Playfully denying that he possessed any celebrity as a writer on legal matters, Yorke, with an assumption of candor, admitted that he had some thoughts of lightening the labors of law-students by turning Coke upon Littleton into verse. Indeed, he confessed that he had already begun the work of versification. Not seeing the nature of the reply, Sir Lyttleton Powys treated the droll fancy as a serious project, and insisted that the author should give a specimen of the style of his contemplated work. Whereupon the young barrister—not pausing to remind a company of lawyers of the words of the original. "Tenant in fee simple is he which hath lands or tenements to hold to him and his heirs forever"—recited the lines—

"He that holdeth his lands in fee
Need neither to quake nor quiver,
*I humbly conceive: for look, do you see*
They are his and his heirs' forever."

The mimicry of voice being not less perfect than the verbal imitation, Yorke's hearers were convulsed with laughter, but so unconscious was Sir Lyttleton of the ridicule which he had incurred, that on subsequently encountering Yorke in London, he asked how "that translation of Coke upon Littleton was getting on." Sir Lyttleton died in 1732, and exactly ten years afterwards appeared the first edition of 'The Reports of Sir Edward Coke, Knt., in Verse'—a work which its author may have been inspired to undertake by Philip Yorke's proposal to versify 'Coke on Littleton.'

Had Yorke's project been carried out, lawyers would have a large supply of that comic but sound literature of which Sir James Burrow's Reports contain a specimen in the following poetical version of Chief Justice Pratt's memorable decision with regard to a woman of English birth, who was the widow of a foreigner:

"A woman having settlement
Married a man with none,
The question was, he being dead,
If what she had was gone.

"Quoth Sir John Pratt, 'The settlement
Suspended did remain,
Living the husband; but him dead
It doth revive again.'

(*Chorus of Puisne Judges.*)

"Living the husband; but him dead
It doth revive again."

Chief Justice Pratt's decision on this point having been reversed by his successor, Chief Justice Ryder's judgment was thus reported:

"A woman having a settlement,
Married a man with none,
He flies and leaves her destitute;
What then is to be done?

"Quoth Ryder, the Chief Justice,
'In spite of Sir John Pratt,
You'll send her to the parish
In which she was a brat.

"'*Suspension of a settlement*
Is not to be maintained;
That which she had by birth subsists
Until another's gained.'

(*Chorus of Puisne Judges.*)

"That which she had by birth subsists
Until another's gained."

In the early months of his married life, whilst playing the part of an Oxford don, Lord Eldon was required to decide in an important action brought by two undergraduates against the cook of University College. The plaintiffs declared that the cook had "sent to their rooms an apple-pie *that could not be eaten*." The defendant pleaded that he had a remarkably fine fillet of veal in the kitchen. Having set aside this plea on grounds obvious to the legal mind, and not otherwise then manifest to unlearned laymen, Mr. John Scott ordered the apple-pie to be brought in court; but the messenger, dispatched to do the judge's bidding, returned with the astounding intelligence that during the progress of the litigation a party of undergraduates had actually devoured the pie—fruit and crust. Nothing but the pan was left. Judgment: "The charge here is, that the cook has sent up an apple-pie that cannot be eaten. Now that cannot be said to have been uneatable which has been eaten; and as this apple-pie has been eaten, it was eatable. Let the cook be absolved."

But of all the judicial decisions on record, none was delivered with more comical effect than Lord Loughborough's decision not to hear a cause brought on a wager about a point in the game of 'Hazard.' A constant frequenter of Brookes's and White's, Lord Loughborough was well known by men of fashion to be fairly versed in the mysteries of gambling, though no evidence has ever been found in support of the charge that he was an habitual dicer. That he ever lost much by play is improbable; but the scandal-mongers of Westminster had some plausible reasons for laughing at the virtuous indignation of the spotless Alexander Wedderburn, who, whilst sitting at *Nisi Prius*, exclaimed, "Do not swear the jury in this case, but let it be struck out of the paper. I will not try it. The administration of justice is insulted by the proposal that I should try it. To my astonishment I find that the action is brought on a wager as to the mode of playing an illegal, disreputable, and mischievous game called 'Hazard;' whether, allowing seven to be the main, and eleven to be a nick to seven, there are more ways than six of nicking seven on the dice? Courts of justice are constituted to try rights and redress injuries, not to solve the problems of the gamesters. The gentlemen of the jury and I may have heard of 'Hazard' as a mode of dicing by which sharpers live, and young men of family and fortune are ruined; but what do any of us know of 'seven being the main,' or 'eleven being the nick to seven?' Do we come here to be instructed in this lore, and are the unusual crowds (drawn hither, I suppose, by the novelty of the expected entertainment) to take a lesson with us in these unholy mysteries, which they are to practice in the evening in the low gaming-houses in St. James Street, pithily called by a name which should inspire a salutary terror of entering them? Again, I say, let the cause be struck out of the paper. Move the court, if you please, that it may be restored, and if my brethren think that I do wrong in the course that I now take, I hope that one of them will officiate for me here, and save me from the degradation of trying 'whether there be more than six ways of nicking seven on the dice, allowing seven to be the main and eleven to be a nick to seven'—a question, after all, admitting of no doubt, and capable of mathematical demonstration."

With equal fervor Lord Kenyon inveighed against the pernicious usage of gambling, urging that the hells of St. James's should, be indicted as common nuisances. The 'legal monk,' as Lord Carlisle stigmatized him for his violent denunciations of an amusement countenanced by women of the highest fashion, even went so far as to exclaim—"If any such prosecutions are fairly brought before me, and the guilty parties are convicted, whatever may be their rank or station in the country, though they may be the first ladies in the land, they shall certainly exhibit themselves in the pillory."

The same considerations, which decided Lord Loughborough not to try an action brought by a wager concerning chicken-hazard, made Lord Ellenborough decline to hear a cause where the plaintiff sought to recover money wagered on a cock-fight. "There is likewise," said Lord Ellenborough, "another principle on which I think an action on such wagers cannot be maintained. They tend to the degradation of courts of justice. It is impossible to be engaged in ludicrous inquiries of this sort consistently with that dignity which it is essential to the public welfare that a court of justice should always preserve. I will not try the plaintiff's right to recover the four guineas, which might involve questions on the weight of the cocks and the construction of their steel spurs."

It has already been remarked that in all ages the wits of Westminster Hall have delighted in puns; and it may be here added, with the exception of some twenty happy verbal freaks, the puns of lawyers have not been remarkable for their excellence. L'Estrange records that when a stone was hurled by a convict from the dock at Charles I.'s Chief Justice Richardson, and passed just over the head of the judge, who happened to be sitting at ease and lolling on his elbow, the learned man smiled, and observed to those who congratulated him on his escape, "You see now, if I had been an *upright judge* I had been slaine." Under George III. Joseph Jekyll[30] was at the same time the brightest wit and most shameless punster of Westminster Hall; and such pride did he take in his reputation as a punster, that after the fashion of the wits of an earlier period he was often at considerable pains to give a pun a well-wrought epigrammatic setting. Bored with the long-winded speech of a prosy sergeant, he wrote on a slip of paper, which was in due course passed along the barristers' benches in the court where he was sitting—

"The sergeants are a grateful race,
Their dress and language show it;
Their purple garments come from *Tyre*,
Their arguments go to it."

When Garrow, by a more skilful than successful cross-examination, was endeavoring to lure a witness (an unmarried lady of advanced years) into an acknowledgment that payment of certain money in dispute had been tendered, Jekyll threw him this couplet—

"Garrow, forbear; that tough old jade
Will never prove a *tender maid*."

So also, when Lord Eldon and Sir Arthur Pigott each made a stand in court for his favorite pronunciation of the word 'lien;' Lord Eldon calling the word *lion* and Sir Arthur maintaining that it was to be pronounced like *lean*, Jekyll, with an allusion to the parsimonious arrangements of the Chancellor's kitchen, perpetrated the *jeu d'esprit*—

"Sir Arthur, Sir Arthur, why what do you mean
By saying the Chancellor's *lion* is *lean*?
D'ye think that his kitchen's so bad as all that,
That nothing within it can ever get fat?"

By this difference concerning the pronunciation of a word the present writer is reminded of an amicable contest that occurred in Westminster Hall between Lord Campbell and a Q.C. who is still in the front rank of court-advocates. In an action brought to recover for damages done to a carriage, the learned counsel repeatedly called, the vehicle in question a broug-ham, pronouncing both syllables of the word *brougham*. Whereupon, Lord Campbell with considerable pomposity observed, "*Broom* is the more usual pronunciation; a carriage of the kind you mean is generally and not incorrectly called a *broom*—that pronunciation is open to no grave objection, and it has the great

[30] One of Jekyll's best displays of brilliant impudence was perpetrated on a Welsh judge, who was alike notorious for his greed of office and his want of personal cleanliness. "My dear sir," Jekyll observed in his most amiable manner to this most unamiable personage, "you have asked the minister for almost everything else, why *don't* you ask him for a piece of soap and a nail-brush?"

advantage of saving the time consumed by uttering an extra syllable." Half an hour later in the same trial Lord Campbell, alluding to a decision given in a similar action, said, "In that case the carriage which had sustained injury was an *omnibus*——" "Pardon me, my lord," interposed the Queen's Counsel, with such promptitude that his lordship was startled into silence, "a carriage of the kind, to which you draw attention is usually termed 'bus;' that pronunciation is open to no grave objection, and it has the great advantage of saving the time consumed by uttering two extra syllables." The interruption was followed by a roar of laughter, in which Lord Campbell joined more heartily than anyone else.

One of Jekyll's happy sayings was spoken at Exeter, when he defended several needlemen who were charged with raising a riot for the purpose of forcing the master-tailors to give higher wages. Whilst Jekyll was examining a witness as to the number of tailors present at the alleged riot, Lord Eldon—then Chief Justice of the Common Pleas—reminded him that three persons can make that which the law regards as a riot; whereupon the witty advocate answered, "Yes, my lord, Hale and Hawkins lay down the law as your lordship states it, and I rely on their authority; for if there must be three men to make a riot, the rioters being *tailors*, there must be nine times three present, and unless the prosecutor make out that there were twenty-seven joining in this breach of the peace, my clients are entitled to an acquittal." On Lord Eldon enquiring whether he relied on common-law or statute-law, the counsel for the defence answered firmly, "My lord, I rely on a well-known maxim, as old as Magna Charta, *Nine Tailors make a Man*." Finding themselves unable to reward a lawyer for so excellent a jest with an adverse verdict, the jury acquitted the prisoners. Towards the close of his career Eldon made a still better jest than this of Jekyll's concerning tailors. In 1829, when Lyndhurst was occupying the woolsack for the first time, and Eldon was longing to recover the seals, the latter presented a petition from the Tailors' Company at Glasgow against Catholic Belief.

"What!" asked Lord Lyndhurst from the woolsack, in a low voice, "do the *tailors* trouble themselves about such *measures*?" Whereto, with unaccustomed quickness, the old Tory of the Tories retorted, "No wonder; you can't suppose that *tailors* like *turncoats*."

As specimens of a kind of pleasantry becoming more scarce every year, some of Sir George Rose's court witticisms are excellent. When Mr. Beams, the reporter, defended himself against the *friction* of passing barristers by a wooden bar, the flimsiness of which was pointed out to Sir George (then Mr. Rose), the wit answered—

> "Yes—the partition is certainly thin—
> Yet thick enough, truly, the Beams within."

The same originator of happy sayings pointed to Eldon's characteristic weakness in the lines—

"Mr. Leach made a speech,
Pithy, clear, and strong;
Mr. Hart, on the other part,
Was prosy, dull, and long;
Mr. Parker made that darker
Which was dark enough without;
Mr. Bell spoke so well,
That the Chancellor said—'I doubt.'"

Far from being offended by this allusion to his notorious mental infirmity, Lord Eldon, shortly after the verses had floated into circulation, concluded one of his decisions by saying, with a significant smile, "And here *the Chancellor does not doubt*."

Not less remarkable for precipitancy than Eldon for procrastination, Sir John Leach, Vice-Chancellor, was said to have done more mischief by excessive haste in a single term than Eldon in his whole life wrought through extreme caution. The holders of this opinion delighted to repeat the poor and not perspicuous lines—

"In equity's high court there are
Two sad extremes, 'tis clear;
Excessive slowness strikes us there,
Excessive quickness here.

"Their source, 'twixt good and evil, brings
A difficulty nice;
The first from Eldon's *virtue*, springs,
The latter from his *vice*."

It is needless to remark that this attempt to gloss the Chancellor's shortcomings is an illustration of the readiness with which censors apologize for the misdeeds of eminently fortunate offenders. Whilst Eldon's procrastination and Leach's haste were thus put in contrast, an epigram also placed the Chancellor's frailty in comparison with the tedious prolixity of the Master of the Rolls—

"To cause delay in Lincoln's Inn
Two diff'rent methods tend:
His lordship's judgments ne'er begin,
His honors never end."

A mirth-loving judge, Justice Powell, could be as thoroughly humorous in private life as he was fearless and just upon the bench. Swift describes him as a surpassingly merry old gentleman, laughing heartily at all comic things, and his own droll stories more than aught else. In court he could not always refrain from jocularity. For instance, when he tried Jane Wenham for witch-craft, and she assured him that she could fly, his eye twinkled as he answered, "Well, then you may; there is no law against flying." When Fowler, Bishop of Gloucester—a thorough believer in what is now-a-days called spiritualism—was persecuting his acquaintance with silly stories about ghosts, Powell gave him a telling reproof for his credulity by describing a horrible apparition which was represented as having disturbed the narrator's rest on the previous night. At the hour of midnight, as the clocks were striking twelve, the judge was roused from his first slumber by a hideous sound. Starting up, he saw at the foot of his uncompanioned bed a figure—dark, gloomy, terrible, holding before its grim and repulsive visage a lamp that shed an uncertain light. "May Heaven have mercy on us!" tremulously ejaculated the bishop at this point of the story. The judge continued his story: "Be calm, my lord bishop; be calm. The awful part of this mysterious interview has still to be told. Nerving myself to fashion the words of inquiry, I addressed the nocturnal visitor thus—'Strange being, why hast thou come at this still hour to perturb a sinful mortal?' You understand, my lord, I said this in hollow tones—in what I may almost term a sepulchral voice." "Ay—ay," responded the bishop, with intense excitement; "go on—I implore you to go on. What did *it* answer?" "It answered in a voice not greatly different from the voice of a human creature—'Please, sir, *I am the watchman on beat, and your street-door is open*.'" Readers will remember the use which Barham has made of this story in the Ingoldsby Legends.

As a Justice of the King's Bench, Powell had in Chief Justice Holt an associate who could not only appreciate the wit of others, but could himself say smart things. When Lacy, the fanatic, forced his way into Holt's house in Bedford Row, the Chief Justice was equal to the occasion. "I come to you," said Lacy, "a prophet from the Lord God, who has sent me to thee and would have thee grant a *nolle prosequi* for John Atkins, his servant, whom thou hast sent to prison." Whereto the judge answered, with proper emphasis, "Thou art a false prophet and a lying knave. If the Lord God had sent thee, it would have been to the Attorney General, for the Lord God knows that it belongeth not to the Chief Justice, to grant a *nolle prosequi*; but I, as Chief Justice, can grant a warrant to commit thee to John Atkins's company." Whereupon the false prophet, sharing the fate of many a true one, was forthwith clapped in prison.

Now that so much has been said of Thurlow's brutal sarcasms, justice demands for his memory an acknowledgment that he possessed a vein of genuine humor that could make itself felt without wounding. In his undergraduate days at Cambridge he is said to have worried the tutors of Caius with a series of disorderly pranks and impudent *escapades*, but on one occasion he unquestionably displayed at the university the quick wit that in after life rescued him from many an embarrassing position. "Sir," observed a tutor, giving the unruly undergraduate a look of disapproval, "I never come to the window without seeing you idling in the court." "Sir," replied young Thurlow, imitating the don's tone, "I never come into the court without seeing you idling at the window."

Years later, when he had become a great man, and John Scott was paying him assiduous court, Thurlow said, in ridicule of the mechanical awkwardness of many successful equity draughtsmen, "Jack Scott, don't you think we could invent a machine to draw bills and answers in Chancery?" Having laughed at the suggestion when it was made, Scott put away the droll thought in his memory; and when he had risen to be Attorney General reminded Lord Thurlow of it under rather awkward circumstances. Macnamara, the conveyancer, being concerned as one of the principals in a Chancery suit, Lord Thurlow advised him to submit the answer to the bill filed against him to the Attorney General. In due course the answer came under Scott's notice, when he found it so wretchedly drawn, that he advised Macnamara to have another answer drawn by someone who understood pleading. On the same day he was engaged at the bar of the House of Lords, when Lord Thurlow came to him, and said, "So I understand you don't think my friend Mac's answer will do?" "Do!" Scott replied, contemptuously. "My Lord, it won't do at all! it must have been drawn by that wooden machine which you once told me might be invented to draw bills and answers." "That's very unlucky," answered Thurlow, "and impudent too, if you had known—*that I drew the answer myself.*"

Lord Lyndhurst used to maintain that it was one of the chief duties of a judge to render it disagreeable to counsel to talk nonsense. Jeffreys in his milder moments no doubt salved his conscience with the same doctrine, when he recalled how, after elating him with a compliment, he struck down the rising junior with "Lord, sir! you must be cackling too. We told you, Mr. Bradbury, your objection was very ingenious; that must not make you troublesome: you cannot lay an egg, but you must be cackling over it." Doubtless, also, he felt it one of the chief duties of a judge to restrain attorneys from talking nonsense when—on hearing that the solicitor from whom he received his first brief had boastfully remarked, in allusion to past services, "My Lord Chancellor! I *made* him!"—he exclaimed, "Well, then, I'll lay my maker by the heels," and forthwith committed his former client and patron to the Fleet prison. If this bully of the bench actually, as he is said to have done, interrupted the venerable Maynard by saying, "You have lost your knowledge of law; your memory, I tell you, is failing through old age," how must every hearer of the speech have exulted when Maynard quietly answered, "Yes, Sir George, I have forgotten more law than you ever learned; but allow me to say, I have not forgotten much."

On the other hand it should be remembered that Maynard was a man eminently qualified to sow violent animosities, and that he was a perpetual thorn in the flesh of the political barristers, whose principles he abhorred. A subtle and tricky man, he was constantly misleading judges by citing fictitious authorities, and then smiling at their professional ignorance when they had swallowed his audacious fabrications. Moreover, the manner of his speech was sometimes as offensive as its substance was dishonest. Strafford spoke a bitter criticism not only with regard to Maynard and Glyn, but with regard to the prevailing tone of the bar, when, describing the conduct of the advocates who managed his prosecution, he said: "Glynne and Maynard used me *like advocates*, but Palmer and Whitelock *like gentlemen*; and yet the latter left out nothing against me that was material to be urged against me." As a Devonshire man Maynard is one of the many cases which may be cited against the smart saying of Sergeant Davy, who used to observe: "The further I journey toward the West, the more convinced I am that the wise men come from the East." But shrewd, observant, liberal though he was in most respects, he was on one matter so far behind the spirit of the age that, blinded and ruled by an unwise sentiment, he gave his parliamentary support to an abortive measure "to prevent further building in London and the neighborhood." In support of this measure he observed, "This building is the ruin of the gentry and ruin of religion, as leaving many good people without churches to go to. This enlarging of London makes it filled with lacqueys and pages. In St. Giles's parish scarce the fifth part come to church, and we shall have no religion at last."

Whilst justice has suffered something in respect of dignity from the overbearing temper of judges to counsel, from collisions of the bench with the bar, and from the mutual hostility of rival advocates, she has at times sustained even greater injury from the jealousies and altercations of judges. Too often wearers of the ermine, sitting on the same bench, nominally for the purpose of assisting each other, have roused the laughter of the bar, and the indignation of suitors, by their petty squabbles. "It now comes to my turn," an Irish judge observed, when it devolved on him to support the decision of one or the other of two learned coadjutors, who had stated with more fervor than courtesy altogether irreconcilable opinions—"It now comes to my turn to declare my view of the case, and fortunately I can be brief. I agree with my brother A, from the irresistible force of my brother B's arguments." Extravagant as this case may appear, the King's Bench of Westminster Hall, under Mansfield and Kenyon, witnessed several not less scandalous and comical differences. Taking thorough pleasure in his work, Lord Mansfield was not less industrious than impartial in the discharge of his judicial functions; so long as there was anything for him to learn with regard to a cause, he not only sought for it with pains but with a manifest pleasure similar to that delight in judicial work which caused the French Advocate, Cottu, to say of Mr. Justice Bayley: "Il s'amuse à juger:" but notwithstanding these good qualities, he was often culpably deficient in respect for the opinions of his subordinate coadjutors. At times a vain desire to impress on the minds of spectators that his intellect was the paramount power of the bench; at other times a personal dislike to one of his *puisnes* caused him to derogate from the dignity of his court, in cases where he was especially careful to protect the interests of suitors. With silence more disdainful than any words could have been, he used to turn away from Mr. Justice Willes, at the moment when the latter expected his chief to ask his opinion; and on such occasions the indignant *puisne* seldom had the prudence and nerve to conceal his mortification. "I have not been consulted, and I will be heard!" he once shrieked forth in a paroxysm of rage caused by Mansfield's contemptuous treatment; and forty years afterwards Jeremy Bentham, who was a witness of the insult and its effect, observed: "At this distance of time—five-and-thirty or forty years—the feminine scream issuing out of his manly frame still tingles in my ears." Mansfield's overbearing demeanor to his *puisnes* was reproduced with less dignity by his successor; but Buller, the judge who wore ermine whilst he was still in his thirty-third year, and who confessed that his "idea of heaven was to sit at Nisi Prius all day, and to play whist all night," seized the first opportunity to give Taffy Kenyon a lesson in good manners by stating, with impressive self-possession and convincing logic, the reasons which induced him to think the judgment delivered by his chief to be altogether bad in law and argument.

*Chapter 41*

# WITS IN 'SILK' AND PUNSTERS IN 'ERMINE'

Whilst Lord Camden held the chiefship of the Common Pleas, he was walking with his friend Lord Dacre on the outskirts of an Essex village, when they passed the parish stocks. "I wonder," said the Chief Justice, "whether a man in the stocks endures a punishment that is physically painful? I am inclined to think that, apart from the sense of humiliation and other mental anguish, the prisoner suffers nothing, unless the populace express their satisfaction at his fate by pelting him with brick-bats." "Suppose you settle your doubts by putting your feet into the holes," rejoined Lord Dacre, carelessly. In a trice the Chief Justice was sitting on the ground with his feet some fifteen inches above the level of his seat, and his ankles encircled by hard wood. "Now, Dacre!" he exclaimed, enthusiastically, "fasten the bolts, and leave me for ten minutes." Like a courteous host Lord Dacre complied with the whim of his guest, and having placed it beyond his power to liberate himself bade him 'farewell' for ten minutes. Intending to saunter along the lane and return at the expiration of the stated period, Lord Dacre moved away, and falling into one of his customary fits of reverie, soon forgot all about the stocks, his friend's freak, and his friend. In the meantime the Chief Justice went through every torture of an agonizing punishment—acute shootings along the confined limbs, aching in the feet, angry pulsations under the toes, violent cramps in the muscles and thighs, gnawing pain at the point where his person came in immediate contact with the cold ground, pins-and-needles everywhere. Amongst the various forms of his physical discomfort, faintness, fever, giddiness, and raging thirst may be mentioned. He implored a peasant to liberate him, and the fellow answered with a shout of derision; he hailed a passing clergyman, and explained that he was not a culprit, but Lord Camden, Chief Justice of the Common Pleas, and one of Lord Dacre's guests. "Ah!" observed the man of cloth, not so much answering the wretched culprit as passing judgment on his case, "mad with liquor. Yes, drunkenness is sadly on the increase; 'tis droll, though, for a drunkard in the stocks to imagine himself a Chief Justice!" and on he passed. A farmer's wife jogged by on her pillion, and hearing the wretched man exclaim that he should die of thirst, the good creature gave him a juicy apple, and hoped that his punishment would prove for the good of his soul. Not ten minutes, but ten hours did the Chief Justice sit in the stocks, and when at length he was carried into Lord Dacre's house, he was in no humor to laugh at his own miserable plight. Not long afterwards he presided at a trial in which a workman brought an action against a magistrate who had wrongfully placed him in the stocks. The counsel for the defence happening to laugh at the statement of the plaintiff, who maintained that he had suffered intense pain during his confinement, Lord Camden leaned forwards and inquired in a whisper, "Brother were you ever in the stocks?" "Never, my lord," answered the advocate, with a look of lively astonishment "I have been," was the whispered reply; "and let me assure you that the agony inflicted by the stocks is—*awful*!"

Of a different sort, but scarcely less intense, was the pain endured by Lord Mansfield whenever a barrister pronounced a Latin word with a false quantity. "My lords," said the Scotch advocate, Crosby, at the bar of the House of Lords, "I have the honor to appear before your lordships as counsel for the Curators." "Ugh!" groaned the Westminster Oxford law-lord, softening his reproof by an allusion to his Scotch nationality, "Curators, Mr. Crosby, Curators: I wish *our* countrymen would pay a little more attention to prosody." "My Lord," replied Mr. Crosby, with delightful readiness and composure, "I can assure you that *our* countrymen are very proud of your lordship as the greatest senator and orator of the present age." The barrister who made Baron Alderson shudder under his robes by applying for a 'nolle prosequi,' was not equally quick at self-defence, when that judge interposed, "Stop, sir—consider that this is the last day of term, and don't make things unnecessarily long." It was Baron Alderson who, in reply to the juryman's confession that he was deaf in one ear, observed, "Then leave the box before the trial begins; for it is necessary that jurymen should *hear both sides*."

Amongst legal wits, Lord Ellenborough enjoys a high place; and though in dealing out satire upon barristers and witnesses, and even on his judicial coadjutors, he was often needlessly severe, he seldom perpetrated a jest the force of which lay solely in its cruelty. Perhaps the most harsh and reprehensible outburst of satiric humor recorded of him is the crushing speech by which he ruined a young man for life. "The *unfortunate* client for whom it is my privilege to appear," said a young barrister, making his first essay in Westminster Hall—"the unfortunate client, my lord, for whom I appear—hem! hem!—I say, my lord, my *unfortunate client*——" Leaning forwards, and speaking in a soft, cooing voice, that was all the more derisive, because it was so gentle, Lord Ellenborough said, "you may go on, sir—so far the court is with you." One would have liked his lordship better had he sacrificed his jest to humanity, and acted as long afterwards that true gentleman, Mr. Justice Talfourd, acted, who, seeing a young barrister overpowered with nervousness, gave him time to recover himself by saying, in the kindest possible manner, "Excuse me for interrupting you—but for a minute I am not at liberty to pay you attention." Whereupon the Judge took up his pen and wrote a short note to a friend. Before the note was finished, the young barrister had completely recovered his self-possession, and by an admirable speech secured a verdict for his client. A highly nervous man, he might on that day have been broken for life, like Ellenborough's victim, by mockery; but fortunate in appearing before a judge whose witty tongue knew not how to fashion unkind words, he triumphed over his temporary weakness, and has since achieved well deserved success in his profession. Talfourd might have made a jest for the thoughtless to laugh at; but he preferred to do an act, on which those who loved him like to think.

When Preston, the great conveyancer, gravely informed the judges of the King's Bench that "an estate in fee simple was the highest estate known to the law of England," Lord Ellenborough checked the great Chancery lawyer, and said with politest irony, "Stay, stay, Mr. Preston, let me take that down. An estate" (the judge writing as he spoke) "in fee simple is—the highest estate—known to—the law of England. Thank you, Mr. Preston! The court, sir, is much indebted to you for the information." Having inflicted on the court an unspeakably dreary oration, Preston, towards the close of the day, asked when it would be their lordship's pleasure to hear the remainder of his argument; whereupon Lord Ellenborough uttered a sigh of resignation, and answered, 'We are bound to hear you, and we will endeavor to give you our undivided attention on Friday next; but as for *pleasure*, that, sir, has been long out of the question.'

Probably mistelling an old story, and taking to himself the merit of Lord Ellenborough's reply to Preston, Sir Vicary Gibbs (Chief of the Common Pleas) used to tell his friends that Sergeant Vaughan—the sergeant who, on being subsequently raised to the bench through the influence of his elder brother, Sir Henry Halford, the court physician, was humorously described by the wits of Westminster Hall as a judge *by prescription*—once observed in a grandiose address to the Judges of the Common Pleas, "For though our law takes cognizance of divers different estates, I may be permitted to say, without reserve or qualification of any kind, that the highest estate known to the law of England is an estate in fee simple." Whereupon Sir Vicary, according to his own account, interrupted the sergeant with an air of incredulity and astonishment. "What is your proposition, brother Vaughan? Perhaps I did not hear you rightly!" Flustered by the interruption, which completely effected its object, the sergeant explained, "My lord, I mean to contend that an estate in fee simple is *one of the highest estates* known to the law of England, that is, my lord, that it may be under certain circumstances—and sometimes is so."

Notwithstanding his high reputation for wit, Lord Ellenborough would deign to use the oldest jests. Thus of Mr. Caldecott, who over and over again, with dull verbosity, had said that certain limestone quarries, like lead and copper mines, "were not rateable, because the limestone could only be reached by boring, which was matter of science," he gravely inquired, "Would you, Mr. Caldecott, have us believe that every kind of *boring* is matter of science?" With finer humor he nipped in the bud one of Randle Jackson's flowery harangues. "My lords," said the orator, with nervous intonation, "in the book of nature it is written——" "Be kind enough, Mr. Jackson," interposed Lord Ellenborough, "to mention the page from which you are about to quote." This calls to mind the ridicule which, at an earlier period of his career, he cast on Sheridan for saying at the trial of Warren Hastings, "The treasures in the Zenana of the Begum are offerings laid by the hand of piety on the altar of a saint." To this not too rhetorical statement, Edward Law, as leading counsel for Warren Hastings, replied by asking, "how the lady was to be considered a saint, and how the camels were to be laid upon the altar?" With greater pungency, Sheridan defended himself by saying, "This is the first time in my life that I ever heard of special pleading on a metaphor, or a bill of indictment against a trope; but such is the turn of the learned gentleman's mind, that when he attempts to be humorous no jest can be found, and when serious no fact is visible."[31] To the last Law delighted to point the absurdities of orators who in aiming at the sublime only achieved the ridiculous. "My lords," said Mr. Gaselee, arguing that mourning coaches at a funeral were not liable to post-horse duty, "it never could have been the intention of a Christian legislature to aggravate the grief which mourners endure whilst following to the grave the remains of their dearest relatives, by compelling them at the same time to pay the horse-duty." Had Mr. Gaselee been a humorist, Lord Ellenborough would have laughed; but as the advocate was well known to have no turn for raillery, the Chief Justice gravely observed, "Mr. Gaselee, you incur danger by sailing in high sentimental latitudes."

To the surgeon in the witness-box who said, "I employ myself as a surgeon," Lord Ellenborough retorted, "But does anybody else employ you as a surgeon?"

The demand to be examined *on affirmation* being preferred by a Quaker witness, whose dress was so much like the costume of an ordinary *conformist* that the officer of the court had begun to administer the usual oath, Lord Ellenborough inquired of the 'friend,' "Do you really mean to impose upon the court by appearing here in the disguise of a reasonable being?" Very pungent was his ejaculation at a cabinet dinner when he heard that Lord Kenyon was about to close his penurious old age by dying. "Die!—why should he die?—what would he get by that?" interposed Lord Ellenborough, adding to the pile of jests by which men have endeavored to keep a grim, unpleasant subject out of sight—a pile to which the latest *mot* was added the other day by Lord Palmerston, who during his last attack of gout exclaimed playfully. "*Die*, my dear doctor! That's the *last* thing I think of doing." Having jested about Kenyon's parsimony, as the old man lay *in*

---

[31] Robert Dallas—one of Edward Law's coadjutors in the defence of Hastings—gave another 'manager' a more telling blow. Indignant with Burke for his implacable animosity to Hastings, Dallas (subsequently Chief Justice of the Common Pleas) wrote the stinging lines—

"Oft have we wondered that on Irish ground
No poisonous reptile has e'er yet been found;
Reveal'd the secret stands of nature's work—
She saved her venom to produce her Burke."

*extremis*, Ellenborough placed another joke of the same kind upon his coffin. Hearing that through the blunder of an illiterate undertaker the motto on Kenyon's hatchment in Lincoln's Inn Fields had been painted '*Mors Janua Vita*,' instead of 'Mors Janua Vitæ,' he exclaimed, "Bless you, there's no mistake; Kenyon's will directed that it should be 'Vita,' so that his estate might be saved the expense of *a diphthong*." Capital also was his reply when Erskine urged him to accept the Great Seal. "How can you," he asked, in a tone of solemn entreaty, "wish me to accept the office of Chancellor, when you know, Erskine, that I am as ignorant of its duties as you are yourself?" At the time of uttering these words, Ellenborough was well aware that if he declined them Erskine would take the seals. Some of his puns were very poor. For instance, his exclamation, "Cite to me the decisions of the judges of the land: not the judgments of the Chief Justice of Ely, who is fit only to *rule* a copybook."

One of the best 'legal' puns on record is unanimously attributed by the gossipers of Westminster Hall to Lord Chelmsford. As Sir Frederick Thesiger he was engaged in the conduct of a cause, and objected to the irregularity of a learned sergeant who in examining his witnesses repeatedly put leading questions. "I have a right," maintained the sergeant, doggedly, "to *deal* with my witnesses as I please." "To that I offer no objection," retorted Sir Frederick; "you may *deal* as you like, but you shan't *lead*." Of the same brilliant conversationalist Mr. Grantley Berkeley has recorded a good story in 'My Life and Recollections.' Walking down St. James's Street, Lord Chelmsford was accosted by a stranger, who exclaimed "Mr. Birch I believe?" "If you believe that, sir, you'll believe anything," replied the ex-Chancellor, as he passed on.

When Thelwall, instead of regarding his advocate with grateful silence, insisted on interrupting him with vexatious remarks and impertinent criticisms, Erskine neither threw up his brief nor lost his temper, but retorted with an innocent flash of merriment. To a slip of paper on which the prisoner had written, "I'll be hanged if I don't plead my own cause," he contented himself with returning answer, "You'll be hanged if you do." His *mots* were often excellent, but it was the tone and joyous animation of the speaker that gave them their charm. It is said that in his later years, when his habitual loquaciousness occasionally sank into garrulity, he used to repeat his jests with imprudent frequency, shamelessly giving his companions the same pun with each course of a long dinner. There is a story that after his retirement from public life he used morning after morning to waylay visitors on their road through the garden to his house, and, pointing to his horticultural attire and the spade in his hand assure them that he was 'enjoying his otium cum *digging a tatie*.' Indeed the tradition lives that before his fall from the woolsack, pert juniors used to lay bets as to the number of times he could fire off a favorite old pun in the course of a sitting in the Court of Chancery, and that wily leaders habitually strove to catch his favor by giving him opportunities for facetious interruptions during their arguments. If such traditions be truthful, it is no matter for surprise that Erskine's court-jokes have come down to us with so many variations. For instance, it is recorded with much circumstantiality that on circuit, accosting a junior who had lost his portmanteau from the back of a post-chaise, he said, with mock gravity, "Young gentlemen, henceforth imitate the elephant, the wisest of animals, who always *carries his trunk before him*;" and on equally good authority it is stated that when Polito, the keeper of the Exeter 'Change Menagerie, met with a similar accident and brought an action for damages against the proprietor of the coach from the hind-boot of which his property had disappeared, Erskine, speaking for the defence, told the jury that they would not be justified in giving a verdict favorable to the man, who, though he actually possessed an elephant, had neglected to imitate its prudent example and carry his trunk before him.

As a *littérateur* Erskine met with meagre success; but some of his squibs and epigrams are greatly above the ordinary level of '*vers de société*.' For instance this is his:—

> "De Quodam Rege.
> "I may not do right, though I ne'er can do wrong;
> I never can die, though I cannot live long;
> My jowl it is purple, my hand it is fat—
> Come, riddle my riddle. What is it? *What? What?*"

The liveliest illustrations of Erskine's proverbial egotism are the squibs of political caricaturists; and from their humorous exaggerations it is difficult to make a correct estimate of the lengths of absurdity to which his intellectual vanity and self-consciousness sometimes carried him. From what is known of his disposition it seems probable that the sarcasms aimed by public writers at his infirmity inclined him to justify their attacks rather than to disprove them by his subsequent demeanor, and that some of his most extravagant outbursts of self-assertion were designed in a spirit of bravado and reckless good-nature to increase the laughter which satirists had raised against him. However this may be, his conduct drew upon him blows that would have ruffled the composure of any less self-complacent or less amiable man. The Tory prints habitually spoke of him as Counsellor Ego whilst he was at the bar; and when it was known that he had accepted the seals, the opposition journals announced that he would enter the house as "Baron Ego, of Eye, in the county of Suffolk." Another of his nicknames was *Lord Clackmannan*; and Cobbett published the following notice of an harangue made by the fluent advocate in the House of Commons:—"Mr. Erskine delivered a most animated speech in the House of Commons on the causes and consequences of the late war, which lasted thirteen hours, eighteen minutes, and a second, by Mr. John Nichol's stop-watch. Mr. Erskine closed his speech with a dignified climax: 'I was born free, and, by G-d, I'll remain so!'—[A loud cry of '*Hear! hear*' in the gallery, in which were citizens Tallien and Barrère.] On Monday three weeks we shall have the extreme satisfaction of laying before the public a brief analysis of the above speech, our letter-founder having entered into an engagement to furnish a fresh font of I's."[32]

From the days of Wriothesley, who may be regarded as the most conspicuous and unquestionable instance of judicial incompetency in the annals of English lawyers, the multitudes have always delighted in stories that illustrate the ignorance and incapacity of men who are presumed to possess, by right of their office, an extraordinary share of knowledge and wisdom. What law-student does not rub his hands as he reads of Lord St. John's trouble during term whilst he held the seals, and of the impatience with which he looked forward to the long vacation, when he would not be required to look wise and speak authoritatively about matters concerning which he was totally ignorant. Delicious are the stories of Francis Bacon's clerical successor, who endeavored to get up a *quantum suff.* of Chancery law by falling on his knees and asking enlightenment of Heaven. Gloomily comical are the anecdotes of Chief Justice Fleming, whose most famous and disastrous blunder was his judgment in Bates's case. Great fun may be gathered from the tales that exemplify the ignorance of law which characterized the military, and also the non-military laymen, who helped to take care of the seals during the civil troubles of the seventeenth century. Capital is Roger North's picture of Bob Wright's ludicrous shiftlessness whenever the influence of his powerful relations brought the loquacious, handsome, plausible fellow a piece of business. "He was a comely fellow," says Roger North, speaking of the Chief Justice Wright's earlier days, "airy and flourishing both in his habits and way of living; and his relation Wren (being a powerful man in those parts) set him in credit with the country; but withal, he was so poor a lawyer that he used to bring such cases as came to him to his friend Mr. North, and he wrote the opinion on the paper, and the lawyer copied it, and signed under the case as if it had been his own. It ran so low with him that when Mr. North was at London he sent up his cases to him, and had opinions returned by the post; and, in the meantime he put off his clients on pretence of taking the matter into serious consideration." Perhaps some readers of this page can point

---

[32] In the 'Anti-Jacobin,' Canning, in the mock report of an imaginary speech, represented Erskine as addressing the 'Whig Club' thus:—"For his part he should only say that, having been, as he had been, both a soldier and a sailor, if it had been his fortune to have stood in either of these relations to the Directory—as *a* man and a major-general he should not have scrupled to direct his artillery against the national representatives:—as a naval officer he would undoubtedly have undertaken for the removal of the exiled deputies; admitting the exigency, under all its relations, as it appeared to him to exist, and the then circumstances of the times with all their bearings and dependencies, branching out into an infinity of collateral considerations and involving in each a variety of objects, political, physical, and moral; and these, again, under their distinct and separate heads, ramifying into endless subdivisions, which it was foreign to his purpose to consider, Mr. Erskine concluded by recapitulating, in a strain of agonizing and impressive eloquence, the several more prominent heads of his speech; he had been a soldier and a sailor, and had a son at Winchester school—he had been called by special retainers, during the summer, into many different and distant parts of the country—traveling chiefly in post-chaises. He felt himself called upon to declare that his poor faculties were at the service of his country—of the free and enlightened part of it at least. He stood there as a man—he stood in the eye, indeed, in the hand of God—to whom (in the presence of the company and the waiters), he solemnly appealed. He was of noble, perhaps royal, blood—he had a house at Hampsted—was convinced of the necessity of a thorough and radical reform. His pamphlets had gone through thirty editions, skipping alternately the odd and even numbers. He loved the Constitution, to which he would cling and grapple—and he was clothed with the infirmities of man's nature."

to juniors of the present date whose professional incapacity closely resembles the incompetence of this gay young barrister of Charles II.'s time. Laughter again rises at the thought of Lord Chancellor Bathurst and the judicial perplexities and blunders which caused Sir Charles Williams to class him with those who

> "Were cursed and stigmatized by power,
> And rais'd to be expos'd."

Much more than an average or altogether desirable amount of amiability has fallen to the reader who can refrain from a malicious smile, when he is informed by reliable history that Lord Loughborough (no mean lawyer or inefficient judge), gave utterance to so much bad law, as Chairman of Quarter Sessions in canny Yorkshire, that when on appeal his decisions were reversed with many polite expressions of *sincere* regret by the King's Bench, all Westminster Hall laughed in concert at the mistakes of the sagacious Chief of the Common Pleas.

But no lawyer, brilliant or dull, has been more widely ridiculed for incompetence than Erskine. Sir Causticus Witherett, being asked some years since why a certain Chancellor, unjustly accused of intellectual dimness by his political adversaries and by the uninformed public, preferred his seat amongst the barons to his official place on the woolsack, is said to have replied: "The Lord Chancellor usually takes his seat amongst the peers whenever he can do so with propriety, because he is a highly nervous man, and when he is on the woolsack, he is apt to be frightened at finding himself all alone—*in the dark*." As soon as Erskine was mentioned as a likely person to be Lord Chancellor, rumors began to circulate concerning his total unfitness for the office; and no sooner had he mounted the woolsack than the wits declared him to be alone and in the dark. Lord Ellenborough's sarcasm was widely repeated, and gave the cue to the advocate's detractors, who had little difficulty in persuading the public that any intelligent law-clerk would make as good a Chancellor as Thomas Erskine. With less discretion than good-humor, Erskine gave countenance to the representations of his enemies by ridiculing his own unfitness for the office. During the interval between his appointment and his first appearance as judge in the Court of Chancery, he made a jocose pretence of 'reading up' for his new duties: and whimsically exaggerating his deficiencies, he represented himself as studying books with which raw students have some degree of familiarity. Caught with 'Cruise's Digest' of the laws relating to real property, open in his hand, he observed to the visitor who had interrupted his studies, "You see, I am taking a little from my *cruise* daily, without any prospect of coming to the end of it."

In the autumn of 1819 two gentlemen of the United States having differed in opinion concerning his incompetence in the Court of Chancery—the one of them maintaining that the greater number of his decrees had been reversed, and the other maintaining that so many of his decisions had not endured reversal—the dispute gave rise to a bet of three dozen of port. With comical bad taste one of the parties to the bet—the one who believed that the Chancellor's judgments had been thus frequently upset—wrote to Erskine for information on the point. Instead of giving the answer which his correspondent desired, Erskine informed him in the following terms that he had lost his wine:—

> "Upper Berkley Street, Nov. 13, 1819.
>
> "Sir:—I certainly was appointed Chancellor under the administration in which Mr. Fox was Secretary of State, in 1806, and could have been Chancellor under no administration in which he had not a post; nor would have accepted without him any office whatsoever. I believe the administration was said, by all the *Blockheads*, to be made up of all the *Talents* in the country.
>
> "But you have certainly lost your bet on the subject of my decrees. None of them were appealed against, except one, upon a branch of Mr. Thellusson's will—but it was affirmed without a dissentient voice, on the motion of Lord Eldon, then and now Lord Chancellor. If you think I was no lawyer, you may continue to think so. It is plain you are no lawyer yourself; but I wish every man to retain his opinion, though at the cost of three dozen of port.
>
> "Your humble servant,
> "Erskine.
>
> "To save you from spending your money on bets which you are sure to lose, remember that no man can be a great advocate who is no lawyer. The thing is impossible."

Of the many good stories current about chiefs of the law who are still alive, the present writer, for obvious reasons, abstains from taking notice; but one humorous anecdote concerning a lively judge may with propriety be inserted in these pages, since it fell from his own lips when he was making a speech from the chair at a public dinner. Between sixty-five and seventy years from the present time, when Sir Frederick Pollock was a boy at St. Paul's school, he drew upon himself the displeasure of Dr. Roberts, the somewhat irascible head-master of the school, who frankly told Sir Frederick's father, "Sir, you'll live to see that boy of yours hanged." Years afterwards, when the boy of whom this dismal prophecy was made had distinguished himself at Cambridge and the bar, Dr. Roberts, meeting Sir Frederick's mother in society, overwhelmed her with congratulations upon her son's success, and fortunately oblivious of his former misunderstanding with his pupil, concluded his polite speeches by saying—"Ah! madam, I always said he'd fill an *elevated* situation." Told by the venerable judge at a recent dinner of 'Old Paulines,' this story was not less effective than the best of those post-prandial sallies with which William St. Julien Arabin—the Assistant Judge of Old Bailey notoriety—used to convulse his auditors something more than thirty years since. In the 'Arabiniana' it is recorded how this judge, in sentencing an unfortunate woman to a long term of transportation, concluded his address with—"You must go out of the country. You have disgraced *even* your own sex."

Let this chapter close with a lawyer's testimony to the moral qualities of his brethren. In the garden of Clement's Inn may still be seen the statue of a negro, supporting a sun-dial, upon which a legal wit inscribed the following lines:—

"In vain, poor sable son of woe,
Thou seek'st the tender tear;
From thee in vain with pangs they flow,
For mercy dwells not here.
From cannibals thou fled'st in vain;
Lawyers less quarter give;
The *first* won't eat you till you're *slain*,
The *last* will do't *alive*."

Unfortunately these lines have been obliterated.

*Chapter 42*

# Witnesses

In the days when Mr. Davenport Hill, the Recorder of Birmingham, made a professional reputation for himself in the committee-rooms of the Houses of Parliament, he had many a sharp tussle with one of those venal witnesses who, during the period of excitement that terminated in the disastrous railway panic, were ready to give scientific evidence on engineering questions, with less regard to truth than to the interests of the persons who paid for their evidence. Having by mendacious evidence gravely injured a cause in which Mr. Hill was interested as counsel, and Mr. Tite, the eminent architect, and present member for Bath, was concerned as a projector, this witness was struck with apoplexy and died—before he could complete the mischief which he had so adroitly begun. Under the circumstances, his sudden withdrawal from the world was not an occasion for universal regret. "Well, Hill, have you heard the news?" inquired Mr. Tite of the barrister, whom he encountered in Middle Temple Lane on the morning after the engineer's death. "Have you heard that —— died yesterday of apoplexy?" "I can't say," was the rejoinder, "that I shall shed many tears for his loss. He was an arrant scoundrel." "Come, come," replied the architect, charitably, "you have always been too hard on that man. He was by no means so bad a fellow as you would make him out. I do verily believe that in the whole course of his life that man never told a lie—*out of the witness-box*." Strange to say, this comical testimony to character was quite justified by the fact. This man, who lied in public as a matter of business, was punctiliously honorable in private life.

Of the simplest method of tampering with witnesses an instance is found in a case which occurred while Sir Edward Coke was Chief Justice of the King's Bench. Loitering about Westminster Hall, one of the parties in an action stumbled upon the witness whose temporary withdrawal from the ways of men he was most anxious to effect. With a perfect perception of the proper use of hospitality, he accosted this witness (a staring, open-mouthed countryman), with suitable professions of friendliness, and carrying him into an adjacent tavern, set him down before a bottle of wine. As soon as the sack had begun to quicken his guest's circulation, the crafty fellow hastened into court with the intelligence that the witness, whom he had left drinking in a room not two hundred yards distant, was in a fit and lying at death's door. The court being asked to wait, the impudent rascal protested that to wait would be useless; and the Chief Justice, taking his view of the case, proceeded to give judgment without hearing the most important evidence in the cause.

In badgering a witness with noisy derision, no barrister of Charles II.'s time could surpass George Jeffreys; but on more than one occasion that gentleman, in his most overbearing moments, met with his master in the witness whom he meant to brow-beat. "You fellow in the leathern doublet," he is said to have exclaimed to a countryman whom he was about to cross-examine, "Pray, what are you paid for swearing?" "God bless you, sir, and make you an honest man," answered the farmer, looking the barrister full in the face, and speaking with a voice of hearty good-humor; "if you had no more for lying than I have for swearing, you would wear a leather doublet as well as I."

Sometimes Erskine's treatment of witnesses was very jocular, and sometimes very unfair; but his jocoseness was usually so distinct from mere flippant derisiveness, and his unfairness was redeemed by such delicacy of wit and courtesy of manner, that his most malicious *jeux d'esprit* seldom raised the anger of the witnesses at whom they were aimed. A religious enthusiast objecting to be sworn in the usual manner, but stating that though he would not "kiss the book," he would "hold up his hand" and swear, Erskine asked him to give his reason for preferring so eccentric a way to the ordinary mode of giving testimony. "It is written in the book of Revelations," answered the man, "that the angel standing on the sea *held up his hand*." "But that does not apply to your case," urged the advocate; "for in the first place, you are no angel; secondly, you cannot tell how the angel would have sworn if he had stood on dry ground, as you do." Not shaken by this reply, which cannot be called unfair, and which, notwithstanding its jocoseness, was exactly the answer which the gravest divine would have made to such scruples, the witness persisted in his position; and on being permitted to give evidence in his own peculiar way, he had enough influence with the jury to induce them to give a verdict adverse to Erskine's wishes.

Less fair but more successful was Erskine's treatment of the commercial traveller, who appeared in the witness box dressed in the height of fashion, and wearing a starched white necktie folded with the 'Brummel fold.' In an instant reading the character of the man, on whom he had never before set eyes, and knowing how necessary it was to put him in a state of extreme agitation and confusion, before touching on the facts concerning which he had come to give evidence, Erskine rose, surveyed the coxcomb, and said, with an air of careless amusement, "You were born and bred in Manchester, *I perceive*." Greatly astonished at this opening remark, the man answered, nervously, that he was "a Manchester man—born and bred in Manchester." "Exactly," observed Erskine, in a conversational tone, and as though he were imparting information to a personal friend— "exactly so; I knew it from the absurd tie of your neckcloth." The roars of laughter which followed this rejoinder so completely effected the speaker's purpose that the confounded bagman could not tell his right hand from his left. Equally effective was Erskine's sharp question, put quickly to the witness, who, in an action for payment of a tailor's bill, swore that a certain dress-coat was badly made—one of the sleeves being longer than the other. "You will," said Erskine, slowly, having risen to cross-examine, "swear—that one of the sleeves was—longer—than the other?" *Witness.* "I do swear it." *Erskine*, quickly, and with a flash of indignation, "Then, sir, I am to understand that you positively deny that one of the sleeves was *shorter* than the other?" Startled into a self-contradiction by the suddenness and impetuosity of this thrust, the witness said, "I do deny it." *Erskine*, raising his voice as the tumultuous laughter died away, "Thank you, sir; I don't want to trouble you with another question." One of Erskine's smartest puns referred to a question of evidence. "A case," he observed, in a speech made during his latter years, "being laid before me by my veteran friend, the Duke of Queensbury—better known as 'old Q'—as to whether he could sue a tradesman for breach of contract about the painting of his house; and the evidence being totally insufficient to support the case, I wrote thus: 'I am of opinion that this action will not *lie* unless the witnesses *do*.'" It is worthy of notice that this witticism was but a revival (with a modification) of a pun attributed to Lord Chancellor Hatton in Bacon's 'Apophthegmes.'

In this country many years have elapsed since duels have taken place betwixt gentlemen of the long robe, or between barristers and witnesses in consequence of words uttered in the heat of forensic strife; but in the last century, and in the opening years of the present, it was no very rare occurrence for a barrister to be called upon for 'satisfaction' by a person whom he had insulted in the course of his professional duty. During George II.'s reign, young Robert Henley so mercilessly badgered one Zephaniah Reeve, whom he had occasion to cross-examine in a trial at Bristol, that the infuriated witness—Quaker and peace-loving merchant though he was—sent his persecutor a challenge immediately upon leaving court. Rather than incur the ridicule of 'going out with a Quaker,' and the sin of shooting at a man whom he had actually treated with unjustifiable freedom, Henley retreated from an embarrassing position by making a handsome apology; and years afterwards, when he had risen to the woolsack, he entertained his old acquaintance, Zephaniah Reeve, at a fashionable dinner-party, when he assembled guests were greatly amused by the Lord Chancellor's account of the commencement of his acquaintance with his Quaker friend.

Between thirty and forty years later Thurlow was 'called out' by the Duke of Hamilton's agent, Mr. Andrew Stewart, whom he had grievously offended by his conduct of the Great Douglas Case. On Jan. 14, 1769-1770, Thurlow and his adversary met in Hyde Park. On his way to the appointed place, the barrister stopped at a tavern near Hyde Park Corner, and "ate an enormous breakfast," after which preparation for business, he hastened to the field of action. Accounts agree in saying that he behaved well upon the ground. Long after the bloodless *rencontre*, the Scotch agent, not a little proud of his 'affair' with a future Lord Chancellor, said, "Mr. Thurlow advanced and stood up to me like an elephant." But the elephant and the mouse parted without hurting each other; the encounter being thus faithfully described in the 'Scots' Magazine:' "On Sunday morning, January 14, the parties met with swords and pistols, in Hyde Park, one of them having for his second his brother, Colonel S——, and the other having for his Mr. L——, member for a city in Kent. Having discharged pistols, at ten yards' distance, without effect, they drew their swords, but the seconds interposed, and put an end to the affair."

One of the best 'Northern Circuit stories' pinned upon Lord Eldon relates to a challenge which an indignant suitor is said to have sent to Law and John Scott. In a trial at York that arose from a horse-race, it was stated in evidence that one of the conditions of the race required that "each horse should be ridden by a gentleman." The race having been run, the holders refused to pay the stakes to the winner on the ground that he was not a gentleman; whereupon the equestrian whose gentility was thus called in question brought an action for the money. After a very humorous inquiry, which terminated in a verdict for the defendants, the plaintiff *was said* to have challenged the defendants' counsel. Messrs. Scott and Law, for maintaining that he was no gentleman; to which invitation, it also averred, reply was made that the challengees "could not think of fighting one who had been found *no gentleman* by the solemn verdict of twelve of his countrymen." Inquiry, however, has deprived this delicious story of much of its piquancy. Eldon had no part in the offence; and Law, who was the sole utterer of the obnoxious words, received no invitation to fight. "No message was sent," says a writer, supposed to be Lord Brougham, in the 'Law Magazine,' "and no attempt was made to provoke a breach of the peace. It is very possible Lord Eldon may have said, and Lord Ellenborough too, that they were not bound to treat one in such a predicament as a gentleman, and hence the story has arisen in the lady's mind. The fact was as well known on the Northern Circuit as the answer of a witness to a question, whether the party had a right by his circumstances to keep a pack of fox-hounds; 'No more right than I to keep a pack of archbishops.'"

Curran is said to have received a call, before he left his bed one morning, from a gentleman whom he had cross-examined with needless cruelty and unjustifiable insolence on the previous day. "Sir!" said this irate man, presenting himself in Curran's bedroom, and rousing the barrister from slumber to a consciousness that he was in a very awkward position, "I am the gintleman whom you insulted yesterday in His Majesty's court of justice, in the presence of the whole county, and I am here to thrash you soundly!" Thus speaking, the Herculean intruder waved a horsewhip over the recumbent lawyer. "You don't mean to strike a man when he is lying down?" inquired Curran. "No, bedad; I'll just wait till you've got out of bed and then I'll give it to you sharp and fast." Curran's eye twinkled mischievously as he rejoined: "If that's the case, by —— I'll lie here all day." So tickled was the visitor with this humorous announcement, that he dropped his horsewhip, and dismissing anger with a hearty roar of laughter, asked the counsellor to shake hands with him.

In the December of 1663, Pepys was present at a trial in Guildhall concerning the fraud of a merchant-adventurer, who having insured his vessel for £2400 when, together with her cargo, she was worth no more than £500, had endeavored to wreck her off the French coast. From Pepys's record it appears that this was a novel piece of rascality at that time, and consequently created lively sensation in general society, as well as in legal and commercial coteries. "All the great counsel in the kingdom" were employed in the cause; and though maritime causes then, as now, usually involved much hard swearing, the case was notable for the prodigious amount of perjury which it elicited. For the most part the witnesses were sailors, who, besides swearing with stolid indifference to truth, caused much amusement by the incoherence of their statements and by their free use of nautical expressions, which were quite unintelligible to Chief Justice (Sir Robert) Hyde. "It was," says Pepys, "pleasant to see what mad sort of testimonys the seamen did give, and could not be got to speak in order; and then their terms such as the judge could not understand, and to hear how sillily the counsel and judge would speak as to the terms necessary in the matter, would make one laugh; and above all a Frenchman, that was forced to speak in French, and took an English oath he did not understand, and had an interpreter sworn to tell us what he said, which was the best testimony of all." A century later Lord Mansfield was presiding at a trial consequent upon a collision of two ships at sea, when a common sailor, whilst giving testimony, said, "At the time I was standing abaft the binnacle;" whereupon his lordship, with a proper desire to master the facts of the case, observed, "Stay, stay a minute, witness: you say that at the time in question you were *standing abaft the binnacle*; now tell me, where is abaft the binnacle?" This was too much for the gravity of 'the salt,' who immediately before climbing into the witness-box had taken a copious draught of neat rum. Removing his eyes from the bench, and turning round upon the crowded court with an expression of intense amusement, he exclaimed at the top of his voice, "He's a pretty fellow for a judge! Bless my jolly old eyes!—[the reader may substitute a familiar form of 'imprecation on eye-sight']—you have got a pretty sort of a land-lubber for a judge! He wants me to tell him where *abaft the binnacle is*!" Not less amused than the witness, Lord Mansfield rejoined, "Well, my friend, you must fit me for my office by telling me where *abaft the binnacle* is; you've already shown me the meaning of *half seas over*."

With less good-humor the same Chief Justice revenged himself on Dr. Brocklesby, who, whilst standing in the witness-box of the Court of King's Bench, incurred the Chief Justice's displeasure by referring to their private intercourse. Some accounts say that the medical witness merely nodded to the Chief Justice, as he might have done with propriety had they been taking seats at a convivial table; other accounts, with less appearance of probability, maintain that in a voice audible to the bar, he reminded the Chief Justice of certain jolly hours which they had spent together during the previous evening. Anyhow, Lord Mansfield was hurt, and showed his resentment in his 'summing-up' by thus addressing the Jury: "The next witness is one *R*ocklesby, or *B*rocklesby—*B*rocklesby or *R*ocklesby, I am not sure which; and first, *he swears that he is a physician*."

On one occasion Lord Mansfield covered his retreat from an untenable position with a sparkling pleasantry. An old witness named *Elm* having given his evidence with remarkable clearness, although he was more than eighty years of age, Lord Mansfield examined him as to his habitual mode of living, and found that he had throughout life been an early riser and a singularly temperate man. "Ay," observed the Chief Justice, in a tone of approval, "I have always found that without temperance and early habits, longevity is never attained." The next witness, the *elder* brother of this model of temperance, was then called, and he almost surpassed his brother as an intelligent and clear-headed utterer of evidence. "I suppose," observed Lord Mansfield, "that you also are an early riser." "No, my lord," answered the veteran, stoutly; "I like my bed at all hours, and special-*lie* I like it of a morning." "Ah; but, like your brother, you are a very temperate man?" quickly asked the judge, looking out anxiously for the safety of the more important part of his theory. "My lord," responded this ancient Elm, disdaining to plead guilty to a charge of habitual sobriety, "I am a very old man, and my memory is as clear as a bell, but I can't remember the night when I've gone to bed without being more or less drunk." Lord Mansfield was silent. "Ah, my lord," Mr. Dunning exclaimed, "this old man's case supports a theory upheld by many persons, that habitual intemperance is favorable to longevity." "No, no," replied the Chief Justice, with a smile, "this old man and his brother merely teach us what every carpenter knows—that Elm, whether it be wet or dry, is a very tough wood." Another version of this excellent story makes Lord Mansfield inquire of the elder Elm, "Then how do you account for your prolonged tenure of existence?" to which question Elm is made to respond, more like a lawyer than a simple witness, "I account for it by the terms of the original lease."

Few stories relating to witnesses are more laughable than that which describes the arithmetical process by which Mr. Baron Perrot arrived at the value of certain conflicting evidence. "Gentlemen of the jury," this judge is reported to have said, in summing up the evidence in a trial where the witnesses had sworn with noble tenacity of purpose, "there are fifteen witnesses who swear that the watercourse used to flow in a ditch on the north side of the hedge. On the other hand, gentlemen, there are nine witnesses who swear that the watercourse used to flow on the south side of the hedge. Now, gentlemen, if you subtract nine from fifteen, there remain six witnesses wholly uncontradicted; and I recommend you to give your verdict for the party who called those six witnesses."

Whichever of the half-dozen ways in which it is told be accepted as the right one, the following story exemplifies the difficulty which occasionally arises in courts of justice, when witnesses use provincial terms with which the judge is not familiar. Mr. William Russell, in past days deputy-surveyor of 'canny Newcastle,' and a genuine Northumbrian in dialect, brogue, and shrewdness, was giving his evidence at an important trial in the Newcastle court-house, when he said—"As I was going along the quay, I saw a hubbleshew coming out of a chare-foot." Not aware that on Tyne-side the word 'hubbleshew' meant 'a concourse of riotous persons;' that the narrow alleys or lanes of Newcastle 'old town' were called by their inhabitants 'chares;' and that the lower end of each alley, where it opened upon quay-side, was termed a 'chare-foot;' the judge, seeing only one part of the puzzle, inquired the meaning of the word 'hubbleshew.' "A crowd of disorderly persons," answered the deputy-surveyor. "And you mean to say," inquired the judge of assize, with a voice and look of surprise, "that you saw a crowd of people come out of a chair-foot?" "I do, my lord," responded the witness. "Gentlemen of the jury," said his lordship, turning to the 'twelve good men' in the box, "it must be needless for me to inform you—*that this witness is insane*!"

The report of a trial which occurred at Newcastle Assizes towards the close of the last century gives the following succession of questions and answers:—*Barrister.*—"What is your name?" *Witness.*—"Adam, sir—Adam Thompson." *Barrister.*—"Where do you live?" *Witness.*—"In Paradise." *Barrister* (with facetious tone).—"And pray, Mr. Adam, how long have you dwelt in Paradise?" *Witness.*—"Ever since the flood." Paradise is the name of a village in the immediate vicinity of Newcastle; and 'the flood' referred to by the witness was the inundation (memorable in local annals) of the Tyne, which in the year 1771 swept away the old Tyne Bridge.

*Chapter 43*

# CIRCUITEERS

Exposed to some of the discomforts, if not all the dangers,[33] of travel; required to ride over black and cheerless tracts of moor and heath: now belated in marshy districts, and now exchanging shots with gentlemen of the road; sleeping, as luck favored them, in way-side taverns, country mansions, or the superior hotels of provincial towns—the circuiteers of olden time found their advantage in cultivating social hilarity and establishing an etiquette that encouraged good-fellowship in their itinerant societies. At an early date they are found varying the monotony of cross-country rides with racing-matches and drinking bouts, cock-fights and fox-hunting; and enlivening assize towns and country houses with balls and plays, frolic and song. A prodigious amount of feasting was perpetrated on an ordinary circuit-round of the seventeenth century; and at circuit-messes, judges' dinners, and sheriffs' banquets, saucy juniors were allowed a license of speech to staid leaders and grave dignitaries that was altogether exceptional to the prevailing tone of manners.

In the days when Chief Justice Hyde, Clarendon's cousin, used to ride the Norfolk Circuit, old Sergeant Earl was the leader, or, to use the slang of the period, 'cock of the round'. A keen, close-fisted, tough practitioner, this sergeant used to ride from town to town, chuckling over the knowledge that he was earning more and spending less than any other member of the circuit. One biscuit was all the refreshment which he permitted himself on the road from Cambridge to Norwich; although he consented to dismount at the end of every ten miles to stretch his limbs. Sidling up to Sergeant Earl, as there was no greater man for him to toady, Francis North offered himself as the old man's travelling companion from the university to the manufacturing town; and when Earl with a grim

---

[33] Lord Eldon, when he was handsome Jack Scott of the Northern Circuit, was about to make a short cut over the sands from Ulverstone to Lancaster at the of the tide, when he was restrained from acting on his rash resolve by the representations of an hotel keeper. "Danger, danger," asked Scott, impatiently—"have you ever *lost* anybody there?" Mine host answered slowly, "Nae, sir, nae body has been *lost* on the sands, *the puir bodies have been found at low water*."

smile accepted the courteous suggestion, the young man congratulated himself. On the following morning, however, he had reason to question his good fortune when the sergeant's clerk brought him a cake, and remarked, significantly, "Put it in your pocket, sir; you'll want it; for my master won't draw bit till he comes to Norwich." It was a hard day's work; but young Frank North was rewarded for his civility to the sergeant, who condescended to instruct his apt pupil in the tricks and chicaneries of their profession. "Sir," inquired North at the close of the excursion, emboldened by the rich man's affability, "by what system do you keep your accounts, which must be very complex, as you have lands, securities, and great comings-in of all kinds?" "Accounts! boy," answered the grey-headed curmudgeon; "I get as much as I can, and I spend as little as I can; that's how I keep my accounts."

When North had raised himself to the Chiefship of the Common Pleas he chose the Western Circuit, "not for the common cause, it being a long circuit, and beneficial for the officers and servants, but because he knew the gentlemen to be loyal and conformable, and that he should have fair quarter amongst them;" and so much favor did he win amongst the loyal and conformable gentry that old Bishop Mew—the prelate of Winchester, popularly known as Bishop *Patch*, because he always wore a patch of black court-plaster over the scar of a wound which he received on one of his cheeks, whilst fighting as a trooper for Charles I.—used to term him the "Deliciæ occidentis, or Darling of the West." On one occasion this Darling of the West was placed in a ludicrous position by the alacrity with which he accepted an invitation from "a busy fanatic," a Devonshire gentleman, of good family, and estate, named Duke. This "busy fanatic" invited the judges on circuit and their officers to dine and sleep at his mansion on their way to Exeter, and subsequently scandalized his guests—all of them of course zealous defenders of the Established Church—by reading family-prayers before supper. "The gentleman," says the historian, "had not the manners to engage the parish minister to come and officiate with any part of the evening service before supper: but he himself got behind the table in his hall, and read a chapter, and then a long-winded prayer, after the Presbyterian way." Very displeased were the Chief Justice and the other Judge of Assize; and their dissatisfaction was not diminished on the following day when on entering Exeter a rumor met them, that "the judges had been at a conventicle, and the grand jury intended to present them and all their retinue for it."

Not many years elapsed before this Darling of the West was replaced, by another Chief Justice who asserted the power of constituted authorities with an energy that roused more fear than gratitude in the breasts of local magistrates. That grim, ghastly, hideous progress, which Jeffreys made in the plenitude of civil and military power through the Western Counties, was not without its comic interludes; and of its less repulsive scenes none was more laughable than that which occurred in Bristol Courthouse when the terrible Chief Justice upbraided the Bristol magistrates for taking part in a slave-trade of the most odious sort. The mode in which the authorities of the western port carried on their iniquitous traffic deserves commemoration, for no student can understand the history of any period until he has acquainted himself with its prevailing morality. At a time when by the wealth of her merchants and the political influence of her inhabitants Bristol was the second city of England, her mayor and aldermen used daily to sit in judgment on young men and growing boys, who were brought before them and charged with trivial offences. Some of the prisoners had actually broken the law: but in a large proportion of the cases the accusations were totally fictitious—the arrests having been made in accordance with the directions of the magistrates, on charges which the magistrates themselves knew to be utterly without foundation. Every morning the Bristol tolsey or court-house saw a crowd of those wretched captives—clerks out of employment, unruly apprentices, street boys without parents, and occasionally children of honest birth, ay, of patrician lineage, whose prompt removal from their native land was desired by brutal fathers or vindictive guardians; and every morning a mockery of judicial investigation was perpetrated in the name of justice. Standing in a crowd the prisoners were informed of the offences charged against them; huddled together in the dock, like cattle in a pen, they caught stray sentences from the lips of the perjured rascals who had seized them in the public ways; and whilst they thus in a frenzy of surprise and fear listened to the statements of counsel for the prosecution, and to the fabrications of lying witnesses, agents of the court whispered to them that if they wished to save their lives they must instantly confess their guilt, and implore the justices to transport them to the plantations. Ignorant, alarmed, and powerless, the miserable victims invariably acted on this perfidious counsel; and forthwith the magistrates ordered their shipment to the West Indies, where they were sold as slaves—the money paid for them by West India planters in due course finding its way into the pockets of the Bristol justices. It is asserted that the wealthier aldermen, through caution, or those few grains of conscience which are often found in the breasts of consummate rogues, forbore to share in the gains of this abominable traffic; but it cannot be gainsaid that the least guilty magistrates winked at the atrocious conduct of their brother-justices.

Vowing vengeance on the Bristol kidnappers Jeffreys entered their court-house, and opened proceedings by crying aloud that "he had brought a broom to sweep them with." The Mayor of Bristol was in those days no common mayor; in Assize Commissions his name was placed before the names of Judges of Assize; and even beyond the limits of his jurisdiction he was a man of mark and influence. Great therefore was this dignitary's astonishment when Jeffreys ordered him—clothed as he was in official scarlet and furs—to stand in the dock. For a few seconds the local potentate demurred; but when the Chief Justice poured upon him a cataract of blasphemy, and vowed to hang him instantly over the entrance to the tolsey unless he complied immediately, the humiliated chief magistrate of the ancient borough took his place at the felon's bar, and received such a rating as no thief, murderer or rebel had ever heard from George Jeffrey's abusive mouth. Unfortunately the affair ended with the storm. Until the arrival of William of Orange the guilty magistrates were kept in fear of criminal prosecution; but the matter was hushed up and covered with amnesty by the new government; so that "the fright only, which was no small one, was all the punishment which these judicial kidnappers underwent; and the gains," says Roger North, "acquired by so wicked a trade, rested peacefully in their pockets." It should be remembered that the kidnapping justices whom the odious Jeffreys so indignantly denounced were tolerated and courted by their respectable and prosperous neighbors; and some of the worst charges, by which the judge's fame has been rendered odious to posterity, depend upon the evidence of men who, if they were not kidnappers themselves, saw nothing peculiarly atrocious in the conduct of magistrates who systematically sold their fellow-countrymen into a most barbarous slavery.

Amongst old circuit stories of questionable truthfulness there is a singular anecdote recorded by the biographers of Chief Justice Hale, who, whilst riding the Western Circuit, tried a half-starved lad on a charges of burglary. The prisoner had been shipwrecked upon the Cornish coast, and on his way through an inhospitable district had endured the pangs of extreme hunger. In his distress, the famished wanderer broke the window of a baker's shop and stole a loaf of bread. Under the circumstances, Hale directed the jury to acquit the prisoner: but, less merciful than the judge, the gentlemen of the box returned a verdict of 'Guilty'—a verdict which the Chief Justice stoutly refused to act upon. After much resistance, the jurymen were starved into submission; and the youth was set at liberty. Several years elapsed; and Chief Justice Hale was riding the Northern Circuit, when he was received with such costly and excessive pomp by the sheriff of a northern county, that he expostulated with his entertainer on the lavish profuseness of his conduct. "My lord," answered the sheriff, with emotion, "don't blame me for showing my gratitude to the judge who saved my life when I was an outcast. Had it not been for you, I should have been hanged in Cornwall for stealing a loaf, instead of living to be the richest landowner of my native county."

A sketch of circuit-life in the middle of the last century may be found in 'A Northern Circuit, Described in a Letter to a Friend: a Poetical Essay. By a Gentleman of the Middle Temple. 1751.'—a piece of doggrel that will meet with greater mercy from the antiquary than the poetical critic.

In seeking to avoid the customary exactions of their office, the sheriffs of the present generation were only following in the steps of sheriffs who, more than a century past, exerted themselves to reduce the expenses of shrievalties, and whose economical reforms were defended by reference to the conduct of sheriffs under the last of the Tudors.—In the days of Elizabeth, the sheriffs demanded and obtained relief from an obligation to supply judges on circuit, with food and lodging; under Victoria they have recently exclaimed against the custom which required them to furnish guards of javelin-bearers for the protection of Her Majesty's representatives; when George II was king, they grumbled against lighter burdens—for instance, the cost of white kid-gloves and payments to bell-ringers. The sheriff is still required by custom to present the judges with white gloves whenever an assize has been held without a single capital conviction; but in past times, on every *maiden* assize, he was expected to give gloves not only to the judges, but to the entire body of circuiteers—barristers as well as officers of court.[34] Wishing to keep his official expenditure down to the lowest possible sum, a certain sheriff for Cumberland—called in 'A Northern Circuit,' Sir Frigid Gripus Knapper—directed his under-sheriff not to give white gloves on the occasion of a maiden assize at Carlisle, and also through the mouth of his subordinate, declined to pay the officers of the circuit certain customary fees. To put the innovator to shame, Sir William Gascoigne, the judge before whom the case was laid, observed in open court, "Though I can compel an immediate payment, it being a demand of right, and not a mere gift, yet I will set him an example by gifts which I might refuse, but will not, because they are customary," and forthwith addressing the steward, added—"Call the sheriff's coachman, his pages, and musicians, singing-boys, and vergers, and give them the accustomed gifts as soon as the sheriff comes." From this direction, readers may see that under the old system of presents a judge was compelled to give away with his left hand much of that which he accepted with his right. It appears that Sir William Gascoigne's conduct had the desired effect; for as soon as the sheriff made his appearance, he repudiated the parsimonious conduct of the under-sheriff—though it is not credible that the subordinate acted without the direction or concurrence of his superior. "I think it," observed the sheriff, in reference to the sum of the customary payments, "as much for the honor of my office, and the country in general, as it is justice to those to whom it is payable; and if any sheriff has been of a different opinion it shall never bias me."

From the days when Alexander Wedderburn, in his new silk gown, to the scandal of all sticklers for professional etiquette, made a daring but futile attempt to seize the lead of

[34] With regard to the customary gifts of white gloves Mr. Foss says:—"Gloves were presented to the judges on some occasions: viz., when a man, convicted for murder, or manslaughter, came and pleaded the king's pardon; and, till the Act of 4 & 5 William and Mary c. 18, which rendered personal appearance unnecessary, an outlawry could not be reversed, unless the defendant came into court, and with a present of gloves to the judges implored their favor to reverse it. The custom of giving the judge a pair of white gloves upon a maiden assize has continued till the present time." An interesting chapter might be written on the ancient ceremonies and usages obsolete and extant, of our courts of law. Here are a few of the practices which such a chapter would properly notice:—The custom, still maintained, which forbids the Lord Chancellor to utter any word or make any sign, when on Lord Mayor's Day the Lord Mayor of London enters the Court of Chancery, and by the mouth of the Recorder prays his lordship to honor the Guildhall banquet with his presence; the custom—extant so late as Lord Brougham's Chancellorship—which required the Holder of the Seals, at the installation of a new Master of Chancery, to install the new master by placing a cap or hat on his head; the custom which in Charles II.'s time, on motion days at the Chancellor's, compelled all barristers making motions to contribute to his lordship's 'Poor's Box'—barristers within the bar paying two shillings, and outer barristers one shilling—the contents of which box were periodically given to magistrates, for distribution amongst the deserving poor of London; the custom which required a newly-created judge to present his colleagues with biscuits and wine; the barbarous custom which compelled prisoners to plead their defence, standing in fetters, a custom enforced by Chief Justice Pratt at the trial of the Jacobite against Christopher Layer, although at the of trial of Cranburne for complicity in the 'Assassination Plot,' Holt had enunciated the merciful maxim, "When the prisoners are tried they should stand at ease;" the custom which—in days when forty persons died of gaol fever caught at the memorable Black Sessions (May, 1759) at the Old Bailey, when Captain Clark was tried for killing Captain Innes in a duel—strewed rue, fennel, and other herbs on the ledge of the dock, in the faith that the odor of the herbage would act as a barrier to the poisonous exhalations from prisoners sick of gaol distemper, and would protect the assembly in the body of the court from the contagion of the disease.

the circuit which seventeen years later he rode as judge, 'The Northern' had maintained the *prestige* of being the most important of the English circuits. Its palmiest and most famous days belong to the times of Norton and Wallace, Jack Lee and John Scott, Edward Law and Robert Graham; but still amongst the wise white heads of the upper house may be seen at times the mobile features of an aged peer who, as Mr. Henry Brougham, surpassed in eloquence and intellectual brilliance the brightest and most celebrated of his precursors on the great northern round. But of all the great men whose names illustrate the annals of the circuit, Lord Eldon is the person most frequently remembered in connexion with the jovial ways of circuiteers in the old time. In his later years the port-loving earl delighted to recall the times when as Attorney General of the Circuit Grand Court he used to prosecute offenders 'against the peace of our Lord the Junior,' devise practical jokes for the diversion of the bar, and over bowls of punch at York, Lancaster, or Kirkby Lonsdale, argue perplexing questions about the morals of advocacy. Just as John Campbell, thirty years later, used to recount with glee how in the mock courts of the Oxford Circuit he used to officiate as crier, "holding a fire-shovel in his hand as the emblem of his office;" so did old Lord Eldon warm with mirth over recollections of his circuit revelries and escapades. Many of his stories were apocryphal, some of them unquestionably spurious; but the least truthful of them contained an element of pleasant reality. Of course Jemmy Boswell, a decent lawyer, though better biographer, was neither duped by the sham brief, nor induced to apply in court for the writ of 'quare adhaesit pavimento;' but it is quite credible that on the morning after his removal in a condition of vinous prostration from the Lancaster flagstones, his jocose friends concocted the brief, sent it to him with a bad guinea, and proclaimed the success of their device. When the chimney-sweeper's boy met his death by falling from a high gallery to the floor of the court-house at the York Assizes, whilst Sir Thomas Davenport was speaking, it was John Scott who—arguing that the orator's dullness had sent the boy to sleep, and so caused his fatal fall—prosecuted Sir Thomas for murder in the High Court, alleging in the indictment that the death was produced by a "certain blunt instrument of *no value*, called a *long speech*." The records of the Northern Circuit abound with testimony to the hearty zeal with which the future Chancellor took part in the proceedings of the Grand Court—paying fines and imposing them with equal readiness, now upholding with mock gravity the high and majestic character of the presiding judge, and at another time inveighing against the levity and indecorum of a learned brother who had maintained in conversation that "no man would be such a——fool as to go to a lawyer for advice who knew how to get on without it." The monstrous offender against religion and propriety who gave utterance to this execrable sentiment was Pepper Arden (subsequently Master of the Rolls and Lord Alvanley), and his punishment is thus recorded in the archives of the circuit:—"In this he was considered as doubly culpable, in the first place as having offended, against the laws of Almighty God by his profane cursing; for which, however, he made a very sufficient atonement by paying a bottle of claret; and secondly, as having made use of an expression which, if it should become a prevailing opinion, might have the most alarming consequences to the profession, and was therefore deservedly considered in a far more hideous light. For the last offence he was fin'd 3 bottles. Pd."

One of the most ridiculous circumstances over which the Northern Circuit men of the last generation delighted to laugh occurred at Newcastle, when Baron Graham—the poor lawyer, but a singularly amiable and placid man, of whom Jeckyll observed, "no one but his sempstress could ruffle him"—rode the circuit, and was immortalized as 'My Lord 'Size,' in Mr. John Shield's capital song—

"The jailor, for trial had brought up a thief,
Whose looks seemed a passport for Botany Bay;
The lawyers, some with and some wanting a brief,
Around the green table were seated so gay;
Grave jurors and witnesses waiting a call;
Attorneys and clients, more angry than wise;
With strangers and town-people, throng'd the Guildhall,
All watching and gaping to see my Lord 'Size.

"Oft stretch'd were their necks, oft erected their ears,
Still fancying they heard of the trumpets the sound,
When tidings arriv'd, which dissolv'd them in tears,
That my lord at the dead-house was then lying drown'd.
Straight left *tête-a-tête* were the jailor and thief;
The horror-struck crowd to the dead-house quick hies;
Ev'n the lawyers, forgetful of fee and of brief,
Set off helter-skelter to view my Lord 'Size.

"And now the Sandhill with the sad tidings rings,
And the tubs of the taties are left to take care;
Fishwomen desert their crabs, lobsters, and lings,
And each to the dead-house now runs like a hare;
The glassmen, some naked, some clad, heard the news,
And off they ran, smoking like hot mutton pies;
Whilst Castle Garth tailors, like wild kangaroos,
Came tail-on-end jumping to see my Lord 'Size.

"The dead-house they reach'd, where his lordship they found,
Pale, stretch'd on a plank, like themselves out of breath,
The coroner and jury were seated around,
Most gravely enquiring the cause of his death.
No haste did they seem in, their task to complete,
Aware that from hurry mistakes often rise;

Or wishful, perhaps, of prolonging the treat
Of thus sitting in judgment upon my Lord 'Size.

"Now the Mansion House butler, thus gravely deposed:—
'My lord on the terrace seem'd studying his charge
And when (as I thought) he had got it compos'd,
He went down the stairs and examined the barge;
First the stem he surveyed, then inspected the stern,
Then handled the tiller, and looked mighty wise;
But he made a false step when about to return,
And souse in the river straight tumbled Lord 'Size.'

"'Now his narrative ended, the butler retir'd,
Whilst Betty Watt, muttering half drunk through her teeth,
Declar'd 'in her breast great consarn it inspir'd,
That my lord should sae cullishly come by his death;'
Next a keelman was called on, Bold Airchy by name,
Who the book as he kissed showed the whites of his eyes,
Then he cut an odd caper attention to claim,
And this evidence gave them respecting Lord 'Size;—

"Aw was settin' the keel, wi' Dick Slavers an' Matt,
An' the Mansion House stairs we were just alongside,
When we a' three see'd somethin', but didn't ken what,
That was splashin' and labberin', aboot i' the tide.
'It's a fluiker,' ki Dick; 'No,' ki Matt, 'its owre big,
It luik'd mair like a skyet when aw furst seed it rise;'
Kiv aw—for aw'd getten a gliff o' the wig—
'Ods marcy! wey, marrows, becrike, it's Lord 'Size.

"'Sae aw huik'd him, an' haul'd him suin into the keel,
An' o' top o' the huddock aw rowl'd him aboot;
An' his belly aw rubb'd, an' aw skelp'd his back weel,
But the water he'd druck'n it wadn't run oot;
So aw brought him ashore here, an' doctor's, in vain,
Furst this way, then that, to recover him tries;
For ye see there he's lyin' as deed as a stane,
An' that's a' aw can tell ye aboot my Lord 'Size.'

"Now the jury for close consultation retir'd:
Some '*Death Accidental*' were willing to find;
'God's Visitation' most eager requir'd;
And some were for 'Fell in the River' inclin'd;
But ere on their verdict they all were agreed,

My Lord gave a groan, and wide opened his eyes;
Then the coach and the trumpeters came with great speed,
And back to the Mansion House carried Lord 'Size."

Amongst memorable Northern Circuit worthies was George Wood, the celebrated Special Pleader, in whose chambers Law, Erskine, Abbott and a mob of eminent lawyers acquired a knowledge of their profession. It is on record that whilst he and Mr. Holroyde were posting the Northern round, they were accosted on a lonely heath by a well-mounted horseman, who reining in his steed asked the barrister "What o'clock it was?" Favorably impressed by the stranger's appearance and tone of voice, Wood pulled out his valuable gold repeater, when the highwayman presenting a pistol, and putting it on the cock, said coolly, "*As you have* a watch, be kind enough to give it me, so that I may not have occasion to trouble you again about the time." To demur was impossible; the lawyer, therefore, who had met his disaster by *going to the country*, meekly submitted to circumstances and surrendered the watch. For the loss of an excellent gold repeater he cared little, but he winced under the banter of his professional brethren, who long after the occurrence used to smile with malicious significance as they accosted him with—"What's the time, Wood?"

Another of the memorable Northern circuiteers was John Hullock, who, like George Wood, became a baron of the Exchequer, and of whom the following story is told on good authority. In an important cause tried upon the Northern Circuit, he was instructed by the attorney who retained him as leader on one side not to produce a certain deed unless circumstances made him think that without its production his client would lose the suit. On perusing the deed entrusted to him with this remarkable injunction, Hullock saw that it established his client's case, and wishing to dispatch the business with all possible promptitude, he produced the parchment before its exhibition was demanded by necessity. Examination instantly detected the spurious character of the deed, which had been fabricated by the attorney. Of course the presiding judge (Sir John Bayley) ordered the deed to be impounded; but before the order was carried out, Mr. Hullock obtained permission to inspect it again. Restored to his hands, the deed was forthwith replaced in his bag. "You must surrender that deed instantly," exclaimed the judge, seeing Hullock's intention to keep it. "My lord," returned the barrister, warmly, "no power on earth shall induce me to surrender it. I have incautiously put the life of a fellow-creature in peril; and though I acted to the best of my discretion, I should never be happy again were a fatal result to ensue." At a loss to decide on the proper course of action, Mr. Justice Bayley retired from court to consult with his learned brother. On his lordship's reappearance in court, Mr. Hullock—who had also left the court for a brief period—told him that during his absence the forged deed had been destroyed. The attorney escaped; the barrister became a judge.

*Chapter 44*

# LAWYERS AND SAINTS

Notwithstanding the close connexion which in old times existed between the Church and the Law, popular sentiment holds to the opinion that the ways of lawyers are far removed from the ways of holiness, and that the difficulties encountered by wealthy travellers on the road to heaven are far greater with rich lawyers than with any other class of rich men. An old proverb teaches that wearers of the long robe never reach paradise *per saltum*, but 'by slow degrees;' and an irreverent ballad supports the vulgar belief that the only attorney to be found on the celestial rolls gained admittance to the blissful abode more by artifice than desert. The ribald broadside runs in the following style:—

"Professions will abuse each other;
The priests won't call the lawyer brother;
While *Salkeld* still beknaves the parson,
And says he cants to keep the farce on.
Yet will I readily suppose
They are not truly bitter foes,
But only have their pleasant jokes,
And banter, just like other folks.
And thus, for so they quiz the law,
Once on a time th' Attorney Flaw,
A man to tell you, as the fact is,
Of vast chicane, of course of practice;
(But what profession can we trace
Where none will not the corps disgrace?
Seduced, perhaps, by roguish client,
Who tempt him to become more pliant),
A notice had to quit the world,
And from his desk at once was hurled.
Observe, I pray, the plain narration:

'Twas in a hot and long vacation,
When time he had but no assistance.
Tho' great from courts of law the distance,
To reach the court of truth and justice
(Where I confess my only trust is);
Though here below the special pleader
Shows talents worthy of a leader,
Yet his own fame he must support,
Be sometimes witty with the court
Or word the passion of a jury
By tender strains, or full of fury;
Misleads them all, tho' twelve apostles,
While with the new law the judge he jostles,
And makes them all give up their powers
To speeches of at least three hours—
But we have left our little man,
And wandered from our purpos'd plan:
'Tis said (without ill-natured leaven)
"If ever lawyers get to heaven,
It surely is by slow degrees"
(Perhaps 'tis slow they take their fees).
The case, then, now I fairly state:
Flaw reached at last to heaven's high gate;
Quite short he rapped, none did it neater;
The gate was opened by St. Peter,
Who looked astonished when he saw,
All black, the little man of law;
But charity was Peter's guide.
For having once himself denied
His master, he would not o'erpass
The penitent of any class;
Yet never having heard there entered
A lawyer, nay, nor ever ventured
Within the realms of peace and love,
He told him mildly to remove,
And would have closed the gate of day,
Had not old Flaw, in suppliant way,
Demurring to so hard a fate,
Begg'd but a look, tho' through the gate.
St. Peter, rather off his guard,
Unwilling to be thought too hard,
Opens the gate to let him peep in.
What did the lawyer? Did he creep in?
Or dash at once to take possession?

Oh no, he knew his own profession:
He took his hat off with respect,
And would no gentle means neglect;
But finding it was all in vain
For him admittance to obtain,
Thought it were best, let come what will,
To gain an entry by his skill.
So while St. Peter stood aside,
To let the door be opened wide,
He skimmed his hat with all his strength
Within the gate to no small length.
St. Peter stared; the lawyer asked him
"Only to fetch his hat," and passed him;
But when he reached the jack he'd thrown,
Oh, then was all the lawyer shown;
He clapt it on, and arms akimbo
(As if he had been the gallant Bembo),
Cry'd out—'What think you of my plan?
Eject me, Peter, if you can.'"

The celestial courts having devised no process of ejectment that could be employed in this unlooked-for emergency, St. Peter hastily withdrew to take counsel's opinion; and during his absence Mr. Flaw firmly established himself in the realms of bliss, where he remains to this day the black sheep of the saintly family.

But though a flippant humorist in these later times could deride the lawyer as a character who had better not force his way into heaven, since he would not find a single personal acquaintance amongst its inhabitants, in more remote days lawyers achieved the honors of canonization, and our forefathers sought their saintly intercession with devout fervor. Our calendars still regard the 15th of July as a sacred day, in memory of the holy Swithin, who was tutor to King Ethelwulf and King Alfred, and Chancellor of England, and who certainly deserved his elevation to the fellowship of saints, even had his title to the honor rested solely on a remarkable act which he performed in the exercise of his judicial functions. A familiar set of nursery rhymes sets forth the utter inability of all the King's horses and men to reform the shattered Humpty-Dumpty, when his rotund highness had fallen from a wall; but when a wretched market-woman, whose entire basketful of new-laid eggs had been wilfully smashed by an enemy, sought in her trouble the aid of Chancery, the holy Chancellor Swithin miraculously restored each broken shell to perfect shape, each yolk to soundness. Saith William of Malmesbury, recounting this marvellous achievement—"statimque porrecto crucis signo, fracturam omnium ovorum consolidat."

Like Chancellor Swithin before him, and like Chancellor Wolsey in a later time, Chancellor Becket was a royal tutor;[35] and like Swithin, who still remains the pluvious saint of humid England, and unlike Wolsey, who just missed the glory of canonization, Becket became a widely venerated saint. But less kind to St. Thomas of Canterbury than to St. Swithin, the Reformation degraded Becket from the saintly rank by the decision which terminated the ridiculous legal proceedings instituted by Henry VIII. against the holy reputation of St. Thomas. After the saint's counsel had replied to the Attorney-General, who, of course, conducted the cause for the crown, the court declared that "Thomas, sometime Archbishop of Canterbury, had been guilty of contumacy, treason and rebellion; that his bones should be publicly burnt, to admonish the living of their duty by the punishment of the dead; and that the offerings made at his shrine should be forfeited to the crown."

After the conclusion of the suit for the saint's degradation—a suit which was an extravagant parody of the process for establishing at Rome a holy man's title to the honors of canonization—proclamation was made that "forasmuch as it now clearly appeared that Thomas Becket had been killed in a riot excited by his own obstinacy and intemperate language, and had been afterwards canonized by the Bishop of Rome as the champion of his usurped authority, the king's majesty thought it expedient to declare to his loving subjects that he was no saint, but rather a rebel and traitor to his prince, and therefore strictly charged and commanded that he should not be esteemed or called a saint; that all images and pictures of him should be destroyed, the festivals in his honor be abolished, and his name and remembrance be erased out of all books, under pain of his majesty's indignation and imprisonment at his grace's pleasure."

But neither St. Swithin nor St. Thomas of Canterbury, lawyers though they were, deigned to take the legal profession under especial protection, and to mediate with particular officiousness between the long robe and St. Peter. The peculiar saint of the profession was St. Evona, concerning whom Carr, in his 'Remarks of the Government of the Severall Parts of Germanie, Denmark, &c.,' has the following passage: And now because I am speaking of Petty-foggers, give me leave to tell you a story I mett with when I lived in Rome. Goeing with a Romane to see some antiquityes, he showed me a chapell dedicated to St. Evona, a lawyer of Brittanie, who, he said, came to Rome to entreat the Pope to give the lawyers of Brittanie a patron, to which the Pope replied, that he knew of no saint but what was disposed to other professions. At which Evona was very sad, and earnestly begd of the Pope to think of one for him. At last the Pope

[35] Swithin was tutor to Ethelwulf and Alfred. Becket was tutor to Henry II.'s eldest son. Wolsey—who took delight in discharging scholastic functions from the days when he birched schoolboys at Magdalen College, Oxford, till the time when in the plenitude of his grandeur he framed regulations for Dean Colet's school of St. Paul's and wrote an introduction to a Latin Grammar for the use of children—acted as educational director to the Princess Mary, and superintended the studies of Henry VIII.'s natural son, the Earl of Richmond. Amongst pedagogue-chancellors, by license of fancy, may be included the Earl of Clarendon, whose enemies used to charge him with 'playing the schoolmaster to his king,' and in their desire to bring him into disfavor at court used to announce his approach to Charles II. by saying, "Here comes your schoolmaster."

proposed to St. Evona that he should go round the church of St. John de Latera blindfold, and after he had said so many Ave Marias, that the first saint he laid hold of should be his patron, which the good old lawyer willingly undertook, and at the end of his Ave Maryes he stopt at St. Michael's altar, where he layed hold of the Divell, under St. Michael's feet, and cry'd out, this is our saint, let him be our patron. So being unblindfolded, and seeing what a patron he had chosen, he went to his lodgings so dejected, that a few moneths after he died, and coming to heaven's gates knockt hard. Whereupon St. Peter asked who it was that knockt so bouldly. He replied that he was St. Evona the advocate. Away, away, said St. Peter, here is but one advocate in Heaven; here is no room for you lawyers. O but, said St. Evona, I am that honest lawyer who never tooke fees on both sides, or pleaded in a bad cause, nor did I ever set my Naibours together by the ears, or lived by the sins of the People. Well, then, said St. Peter, come in. This newes coming down to Rome, a witty poet wrote on St. Evona's tomb these words:—

'St. Evona un Briton,
Advocat non Larron.
Hallelujah.'

This story put me in mind of Ben Jonson goeing throw a church in Surrey, seeing poore people weeping over a grave, asked one of the women why they wept. Oh, said shee, we have lost our pretious lawyer, Justice Randall; he kept us all in peace, and always was so good as to keep us from goeing to law; the best man ever lived. Well, said Ben Jonson, I will send you an epitaph to write upon his tomb, which was—

'God works wonders now and then,
Here lies a lawyer an honest man.'

An important vestige of the close relations which formerly existed between the Law and the Church is still found in the ecclesiastical patronage of the Lord Chancellor; and many are the good stories told of interviews that took place between our more recent chancellors and clergymen suing for preferment. "Who sent you, sir?" Thurlow asked savagely of a country curate, who had boldly forced his way into the Chancellor's library in Great Ormond Street, in the hope of winning the presentation to a vacant living. "In whose *name* do you come, that you venture to pester me about your private affairs? I say, sir—what great lords sent you to bother me in my house?" "My Lord," answered the applicant, with a happy combination of dignity and humor, "no great man supports my entreaty; but I may say with honesty, that I come to you in the name of the Lord of Hosts." Pleased by the spirit and wit of the reply, Thurlow exclaimed, "The Lord of Hosts! the Lord of Hosts! you are the first parson that ever applied to me in that Lord's name; and though his title can't be found in the Peerage, by —— you shall have the living." On another occasion the same Chancellor was less benign, but not less just to a clerical applicant. Sustained by Queen Charlotte's personal favor and intercession with Thurlow, the clergyman in question felt so sure of obtaining the valuable living which was the object of his ambition, that he regarded his interview with the Chancellor as a purely formal affair. "I have, sir," observed Lord Thurlow, "received a letter from the curate of the parish to which it is my intention to prefer you, and on inquiry I find him to be a very worthy man. The father of a large family, and a priest who has labored zealously in the parish for many years, he has written to me—not asking for the living, but modestly entreating me to ask the new rector to retain him as curate. Now, sir, you would oblige me by promising me to employ the poor man in that capacity." "My lord," replied Queen Charlotte's pastor, "it would give me great pleasure to oblige your lordship in this matter, but unfortunately I have arranged to take a personal friend for my curate." His eyes flashing angrily, Thurlow answered, "Sir, I cannot force you to take this worthy man for your curate, but I can make him the rector; and by —— he shall have the living, and be in a position to offer you the curacy."

Of Lord Loughborough a reliable biographer records a pleasant and singular story. Having pronounced a decision in the House of Lords, which deprived an excellent clergyman of a considerable estate and reduced him to actual indigence, the Chancellor, before quitting the woolsack, addressed the unfortunate suitor thus:—"As a judge I have decided against you, whose virtues are not unknown to me; and in acknowledgment of those virtues I beg you to accept from me a presentation to a living now vacant, and worth £600 per annum."

Capital also are the best of many anecdotes concerning Eldon and his ecclesiastical patronage. Dating the letter from No. 2, Charlotte Street, Pimlico, the Chancellor's eldest son sent his father the following anonymous epistle:—

"Hear, generous lawyer! hear my prayer,
Nor let my freedom make, you stare,
In hailing you Jack Scott!
Tho' now upon the woolsack placed,
With wealth, with power, with title graced,
*Once* nearer was our lot.

"Say by what name the hapless bard
May best attract your kind regard—
Plain Jack?—Sir John?—or Eldon?
Give from your ample store of giving,
A starving priest some little living—
The world will cry out 'Well done.'

"In vain, without a patron's aid,
I've prayed and preached, and preached and prayed—
*Applauded* but *ill-fed*.
Such vain *éclat* let others share;
Alas, I cannot feed on air—
I ask not *praise*, but *bread*."

Satisfactorily hoaxed by the rhymer, the Chancellor went to Pimlico in search of the clerical poetaster, and found him not.

Prettier and less comic is the story of Miss Bridge's morning call upon Lord Eldon. The Chancellor was sitting in his study over a table of papers when a young and lovely girl—slightly rustic in her attire, slightly embarrassed by the novelty of her position, but thoroughly in command of her wits—entered the room, and walked up to the lawyer's chair. "My dear," said the Chancellor, rising and bowing with old-world courtesy, "who *are* you?" "Lord Eldon," answered the blushing maiden, "I am Bessie Bridge of Weobly, the daughter of the Vicar of Weobly, and papa has sent me to remind you of a promise which you made him when I was a little baby, and you were a guest in his house on the occasion of your first election as member of Parliament for Weobly." "A promise, my dear young lady?" interposed the Chancellor, trying to recall how he had pledged himself. "Yea, Lord Eldon, a promise. You were standing over my cradle when papa said to you, 'Mr. Scott, promise me that if ever you are Lord Chancellor, when my little girl is a poor clergyman's wife, you will give her husband a living;' and you answered, 'Mr. Bridge, my promise is not worth half-a-crown, but I give it to you, wishing it were worth more.'" Enthusiastically the Chancellor exclaimed, "You are quite right. I admit the obligation. I remember all about it;" and, then, after a pause, archly surveying the damsel, whose graces were the reverse of matronly, he added, "But surely the time for keeping my promise has not yet arrived? You cannot be any one's wife at present?" For a few seconds Bessie hesitated for an answer, and then, with a blush and a ripple of silver laughter she replied, "No, but I do so wish to be *somebody's* wife. I am engaged to a young clergyman; and there's a living in Herefordshire near my old home that has recently fallen vacant, and if you'll give it to Alfred, why then, Lord Eldon, we shall marry before the end of the year." Is there need to say that the Chancellor forthwith summoned his Secretary, that the secretary forthwith made out the presentation to Bessie's lover, and that having given the Chancellor a kiss of gratitude, Bessie made good speed back to Herefordshire, hugging the precious document the whole way home?

A bad but eager sportsman, Lord Eldon used to blaze away at his partridges and pheasants with such uniform want of success that Lord Stowell had truth as well as humor on his side when he observed, "My brother has done much execution this shooting season; with his gun he has *killed a great deal of time*." Having ineffectually discharged two barrels at a covey of partridges, the Chancellor was slowly walking to the gate of one of his Encome turnip-fields when a stranger of clerical garb and aspect hailed him from a distance, asking, "Where is Lord Eldon?" Not anxious to declare himself to the witness of his ludicrously bad shot, the Chancellor answered evasively, and with scant courtesy, "Not far off." Displeased with the tone of this curt reply, the clergyman rejoined, "I wish you'd use your tongue to better purpose than you do your gun, and tell me civily where I can find the Chancellor." "Well," responded the sportsman, when he had slowly approached his questioner, "here you see the Chancellor—I am Lord Eldon." It was an untoward introduction to the Chancellor for the strange clergyman who had traveled from the North of Lancashire to ask for the presentation to a vacant living. Partly out of humorous compassion for the applicant who had offered rudeness, if not insult to the person whom he was most anxious to propitiate; partly because on inquiry he ascertained the respectability of the applicant; and partly because he wished to seal by kindness the lips of a man who could report on the authority of his own eyes that the best lawyer was also the worst shot in all England, Eldon gave the petitioner the desired preferment. "But now," the old Chancellor used to add in conclusion, whenever he told the story, "see the ingratitude of mankind. It was not long before a large present of game reached me, with a letter from my new-made rector, purporting that he had sent it to me, because *from what he had seen of my shooting he* supposed I must be badly off for game. Think of turning upon me in this way, and wounding me in my tenderest point."

Amongst Eldon's humorous answers to applications for preferment should be remembered his letter to Dr. Fisher of the Charterhouse: on one side of a sheet of paper, "Dear Fisher, I cannot, to-day, give you the preferment for which you ask.—I remain your sincere friend, Eldon.—*Turn over*;" and on the other side, "I gave it to you yesterday." This note reminds us of Erskine's reply to Sir John Sinclair's solicitation for a subscription to the testimonial which Sir John invited the nation to present to himself. On the one side of a sheet of paper it ran, "My dear Sir John, I am certain there are few in this kingdom who set a higher value on your services than myself, and I have the honor to subscribe," and on the other side it concluded, "myself your obedient faithful servant, Erskine."

# Part 9. At Home: In Court: And in Society

*Chapter 45*

# LAWYERS AT THEIR OWN TABLES

A long list, indeed, might be made of abstemious lawyers; but their temperance is almost invariably mentioned by biographers as matter for regret and apology, and is even made an occasion for reproach in cases where it has not been palliated by habits of munificent hospitality. In the catalogue of Chancellor Warham's virtues and laudable usages, Erasmus takes care to mention that the primate was accustomed to entertain his friends, to the number of two hundred at a time: and when the man of letters notices the archbishop's moderation with respect to wines and dishes—a moderation that caused his grace to eschew suppers, and never to sit more than an hour at dinner—he does not omit to observe that though the great man "made it a rule to abstain entirely from supper, yet if his friends were assembled at that meal he would sit down along with them and promote their conviviality."

Splendid in all things, Wolsey astounded envious nobles by the magnificence of his banquets, and the lavish expenses of his kitchens, wherein his master-cooks wore raiment of richest materials—the *chef* of his private kitchen daily arraying himself in a damask-satin or velvet, and wearing on his neck a chain of gold. Of a far other kind were the tastes of Wolsey's successor, who, in the warmest sunshine of his power, preferred a quiet dinner with Erasmus to the pompous display of state banquets, and who wore a gleeful light in his countenance when, after his fall, he called his children and grandchildren about him, and said: "I have been brought up at Oxford, at an Inn of Chancery, at Lincoln's Inn, and in the King's Court—from the lowest degree to the highest, and yet have I in yearly revenues at this present, little left me above a hundred pounds by the year; so that now, if we wish to live together, you must be content to be contributaries together. But my counsel is that we fall not to the lowest fare first; we will not, therefore, descend to Oxford fare, nor to the fare of New Inn, but we will begin with Lincoln's Inn diet, where many right worshipful men of great account and good years do live full well; which if we find ourselves the first year not able to maintain, then will we in the next year come down to Oxford fare, where many great, learned, and ancient fathers and doctors are continually conversant; which if our purses stretch not to maintain neither, then may we after, with bag and wallet, go a-begging together, hoping that for pity some good folks will give us their charity and at every man's door to sing a *Salve Regina*, whereby we shall keep company and be merry together."

Students recalling the social life of England should bear in mind the hours kept by our ancestors in the fourteenth and two following centuries. Under the Plantagenets noblemen used to sup at five P.M., and dine somewhere about the breakfast hour of Mayfair in a modern London season. Gradually hours became later; but under the Tudors the ordinary dinner hour for gentlepeople was somewhere about eleven A.M., and their usual time for supping was between five P.M. and six P.M., tradesmen, merchants and farmers dining and supping at later hours than their social superiors. "With us," says Hall the chronicler, "the nobility, gentry, and students, do ordinarily go to dinner at eleven before noon, and to supper at five, or between five and six, at afternoon. The merchants dine and sup seldom before twelve at noon and six at night. The husbandmen also dine at high noon as they call it, and sup at seven or eight; but out of term in our universities the scholars dine at ten." Thus whilst the idlers of society made haste to eat and drink, the workers postponed the pleasures of the table until they had made a good morning's work. In the days of morning dinners and afternoon suppers, the law-courts used to be at the height of their daily business at an hour when Templars of the present generation have seldom risen from bed. Chancellors were accustomed to commence their daily sittings in Westminster at seven A.M. in summer, and at eight A.M. in winter months. Lord Keeper Williams, who endeavored to atone for want of law by extraordinarily assiduous attention to the duties of his office, used indeed to open his winter sittings by candlelight between six and seven o'clock.

Many were the costly banquets of which successive Chancellors invited the nobility, the judges, and the bar, to partake at old York House; but of all the holders of the Great Seal who exercised pompous hospitality in that picturesque palace, Francis Bacon was the most liberal, gracious, and delightful entertainer. Where is the student of English history who has not often endeavored to imagine the scene when Ben Jonson sat amongst the honored guests of

> "England's high Chancellor, the destin'd heir,
> In his soft cradle, to his father's chair,"

and little prescient of the coming storm, spoke of his host as one

> "Whose even thread the Fates spin round and full,
> Out of their choicest and their whitest wool."

Even at the present day lawyers have reason to be grateful to Bacon for the promptitude with which, on taking possession of the Marble Chair, he revived the ancient usages of earlier holders of the seal, and set an example of courteous hospitality to the bar, which no subsequent Chancellor has been able to disregard without loss of respect and *prestige*. Though a short attack of gout qualified the new pleasure of his elevation—an attack attributed by the sufferer to his removal "from a field air to a Thames air," i.e., from Gray's Inn to the south side of the Strand—Lord Keeper Bacon lost no time in summoning the judges and most eminent barristers to his table; and though the gravity of his indisposition, or the dignity of his office, forbade him to join in the feast, he sat and spoke pleasantly with them when the dishes had been removed. "Yesterday," he wrote to Buckingham, "which was my weary day, I bid all the judges to dinner, which was not used to be, and entertained them in a private withdrawing chamber with the learned counsel. When the feast was past I came amongst them and sat me down at the end of the table, and prayed them to think I was one of them, and but a foreman." Nor let us, whilst recalling Bacon's bounteous hospitalities, fail in justice to his great rival, Sir Edward Coke—-who, though he usually held himself aloof from frivolous amusements, and cared but little for expensive repasts, would with a liberal hand place lordly dishes before lordly guests; and of whom it is recorded in the 'Apophthegmes,' that when any great visitor dropped in upon him for pot-luck without notice he was wont to say, "Sir, since you sent me no notice of your coming, you must dine with me; but if I had known of it in due time I would have dined with you."

From such great men as Lord Nottingham and Lord Guildford, who successively kept high state in Queen Street, Lincoln's Inn Fields, to fat *puisnes* occupying snug houses in close proximity to the Inns of Court, and lower downwards to leaders of the bar and juniors sleeping as well as working in chambers, the Restoration lawyers were conspicuous promoters of the hilarity which was one of the most prominent and least offensive characteristics of Charles II.'s London. Lord Nottingham's sumptuous hospitalities were the more creditable, because he voluntarily relinquished his claim to £4000 per annum, which the royal bounty had assigned him as a fund to be expended in official entertainments. Similar praise cannot be awarded to Lord Guildford; but justice compels the admission that, notwithstanding his love of money, he maintained the *prestige* of his place, so far as a hospitable table and profuse domestic expenditure could support it.

Contrasting strongly with the lawyers of this period, who copied in miniature the impressive state of Clarendon's princely establishments, were the jovial, catch-singing, three-bottle lawyers—who preferred drunkenness to pomp; an oaken table, surrounded by jolly fellows, to ante-rooms crowded with obsequious courtiers; a hunting song with a brave chorus to the less stormy diversion of polite conversation. Of these free-living lawyers, George Jeffreys was a conspicuous leader. Not averse to display, and not incapable of shining in refined society, this notorious man loved good cheer and jolly companions beyond all other sources of excitement; and during his tenure of the seals, he was never more happy than when he was presiding over a company of sharp-witted men-about-town whom he had invited to indulge in wild talk and choice wine at his mansion that overlooked the lawns, the water, and the trees of St. James's Park. On such occasions his lordship's most valued boon companion was Mountfort, the comedian, whom he had taken from the stage and made a permanent officer of the Duke Street household. Whether the actor was required to discharge any graver functions in the Chancellor's establishment is unknown; but we have Sir John Reresby's testimony that the clever mimic and brilliant libertine was employed to amuse his lordship's guests by ridiculing the personal and mental peculiarities of the judges and most eminent barristers. "I dined," records Sir John, "with the Lord Chancellor, where the Lord Mayor of London was a guest, and some other gentlemen. His lordship having, according to custom, drunk deep at dinner, called for one Mountfort, a gentleman of his, who had been a comedian, an excellent mimic; and to divert the company, as he was pleased to term it, he made him plead before him in a feigned cause, during which he aped the judges, and all the great lawyers of the age, in tone of voice and in action and gesture of body, to the very great ridicule, not only of the lawyers, but of the law itself, which to me did not seem altogether prudent in a man in his lofty station in the law; diverting it certainly was, but prudent in the Lord Chancellor I shall never think it." The fun of Mountfort's imitations was often heightened by the presence of the persons whom they held up to derision—some of whom would see and express natural displeasure at the affront; whilst others, quite unconscious of their own peculiarities, joined loudly in the laughter that was directed against themselves.

As pet buffoon of the tories about town, Mountfort was followed, at a considerable distance of time, by Estcourt—an actor who united wit and fine humor with irresistible powers of mimicry; and who contrived to acquire the respect and affectionate regard of many of those famous Whigs whom it was alike his pleasure and his business to render ridiculous. In the *Spectator* Steele paid him a tribute of cordial admiration; and Cibber, noticing the marvellous fidelity of his imitations, has recorded, "This man was so amazing and extraordinary a mimic, that no man or woman, from the coquette to the privy counsellor, ever moved or spoke before him, but he could carry their voice, look, mien, and motion instantly into another company. I have heard him make long harangues, and form various arguments, even in the manner of thinking of an eminent pleader at the bar, with every the least article and singularity of his utterance so perfectly imitated, that he was the very *alter ipse*, scarce to be distinguished from the original."

With the exception of Kenyon and Eldon, and one or two less conspicuous instances of judicial penuriousness, the judges of the Georgian period were hospitable entertainers. Chief Justice Lee, who died in 1754, gained credit for an adequate knowledge of law by the sumptuousness and frequency of the dinners with which he regaled his brothers of the bench and learned counsellors. Chief Justice Mansfield's habitual temperance and comparative indifference to the pleasures of the table did not cause him to be neglectful of hospitable duties. Notwithstanding the cold formality of Lord Hardwicke's entertainments, and the charges of niggardliness preferred against Lady Hardwicke's domestic system by Opposition satirists, Philip Yorke used to entertain the chiefs of his profession with pomp, if not with affability. Thurlow entertained a somewhat too limited circle of friends with English fare and a superabundance of choice port in Great Ormond Street. Throughout his public career, Alexander Wedderburn was a lavish and delightful host, amply atoning in the opinion of frivolous society for his political falsity by the excellence and number of his grand dinners. On entering the place of Solicitor-General, he spent £8000 on a service of plate; and as Lord Loughborough he gratified the bar and dazzled the fashionable world by hospitality alike sumptuous and brilliant.

Several of the Georgian lawyers had strong predilections for particular dishes or articles of diet. Thurlow was very fanciful about his fruit; and in his later years he would give way to ludicrous irritability, if inferior grapes or faulty peaches were placed before him. At Brighton, in his declining years, the ex-Chancellor's indignation at a dish of defective wall-fruit was so lively that—to the inexpressible astonishment of Horne Tooke and other guests—he caused the whole of a very fine dessert to be thrown out of the window upon the Marine Parade. Baron Graham's weakness was for oysters, eaten as a preparatory whet to the appetite before dinner; and it is recorded of him that on a certain occasion, when he had been indulging in this favorite pre-prandial exercise, he observed with pleasant humor—"Oysters taken before dinner are said to sharpen the appetite; but I have just consumed half-a-barrel of fine natives—and speaking honestly, I am bound to say that I don't feel quite as hungry as when I began." Thomas Manners Button's peculiar *penchant* was for salads; and in a moment of impulsive kindness he gave Lady Morgan the recipe for his favorite salad—a compound of rare merit and mysterious properties. Bitterly did the old lawyer repent his unwise munificence when he read 'O'Donnell.' Warmly displeased with the political sentiments of the novel, he ordered it to be burnt in the servants' hall, and exclaimed, peevishly, to Lady Manners, "I wish I had not given her the secret of my salad." In no culinary product did Lord Ellenborough find greater delight than lobster-sauce; and he gave expression to his high regard for that soothing and delicate compound when he decided that persons engaged in lobster-fishery were exempt from legal liability to impressment. "Then is not," inquired his lordship, with solemn pathos, "the lobster-fishery a fishery, and a most important fishery, of this kingdom, though carried on in shallow water? The framers of the law well knew that the produce of the deep sea, without the produce of the shallow water, would be of comparatively small value, and intended that turbot, when placed upon our tables, should be flanked by good lobster-sauce." Eldon's singular passion for fried 'liver and bacon' was amongst his most notorious and least pleasant peculiarities. Even the Prince Regent condescended to humor this remarkable taste by ordering a dish of liver and bacon to be placed on the table when the Chancellor dined with him at Brighton. Sir John Leach, Master of the Rolls, was however less ready to pander to a depraved appetite. Lord Eldon said, "It will give me great pleasure to dine with you, and since you are good enough to ask me to order a dish that shall test your new *chef's* powers—I wish you'd tell your Frenchman to fry some liver and bacon for me." "Are you laughing at me or my cook?" asked Sir John Leach, stiffly, thinking that the Chancellor was bent on ridiculing his luxurious mode of living. "At neither," answered Eldon, with equal simplicity and truth; "I was only ordering the dish which I enjoy beyond all other dishes."

Although Eldon's penuriousness was grossly exaggerated by his detractors, it cannot be questioned that either through indolence, or love of money, or some other kind of selfishness, he was very neglectful of his hospitable duties to the bench and the bar. "Verily he is working off the arrears of the Lord Chancellor," said Romilly, when Sir Thomas Plummer, the Master of the Rolls, gave a succession of dinners to the bar; and such a remark would not have escaped the lips of the decorous and amiable Romilly had not circumstances fully justified it. Still it is unquestionable that Eldon's Cabinet dinners were suitably expensive; and that he never grudged his choicest port to the old attorneys and subordinate placemen who were his obsequious companions towards the close of his career. For the charges of sordid parsimony so frequently preferred against Kenyon it is to be feared there were better grounds. Under the steadily strengthening spell of avarice he ceased to invite even old friends to his table; and it was rumored that in course of time his domestic servants complained with reason that they were required to consume the same fare as their master deemed sufficient for himself. "In Lord Kenyon's house," a wit exclaimed, "all the year through it is Lent in the kitchen, and Passion Week in the Parlor." Another caustic quidnunc remarked, "In his lordship's kitchen the fire is dull, but the spits are always bright;" whereupon Jekyll interposed with an assumption of testiness, "Spits! in the name of common sense I order you not to talk about *his* spits, for nothing turns upon them."

Very different was the temper of Erskine, who spent money faster than Kenyon saved it, and who died in indigence after holding the Great Seal of England, and making for many years a finer income at the bar than any of his contemporaries not enjoying crown patronage. Many are the bright pictures preserved to us of his hospitality to politicians and lawyers, wits, and people of fashion; but none of the scenes is more characteristic than the dinner described by Sir Samuel Romilly, when that good man met at Erskine's Hampstead villa the chiefs of the opposition and Mr. Pinkney, the American Minister. "Among the light, trifling topics of conversation after dinner," says Sir Samuel Romilly, "it may be worth while to mention one, as it strongly characterizes Lord Erskine. He has always expressed and felt a strong sympathy with animals. He has talked for years of a bill he was to bring into parliament to prevent cruelty towards them. He has always had some favorite animals to whom he has been much attached, and of whom all his acquaintance have a number of anecdotes to relate; a favorite dog which he used to bring, when he was at the bar, to all his consultations; another favorite dog, which, at the time when he was Lord Chancellor, he himself rescued in the street from some boys who were about to kill it under the pretence of its being mad; a favorite goose, which followed him wherever he walked about his grounds; a favorite macaw, and other dumb favorites without number. He told us now that he had got two favorite leeches. He had been blooded by them last autumn when he had been taken dangerously ill at Portsmouth; they had saved his life, and he had brought them with him to town, had ever since kept them in a glass, had himself every day given them fresh water, and had formed a friendship for them. He said he was sure they both knew him and were grateful to him. He had given them different names, 'Home' and 'Cline' (the names of two celebrated surgeons), their dispositions being quite different. After a good deal of conversation about them, he went himself, brought them out of his library, and placed them in their glass upon the table. It is impossible, however, without the vivacity, the tones, the details, and the gestures of Lord Erskine, to give an adequate idea of this singular scene." Amongst the listeners to Erskine, whilst he spoke eloquently and with fervor of the virtues of his two leeches, were the Duke of Norfolk, Lord Grenville, Lord Grey, Lord Holland, Lord Ellenborough, Lord Lauderdale, Lord Henry Petty, and Thomas Grenville.

*Chapter 46*

# WINE

From the time when Francis Bacon attributed a sharp attack of gout to his removal from Gray's Inn Fields to the river side, to a time not many years distant when Sir Herbert Jenner Fust[36] used to be brought into his court in Doctors' Commons and placed in the judicial seat by two liveried porters, lawyers were not remarkable for abstinence from the pleasures to which our ancestors were indebted for the joint-fixing, picturesque gout that has already become an affair of the past. Throughout the long period that lies between Charles II.'s restoration and George III.'s death, an English judge without a symptom of gout was so exceptional a character that people talked of him as an interesting social curiosity. The Merry Monarch made Clarendon's bedroom his council-chamber when the Chancellor was confined to his couch by *podagra*. Lord Nottingham was so disabled by gout, and what the old physicians were pleased to call a 'perversity of the humors,' that his duties in the House of Lords were often discharged by Francis North, then Chief Justice of the Common Pleas; and though he persevered in attending to the business of his court, a man of less resolution would have altogether succumbed to the agony of his disease and the burden of his infirmities. "I have known him," says Roger North, "sit to hear petitions in great pain, and say that his servants had let him out, though he was fitter for his chamber." Prudence saved Lord Guildford from excessive intemperance; but he lived with a freedom that would be remarkable in the present age. Chief Justice Saunders

---

[36] In old Sir Herbert's later days it was a mere pleasantry, or bold figure of speech to say that his court had risen, for he used to be lifted from his chair and carried bodily from the chamber of justice by two brawny footmen. Of course, as soon as the judge was about to be elevated by his bearers, the bar rose; and also as a matter of course the bar continued to stand until the strong porters had conveyed their weighty and venerable burden along the platform behind one of the rows of advocates and out of sight. As the *trio* worked their laborious way along the platform, there seemed to be some danger that they might blunder and fall through one of the windows into the space behind the court; and at a time when Sir Herbert and Dr. —— were at open variance, that waspish advocate had on one occasion the bad taste to keep his seat at the rising of the court, and with characteristic malevolence of expression to say to the footmen, "Mind, my men, and take care of that judge of yours—or, by Jove, you'll pitch him out of the window." It is needless to say that this brutal speech did not raise the speaker in the opinion of the hearers.

was a confirmed sot, taking nips of brandy with his breakfast, and seldom appearing in public "without a pot of ale at his nose or near him." Sir Robert Wright was notoriously addicted to wine; and George Jeffreys drank, as he swore, like a trooper. "My lord," said King Charles, in a significant tone, when he gave Jeffreys the *blood-stone* ring, "as it is a hot summer, and you are going the circuit, I desire you will not drink too much."

Amongst the reeling judges of the Restoration, however, there moved one venerable lawyer, who, in an age when moralists hesitated to call drunkenness a vice, was remarkable for sobriety. In his youth, whilst he was indulging with natural ardor in youthful pleasures, Chief Justice Hale was so struck with horror at seeing an intimate friend drop senseless, and apparently lifeless, at a student's drinking-bout, that he made a sudden but enduring resolution to conquer his ebrious propensities, and withdraw himself from the dangerous allurements of ungodly company. Falling upon his knees he prayed the Almighty to rescue his friend from the jaws of death, and also to strengthen him to keep his newly-formed resolution. He rose an altered man. But in an age when the barbarous usage of toast-drinking was in full force, he felt that he could not be an habitually sober man if he mingled in society, and obeyed a rule which required the man of delicate and excitable nerves to drink as much, bumper for bumper, as the man whose sluggish system could receive a quart of spirits at a sitting and yet scarcely experience a change of sensation. At that time it was customary with prudent men to protect themselves against a pernicious and tyrannous custom, by taking a vow to abstain from toast-drinking, or even from drinking wine at all, for a certain stated period. Readers do not need to be reminded how often young Pepys was under a vow not to drink; and the device by which the jovial admiralty clerk strengthened an infirm will and defended himself against temptation was frequently employed by right-minded young men of his date. In some cases, instead of *vowing* not to drink, they *bound* themselves not to drink within a certain period; two persons, that is to say, agreeing that they would abstain from wine and spirits for a certain period, and each *binding* himself in case he broke the compact to pay over a certain sum of money to his partner in the bond. Young Hale saw that to effect a complete reformation of his life it was needful for him to abjure the practice of drinking healths. He therefore vowed *never again* to drink a health; and he kept his vow. Never again did he brim his bumper and drain it at the command of a toast-master, although his abstinence exposed him to much annoyance; and in his old age he thus urged his grandchildren to follow his example—"I will not have you begin or pledge any health, for it is become one of the greatest artifices of drinking, and occasions of quarrelling in the kingdom. If you pledge one health you oblige yourself to pledge another, and a third, and so onwards; and if you pledge as many as will be drunk, you must be debauched and drunk. If they will needs know the reason of your refusal, it is a fair answer, 'that your grandfather that brought you up, from whom, under God, you have the estate you enjoy or expect, left this in command with you, that you should never begin or pledge a health.'"

Jeffrey's *protégé*, John Trevor, liked good wine himself, but emulated the virtuous Hale in the pains which he took to place the treacherous drink beyond the reach of others—whenever they showed a desire to drink it at his expense. After his expulsion from the House of Commons, Sir John Trevor was sitting alone over a choice bottle of claret, when his needy kinsman, Roderic Lloyd, was announced. "You rascal," exclaimed the Master of the Rolls, springing to his feet, and attacking his footman with furious language, "you have brought my cousin, Roderic Lloyd, Esquire, Prothonotary of North Wales, Marshal to Baron Price, up my back stairs. You scoundrel, hear ye, I order you to take him this instant down my *back stairs*, and bring him up my *front stairs*." Sir John made such a point of showing his visitor this mark of respect, that the young barrister was forced to descend and enter the room by the state staircase; but he saw no reason to think himself honored by his cousin's punctilious courtesy, when on entering the room a second time he looked in vain for the claret bottle.

On another occasion Sir John Trevor's official residence afforded shelter to the same poor relation when the latter was in great mental trouble. "Roderic," saith the chronicler, "was returning rather elevated from his club one night, and ran against the pump in Chancery Lane. Conceiving somebody had struck him, he drew and made a lunge at the pump. The sword entered the spout, and the pump, being crazy, fell down. Roderic concluded he had killed his man, left, his sword in the pump, and retreated to his old friend's house at the Rolls. There he was concealed by the servants for the night. In the morning his Honor, having heard the story, came himself to deliver him from his consternation and confinement in the coal-hole."

Amongst the eighteenth century lawyers there was considerable difference of taste and opinion on questions relating to the use and abuse of wine. Though he never, or very seldom, exceeded the limits of sobriety, Somers enjoyed a bottle in congenial society; and though wine never betrayed him into reckless hilarity, it gave gentleness and comity to his habitually severe countenance and solemn deportment—if reliance may be placed on Swift's couplet—

> "By force of wine even Scarborough is brave,
> Hall grows more pert, and Somers not so grave."

A familiar quotation that alludes to Murray's early intercourse with the wits warrants an inference that in opening manhood he preferred champagne to every other wine; but as Lord Mansfield he steadily adhered to claret, though fashion had taken into favor the fuller wine stigmatized as poison by John Home's famous epigram—

> "Bold and erect the Caledonian stood;
> Old was his mutton, and his claret good.
> 'Let him drink port,' an English statesman cried:
> He drunk the poison and his spirit died."

Unlike his father, who never sinned against moderation in his cups, Charles Yorke was a deep drinker as well as a gourmand. Hardwicke's successor, Lord Northington, was the first of a line of port-wine-drinking judges that may at the present time be fairly said to have come to an end—although a few reverend fathers of the law yet remain, who drink with relish the Methuen drink when age has deprived it of body and strength. Until Robert Henley held the seals, Chancellors continued to hold after-dinner sittings in the Court of Chancery on certain days of the week throughout term. Hardwicke, throughout his long official career, sat on the evenings of Wednesdays and Fridays hearing causes, while men of pleasure were fuddling themselves with fruity vintages. Lord Northington, however, prevailed on George III to let him discontinue these evening attendances in court. "But why," asked the monarch, "do you wish for a change?" "Sir," the Chancellor answered, with delightful frankness, "I want the change in order that I may finish my bottle of port at my ease; and your majesty, in your parental care for the happiness of your subjects, will, I trust, think this a sufficient reason." Of course the king's laughter ended in a favorable answer to the petition for reform, and from that time the Chancellor's evening sittings were discontinued. But ere he died, the jovial Chancellor paid the penalty which port exacts from all her fervent worshippers, and he suffered the acutest pangs of gout. It is recorded that as he limped from the woolsack to the bar of the House of Lords, he once muttered to a young peer, who watched his distress with evident sympathy—"Ah, my young friend, if I had known that these legs would one day carry a Chancellor, I would have taken better care of them when I was at your age." Unto this had come the handsome legs of young Counsellor Henley, who, in his dancing days, stepped minuets to the enthusiastic admiration of the *belles* of Bath.

Some light is thrown on the manners of lawyers in the eighteenth century by an order made by the authorities of Barnard's Inn, who, in November, 1706, named two quarts as the allowance of wine to be given to each mess of four men by two gentlemen on going through the ceremony of 'initiation.' Of course, this amount of wine was an 'extra' allowance, in addition to the ale and sherry assigned to members by the regular dietary of the house. Even Sheridan, who boasted that he could drink any *given* quantity of wine, would have thought twice before he drank so large a given quantity, in addition to a liberal allowance of stimulant. Anyhow, the quantity was fixed—a fact that would have elicited an expression of approval from Chief Baron Thompson, who, loving port wine wisely, though too well, expressed at the same time his concurrence with the words, and his dissent from the opinion of a barrister, who observed—"I hold, my lord, that after a good dinner a certain quantity of wine does no harm." With a smile, the Chief Baron rejoined—"True, sir; it is the *uncertain* quantity that does the mischief."

The most temperate of the eighteenth-century Chancellors was Lord Camden, who required no more generous beverage than sound malt liquor, as he candidly declared, in a letter to the Duke of Grafton, wherein he says—"I am, thank God, remarkably well, but your grace must not seduce me into my former intemperance. A plain dish and a draught of porter (which last is indispensable), are the very extent of my luxury." For porter, Edward Thurlow, in his student days, had high respect and keen relish; but in his mature years, as well as still older age, full-bodied port was his favorite drink, and under its influence were seen to the best advantage those colloquial powers which caused Samuel Johnson to exclaim—"Depend upon it, sir, it is when you come close to a man in conversation that you discover what his real abilities are; to make a speech in a public assembly is a knack. Now, I honor Thurlow, sir; Thurlow is a fine fellow: he fairly puts his mind to yours." Of Thurlow, when he had mounted the woolsack, Johnson also observed—"I would prepare myself for no man in England but Lord Thurlow. When I am to meet him, I would wish to know a day before." From the many stories told of Thurlow and ebriosity, one may be here taken and brought under the reader's notice—not because it has wit or humor to recommend it, but because it presents the Chancellor in company with another port-loving lawyer, William Pitt, from whose fame, by-the-by, Lord Stanhope has recently removed the old disfiguring imputations of sottishness. "Returning," says Sir Nathaniel Wraxall, a poor authority, but piquant gossip-monger, "by way of frolic, very late at night, on horseback, to Wimbledon, from Addiscombe, the seat of Mr. Jenkinson, near Croydon, where the party had dined, Lord Thurlow, the Chancellor, Pitt, and Dundas, found the turnpike gate, situate between Tooting and Streatham, thrown open. Being elevated above their usual prudence, and having no servant near them, they passed through the gate at a brisk pace, without stopping to pay the toll, regardless of the remonstrances and threats of the turnpike man, who running after them, and believing them to belong to some highwaymen who had recently committed some depredation on that road, discharged the contents of his blunderbuss at their backs. Happily he did no injury."

Throughout their long lives the brothers Scott were steady, and, according to the rules of the present day, inordinate drinkers of port wine. As a young barrister, John Scott could carry more port with decorum than any other man of his inn; and in the days when he is generally supposed to have lived on sprats and table-beer, he seldom passed twenty-four hours without a bottle of his favorite wine. Prudence, however, made him careful to avoid intoxication, and when he found that a friendship often betrayed him into what he thought excessive drinking, he withdrew from the dangerous connexion. "I see your friend Bowes very often," he wrote in May, 1778, a time when Mr. Bowes was his most valuable client; "but I dare not dine with him above once in three months, as there is no getting away before midnight; and, indeed, one is sure to be in a condition in which no man would wish to be in the streets at any other season." Of the quantities imbibed at these three-monthly dinners, an estimate may be formed from the following story. Bringing from Oxford to London that fine sense of the merits of port wine which characterized the thorough Oxonion of a century since, William Scott made it for some years a rule to dine with his brother John on the first day of term at a tavern hard by the Temple; and on these occasions the brothers used to make away with bottle after bottle not less to the astonishment than the approval of the waiters who served them. Before the decay of his faculties, Lord Stowell was recalling these terminal dinners to his son-in-law, Lord Sidmouth, when the latter observed, "You drank some wine together, I dare say?" Lord Stowell, modestly, "Yes, we drank some wine." Son-in-law, inquisitively, "Two bottles?" Lord Stowell, quickly putting away the imputation of such abstemiousness, "More than that." Son-in-law, smiling, "What, three bottles?" Lord Stowell, "More." Son-in-law, opening his eyes with astonishment, "By Jove, sir, you don't mean to say that you took four bottles?" Lord Stowell, beginning to feel ashamed of himself, "More; I mean to say we had more. Now don't ask any more questions."

Whilst Lord Stowell, smarting under the domestic misery of which his foolish marriage with the Dowager Marchioness of Sligo was fruitful, sought comfort and forgetfulness in the cellar of the Middle Temple, Lord Eldon drained magnums of Newcastle port at his own table. Populous with wealthy merchants, and surrounded by an opulent aristocracy, Newcastle had used the advantages given her by a large export trade with Portugal to draw to her cellars such superb port wine as could be found in no other town in the United Kingdom; and to the last the Tory Chancellor used to get his port from the canny capital of Northumbria. Just three weeks before his death, the veteran lawyer, sitting in his easy-chair and recalling his early triumphs, preluded an account of the great leading case, "Akroyd *v.* Smithson," by saying to his listener, "Come, Farrer, help yourself to a glass of Newcastle port, and help me to a little." But though he asked for a little, the old earl, according to his wont, drank much before he was raised from his chair and led to his sleeping-room. It is on record, and is moreover supported by unexceptionable evidence, that in his extreme old age, whilst he was completely laid upon the shelf, and almost down to the day of his death, which occurred in his eighty-seventh year, Lord Eldon never drank less than three pints of port daily with or after his dinner.

Of eminent lawyers who were steady port-wine drinkers, Baron Platt—the amiable and popular judge who died in 1862, aged seventy-two years—may be regarded as one of the last. Of him it is recorded that in early manhood he was so completely prostrated by severe illness that beholders judged him to be actually dead. Standing over his silent body shortly before the arrival of the undertaker, two of his friends concurred in giving utterance to the sentiment: "Ah, poor dear fellow, we shall never drink a glass of wine with him again;" when, to their momentary alarm and subsequent delight, the dead man interposed with a faint assumption of jocularity, "But you will though, and a good many too, I hope." When the undertaker called he was sent away a genuinely sorrowful man; and the young lawyer, who was 'not dead yet,' lived to old age and good purpose.

*Chapter 47*

# LAW AND LITERATURE

At the present time, when three out of every five journalists attached to our chief London newspapers are Inns-of-Court men; when many of our able and successful advocates are known to ply their pens in organs of periodical literature as regularly as they raise their voices in courts of justice; and when the young Templar, who has borne away the first honors of his university, deems himself the object of a compliment on receiving an invitation to contribute to the columns of a leading review or daily journal—it is difficult to believe that strong men are still amongst us who can remember the days when it was the fashion of the bar to disdain law-students who were suspected of 'writing for hire' and barristers who 'reported for the papers.' Throughout the opening years of the present century, and even much later, it was almost universally held on the circuits and in Westminster Hall, that Inns-of-Court men lowered the dignity of their order by following those literary avocations by which some of the brightest ornaments of the law supported themselves at the outset of their professional careers. Notwithstanding this prejudice, a few wearers of the long robe, daring by nature, or rendered bold by necessity, persisted in 'maintaining a connexion with the press, whilst they sought briefs on the circuit, or waited for clients in their chambers. Such men as Sergeant Spankie and Lord Campbell, as Master Stephen and Mr. Justice Talfourd, were reporters for the press whilst they kept terms; and no sooner had Henry Brougham's eloquence charmed the public, than it was whispered that for years his pen, no less ready than his tongue, had found constant employment in organs of political intelligence.

But though such men were known to exist, they were regarded as the 'black sheep' of the bar by a great majority of their profession. It is not improbable that this prejudice against gownsmen on the press was palliated by circumstances that no longer exist. When political writers were very generally regarded as dangerous members of society, and when conductors of respectable newspapers were harassed with vexatious prosecutions and heavy punishments for acts of trivial inadvertence, or for purely imaginary offences, the average journalist was in many respects inferior to the average journalist working under the present more favorable circumstances. Men of culture, honest purpose, and fine feeling were slow to enrol themselves members of a despised and proscribed fraternity; and in the dearth of educated gentlemen ready to accept literary employment, the task of writing for the public papers too frequently devolved upon very unscrupulous persons, who rendered their calling as odious as themselves. A shackled and persecuted press is always a licentious and venal press; and before legislation endowed English journalism with a certain measure of freedom and security, it was seldom manly and was often corrupt. It is therefore probable that our grandfathers had some show of reason for their dislike of contributors to anonymous literature. At the bar men of unquestionable amiability and enlightenment were often the loudest to express this aversion for their scribbling brethren. It was said that the scribblers were seldom gentlemen in temper; and that they never hesitated to puff themselves in their papers. These considerations so far influenced Mr. Justice Lawrence that, though he was a model of judicial suavity to all other members of the bar, he could never bring himself to be barely civil to advocates known to be 'upon the press.'

At Lincoln's Inn this strong feeling against journalists found vent in a resolution, framed in reference to a particular person, which would have shut out journalists from the Society. It had long been understood that no student could be called to the bar *whilst* he was acting as a reporter in the gallery of either house; but the new decision of the benchers would have destroyed the ancient connexion of the legal profession and literary calling. Strange to say this illiberal measure was the work of two benchers who, notwithstanding their patrician descent and associations, were vehement asserters of liberal principles. Mr. Clifford—'O.P.' Clifford—was its proposer and Erskine was its seconder. Fortunately the person who was the immediate object of its provisions petitioned the House of Commons upon the subject, and the consequent debate in the Lower House decided the benchers to withdraw from their false position; and since their silent retreat no attempt has been made by any of the four honorable societies to affix an undeserved stigma on the followers of a serviceable art. Upon the whole the literary calling gained much from the discreditable action of Lincoln's Inn; for the speech in which Sheridan covered with derision this attempt to brand parliamentary reporters as unfit to associate with members of the bar, and the address in which Mr. Stephen, with manly reference to his own early experiences, warmly censured the conduct of the society of which he was himself a member, caused many persons to form a new and juster estimate of the working members of the London press. Having alluded to Dr. Johnson and Edmund Burke, who had both acted as parliamentary reporters, Sheridan stated that no less than twenty-three graduates of universities were then engaged as reporters of the proceedings of the house.

The close connexion which for centuries has existed between men of law and men of letters is illustrated on the one hand by a long succession of eminent lawyers who have added to the lustre of professional honors the no less bright distinctions of literary achievements or friendships, and on the other hand by the long line of able writers who either enrolled themselves amongst the students of the law, or resided in the Inns of Court, or cherished with assiduous care the friendly regard of famous judges. Indeed, since the days of Chancellor de Bury, who wrote the 'Philobiblon,' there have been few Chancellors to whom literature is not in some way indebted; and the few Keepers of the Seal who neither cared for letters nor cultivated the society of students, are amongst the judges whose names most Englishmen would gladly erase from the history of their country. Jeffreys and Macclesfield represent the unlettered Chancellors; More and Bacon the lettered. Fortescue's 'De Laudibus' is a book for every reader. To Chancellor Warham, Erasmus—a scholar not given to distribute praise carelessly—dedicated his 'St. Jerom,' with cordial eulogy. Wolsey was a patron of letters. More may be said to have revived, if he did not create, the literary taste of his contemporaries, and to have transplanted the novel to English soil. Equally diligent as a writer and a collector of books, Gardyner spent his happiest moments at his desk, or over the folios of the magnificent library which was destroyed by Wyat's insurgents. Christopher Hatton was a dramatic author. To one person who can describe with any approach to accuracy Edward Hyde's conduct in the Court of Chancery, there are twenty who have studied Clarendon's 'Rebellion.' At the present date Hale's books are better known than his judgments, though his conduct towards the witches of Bury St. Edmunds conferred an unenviable fame on his judicial career. By timely assistance rendered to Burnet, Lord Nottingham did something to atone for his brutality towards Milton, whom, at an earlier period of his career, he had declared worthy of a felon's death, for having been Cromwell's Latin secretary. Lord Keeper North wrote upon 'Music;' and to his brother Roger literature is indebted for the best biographies composed by any writer of his period. In his boyhood Somers was a poet; in his maturer years the friend of poets. The friend of Prior and Gay, Arbuthnot and Pope, Lord Chancellor Harcourt, wrote verses of more than ordinary merit, and alike in periods of official triumph and in times of retirement valued the friendship of men of wit above the many successes of his public career. Lord Chancellor King, author of 'Constitution and Discipline of the Primitive Church,' was John Locke's dutiful nephew and favorite companion. King's immediate successor was extolled by Pope in the lines,

> O teach us, Talbot! thou'rt unspoil'd by wealth,
> That secret rare, between the extremes to move,
> Of mad good-nature and of mean self-love.
> Who is it copies Talbot's better part,
> To ease th' oppress'd, and raise the sinking heart?

But Talbot's fairest eulogy was penned by his son's tutor, Alexander Thomson—a poet who had no reason to feel gratitude to Talbot's official successor. Ere he thoroughly resolved to devote himself to law, the cold and formal Hardwicke had cherished a feeble ambition for literary distinction; and under its influence he wrote a paper that appeared in the *Spectator*. Blackstone's entrance at the Temple occasioned his metrical 'Farewell' to his muse. In his undergraduate days at Cambridge Lord Chancellor Charles Yorke was a chief contributor to the 'Athenian Letters,' and it would have been well for him had he in after-life given to letters a portion of the time which he sacrificed to ambition. Thurlow's churlishness and overbearing temper are at this date trifling matters in comparison with his friendship for Cowper and Samuel Johnson, and his kindly aid to George Crabbe. Even more than for the wisdom of his judgments Mansfield is remembered for his intimacy with 'the wits,' and his close friendship with that chief of them all, who exclaimed, "How sweet an Ovid, Murray, was our boast," and in honor of that "Sweet Ovid" penned the lines,

> "Graced as thou art, with all the power of words,
> So known, so honored in the House of Lords"—

verses deliciously ridiculed by the parodist who wrote,

> "Persuasion tips his tongue whene'er he talks:
> And he has chambers in the King's Bench walks."

As an atonement for many defects, Alexander Wedderburn had one virtue—an honest respect for letters that made him in opening manhood seek the friendship of Hume, at a later date solicit a pension for Dr. Johnson, and after his elevation to the woolsack overwhelm Gibbon with hospitable civilities. Eldon was an Oxford Essayist in his young, the compiler of 'The Anecdote Book' in his old days; and though he cannot be commended for literary tastes, or sympathy with men of letters, he was one of the many great lawyers who found pleasure in the conversation of Samuel Johnson. Unlike his brother, Lord Stowell clung fast to his literary friendships, as 'Dr. Scott of the Commons' priding himself more on his membership in the Literary Club than on his standing in the Prerogative Court; and as Lord Stowell evincing cordial respect for the successors of Reynolds and Malone, even when love of money had taken firm hold of his enfeebled mind. Archdeacon Paley's London residence was in Edward Law's house in Bloomsbury Square. In Erskine literary ambition was so strong that, not content with the fame brought to him by excellent *vers de société*, he took pen in hand when he resigned the seals, and—more to the delight of his enemies than the satisfaction of his friends—wrote a novel, which neither became, nor deserved to be, permanently successful. With similar zeal and greater ability the literary reputation of the bar has been maintained by Lord Denman, who was an industrious *littérateur* whilst he was working his way up at the bar; by Sir John Taylor Coleridge, whose services to the *Quarterly Review* are an affair of literary history; by Sir Thomas Noon Talfourd, who, having reported in the gallery, lived to lake part in the debates of the House of Commons, and who, from the date of his first engagement on the *Times* till the sad morning when "God's finger touched him," while he sat upon the bench, never altogether relinquished those literary pursuits, in which he earned well-merited honor; by Lord Macaulay, whose connexion with the legal profession is almost lost sight of in the brilliance of his literary renown; by Lord Campbell, who dreamt of living to wear an SS collar in Westminster Hall whilst he was merely John Campbell the reporter; by Lord Brougham, who, having instructed our grandfathers with his pen, still remains upon the stage, giving their grandsons wise lessons with his tongue; and by Lord Romilly, whose services to English literature have won for him the gratitude of scholars.

Of each generation of writers between the accession of Elizabeth and the present time, several of the most conspicuous names are either found on the rolls of the inns, or are closely associated in the minds of students with the life of the law-colleges. Shakspeare's plays abound with testimony that he was no stranger in the legal inns, and the rich vein of legal lore and diction that runs through his writings has induced more judicious critics than Lord Campbell to conjecture that he may at some early time of his career have directed his mind to the study, if not the practice, of the law. Amongst Elizabethan writers who belonged to inns may be mentioned—George Ferrars, William Lambarde, Sir Henry Spelman, and that luckless pamphleteer John Stubbs, all of whom were members of Lincoln's Inn; Thomas Sackville, Francis Beaumont the Younger, and John Ferne, of the Inner Temple; Walter Raleigh, of the Middle Temple; Francis Bacon, Philip Sidney, George Gascoyne, and Francis Davison, of Gray's Inn. Sir John Denham, the poet, became a Lincoln's-Inn student in 1634; and Francis Quarles was a member of the same learned society. John Selden entered the Inner Temple in the second year of James I., where in due course he numbered, amongst his literary contemporaries,—William Browne, Croke, Oulde, Thomas Gardiner, Dynne, Edward Heywood, John Morgan, Augustus Cæsar, Thomas Heygate, Thomas May, dramatist and translator of Lucan's 'Pharsalia,' William Rough and Rymer were members of Gray's Inn. Sir John David and Sir Simonds D'Ewes belonged to the Middle Temple. Massinger's dearest friends lived in the Inner Temple, of which society George Keate, the dramatist, and Butler's staunch supporter William Longueville, were members. Milton passed the most jocund hours of his life in Gray's Inn, in which college Cleveland and the author of 'Hudibras' held the meetings of their club. Wycherley and Congreve, Aubrey and Narcissus Luttrell were Inns-of-Court men. In later periods we find Thomas Edwards, the critic; Murphy, the dramatic writer; James Mackintosh, Francis Hargrave, Bentham, Curran, Canning, at Lincoln's Inn. The poet Cowper was a barrister of the Temple. Amongst other Templars of the eighteenth century, with whose names the literature of their time is inseparably associated, were Henry Fielding, Henry Brooke, Oliver Goldsmith, and Edmund Burke. Samuel Johnson resided both in Gray's Inn and the

Temple, and his friend Boswell was an advocate of respectable ability as well as the best biographer on the roll of English writers.

The foregoing are but a few taken from hundreds of names that illustrate the close union of Law and Literature in past times. To lengthen the list would but weary the reader; and no pains would make a perfect muster roll of all the literary lawyers and *legal littérateurs* who either are still upon the stage, or have only lately passed away. In their youth four well-known living novelists—Mr. William Harrison Ainsworth, Mr. Shirley Brooks, Mr. Charles Dickens, and Mr. Benjamin Disraeli—passed some time in solicitors' offices. Mr. John Oxenford was articled to an attorney. Mr. Theodore Martin resembles the authors of 'The Rejected Addresses' in being a successful practitioner in the inferior branch of the law. Mr. Charles Henry Cooper was a successful solicitor. On turning over the leaves to that useful book, 'Men of the Time,' the reader finds mention made of the following men of letters and law—Sir Archibald Alison, Mr. Thomas Chisholm Anstey, Mr. William Edmonstone Aytoun, Mr. Philip James Bailey, Mr. J.N. Ball, Mr. Sergeant Peter Burke, Sir J.B. Burke, Mr. John Hill Burton, Mr. Hans Busk, Mr. Isaac Butt, Mr. George Wingrove Cooke, Sir E.S. Creasy, Dr. Dasent, Mr. John Thaddeus Delane, Mr. W. Hepworth Dixon, Mr. Commissioner Fonblanque, Mr. William Forsyth, Q.C., Mr. Edward Foss, Mr. William Carew Hazlitt, Mr. Thomas Hughes, Mr. Leone Levi, Mr. Lawrence Oliphant, Mr. Charles Reade, Mr. W. Stigant, Mr. Tom Taylor, Mr. McCullagh Torrens, Mr. M.F. Tupper, Dr. Travers, Mr. Samuel Warren, and Mr. Charles Weld. Some of the gentlemen in this list are not merely nominal barristers, but are practitioners with an abundance of business. Amongst those to whom the editor of 'Men of the Time' draws attention as 'Lawyers,' and who either are still rendering or have rendered good service to literature, occur the names of Sir William A'Beckett, Mr. W. Adams, Dr. Anster, Sir Joseph Arnould, Sir George Bowyer, Sir John Coleridge, Mr. E. W. Cox, Mr. Wilson Gray, Mr. Justice Haliburton, Mr. Thomas Lewin, Mr. Thomas E. May, Mr. J.G. Phillimore, Mr. James Fitz James Stephen, Mr. Vernon Harcourt, Mr. James Whiteside. Some of the distinguished men mentioned in this survey have already passed to another world since the publication of the last edition of 'Men of the Time;' but their recorded connexion with literature as well as law no less serves to illustrate an important feature of our social life. It is almost needless to remark that the names of many of our ablest anonymous writers do not appear in 'Men of the Time.'

# INDEX


## A

abolition, 112, 143
accommodation, 15, 16, 18, 172, 225
acquaintance, 27, 64, 153, 208, 252, 269, 287, 300
age, 10, 17, 19, 27, 29, 35, 53, 54, 56, 57, 70, 76, 80, 82, 87, 121, 126, 132, 160, 167, 180, 193, 209, 215, 219, 254, 258, 272, 298, 303, 304, 306, 307
ancestors, 5, 101, 187, 205, 296, 303
anger, 61, 66, 167, 268, 271
anxiety, 125, 170, 239
appointments, 72, 138
arbitration, 71, 77, 84, 102
architect, 19, 24, 267
atmosphere, 20, 23, 76, 87, 144, 215, 226
aversion, 143, 149, 310

## B

blood, 43, 70, 199, 200, 201, 238, 263, 304
brain, 12, 33, 35, 37, 236
bribes, 85, 88, 89, 91, 99, 101
brutality, 98, 143, 311
butcher, 101, 200
buttons, 144, 159

## C

candidates, 137, 161, 202
Canterbury, 13, 70, 160, 161, 212, 221, 288
Chief Justice, vi, 18, 19, 20, 25, 26, 40, 46, 49, 58, 70, 75, 79, 87, 88, 89, 93, 96, 101, 103, 108, 111, 112, 121, 126, 127, 128, 134, 139, 144, 146, 152, 156, 161, 170, 171, 185, 200, 201, 209, 210, 215, 222, 242, 243, 246, 247, 248, 250, 252, 257, 260, 261, 263, 267, 271, 272, 275, 276, 277, 278, 279, 298, 303, 304
childhood, 63
children, 5, 6, 7, 8, 19, 34, 35, 36, 43, 47, 49, 53, 61, 64, 65, 151, 160, 167, 168, 170, 198, 201, 203, 207, 277, 288, 295
Christians, 180
Cicero, v, 49, 51
circulation, 251, 268
clients, 3, 4, 10, 44, 46, 56, 61, 69, 70, 71, 76, 77, 79, 80, 82, 86, 93, 135, 150, 208, 209, 215, 250, 263, 281, 309
coal, 24, 187, 229, 305
coffee, 9, 55, 145, 155, 226
collateral, 204, 263
colleges, 3, 4, 18, 20, 100, 149, 188, 192, 193, 199, 200, 211, 212, 214, 216, 219, 220, 313
commercial, 82, 202, 212, 268, 271
common law, 11, 26, 84, 96, 109, 122, 124, 125, 127, 166, 192, 225, 233
common sense, 206, 300
communication, 66, 141
compassion, 34, 35, 46, 292
compensation, 64, 66, 79, 112
compliance, 92, 93, 137, 167, 220
composition, 45, 222
conference, 122, 240
conviction, 77, 103, 240, 242, 279
corruption, 85, 86, 93, 97, 99, 103, 110, 124
cost, 8, 18, 26, 72, 86, 99, 108, 139, 176, 177, 181, 200, 212, 221, 242, 265, 278

counsel, v, 29, 30, 34, 41, 45, 50, 65, 69, 70, 71, 72, 73, 74, 75, 76, 77, 78, 79, 80, 81, 82, 84, 87, 92, 111, 124, 127, 128, 136, 137, 138, 139, 143, 144, 145, 166, 185, 206, 209, 210, 215, 222, 235, 238, 239, 240, 249, 250, 253, 254, 258, 260, 267, 270, 271, 277, 287, 288, 295, 297
criticism, 65, 95, 168, 253
crown, 14, 20, 69, 73, 75, 92, 108, 110, 125, 138, 288, 291, 300

## D

dances, 11, 176, 183, 188
danger, 30, 212, 233, 260, 275, 303
decoration, 8, 117, 126, 134
defence, 28, 69, 74, 79, 83, 98, 125, 213, 250, 258, 260, 262, 279
degradation, 11, 43, 64, 96, 202, 248, 288
dignity, 36, 45, 101, 108, 129, 165, 166, 182, 200, 201, 202, 217, 221, 223, 239, 248, 254, 289, 297, 309
disappointment, 58, 156
discomfort, 3, 47, 154, 257
disgust, 131, 144, 239, 241
disorder, 187, 221
disposition, 135, 262
dissatisfaction, 27, 65, 96, 127, 226, 276
distress, 167, 278, 306
distribution, 137, 279

## E

earnings, 75, 78, 81, 107
education, 34, 193, 199, 205, 219, 225
ejaculation, 260
election, 56, 161, 166, 221, 237, 291
employment, 46, 78, 83, 155, 202, 216, 277, 309, 310
encouragement, 142, 210, 217
enemies, 25, 27, 96, 100, 143, 200, 264, 288, 312
England, 14, 20, 28, 35, 53, 54, 70, 75, 82, 89, 90, 98, 102, 110, 111, 125, 126, 127, 128, 131, 132, 133, 139, 151, 154, 172, 186, 192, 193, 198, 201, 205, 206, 211, 212, 213, 215, 233, 235, 259, 277, 287, 288, 292, 296, 300, 307
equity, 91, 221, 229, 251, 253
etiquette, 70, 74, 77, 82, 136, 137, 149, 220, 227, 230, 237, 239, 275, 279
evidence, 29, 54, 58, 59, 69, 81, 98, 120, 131, 146, 166, 191, 200, 210, 247, 267, 268, 270, 272, 273, 278, 282, 308
evil, 10, 98, 100, 118, 143, 179, 251
execution, 155, 209, 233, 243, 291
exercise, 7, 90, 96, 99, 111, 152, 198, 206, 216, 220, 222, 287, 299
exercises, 151, 208, 219, 220, 222, 226
expulsion, 15, 46, 119, 192, 214, 305
extraction, 78, 96, 200, 205

## F

families, 3, 7, 11, 23, 29, 45, 57, 153, 197, 205, 215
fear, 30, 33, 117, 212, 220, 240, 276, 278
fears, 49, 96, 240
feelings, 66, 167, 214
fever, 75, 182, 257, 279
freedom, 77, 82, 117, 193, 215, 269, 290, 303, 310
friendship, 47, 56, 57, 301, 307, 311, 312
full employment, 137
funds, 28, 63, 97

## G

God, 4, 36, 47, 75, 96, 121, 151, 168, 192, 216, 242, 252, 263, 268, 280, 282, 289, 304, 306, 313
goose, 228, 301
gout, 15, 27, 260, 297, 303, 306
gravity, 8, 133, 144, 151, 242, 262, 271, 280, 297
growth, 85, 118, 119, 138, 202, 238
guilty, 6, 24, 91, 97, 98, 156, 242, 248, 272, 277, 278, 288

## H

hair, 33, 76, 117, 119, 120, 125, 126, 127, 129, 131, 141, 144, 160
happiness, 35, 61, 216, 227, 306
harmony, 150, 152, 199, 203
health, 19, 33, 54, 76, 142, 242, 304
height, 13, 27, 75, 98, 165, 268, 296
history, ix, 15, 17, 29, 38, 39, 49, 64, 69, 75, 85, 89, 91, 103, 121, 141, 170, 193, 220, 264, 277, 296, 311, 313
honesty, 63, 99, 101, 135, 166, 203, 289
horses, 109, 177, 182, 287

hospitality, 5, 27, 88, 90, 170, 171, 185, 186, 188, 221, 267, 295, 296, 297, 299, 300
human, 5, 33, 35, 38, 65, 120, 125, 141, 142, 168, 237, 252
human nature, 120, 142, 237
hunting, 173, 205, 275, 297
husband, 3, 5, 7, 11, 27, 34, 35, 38, 39, 41, 44, 47, 50, 51, 54, 57, 62, 63, 64, 88, 128, 141, 208, 216, 229, 234, 246, 291
Hyde Park, 7, 26, 269

## I

imitation, 131, 180, 246
imprisonment, 51, 66, 96, 98, 199, 288
income, 7, 11, 47, 50, 56, 64, 65, 72, 73, 74, 75, 80, 84, 92, 96, 107, 108, 109, 110, 112, 145, 216, 300
industry, 61, 96, 103, 150, 160, 217, 222
injury, iv, 24, 110, 132, 143, 202, 250, 254, 307
institutions, 10, 25, 100, 192
intelligence, 11, 34, 36, 101, 209, 247, 268, 309
intercourse, 38, 49, 50, 54, 55, 57, 65, 77, 142, 215, 222, 240, 271, 305
irony, 38, 233, 259
irritability, 47, 299

## J

joint demand, 236
journalism, 310
journalists, 309, 310
judicial corruption, v, 85, 86, 99
juries, 84, 145, 167
jurisdiction, 17, 90, 132, 277

## K

Kensington Gardens, 7
knees, 38, 47, 173, 263, 304

## L

laws, 38, 86, 152, 203, 207, 208, 264, 280
lawyers, ix, 4, 6, 7, 8, 9, 13, 17, 18, 19, 20, 23, 24, 29, 30, 37, 46, 49, 50, 57, 58, 63, 70, 72, 75, 76, 79, 80, 81, 82, 83, 98, 99, 100, 108, 110, 112, 117, 119, 120, 123, 132, 133, 135, 136, 137, 141, 143, 149, 150, 152, 155, 166, 169, 170, 171, 176, 179, 180, 181, 183, 185, 186, 187, 188, 191, 192, 193, 197, 199, 202, 203, 205, 207, 208, 209, 211, 212, 220, 221, 222, 236, 237, 245, 246, 248, 263, 281, 283, 285, 286, 287, 288, 295, 297, 299, 300, 303, 305, 306, 308, 310, 312, 314
learning, 39, 61, 135, 180, 191, 194, 197, 202, 206, 219, 220, 221, 222, 225, 229, 238
legal education, vi, 189, 199
legal profession, 17, 24, 64, 74, 82, 108, 179, 201, 202, 203, 288, 310, 313
legs, 127, 165, 173, 306
leisure, 47, 55, 75, 240
liberty, 36, 39, 44, 87, 234, 258, 278
light, 5, 17, 18, 33, 71, 99, 103, 121, 159, 166, 181, 209, 213, 220, 230, 252, 281, 295, 300, 306
London, ix, 3, 4, 11, 13, 15, 16, 17, 18, 20, 23, 24, 25, 26, 27, 29, 39, 43, 45, 46, 47, 55, 56, 57, 62, 64, 70, 71, 100, 109, 120, 133, 134, 135, 138, 142, 143, 149, 153, 154, 157, 177, 180, 191, 195, 197, 198, 199, 201, 202, 211, 215, 216, 219, 225, 234, 240,246, 254, 263, 279, 296, 297, 298, 307, 309, 310, 312
longevity, 272
love, 11, 28, 33, 34, 37, 38, 40, 43, 46, 57, 61, 77, 117, 149, 151, 152, 179, 187, 200, 228, 286, 297, 300, 311, 312
loyalty, 61, 177
lying, 9, 11, 14, 18, 24, 118, 159, 193, 252, 268, 270, 277, 281

## M

marriage, 6, 18, 34, 35, 38, 39, 40, 41, 43, 45, 50, 53, 54, 55, 57, 62, 63, 64, 65, 66, 177, 308
materials, 110, 146, 295
matter, iv, 36, 55, 69, 70, 71, 91, 102, 124, 131, 136, 152, 160, 171, 202, 206, 207, 219, 225, 238, 239, 240, 254, 259, 261, 263, 267, 271, 278, 290, 295, 303
memory, 4, 14, 20, 125, 137, 252, 253, 272, 287
morality, 45, 49, 78, 88, 100, 242, 277
mother tongue, 206, 208, 209
murder, 58, 59, 104, 210, 241, 279, 280
music, 149, 151, 152, 153, 156, 159, 160, 169, 183, 186, 188
musicians, 151, 153, 155, 170, 171, 172, 176, 177, 182, 187, 188, 211, 279

## N

national expenditure, 110
nobility, 92, 169, 185, 198, 203, 221, 222, 296

## O

offenders, 39, 86, 199, 212, 251, 280
old age, 35, 63, 65, 98, 103, 142, 153, 166, 242, 253, 260, 304, 308
organ, 149, 153, 154, 155, 156
organs, 149, 154, 156, 309

## P

pain, 35, 65, 118, 119, 235, 237, 257, 258, 288, 303
parentage, 200, 202, 212
parents, 62, 65, 201, 227, 277
peace, 47, 51, 56, 104, 123, 149, 156, 199, 209, 250, 269, 270, 280, 286, 289
pedigree, 78, 202, 204, 207, 229
permission, iv, 9, 65, 128, 136, 283
pleasure, 7, 11, 16, 24, 40, 45, 54, 64, 65, 74, 80, 82, 108, 123, 136, 143, 179, 188, 198, 220, 254, 259, 288, 290, 297, 298, 300, 306, 312
politics, 37, 51, 55, 212, 215
poverty, 26, 63, 64, 183
prayer, 128, 276, 290
prejudice, 58, 93, 309
preparation, iv, 193, 269
preservation, 30, 149, 198
prestige, 56, 197, 199, 280, 297
principles, 123, 142, 152, 179, 185, 219, 233, 253, 310
prisoners, 58, 144, 242, 250, 277, 279
proposition, 44, 153, 259
prosperity, 26, 69, 81, 100, 202
protection, 76, 90, 125, 160, 278, 288
punishment, 11, 85, 86, 117, 199, 242, 257, 278, 280, 288
purity, 23, 89, 91, 120

## Q

Quakers, 58

## R

race, 85, 205, 206, 229, 249, 270
reading, 4, 63, 198, 221, 223, 264, 268, 276
recalling, 5, 11, 205, 209, 220, 296, 297, 308
reception, 4, 11, 101, 127, 128, 187, 191
reform, 80, 90, 96, 110, 111, 118, 207, 208, 242, 263, 287, 306
rent, 4, 5, 26, 192, 194, 251
reputation, 14, 53, 56, 58, 90, 101, 107, 120, 143, 156, 222, 236, 238, 249, 259, 267, 288, 312
resolution, 38, 208, 221, 303, 304, 310
retirement, 27, 35, 108, 111, 112, 214, 261, 311
revenue, 73, 75, 89, 92, 216, 222
rights, iv, 102, 248
rules, 79, 117, 119, 167, 208, 307

## S

saints, vii, 285, 287
salaries, vi, 73, 87, 89, 107, 109, 111, 112, 165
sarcasm, 65, 144, 237, 264
school, 23, 66, 118, 159, 160, 161, 191, 194, 195, 203, 216, 219, 263, 265, 288
science, 20, 139, 149, 152, 259
services, iv, 3, 44, 56, 71, 73, 77, 79, 87, 88, 112, 121, 151, 171, 222, 253, 292, 312
showing, 96, 98, 117, 118, 133, 181, 241, 278, 305
silk, 4, 76, 82, 83, 119, 124, 125, 136, 137, 138, 139, 145, 279
silver, 70, 74, 87, 89, 95, 126, 131, 146, 171, 177, 181, 182, 192, 216, 225, 291
society, 3, 4, 7, 8, 9, 10, 11, 27, 35, 39, 40, 45, 47, 49, 62, 64, 65, 66, 77, 84, 89, 91, 95, 97, 118, 119, 120, 128, 131, 133, 141, 151, 155, 156, 169, 170, 176, 179, 180, 185, 186, 187, 188, 191, 193, 194, 197, 199, 200, 205, 214, 222, 225, 226, 235, 242, 265, 271, 296, 297, 299, 304, 305, 309, 310, 311, 313
Solicitor General, 44, 45, 50, 72, 73, 80, 81, 83, 93, 138, 139, 168, 229
species, 23, 30, 132, 137, 141
speech, 10, 55, 57, 72, 74, 82, 83, 129, 133, 165, 167, 238, 239, 240, 241, 249, 251, 253, 258, 262, 263, 265, 269, 275, 280, 303, 307, 310
statesmen, 16, 51
stigmatized, 248, 264, 305

style, 20, 57, 64, 66, 169, 171, 173, 177, 180, 197, 216, 230, 245, 285
succession, 14, 49, 61, 95, 108, 187, 212, 225, 273, 300, 310
sympathy, 35, 167, 168, 205, 300, 306, 312

## T

teachers, 153, 167, 221
tenants, 4, 14, 72, 150, 192, 193, 206
tenure, 13, 21, 26, 73, 75, 80, 87, 101, 107, 109, 138, 151, 221, 236, 272, 298
theatre, 167, 180
theatrical decoration, 177
thoughts, 40, 44, 59, 245
tones, 21, 74, 153, 160, 167, 252, 301
trade, 133, 203, 206, 211, 225, 227, 276, 278, 308
traditions, 37, 122, 261
transactions, 76, 98, 104
translation, 198, 233, 246
trial, 56, 57, 58, 66, 79, 83, 91, 97, 101, 136, 155, 168, 210, 215, 234, 236, 242, 250, 258, 260, 269, 270, 271, 272, 273, 279, 281

## U

unhappiness, 35
uniform, 118, 127, 176, 187, 197, 226, 291
universities, 194, 197, 203, 215, 296, 310

## V

velvet, 13, 50, 119, 120, 124, 126, 145, 173, 295
victims, 44, 97, 100, 234, 240, 277
violence, 21, 38, 214

## W

walking, 8, 152, 188, 237, 257, 291
water, 59, 176, 185, 214, 233, 275, 282, 298, 299, 301
weakness, 250, 259, 299
wealth, 29, 38, 43, 56, 65, 83, 84, 89, 97, 99, 100, 107, 181, 197, 201, 206, 217, 277, 290, 311
weapons, 119
wear, 118, 119, 120, 121, 125, 127, 128, 133, 134, 139, 144, 180, 268, 313
weeping, 47, 86, 289
wine, vii, 7, 9, 27, 46, 72, 88, 91, 92, 102, 109, 124, 133, 171, 187, 188, 212, 220, 221, 222, 239, 245, 265, 268, 279, 298, 303, 304, 305, 306, 307, 308
witnesses, vii, 45, 144, 146, 210, 258, 261, 267, 268, 269, 271, 272, 277, 281